The Unpublished Opinions of the Burger Court

The Unpublished Opinions of the

BURGER
COURT

BERNARD SCHWARTZ

OXFORD UNIVERSITY PRESS
New York   Oxford
1988

More than ever, for Aileen

OXFORD UNIVERSITY PRESS

Oxford New York Toronto
Delhi Bombay Calcutta Madras Karachi
Petaling Jaya Singapore Hong Kong Tokyo
Nairobi Dar es Salaam Cape Town
Melbourne Auckland

and associated companies in
Beirut Berlin Ibadan Nicosia

Published by Oxford University Press, Inc.,
200 Madison Avenue, New York, New York 10016

Library of Congress Cataloging-in-Publication Data
The Unpublished opinions of the Burger court
[compiled] by Bernard Schwartz.
p. cm.
ISBN 0-19-505317-6
1. Judicial opinions—United States. I. Schwartz, Bernard,
1923– . II. United States. Supreme Court.
KF101.8.S37 1988
347.73'26—dc 19   [347.30735]   87-30294

1 2 3 4 5 6 7 8 9

Printed in the United States of America
on acid-free paper

Sources and Acknowledgments

This book is based upon both oral and documentary sources. The oral sources consisted of personal interviews. I interviewed members of the Supreme Court and former law clerks, as well as others. Every statement not otherwise identified was made to me personally. I have tried to identify the statements made by different people, except where they were made upon a confidential basis. In the latter case, I have given the position of the person involved, but not his name. This book could never have been written without the cooperation of those who shared their time and experience so generously with me.

The documentary sources are conference notes, docket books, correspondence, notes, memoranda, and draft opinions. The documents used and their location are identified, except where they were made available upon a confidential basis. Most of these documents have never before been published.

All but seven of the draft opinions in this book are reproduced directly from the originals as printed by the Supreme Court print shop. The others are in typewritten form and have been reset as they were originally typed, including the typographical and other errors contained in the originals.

I have been afforded generous access to the papers of the Justices and gratefully acknowledge the help given by the Manuscript Division, Library of Congress. I also wish to acknowledge the efforts of my editors, Susan Rabiner and Paul E. Schlotthauer, the staff of Oxford University Press, my literary agent, Gerard McCauley, the support of Dean Norman Redlich and the New York University School of Law, the work of my tireless secretary, Mrs. Barbara Ortiz, and the generous help of the Filomen d'Agostino and Max E. Greenberg Research Fund of New York University School of Law.

New York
February 1988

B. S.

Contents

The Unpublished Opinions of the Burger Court

Introduction

On June 17, 1986, President Ronald Reagan announced the retirement of Warren E. Burger as Chief Justice of the United States and his intention to nominate Justice William H. Rehnquist to succeed to the Supreme Court's central chair. Burger said he was retiring to devote his time entirely to his work as chairman of the Commission on the Bicentennial of the U.S. Constitution. He denied that he was leaving the Court because of his health or because of fatigue. "I wasn't weary of being Chief Justice," he told the press. "It's a lot of fun."[1]

The Burger retirement marked the end of an era in the Marble Palace. With the confirmation of his successor, the Burger Court has now given way to the Rehnquist Court, though there will inevitably be a transition period while the new Chief Justice seeks to establish his own mark on the highest tribunal. Such a period is particularly appropriate for publication of a book on the Burger Court, especially one that focuses on the Supreme Court's inner workings.

This study is a companion to my book *The Unpublished Opinions of the Warren Court*.[2] Like that volume, this one contains the draft opinions that were prepared by the Justices in the cases that are included. Such draft opinions are, of course, private Court papers. They have not been published until now. All of the opinions were made available to me on a confidential basis and are not in a collection to which the public has access. Reference is also made throughout the book to conference discussions and communications among the Justices. Their source is contained in the notes except when conference notes or other documents were given to me in confidence. In such instances, I have tried to identify the documents, usually by title and date. I have personally examined every document to which reference is made.

In presenting the draft opinions in this work, I have followed the format of my Warren Court Opinions book. The opinions are prefaced by a statement containing a short history of the case as well as the setting in which the drafts were circulated. Following the opinions, there is an analysis of what took place after the drafts were sent around to the Justices. As in the Warren Court book, I try to explain why the drafts were not issued as the final opinions and dissents in these cases. In particular, I try to show what would have happened if the draft opinions had come down as they are reprinted herein. The contrast between the drafts and the final opinions has made for a substantial difference in the law in the various fields involved. The law and even our society might be very different today if the original drafts in *Roe* v. *Wade*[3] and *United States* v. *Nixon*[4] had been issued as the final opinions of the Court.

I have not reproduced these unpublished draft opinions and told what happened in the Court in these cases in an effort to produce a mini-*Brethren.*[5] Rather, my purpose is to give students of the Supreme Court further insight into the Court's largely unrevealed decision process. Even Court specialists who have been made privy to the Court's internal workings do not seem to fully realize that Court decisions are basically collaborative efforts in which nine individualists must cooperate to bring about the desired result. Before the final opinions are issued, there may be politicking, vote switches, and horse trading to secure them; ultimately, there are usually compromises to obtain the necessary working majority. In the process, the quondam opinion of the Court may become the ultimate dissent—and vice versa—or the potential constitutional landmark may become a minor footnote in Supreme Court history. It is my hope, as in my Warren Court book, that the actual operation of the Court's decision process will be made clearer by this account of these ten cases and the respective opinions that never came down.

In addition to revealing the operation of the Court's decision process, the Warren Court book offers a unique picture of the leadership of Earl Warren as Chief Justice. This volume, too, presents hitherto unrevealed material from which the role of Chief Justice Burger as head of the Court may be weighed. His part in these cases lends vivid evidence to the type of leadership that he felt the Chief Justice should exercise.

A Casting Ideal

It is customary to designate a Supreme Court by the name of its Chief Justice. During the tenure of a strong Chief Justice, such as Earl Warren, this is more than a mere formality. While Warren was at its head, the Supreme Court bore the image of its Chief Justice as unmistakably as the earlier Courts of John Marshall and Roger B. Taney reflected their unique leadership. During his tenure, the high bench was emphatically the *Warren* Court, and he as well as the country knew it.

This is plainly not as true during the time that Chief Justice Burger occupied the Court's central chair. To be sure, Chief Justice Warren was inevitably a tough act to follow. But, even on its own terms, the Burger tenure was not marked by strong leadership in molding Supreme Court jurisprudence.

Chief Justice Burger's career is a contemporary Horatio Alger story.

He grew up in St. Paul, attended the University of Minnesota for two years, and then went to law school at night. To support himself he sold life insurance by day. During the depression, he practiced law in nearby St. Paul, where he became involved in Republican party politics. He was active in Harold E. Stassen's successful campaign for governor and in his later unsuccessful presidential bids. In 1952, Burger was Stassen's floor manager at the Republican National Convention.

After Dwight D. Eisenhower's election, Burger was appointed assistant attorney general in charge of the Claims Division of the Department of Justice. In 1956, he was named to the U.S. Court of Appeals in Washington, D.C., where he developed a reputation as a conservative, particularly in criminal cases. Then, in 1969, came what Justice John M. Harlan once called his "ascendancy to the Jupitership of Mount Olympus."[6] Burger was sworn in as Chief Justice on June 23, 1969, and headed the Court until his 1986 retirement.

Observers noted that Chief Justice Burger's white-haired broad-shouldered presence on the bench was very reminiscent of his predecessor's. Burger was the casting director's ideal of a Chief Justice. On the bench and at public functions, Burger was an almost too-perfect symbol of the law's dignity. His critics contend that he stood too much on the dignity of his office and was more often than not, aloof and unfeeling. Intimates, however, stress his courtesy and kindness and assert that it was the office, not the man, that may have made for a different impression. "The Chief," says Justice Harry A. Blackmun, who has known Burger far longer than anyone else on the Court, "has a great heart in him, and he's a very fine human being when you get to know him, when the tensions are off. One has to remember, too, that he's under strain almost constantly."[7]

His law clerks, particularly, speak of Burger with affection. One of them, whose views usually differed from those of the Chief Justice, tells how Burger used him in the role of devil's advocate during his clerkship year. When the year ended, the Chief Justice put his arm around him and said, "I must have one of you crazies every year so that I can get ready for Brennan."

Burger is not a person to develop intimate relationships with those with whom he works; yet he was as close to his clerks as to anyone in the Marble Palace. An Allen Drury novel tells of a "tiny kitchen installed in his office by Warren E. Burger who loved to cook and often prepared lunch for himself or an occasional guest."[8] Every Saturday at noon, Burger made soup in such a kitchen for his clerks. They never knew what was in it, one of them told me, but they ate it without question or complaint. Then Burger would sit and talk informally with them for hours, usually with colorful reminiscences about his career. The one rule at these sessions was that no one would talk about the cases before the Court on which they were currently working.

The basic Burger kindness is also illustrated by another clerk anecdote. It happened soon after the clerk reported for work in August. An emergency matter that required the Chief Justice's attention arose late one afternoon. The clerk drove out to Burger's home with the necessary papers. Since it was the clerk's wedding anniversary and he had planned to spend the evening with his wife, she went along. The wife waited in the car while her husband carried out his errand. Burger answered the door dressed in a colorful Hawaiian shirt and shorts. The emergency matter was disposed of quickly. The Chief Justice then invited the young man to sit in the garden, where he regaled the clerk with tales about his experiences.

This went on for some time and the clerk was getting increasingly nervous about his waiting wife. Finally, he interrupted the Chief Justice and said that he thought he should rejoin his wife in their car since it was their anniversary. At this Burger interposed with mock solemnity, "I should hold you in contempt!" The Chief Justice put on trousers and went out to invite the wife into his home. The three of them spent what the clerk calls a wonderful time together, with the Chief Justice at his avuncular best—the moment of good cheer improved by a rare wine from the Burger wine cellar.

From his "Middle Temple" Cheddar—made, according to the Burger recipe, "with English Cheddar, Ruby Port, Brandy and a few other ingredients"[9]—to the finest wines, the Chief Justice is somewhat of an epicure. One of the social high points of a 1969 British-American conference at Ditchley, Oxfordshire, attended by the newly appointed Chief Justice, was the learned discussion about vintage clarets that took place between Burger and Sir George Coldstream, head of the lord chancellor's office and in charge of the wine cellar at his Inn of Court. The Chief Justice was particularly proud of his coup in snaring some cases of rare Lafite in an off-the-beaten-path Washington wineshop.

The effectiveness of a Chief Justice, of course, is not aided by his reputation as a world-class epicure. Certainly, Burger in action cannot be compared with past virtuosos of the conference, such as Earl Warren. Indeed, the one Justice who was willing to talk to me frankly about Burger's performance spoke of it in a most denigratory fashion. "The great thing about Earl Warren," said this Justice, "was that he was so considerate of all his colleagues. He was so meticulous on assignments." Now, the Justice went on, "all too damned often the Chief Justice [Burger] will vote with the majority so as to assign the opinion, and then he ends up in dissent."

Burger, according to this Justice, "will assign to someone without letting the rest know, and he has five [votes for the opinion] before the rest of us see it." The Justice also complained about the Burger conduct of conferences in criminal law cases. "If it's a case in which a warden is the petitioner, the Chief Justice goes on and on until the rest are driven to distraction."

It should be pointed out that this Justice was not a Burger supporter but rather one whose vote would be expected to differ from that of the Chief Justice in many cases of consequence. We should, on the other hand, recognize that the Chief Justice's votes were based on his own scale of values, which were different from those that had motivated most members of the Warren Court. When what he considered to be a fundamental value was at stake, Burger could be as stubborn as his predecessor in sticking to his views. "Someone," he insisted to a law clerk in discussing a case, "must draw the line in favor of basic values and, even if the vote is eight-to-one, I will do it." As Justice William O. Douglas once put it in a case on which the Chief Justice had strong views that differed from those expressed by a lower court, "The CJ would rather die than affirm."[10]

As far as the Court itself is concerned, foremost in the Burger scale of values was the privacy and dignity of the Court. The Chief Justice always felt that protecting the privacy of the Court and the confidentiality of its nonpublic processes was essential to the Court's functioning. The posture of prohibiting media coverage of Supreme Court proceedings, even those open to the public, predates Chief Justice Burger. The Court has always refused to allow broadcasting of its sessions. Chief Justice Warren once turned down a CBS request to televise the Supreme Court arguments in an important case. Warren wrote that "the Court has had an inflexible rule to the effect that it will not permit photographs or broadcasting from the courtroom when it is in session." He was sure that the Court "[had] no intention of changing that rule."[11]

Chief Justice Burger carried on this tradition. In 1986, a network asked permission to carry live radio coverage of the arguments in what promised to be a landmark case. The network received a one-sentence reply from the Chief Justice: "It is not possible to arrange for any broadcast of any Supreme Court proceeding." Handwritten at the bottom of the letter was a postscript, "When you get the Cabinet meetings on the air, call me!"[12]

Chief Justice Burger was particularly concerned about the possibility of leaks from the Marble Palace to the press. On March 25, 1971, a Burger *MEMORANDUM TO THE CONFERENCE*, headed *CONFIDENTIAL*, was circulated. The memo was called forth by a reporter's attempt to interview law clerks.

> I have categorically directed that none of my staff have any conversation on any subject with any reporter. This directive was really not necessary since this is a condition of employment. I know of no one who is skilled enough to expose himself to any conversation with a reporter without getting into "forbidden territory". The reporter will inevitably extract information on the internal mechanisms of the Court, one way or another, to our embarrassment.

In assessing Burger's work as Chief Justice, we must consider his exercise of the power to assign the writing of Court opinions. This function has been called the most important of all those reserved to the office of the Chief Justice. In discharging it, a great Chief Justice acts as would a general deploying his army. It is he who determines what use will be made of the Court's personnel; the particular decisions he assigns to each Justice in distributing the work load will influence both the growth of the law and his own relations with his colleagues.

Here we come to a point that is controversial about the leadership of Chief Justice Burger. Almost as old as the tradition that the Chief Justice has the authority to assign opinions is the tradition that limits this authority to those cases in which the Chief Justice has voted with the majority. When he did not so vote, the opinion was assigned by the senior Justice in the majority. I have traced the Chief Justice's assigning power and have found that the limitation of that power to cases in which the Chief Justice had voted with the majority was developed at the time of Chief Justice Taney.[13]

By the present century, this had become uniform practice. The situation was summarized in 1928 by former Associate Justice Charles E. Hughes:

> After a decision has been reached, the Chief Justice assigns the case for opinion to one of the members of the Court, that is, of course, to one of the majority if there is a division and the Chief Justice is a member of the majority. If he is in a minority, the senior Associate Justice in the majority assigns the case for opinion.[14]

It is said that Chief Justice Burger did not follow the established practice in his assignment of opinions. It is alleged that he voted with the majority in order to control the assignment of opinions, even though his true sentiments were the other way.[15] This appears contrary to the spirit if not the letter of the Court's assignment practice. But the Chief Justice went beyond the letter of the tradition as well as its spirit. A striking illustration is contained in the *Swann* school-busing case in which (as I have shown elsewhere) Burger assigned the opinion to himself, even though he had supported the minority view at the conference.[16]

"He does it all the time," one of the Justices told me about Chief Justice Burger's assignment practice. This is doubtless an exaggeration, but there is no doubt that the Chief Justice did assign opinions in other cases when he was not in the majority. Two examples are contained in this book. In Chapter 4—devoted to the 1973 abortion case of *Roe* v. *Wade*—we shall see that the Chief Justice assigned the opinion to Justice Blackmun, though it was not clear that Burger was then part of the majority. A similar situation occurred in *O'Connor* v. *Donaldson* (Chapter 6) when the Chief Justice took the opinion himself, even though he had not voted with the majority.

Of course, Chief Justice Burger also made use of more traditional assignment techniques. He took the most important institutional cases, such as the *Nixon* case, for himself (the Court in these cases probably should speak through its head); he assigned the more significant cases to his allies, such as Justice Blackmun (early on) and Justice Rehnquist (more recently); and he left lesser cases to his opponents on the Court, notably Justice William J. Brennan, Jr.

The Chief Justice also employed the technique of assigning a case to the most lukewarm member of the majority. An illustration can be found in a November 14, 1978, Burger letter to Justice Brennan:

> Apropos your question (I believe at lunch Monday) whether Bill Rehnquist was an appropriate assignee of the above case, I had discussed this with Bill. He prefers his first choice disposition, i.e., no judicial review, but he was willing to write the holding to reflect the majority view otherwise. There were 8 to affirm and he fits the old English rule-of-thumb as the "least persuaded", hence likely to write narrowly.

The Warren Liberals

Justice Felix Frankfurter once compared the Court to a family.[17] The Court "family" is composed of nine very human, often idiosyncratic individuals. At the head of a very special hierarchical arrangement (*primus inter pares*) sits the Chief Justice. But the Associate Justices play crucial supporting roles and, all too often, steal the scene from the nominal lead.

When Chief Justice Burger took his place in the Court's center chair, the remaining seats were occupied by holdovers from the Warren Court. Two of them—Justices Hugo L. Black and John M. Harlan—were among the most noted modern Justices, but they retired after the second Burger term and did not play a significant part in the cases covered in this book.

In dealing with three of the other five Warren holdovers, we can start with a recent analysis by Justice Harry A. Blackmun of the divisions within the Court. Speaking of the Justices who sat in the cases covered in the last four chapters of this book, Blackmun noted, "I had always put on the left" Justices Brennan and Marshall, and on the right Chief Justice Burger and Justice Rehnquist. "Five of us," Blackmun said, were "in the middle"—referring to Justices Stewart, White, Powell, Stevens, and himself.[18]

In the first five cases in this book, it was another Warren holdover, Justice Douglas, who sat instead of Justice Stevens, who was appointed after Douglas retired. Using the Blackmun tripartite division, Douglas must, of course, be put on the left with Justices Brennan and Marshall. Those three constituted the liberal bloc on the early Burger Court and attention must be devoted to them, particularly to Douglas and Brennan who played an important part in many of the cases in the chapters that follow.

William O. Douglas was one of the famous names in modern Supreme Court history. Even more so than the Chief Justice, he was the Court's Horatio Alger, having overcome early polio and poverty to become a noted outdoorsman and legal light. Douglas's impressive physical vitality always seemed out of place in the Court's monastic atmosphere. To the public he was noted as much for his books describing his peripatetic wandering and mountain climbing as for his judicial work. He reveled in exotic and dangerous travels that would have daunted his less adventurous colleagues. When I delivered the Tagore Law Lectures at Calcutta in January 1984, my hosts delighted in telling me how my American predecessor, Justice Douglas, had insisted in 1955 on lecturing in July when even most Indians were overcome by the unbearable heat.

There is no doubt that Justice Douglas had a brilliant mind, but he was erratic. He could whip up opinions faster than any of the Justices and did almost all the work himself, relying less on his clerks than any other Justice. But his opinions were too often unpolished, as though he lacked the interest for the sustained work involved in transforming first drafts into finished products. Lack of interest in the Court's work was, indeed, apparent in Douglas's very attitude as a judge. During oral argument, Douglas seemed to spend most of his time writing. One knew he was writing letters because, every once in a while, he would lift his head from his scribbling and ostentatiously lick an envelope from side to side and seal it. At the same time, every now and then he would lift his head and direct an acute question to counsel. As one of the Justices put it, "Bill could listen with one ear." Chief Justice Warren always felt that the peripatetic Justice spent too much time writing books and doing things that were not related to the Court.

After Black resigned, Douglas was the senior Associate Justice on the Burger Court, and the public considered him the leader of its liberal wing. Douglas was, however, too much the loner to play the leadership role. Instead, that role was assumed by Justice Brennan, who had developed into the Chief Justice's most effective ally while Earl Warren sat in the Court's center chair.

William J. Brennan, Jr., had been Justice Frankfurter's student at Harvard Law School; on Brennan's appointment, his former professor wrote a friend, "It makes me feel like an old man to think of having a former student on the Court and, of course, it gives me great pleasure to find myself on the Court with a former student."[19] Yet, the new Justice showed that he was anything but a Frankfurter acolyte. He quickly became an active Warren supporter and was responsible for some of the most important opinions of the Warren Court. When Justice Harold H. Burton went to see President Eisenhower in 1958 about his resignation from the Court, the President complained as much about Brennan's decisions as he did about Warren's.

Justice Brennan's role changed drastically after Warren's retirement. Now he was no longer the Chief Justice's trusted insider. Instead, he became the Justice who tried above all to keep the Warren flame burning, and as a consequence, he became Burger's leading opponent on the Court. Both Brennan and the Chief Justice accepted this over the years that the two sat together. One year the Brennan law clerks had been guests at a convivial Burger luncheon. The Chief Justice telephoned Brennan to tell him what fine gentlemen his clerks were. When the clerks returned, however, the Justice stood waiting for them, hands on hips. "You turncoats," he reproved them, "what did you do over there?"

The last left-bank Justice in Blackmun's division was Justice Marshall. In many ways, his pre-Court career was more interesting than his contribution to Supreme Court jurisprudence, for it added a racial dimension to the oblivion-to-prominence American success story. The first black appointed to the Court, Marshall was the great-grandson of a slave and the son of a Pullman car steward. Justice Blackmun relates this story:

> When we went up [to Baltimore, Justice Marshall's native city] for the ceremony in connection with the dedication of [Marshall's] statue up there in front of the Federal building, he and I were sitting next to each other and he said, "Why do you think that fellow asked me what high school here in Baltimore I went to? Hell, there was only one I could go to!"[20]

Before his appointment, Marshall was best known as the first head of the National Association for the Advancement of Colored People's Legal Defense Fund staff—a position he held for over twenty years—and chief counsel in the *Brown* school-segregation case.[21] On the Court, he has always been a firm vote for the liberal bloc; so firm, in fact, that in the Burger Court he was seen almost as a judicial adjunct to Justice Brennan.

The Nixon Right and Center

In the Blackmun analysis as well as in the view of most Court watchers, Justice Rehnquist stood on the right of the Burger Court with the Chief Justice. A *Newsweek* article dubbed Rehnquist, "The Court's Mr. Right."[22] According to the *New York Times,*

> William H. Rehnquist is a symbol. People who have trouble naming all nine Supreme Court Justices quickly identify him as its doctrinaire, right-wing anchor. . . . Justice Rehnquist is the Court's most predictably conservative member, using his considerable intelligence, energy and verbal facility to shape the law to his vision.[23]

By the time of his nomination to the Chief Justiceship, Rehnquist had become a most influential member of the Burger Court, both because he stood out among a group of Associate Justices of generally bland personalities—none of whom seemed prepared to offer a firm sense of direction—and because he was closely allied with the Chief Justice. But the Rehnquist influence was not apparent in the cases chosen for this book. Indeed, except for his vote in *Kirby* v. *Illinois* (Chapter 2), he played no significant part in determining how these cases would be decided.

In the Burger Court's first decade, the majority remained largely unsympathetic to the Rehnquist entreaties from the right. During the period covered by the cases in this book, it was the Justices in the center who held the balance of power. According to Justice Blackmun, "I with others have been trying to hold the center." Those "in the middle" referred to Justices Stewart and White, Warren Court holdovers; Powell and Blackmun, Nixon appointees; and Stevens, appointed by President Gerald R. Ford.[24]

Of the center bloc in the Burger Court, the one who came to play the most important role was Justice Blackmun himself. The second Nixon appointee, Harry A. Blackmun, had served eleven years on the U.S. Court of Appeals for the Eighth Circuit when the call came from Washington in 1970. He was raised in Minnesota and went to grade school with Warren E. Burger. The two remained close friends thereafter, with Blackmun serving as best man at Burger's wedding. After graduation from Harvard Law School, Blackmun served as a law clerk in the Court of Appeals for the Eighth Circuit (to which he would later be appointed), spent sixteen years with a Minneapolis law firm, and was counsel to the famous Mayo Clinic for almost ten years.

In his early years on the Court, few expected Justice Blackmun to be more than an appendage of the Chief Justice. He was then virtually Burger's disciple, almost always to be found on the same side of an issue as his old friend. The press had typecast Blackmun as the subordinate half of the Minnesota Twins—after the baseball team from their hometowns, the Twin Cities of Minneapolis and St. Paul.

All this was to change during the period covered in this book. One can indeed see Justice Blackmun's development in some of the cases that follow. The Blackmun opinions in *Roe* v. *Wade*, the abortion case treated in Chapter 4, sound the first Blackmun declaration of independence from the Chief Justice. Burger had assigned the case to his fellow Minnesotan in the hope that he would write an opinion more to the Chief Justice's liking than might one of the Justices who was for a flat invalidation of abortion laws. Instead, Blackmun wrote an opinion striking down the laws: first, on limited grounds and then—in a revised draft—with a categorical holding of the absolute right to an abortion during the early stages of pregnancy.

In *United States* v. *Nixon* (Chapter 5), Justice Blackmun dealt the final blow to Burger's hope to mold the Court's opinion by handing the Chief Justice a complete revision of the statement of facts in the case. Thereafter, the Chief Justice had to yield to a thorough rewriting by the Justices of the other parts of his original draft opinion. It is said that within the Court the incident came to be told as the "Et Tu Harry" story.[25] "I am fairly positive," Blackmun himself says, "that [the Chief Justice] feels I have not been the supportive arm he would have liked me to be."[26]

By the time of the last case in this book, *Gannett Co.* v. *DePasquale* (Chapter 10), Justice Blackmun was completely his own man. He wrote a draft opinion that contained a broadside vindication of the right to open courts. It was as liberal as any that the Justices on the left might have written. One can also see an improvement in Blackmun's work as time went on. If we compare his hesitant first draft in *Roe* v. *Wade* with his self-assured draft in *Gannett Co.* v. *DePasquale*, we see how the Justice's competence grew with increasing experience and self-confidence. A comparison of the two drafts bears out a conclusion offered in a 1983 *New York Times Magazine* article, "Justice Blackmun's evolution as a jurist and prominence on the Court represent one of the most important developments in the judiciary's recent history."[27]

The fourth Nixon appointee on the Court, Justice Powell, was also one of those who, in the Blackmun phrase, "hold the center." But, if Justice Blackmun has tended to gravitate more to the left of the center bloc, Powell was more to its right. Powell himself came to the Court after a career in private practice with one of Virginia's most prestigious law firms, a career capped by his term as president of the American Bar Association (ABA). In a society in which lawyers play so prominent a part, surprisingly few Supreme Court Justices have been drawn directly from the practicing bar. During the past half century, only Justices Lewis F. Powell, Jr., and Abe Fortas were in private practice when they were appointed.

On the bench, Justice Powell followed the pragmatic approach developed by his thirty-five years of practice. He avoided doctrinaire positions and hard-edged ideological decisions, and he gained a reputation as a moderate, though he voted more often with Chief Justice Burger than some of the others in the center bloc. His quest for the middle ground is best illustrated by his most famous opinion—that in the *Bakke* case.[28] It was his vote that decided the particular issue before the Court: Had Bakke been unconstitutionally denied admission to medical school? Though the Powell *Bakke* opinion was joined by no other Justice, it is considered by most commentators as having laid down the authoritative statement of the law in the case.

Justice Powell displayed the true conservative's concern for upholding deeply felt traditional values, such as free speech, family life, and procedural safeguards against the whims of governmental functionaries. Powell objected to a "serious procedural omission" when the Court was faced with the Occupational Safety and Health Act, under which a fine could be assessed by a single hearing officer, with no right of appeal to the commission. "The net effect of the procedure under this Act," Powell asserted, "is to vest enormous power in a single individual, who may or may not be well qualified, without the procedural and other protections that are available in a court or in most administrative agencies."[29]

The Other Justices

The remaining three Justices who sat during the years covered by this book were also placed, in the Blackmun analysis, in the center of the Court. Two of them, Justices Stewart and White, had been members of the Warren Court; one, Justice Stevens, was appointed by President Ford.

Potter Stewart was not only one of the youngest Justices (at the time of his appointment, he was only forty-three), he also was one of the youngest to retire (only two Justices had retired at a younger age than Stewart's sixty-six). When he first took his seat, Stewart's youth and handsome appearance added an unusual touch to the highest bench, showing that it need not always be composed of nine old men. To those who knew him in those days, it was painful to see his physical decline before he died in 1985.

Before then, people who met Justice Stewart were surprised by his vigor and clearly expressed views. They contrasted sharply with his public image as an indecisive centrist without clearly defined conceptions. Unlike Justices Brennan and Rehnquist, Stewart never acted on the basis of a deep-seated philosophy regarding the proper relationship between the state and its citizens. When asked if he was a liberal or a conservative, he answered, "I am a lawyer." He went on to say, "I have some difficulty understanding what those terms mean even in the field of political life. . . . And I find it impossible to know what they mean when they are carried over to judicial work."[30]

If we must place Justices on a right-left continuum, it may be said of Stewart that he was a moderate with a commonsense approach to issues that polarized others. Under Chief Justice Warren, Stewart remained in the center as the rest of the middle moved to the left. His center position, as we shall see in Chapter 5, enabled him to play the pivotal role in rewriting the draft opinion's crucial section on executive privilege in the *Nixon* case.

To the public, Stewart was best known for his comment in a 1964 obscenity case, "I know it when I see it"[31]—a punchy though legally flawed phrase that he later lamented might well become his epitaph.[32] Stewart's aptness for the well-turned phrase helped make him the press's favorite Justice. Stewart was more accessible to reporters than any of his colleagues. I recall with gratitude his willingness to talk to me about the work of the Justices and cases I was writing about. He never expressed any doubts to me about the public's right to know—even what went on inside the Marble Palace.

Throughout his career, Justice Stewart wrote or joined in opinions upholding the First Amendment claims of the press. It is, therefore, paradoxical that his most important role in this book (aside from that in the *Nixon* case) is to be found in *Gannett Co.* v. *DePasquale* (Chapter 10), in which his opinion restricted the press's right of access to court proceedings.

The last of the Warren holdovers was Justice White. When he was selected by President Kennedy in 1962, Byron R. White was certainly not the typical Supreme Court appointee. He was known to most Americans as "Whizzer" White—the all-American back who became the National Football League rookie of the year in 1938. Physically, White is most impressive. At six feet two and a muscular 190 pounds, he has maintained the constitution that made him a star football player. Even as a Justice, White has retained his athletic competitiveness, never hesitating to take part in the clerks' basketball games in the gymnasium at the top of the Court building—which Court personnel like to call "the highest Court in the land."

As a Justice, White, like Stewart, has defied classification. He, too, tends to take a lawyerlike approach to individual cases without trying to fit them into any overall judicial philosophy. White is considered by some to be one of the more conservative Justices in the Burger Court's center, particularly in criminal cases. "In the criminal field," as Justice Blackmun sees it, "I think Byron White is distinctly a conservative."[33] On the other hand, White tends to disagree with the Chief Justice on the cases the Court should hear. Burger, according to Blackmun, feels it is not necessary to take some cases because it is acceptable to allow "tolerable conflict out there" in lower court rulings. "Justice White feels that no conflict is tolerable."[34]

The last of the Burger Court members to participate in the cases in this book is Justice Stevens. John Paul Stevens was a judge on the U.S. Court of Appeals for the Seventh Circuit when he was selected by President Ford, largely on the recommendation of Attorney General Edward H. Levi. He was appointed as a moderate and was one of those listed by Justice Blackmun as in the Court's center. It is, however, even harder to classify Stevens than the others on the Burger Court. "On a Court that everyone likes to divide into liberal and conservative, Justice Stevens has acquired a list of labels all his own: enigmatic, unpredictable, maverick, a wild card, a loner."[35]

Stevens as a loner reminds one of Justice Douglas, to whose seat Stevens was appointed. Like his predecessor, Stevens makes little effort to win over other members of the Court. What a law clerk once told me about Douglas applies equally to Stevens, "Douglas was just as happy signing a one-man dissent as picking up four more votes." Stevens writes more dissents than any other member of the Court; he is often a lone dissenter. A book on the Burger Court concludes that although Stevens was once viewed as a potential leader of the Court "the effect of his independence of mind often has been to fragment potential majorities and leave the state of the law indeterminate."[36]

Stevens is idiosyncratic in more than his decisions. He hires only two law clerks instead of the usual four and drafts more of his own opinions than any of the others. He also deviates from the Court's unwritten conservative dress code; his constant bow tie (worn even under the judicial robe) gives him a perpetual sophomoric appearance. In 1986, the Justices were hearing arguments on whether Orthodox Jews, with their religious duty to wear yarmulkes, should be exempt from the military dress code's ban on hats indoors. Counsel for the government told the Justices, "It's only human nature to resent being told what to wear, when to wear it, what to eat—"

"Or whether you can wear a bow tie?" chimed in Justice Stevens.[37]

Clerk Power

"Alone among Government agencies," Anthony Lewis wrote in the *New York Times* in 1962, "the court seems to have escaped Parkinson's Law. The work is still done by nine men, assisted by eighteen young law clerks. Nothing is delegated to committees or ghostwriters or task forces."[38]

The only professional help Supreme Court Justices receive is that provided by their law clerks. The work of these clerks plays an important and substantial part in the functioning of the Court. In a 1979 speech, Justice Brennan referred to his opinions on the Court as

> opinions that came from the Brennan chambers over the past 23 years. I say from the "Brennan chambers" because, as Bentham said, the "law is not the work of judges alone but of judge and company." The company in this case consisted of the 65 law clerks who have been associated with me on the Court.[39]

In a perfect legal world, the law clerk would perform the functions of an associate in a law firm, that is, research for senior members and assistance generally in the firm's work. But the tasks assigned clerks at the Supreme Court depend solely on the view of the job held by the individual Justice for whom they are working. Inevitably, the scope of a clerk's responsibility expands in inverse ratio to the caliber of the Justice. It may be doubted that the great Justices, such as Oliver W. Holmes or Louis D. Brandeis, used their clerks as more than research assistants. More run-of-the-mill Justices have given their clerks a larger share of responsibility, including (in some cases) the writing of opinions. The system was described a few years ago as out of control, with many clerks running amok and virtually exercising the roles of junior (at times even senior) Justices.[40]

Complaints of this sort against the clerks' roles have been common over the years. A noted 1957 article in *U.S. News & World Report* by William H. Rehnquist—who had clerked for Justice Robert H. Jackson and was himself to be named to the Burger Court—was entitled "Who Writes Decisions of the Supreme Court?"[41] Rehnquist stated that the

Justices were delegating substantial responsibility to their clerks, who unconsciously slanted materials to accord with their own views. The result, he argued, was that a younger, generally more liberal point of view that was held by the vast majority of the clerks had become the philosophy espoused by the Warren Court. The Rehnquist thesis had been taken up earlier in a satirical vein by Justice Jackson, "A suspicion has grown at the bar that the law clerks . . . constitute a kind of junior court which decides the fate of the certiorari petitions. This idea of the law clerks' influence gave rise to a lawyer's waggish statement that the Senate no longer need bother about confirmation of justices but ought to confirm the appointment of law clerks."[42] Not only wags stated that view. Senator John C. Stennis of Mississippi once urged that law clerks should be confirmed by the Senate because of their rising importance and influence.[43]

A reply to Rehnquist was made, largely under Justice Frankfurter's instigation, by Alexander M. Bickel, a former Frankfurter clerk, who had become a leading constitutional scholar. In a 1958 *New York Times* article, he asserted that "the law clerks are in no respect any kind of a kitchen cabinet." Their job is only to "generally assist their respective Justices in researching the law books and other sources for materials relevant to the decision of cases before the Court." They also "go over drafts of opinions and may suggest changes."[44]

In the Burger Court, the truth was often closer to the Rehnquist than the Bickel picture, especially with regard to two of the most important functions of the Justices: (1) the screening of cases to determine those the Court would hear and decide, and (2) the drafting of opinions.

A few years ago, Justice Stevens publicly conceded that he read only twenty percent of the certiorari petitions presented to the Court.[45] The petitions are gone over by his clerks, who prepare memoranda summarizing the cases and issues and recommending whether or not cert should be granted; only those in which the granting of cert is recommended are read by Stevens. The only member of the Burger Court who has personally gone over petitions for review has been Justice Brennan, who has customarily shared the work with his law clerks. The others have followed the Stevens practice of having the petitions screened by their clerks in the first instance.

In the 1972 Term, Chief Justice Burger instituted an important innovation in the handling of cert petitions. He suggested that the Justices combine their efforts in the screening process by having their clerks work together in one cert pool. The petitions would be divided equally among all the clerks in the pool and the cert memos prepared by them would be circulated to each of the Justices participating. The other Nixon appointees (Justices Blackmun, Powell, and Rehnquist) and Justice White agreed to join the Chief Justice in the cert pool. Justices Douglas, Brennan, Stewart, and Marshall declined to participate, as did Justice Stevens, who was appointed after Douglas resigned.[46]

It is true that the Justices—both those in and outside the cert pool—

make the final decision on what cert petitions to grant. In practice, however, the work on the petitions is done by the law clerks. In the vast majority of cases, the Justices must rely on the clerks' cert memos for information about the petitions and the issues they present, and they normally follow the memos' recommendations. Sheer volume, if nothing else, has helped enshrine this practice.

The Justices themselves have expressed qualms about this delegation of the screening task. In a 1960 letter to Justice Stewart, Justice Frankfurter wrote:

> The appraisal and appreciation of a record as a basis for exercising our discretionary jurisdiction is, I do not have to tell you, so dependent on a seasoned and disciplined professional judgment that I do not believe that lads—most of them fresh out of law school and with their present tendentiousness—should have any routine share in the process of disemboweling a record, however acute and stimulating their power of reasoning may be and however tentative and advisory their memos on what is reported in the record and what is relevant to our taking a case may be.

Referring to a recent case, he told Stewart:

> [I]t is a striking illustration of which I have found many over the years, Term after Term, of the slanted way in which, through compassionate feelings and inexperienced predispositions, these . . . cases are reported to us on the strength of which, so predominantly, action is taken by the court.[47]

An equally important delegation involves the opinion-writing process itself. "As the years passed," says Justice Douglas in his *Autobiography*, "it became more and more evident that the law clerks were drafting opinions."[48] Even the better Justices have made more extensive use of their clerks in the drafting process than outside observers have realized. In the Burger Court, indeed, except in the Douglas chambers, the routine procedure was for the clerks to draft virtually all opinions.

Not long ago, Justice Rehnquist described the opinion-writing process in his chambers. "In my case," he said, "the clerks do the first draft of almost all cases to which I have been assigned to write the Court's opinion." It is only "when the case-load is heavy [that I sometimes] help by doing the first draft of a case myself."[49]

Because this practice has been the standard routine in the Burger Court, the first drafts of virtually all the opinions reprinted in this book are most likely the work of law clerks, not of the Justices who were their ostensible authors. The one case in which this is not true is *Roe v. Wade* (Chapter 4); the first Blackmun drafts were entirely the handiwork of the Justice himself. At that time, Justice Blackmun was trying as much as he could to do his first drafts himself. He refused to allow his clerks to work on the abortion case drafts. Justice Douglas, known for writing his own opinions, also undoubtedly composed his own *Roe v. Wade* draft.

It is true, of course, that the decisions in cases are made by the Justices themselves—though, even with regard to them, the weaker Justices have abdicated much of their authority to their clerks. In most chambers, the clerks, to use a favorite expression of Chief Justice Warren, are not "unguided missiles." The Justices normally outline the way they want opinions drafted. But the drafting clerk is left with a great deal of discretion on the details of the opinion, particularly the specific reasoning and research supporting the decision. The technical minutiae and footnotes that are so dear to law professors are left almost completely to the clerks. Footnote 11 of the *Brown* school-segregation opinion[50]—perhaps the most famous footnote in Supreme Court history—was entirely the product of a Warren law clerk.

To be sure, the Justices themselves go over the drafts prepared by their clerks. "When a clerk writes the first draft," says Justice Rehnquist, "I may revise it in toto." But that does not happen in many cases, where, states Rehnquist: "I may leave it [the clerk's draft] relatively unchanged."[51] Too many of the Justices circulate drafts that are almost wholly the work of their clerks.

Despite Anthony Lewis, the Supreme Court has started to succumb to Parkinson's Law. The growing number of law clerks has led to an increase in the length, though plainly not the quality, of opinions. What Justice Douglas once wrote about Court opinions has become increasingly true: "We have tended more and more to write a law-review-type of opinion. They plague the Bar and the Bench. They are so long they are meaningless. They are filled with trivia and nonessentials."[52]

The product of the Douglas animadversion has been one result of the burgeoning bureaucratization of the Court. As in most institutions, the balance of power has shifted increasingly to the bureaucrats and away from nominal heads. The domain of the law clerks has grown so wide that they now have tremendous influence. All too often it is the clerk corps as much as the Justices who set the tone in the Marble Palace. Asked about the shrillness that some observers have perceived in Burger Court opinions, Justice Rehnquist concedes, "The shrillness is there." However, the Justice goes on, "It may reflect conflict among law clerks rather than acerbity or lack of civility among the judges."[53]

The Changed Judicial Agenda

William Howard Taft, the only man who was both President and Chief Justice, once said that the Supreme Court was his idea of what heaven must be like.[54] Justice Blackmun, on the other hand, has said of being a Justice, "It's a rotten way to earn a living."[55]

In large part, the change in the judicial attitude is a reflection of the Court's ever-increasing caseload. In its early years, the Court had relatively few cases on its docket. Thus, in 1803, there were only 51 cases on the docket; seven years later, the number was 98. The numbers increased as the years went on—but not by that much. There were 723 cases on the Court's docket in 1900 and 1,039 in 1930 when Chief Justice Taft died. More recently, however, the caseload has increased dramatically. In the 1953 Term, Chief Justice Warren's first, 1,293 cases were disposed of; in the 1968 Term, Warren's last, 3,117 cases were disposed of.

The increase continued during Chief Justice Burger's tenure. In the period covered by this book, the cases disposed of increased from 3,357 in 1969 to 3,943 in 1979. The Court's caseload has more than tripled during the past three decades. The burgeoning work load has been responsible for advancing the Court's first conference from early October to the last week in September, for the inclusion of Wednesdays in the conference schedule, and for increasing the number of staff members. In the Warren Court, each Justice had two law clerks; in the Burger Court, the number was increased to four.

Chief Justice Burger warned repeatedly that unless the work load was curbed it would soon be "impossible" for the Justices "to perform [their] duties well and survive very long." Not all the Justices agreed. But the pressures of the docket certainly changed the Court atmosphere from what it was in Chief Justice Taft's day. In a recent speech, Justice Blackmun described the Court as weary and overworked. He asserted that he was "never so tired" as he was at the end of the 1984 Court Term.[56]

It is, however, not only the volume of cases that has changed in recent years. There has been an even more dramatic change in the quality of the cases decided in the Marble Palace. The Court has, of course, always played a pivotal role in the American polity—a role encapsulated in de Tocqueville's famous statement that "scarcely any political question arises in the United States that is not resolved sooner or later into a judicial question."[57] From this point of view, the Supreme Court is primarily a political institution. Because its decrees mark the boundaries between the great departments of government and because on its actions depend the proper functioning of federalism and the scope to be given to the rights of the individual, a judge on such a tribunal has an opportunity to leave his imprint on the life of the nation as no mere master of the common law possibly could. Certainly, as an English writer noted not long ago, "[I]n America, the Supreme Court is supreme. In no other democratic country do nine judges, none of them elected, tell the president and the legislature what each may or may not do."[58]

Yet that is precisely what the Justices have done in the cases in this book. In the *Nixon* case (Chapter 5), the Court not only told the President what he must do, its decision led directly to his forced departure from the White House. In *Roe* v. *Wade* (Chapter 4), the Justices not only told the legislatures they might not restrict the right to abortions, their decision caused a social schism that has remained a major divisive factor in our society. The other cases covered may not be as dramatic, yet each illustrates some facet of the Court's crucial place in the polity.

It may be said that the Court has decided landmark cases throughout its history. Here, too, there has been a difference. In the past, a *Dred Scott* case[59] or an *Income Tax* case[60] would come up every quarter century or so, but the time of the Court would be occupied mainly with lesser cases. During this century, however, the pace of landmark decision making has increased tremendously. This has been particularly true of decision making since Chief Justice Warren took his seat. From the *Brown* case[61] at the beginning of the Chief Justice's tenure to the *Powell* case[62] at its end, the Warren years saw a judicial revolution that transformed both the law and the society that it served—a member of the Warren Court once termed it "the most profound and pervasive revolution ever achieved by substantially peaceful means."[63] Leading case after leading case was decided at a pace that would have astounded Court observers in an earlier day.

The pace did not decrease under Warren's successor. Scarcely a term passed in the Burger Court without decisions that would be landmarks in all but a jaded age. Certainly, the Burger Court was as much in the spotlight of press attention as its precedent-shattering predecessor.

Since Chief Justice Warren's day, there has been a substantial change not only in the volume of leading cases, but also in their quality. In earlier Courts, the important cases involved property rights. In the first part of the century, the Justices used the Due Process Clause to strike down laws regulating economic activity. More recently, the Court came to accept governmental restrictions on the free exercise of property rights to an extent never before permitted in American law. But this has not led to a lessening of the Court's role in the constitutional system. Instead, there has been a shift in judicial emphasis from the protection of property rights to protection of personal rights. Such protection has, indeed, been elevated to the top of the judicial agenda during the past quarter century.

The development in this respect has been accompanied by a continuing rights explosion; as never before, new interests have pressed upon the law to seek recognition in the form of legal rights. The Burger Court recognized rights that had previously scarcely even pressed for recognition, raising ever more rights to the legally protected plane. The rights in question cut across the entire legal spectrum, ranging from extensions of traditional rights, such as those to freedom of expression and equal protection, to newly emerging rights not previously vindicated by law.

The cases in this book well illustrate the changed nature of the rights now asserted before the Court. Most of the cases arose out of alleged infringements on personal rights, particularly the newer rights that have been pressing for legal recognition. Among these rights are those to sexual equality (Chapter 3), to bodily autonomy and privacy (Chapter 4), to treatment by committed persons (Chapter 6), to access to news (Chapter 8), to notice and hearing before even a "privilege" may be taken away (Chapter 9), and to access to court proceedings (Chapter 10). Also included are cases on more traditional rights—the right to seek judicial review of administrative action (Chapter 1) and that to counsel in criminal proceedings (Chapter 2).

The shift in judicial emphasis to protection of personal rights reflects the Justices' concern with the changing nature of our society. With property rights constitutionally curtailed, compensatory scope had to be given to personal rights if the ultimate social interest—that in the individual life—was not to be lost sight of. The need to broaden the constitutional protection of personal rights has received added emphasis from the growth and misuse of governmental power in the twentieth-century world. Totalitarian systems have shown dramatically what it means for the individual to live in a society in which Leviathan had become a reality. The "Blessings of Liberty," which the Constitution's framers took such pains to safeguard, were placed in even sharper relief in a world that has seen so clearly the consequences of their denial.

When the Constitution and the Bill of Rights were written, government was only an arbiter that allowed the individual to go unrestrained except at extreme limits of conduct. In the century and a half that followed, the system gradually shifted to one in which government had a positive duty to promote the welfare of the community, even at the cost of individual property rights. From a constitutional as from a political point of view, the welfare state was by midcentury an established fact.

But the problem had ceased to be one of the exertion of governmental authority over property rights to further the public welfare. In the words of Justice Douglas, "[T]he welfare state is a side issue. The central problem of the age is the scientific revolution and all the wonders and the damage it brings."[64] The "Machine, the genie that man has thoughtlessly let out of its bottle and cannot put back again,"[65] created new concentrations of power, particularly in government, that utterly dwarfed the individual and threatened individuality as never before. "Where in this tightly knit regime," asks Douglas, "is man to find liberty?"[66] The Justices, like the rest of us, have been disturbed by the growth of governmental authority and have sought to preserve a sphere for individuality even in a society in which individuals stand dwarfed by the power concentrations that confront them.

Mea Culpa?

Anthony Lewis has argued that a book such as this, which reveals what goes on during the Justices' decision process, may make it difficult for the Court to perform its crucial function effectively. Speaking of the notes, documents, and discussions revealed in *The Unpublished Opinions of the Warren Court*, the predecessor to this volume, Lewis asks:

> What effect will such disclosures have on the work of the Court? Will the justices be able to argue among one another with the candor that may

change minds if they think their words will soon be retailed to the public? Or will their conferences degenerate into posturing, like most Congressional debates?[67]

Lewis refers to the spate of recent books that purport to penetrate the Court's decision process, from *The Brethren*[68] to my own *Super Chief*.[69] Lewis terms the latter,

a massive book on the Warren Court [in which] Mr. Schwartz reconstructed what purported to be verbatim quotations from the justices' conferences. In important instances he did not disclose his sources, making it difficult to judge the fairness of the accounts; might they have come from one side in a hotly disputed case?[70]

Lewis goes on:

It is no doubt old-fashioned to worry about such things. But the Supreme Court is one institution that works in this country, and I think scholars should be wary of distorting the conference that is so essential to its work.[71]

Of course, it will be said in reply, the claim for secrecy is routinely made in other governmental institutions, from the White House down. Lewis, however, notes an essential difference in this respect in the Supreme Court's operation:

After all, the Court, unlike say, the President, does not in the end act in secret. It acts only through published judgments, and it is held accountable by their persuasiveness.[72]

Yet, Lewis's comment is the whole point about this kind of book. It shows that the published opinions reveal only a small part of the Court's decision process. In practice, the only things known to the public about the Court's functioning are the briefs, the oral arguments, and the published judgments and opinions. Everything else in the Court takes place behind the scenes—as removed from the public gaze as the decision process in the Kremlin.

In particular, the postargument decision process is completely closed. The next knowledge the outside world has about a case occurs with the public announcement of the decision and the opinions filed by the Justices. It is known that the Justices discuss the cases argued at conference sessions that are totally private and attended only by them. The privacy of the conference is one of the most cherished traditions at the Court. In addition to the conference discussion, ideas are exchanged through memoranda and draft opinions. These, too, are completely private and unknown outside the Marble Palace itself.

The Court practice in this respect led another *New York Times* article to describe the situation in the Court quite differently than Lewis:

> There is probably no more secret society in America than the Supreme
> Court. Its nine Justices are among the most powerful, yet least visible, men
> in the United States. It is unheard of for a Justice to reveal anything spe-
> cific about the Court's case work; law clerks, too, are sworn to secrecy.
> The Court's written decisions are supposed to speak for themselves. It is
> the least accountable branch of Government.[73]

In an age of open government and sunshine laws, it is anomalous that
almost nothing is known about the internal functioning of the fulcrum
on which the entire constitutional system turns. This book is an attempt
to help change that situation—to lift the Court's curtain of secrecy somewhat so that the Justices and their work may be better understood.

But what about the effect of revealing the Court's internal operations
on the Justices themselves and the freedom of their deliberations? In a
review of my book on the inner workings of the Warren Court, Erwin
N. Griswold, former solicitor general and Harvard Law School dean,
voiced a concern similar to that expressed by Lewis. "One wonders," he
wrote, "what effect this sort of presentation of documents, interviews and
so on, so soon after the events, has on freedom of exchange, frankness,
trust, common understanding, even bonhomie, among present and future
justices." Griswold then posed a question similar to those of Lewis, "Is
there not an appreciable risk that there may be a similiar chilling effect in
interchange even among Supreme Court justices? Sunshine can be car-
cinogenic as well as antiseptic."[74]

In answer to queries such as these, certain things should be said. The
first is that they are based on an a priori assumption that may or may not
be consistent with the facts of judicial life. Is it proved that the Justices
will be less candid if their decision process is no longer completely sealed?
Will a conscientious judge really be affected by the possibility that the
position he takes in a conference or a draft may some day see the light
of day?

The candor claim has also been asserted to shield executive communications from public disclosure. The argument in support of the claim
was summarized some years ago by an English judge, Lord Pearce,
"[T]he necessary candour cannot be obtained from civil servants if their
documents are to be subjected to an outside chance of production in a
court of law."[75]

This argument was accepted, at least in part, by Chief Justice Burger
in the *Nixon* case (discussed in Chapter 5), where he asserted, "[T]he
importance of this confidentiality is too plain to require further discussion." Without it, officials "may well temper candor with a concern for
appearances."[76] One may wonder, however, whether a more realistic view
is not that followed by the English courts; they reject the candor claim.
In the leading English case, the entire House of Lords agreed with the
view expressed by one of them that the claim is "of doubtful validity."[77]

More recently, Lord Keith, a member of the highest English court
declared in strong language:

[T]he candour contention must now be treated as having little weight, if any. The notion that any competent and conscientious public servant would be inhibited at all in the candour of his writings by consideration of the off-chance that they might have to be produced in a litigation is in my opinion grotesque. To represent that the possibility of it might significantly impair the public service is even more so. Nowadays the state in multifarious manifestations impinges closely upon the lives and activities of individual citizens. Where this has involved a citizen in litigation with the state or one of its agencies, the candour argument is an utterly insubstantial ground for denying him access to relevant documents.[78]

Is the argument really stronger in the case of the Supreme Court? The nine Justices, it should be stressed, are not mere friends exchanging gossip at a social gathering. They are deciding the most vital questions that arise in our society and they are deciding them conclusively, because there is no way the Court's decisions can be overruled except by constitutional amendment. One is reminded of Justice Jackson's famous statement some years ago, "There is no doubt that if there were a super-Supreme Court, a substantial proportion of our reversals of state courts would also be reversed. We are not final because we are infallible, but we are infallible only because we are final."[79]

It is important that we know as much as possible about how people placed in such a position of infallibility exercise their awesome power. Lord Acton's dictum that great men are almost always bad men does not necessarily apply to Supreme Court Justices. But our attitude toward them should still be based on some such assumption. Today, we must not judge those in possession of public power by the maxim that the king can do no wrong. On the contrary, if there is any presumption it should be the other way, against the holders of power, and increasing as the power increases.

Are the Court and the country harmed if it becomes known what a sitting Justice reveals in conference—for example, that had he been on the Court in 1954 he would not have agreed with *Brown* v. *Board of Education*'s famous footnote 11[80] because he feels modern sociological and psychological data do not support the notion of stigma relied on by Chief Justice Warren's *Brown* opinion?[81] Or if a letter of another Court member is published when it contains an animadversion on women's lib?[82] Or even if it is made known that a Justice wrote about one of his colleagues, "[Y]ou would no more heed [his] tripe than you would be seen naked at Dupont Circle at high noon tomorrow?"[83]

Is the public interest really served if such things are kept behind a veil of secrecy? If possible disclosure may lead to more restraint by the Justices, that is not necessarily undesirable. It is hard to see how the work of the Court will be hurt if the decision process is purged of the intemperate type of comment that Court revelations sometimes bring to light.

In addition, one may wonder whether the disseminator of news should be criticized for its content. I have always seen my role in writing about the Court's decision process as that of a reporter who describes what went on in the cases under scrutiny. My function is to tell what happened, not to shield the Court's inner processes from public view. I have been fortunate in having documents made available to me, such as those used throughout this book. But the decision to make them available as well as to discuss the cases involved, was not made by me but by people within the Court community—particularly by Justices who believed that the claims of history were more important than those of judicial secrecy.

My primary purpose in writing this book is to show how the highest Court operates. The documents published—the drafts and internal memoranda, the extracts from letters and conference notes—these all help to explain the workings of the Court: How the Justices vote and change their votes and how opinions are drafted and redrafted before they are finally issued. The Court's decision process is made clearer by this sort of material than it possibly can be by analysis, acute though it may be, of only the opinions published in the *United States Reports.* Other students of the Court have also written books on its inner workings that are based on the kinds of materials used by me, particularly draft opinions and memoranda.[84] From this point of view, I am in good scholarly company.

The bottom line, however, is ultimately to be found in the claims of history—even vis-à-vis the highest Court. The right of the people to know does not degenerate into a mere slogan where the work of the Justices is concerned. The country has the same right to information on how the Supreme Court operates that it has with regard to other governmental institutions. Contrary to the Lewis claim, dissemination of such information will help more than it will hinder the work of the Justices.

It should not be forgotten that the Court is ultimately, in Hamilton's phrase, "the weakest of the three departments."[85] The Justices themselves have recognized this. In Justice Frankfurter's words, "The Court's authority—possessed of neither the purse nor the sword—ultimately rests on sustained public confidence in its moral sanction."[86] The authority of the Court is moral, not physical. It operates by its influence, not by its power alone. The Justices must depend on public support for the ultimate efficacy of their judgments.

Public support depends on an informed public opinion. "What strikes me increasingly, in writings on the work of the Court," Justice Frankfurter once complained, "is their unrelatedness to actuality."[87] For the country to find out how the highest bench actually operates can only increase understanding of the Court's crucial role "in guarding the ark of the Constitution."[88] It must be admitted that my intention was not to solidify popular support for the Court, but to tell what actually happened in these cases and let the chips fall where they may. In fact, they do fall in a way that reflects favorably on the Court. One is constantly impressed by the willingness of Justices to change their views owing to the intellectual arguments made by their colleagues. No other governmental institution could be subjected to comparable scrutiny of its internal processes and come out so well.

The public may conclude from this book that the Court does not work at all in the cold, purely logical way that most people think it does, but that it does work—through the constant give and take between the Justices—in a way that ultimately serves the best interests of the country. Surely, it is better for Court and country that this be made known than for it to be kept concealed behind the red velour curtain.

Notes

1. *New York Times*, June 18, 1986, p. 1.
2. Schwartz, Oxford University Press, 1985.
3. Infra Chapter 4.
4. Infra Chapter 5.
5. Woodward and Armstrong, *The Brethren: Inside the Supreme Court* (1979).
6. John M. Harlan–Warren E. Burger, May 21, 1970. Harlan Papers, Princeton.
7. *New York Times Magazine*, February 20, 1983, p. 20.
8. Drury, *Decision 61* (1983).
9. Warren E. Burger–John M. Harlan, n.d. 1971 Burger File. Harlan Papers, Princeton.
10. William O. Douglas–William J. Brennan, April 24, [1972].
11. *New York Times*, June 14, 1965, p. 38.
12. *New York Times*, March 13, 1986, p. A24.
13. Schwartz, *Swann's Way: The School Busing Case and the Supreme Court* 29 (1986).
14. Hughes, *The Supreme Court of the United States* 58–59 (1928).
15. See, e.g., *New York Times*, May 1, 1984, p. A18.
16. Schwartz, op. cit. supra note 13, at 110–12.
17. Felix Frankfurter–Fred M. Vinson, n.d. Frankfurter Papers, Library of Congress.
18. *New York Times*, March 8, 1986, p. 7.
19. Felix Frankfurter–George W. Pepper, October 19, 1956. Frankfurter Papers, Library of Congress.
20. Supra note 7.
21. *Brown v. Board of Education*, 347 U.S. 483 (1954).
22. *Newsweek*, July 23, 1979, p. 68.
23. *New York Times*, July 12, 1981, section 4, p. 22.
24. Supra note 18.
25. Woodward and Armstrong, op. cit. supra note 5, at 322.
26. Supra note 7.
27. Ibid.
28. *Regents v. Bakke*, 438 U.S. 265 (1978).
29. Lewis F. Powell–Byron R. White, February 11, 1977.
30. Clayton, *The Making of Justice: The Supreme Court in Action* 217 (1964).
31. *Jacobellis v. Ohio*, 378 U.S. 184, 197 (1964).

32. *New York Times*, December 8, 1985, p. 1.
33. Supra note 18.
34. Ibid.
35. *New York Times*, July 23, 1984, p. 8.
36. Blasi, ed., *The Burger Court: The Counter Revolution that Wasn't* 252 (1983).
37. *New York Times*, January 17, 1986, p. A14.
38. *New York Times*, April 21, 1962, p. 17.
39. Brennan, Address at Dean's Day, NYU Law School (1979).
40. Woodward and Armstrong, op. cit. supra note 5, passim.
41. *U.S. News & World Report*, December 13, 1957, p. 74.
42. Quoted in Clark, "Internal Operation of the United States Supreme Court," 43 *Journal of the American Judicature Society*, pp. 45, 48 (1959).
43. *New York Times*, May 1, 1958, p. 27.
44. *New York Times Magazine*, April 17, 1958, p. 16.
45. Stevens, 1982 Madison Lecture at NYU Law School.
46. Justice O'Connor also joined the cert pool, so, it ultimately consisted of six Justices.
47. Felix Frankfurter–Potter Stewart, April 29, 1960. Frankfurter Papers, Library of Congress.
48. Douglas, *The Court Years 1939–1975*, 173 (1980).
49. *Harvard Law School Bulletin*, Winter 1986, p. 28.
50. *Brown* v. *Board of Education*, 347 U.S. 483, 494, n.11 (1954).
51. *Harvard Law School Bulletin*, Winter 1986, p. 28.
52. Douglas, *Memorandum to the Conference*, October 23, 1961. Hugo Black Papers, Library of Congress.
53. *Harvard Law School Bulletin*, Winter 1986, p. 29.
54. *Felix Frankfurter Reminisces* 86 (1960).
55. *Washington Post National Weekly Edition*, October 1, 1984, p. 33.
56. Ibid.
57. 1 de Tocqueville, *Democracy in America* 290 (Bradley ed. 1954).
58. *Economist*, July 12, 1983, p. 16.
59. *Dred Scott* v. *Sandford*, 19 How. 393 (U.S. 1857).
60. *Pollock* v. *Farmers' Loan & Trust Co.*, 157 U.S. 429 (1895).
61. *Brown* v. *Board of Education*, 347 U.S. 483 (1954).
62. *Powell* v. *McCormack*, 395 U.S. 486 (1969).
63. Justice Fortas, quoted in *The Fourteenth Amendment Centennial Volume* 34 (Schwartz ed. 1970).
64. Douglas, in *The Great Rights* 148 (Cahn ed. 1963).
65. 4 *The Collected Essays Journalism and Letters of George Orwell* 75 (1968).
66. Loc. cit. supra note 64.
67. Lewis, *New York Times Book Review*, December 29, 1985, p. 20.
68. Woodward and Armstrong, op. cit. supra note 5.
69. Schwartz, *Super Chief: Earl Warren and His Supreme Court—a Judicial Biography* (1983).
70. Lewis, supra note 67.
71. Ibid.
72. Ibid.
73. *New York Times Magazine*, March 16, 1975, p. 15.
74. Griswold, 69 *American Bar Association Journal* 1506 (1983).

75. *Conway* v. *Rimmer,* [1968] A.C. 910, 984.
76. *United States* v. *Nixon,* 418 U.S. 683, 705 (1974).
77. *Burmah Oil Co.* v. *Bank of England,* [1980] A.C. 1090, 1132.
78. Id. at 1132–1133.
79. *Brown* v. *Allen,* 344 U.S. 443, 540 (1953).
80. Supra note 50.
81. Schwartz, op. cit. supra note 69, at 705.
82. Infra p. 81.
83. Schwartz, op. cit. supra note 69, at 268.
84. E.g., Mason, *Harlan Fiske Stone: Pillar of the Law* (1956); Bickel, *The Unpublished Opinions of Mr. Justice Brandeis* (1957).
85. *The Federalist,* No. 78.
86. Dissenting in *Baker* v. *Carr,* 369 U.S. 186, 267 (1962).
87. Felix Frankfurter–Herbert Wechsler, September 27, 1954. Frankfurter Papers, Library of Congress.
88. 1 Bryce, *The American Commonwealth* 242 (1917 ed.).

1

Barlow v. Collins (1970): Standing and Access to the Courts

Justice Louis D. Brandeis used to say that what the Supreme Court did not do was often more important than what it did do. One thing the Court does not do is deal with disputes that are not presented to it in the form of "cases" or "controversies" as required by Article III of the U.S. Constitution. The Court's only power is "to determine actual controversies arising between adverse litigants"[1] with real interests at stake.

"As an incident to the elaboration of this bedrock requirement," Justice William H. Rehnquist tells us, "this Court has always required that a litigant have 'standing' to challenge the action sought to be adjudicated in the lawsuit."[2] In the settled view of the Supreme Court, there can be no actual "case" or "controversy" if the individual bringing the particular action does not have a personal interest in the act that he challenges. "[T]he party who invokes the court's authority [must] 'show that he personally has suffered some actual or threatened injury as a result of the putatively illegal conduct of the defendant'."[3] Unless he is adversely affected personally, as an individual, plaintiff is seeking a judgment only in the abstract on the legality of the act that he challenges. Such a proceeding is not enough to call for the exercise by the Court of its judicial power.[4]

The law governing standing has a direct relation to the ability of people to vindicate their constitutional rights. Unless standing exists, the litigant is not entitled to have the Court decide the merits of even the most important constitutional issue. Thus, were the federal government, in violation of the Establishment Clause of the First Amendment,[5] to grant property to a Church-related college, this action would be rendered immune from judicial review—even if such review might find it blatantly unconstitutional—if there were no plaintiff with standing to challenge it.

A narrow concept of standing may have been appropriate in an earlier day when the legal system was geared only to hearing John Doe's private law claims against Richard Roe. Many feel that if public interest claims are to be adequately considered in today's legal system, the concept of those able to vindicate the public interest must be accordingly expanded.

One of the criticisms often leveled at the Burger Court is that it unduly restricted the liberalized approach to standing adopted by its predecessor Court under Chief Justice Warren. In *Barlow* v. *Collins*,[6] however, decided during the new Chief Justice's first year, the draft opinion of the Court by Justice Brennan took a more expansive approach to standing than had theretofore been taken in Supreme Court jurisprudence. And, even after the opinions were revised, it turns out that the decisions on standing during the first Burger Term were in their results more favorable to standing than would appear from the language of the opinions finally issued by the Court.

Two standing cases were presented to the Court during the 1969 Term. They were *Associated Data Processing Organizations* v. *Camp*[7] and *Barlow* v. *Collins* itself. In *Data Processing*, companies that sold data processing services to businesses sought to challenge a ruling by the comptroller of the currency that permitted national banks to make data processing services available to other banks and to bank customers. In *Barlow*, tenant farmers challenged the validity of a regulation by the secretary of agriculture regarding the conditions under which federal payments to farmers could be assigned to third parties. The secretary had acted under a statute limiting these assignments to those business transactions that financed "making a crop." Although previously this regulation had excluded assignments to secure payment of farm rent, the regulation as revised expressly defined "making a crop" to include assignments to secure "the payment of cash rent for [farm]land," something the tenant farmers did not want. Plaintiffs alleged that they had been injured by the revised regulation because once the landlords knew that farmers could assign the payments for the rent, they started to pressure them to do so. The effect of the new regulation, therefore, was to take away from the farmers their freedom to use their authority to assign payments as a bargaining tool with the merchants with whom they dealt.

The lower courts in both cases had held that plaintiffs lacked standing. In *Barlow*, the court of appeals found that plaintiffs alleged no invasion of a legally protected interest and that the governing statute did not give them standing. In *Data Processing*, the court of appeals had followed a similar approach. At the conference following arguments in the cases, the Justices all voted to reverse. But this did not lead to a simple opinion rejecting the reasoning upon which the courts of appeals had acted. Instead, there were two separate draft opinions, each following a different approach to the law of standing.

Despite the fact that both *Data Processing* and *Barlow* involved the same issue of standing and the opinions in each should have been assigned to one Justice, who would articulate a uniform Court approach to the issue, the Chief Justice assigned the opinions in the two cases to different Justices: *Data Processing* to Justice William O. Douglas and *Barlow* to

Justice William J. Brennan, Jr. According to one Justice, "The separate assignment of the cases led to much confusion and turmoil before the Court arrived at a single approach for use in both cases."

As it turned out, Justice Brennan had the most liberal approach to standing among the Justices. The Brennan approach may be seen from his draft *Barlow* opinion, which he prepared in early January 1970 and is reprinted on p. 33. On top of the draft copy I used was written, "Not Circulated Sent Copy to Douglas only."

This statement is borne out by a January 5 "Dear Bill" letter from Brennan to Douglas:

> Enclosed is No. 249—*Barlow* v. *Collins* involving the "standing" question you dealt with in No. 85—*Data Processing* v. *Camp*.
>
> I am not going to circulate this until I've had your view of how we ought to coordinate this with No. 85. And, of course, it's going to need a lot of polishing in any event.

The Brennan draft states a simple standing test. "This test is satisfied when the plaintiff alleges, as petitioners complaint alleged here, that the challenged action has caused him substantial injury in fact." This test, says Brennan, would ensure plaintiffs with the proper adversary zeal. "We may reasonably expect that a person so harmed will frame the relevant questions with the necessary specificity, contest the issues with the necessary adverseness, and pursue the litigation vigorously."

Nor, according to the Brennan draft, is more required than injury in fact to meet the Article III "case" or "controversy" requirement. A plaintiff with such an injury "may therefore 'be deemed to have the personal stake and interest that imparts the concrete adverseness . . .'" required by Article III. "Recognition of his standing is then consistent with the constitutional limitations of Article III."

Under his test, Justice Brennan concludes, the *Barlow* plaintiffs had standing. Nor did it make any difference that plaintiffs had failed to show that defendant's action invaded one of their legally protected interests. To hold otherwise would unduly restrict standing. "To insist that a plaintiff show invasion of a legally protected interest confuses the merits of the controversy with the standing of the party to litigate them. Just as standing is a question apart from other aspects of justiciability, so it is unconcerned with whether the plaintiff has stated a claim upon which relief can be granted."

SUPREME COURT OF THE UNITED STATES

No. 249.—OCTOBER TERM, 1969

Clemon Barlow et al., Petitioners, *v.* B. L. Collins, etc., et al.	On Writ of Certiorari to the United States Court of Appeals for the Fifth Circuit.

[January —, 1970]

MR. JUSTICE BRENNAN delivered the opinion of the Court.

The questions to be decided in this case are (1) whether tenant farmers eligible for payments under the Upland Cotton Program enacted by the Food and Agriculture Act of 1965, 7 U. S. C. § 1444 (d), 79 Stat. 1194, have standing to challenge the validity of certain amended regulations promulgated by the respondent Secretary of Agriculture in 1966, and (2) whether in any event judicial review of the Secretary's action at the instance of these petitioners is precluded by the pertinent statutes.

The Upland Cotton Program incorporates a 1938 statute, § 8 (g) of the Soil Conservation and Domestic Allotment Act as amended, 16 U. S. C. § 590h (g), which limits the payments which are made assignable by § 1444 (d)(13) of the 1965 Act to a single assignment of payments during the crop year "as security for cash or advances to finance making a crop." [1] The regulations

---

[1] The Secretary of Agriculture is authorized by § 1444 (d)(5) of the 1965 Act in advance of the growing season to pay a farmer up to 50% of the estimated benefits due him. Section 1444 (d)(13) authorizes the farmer to assign such benefits subject to the limitations of § 8 (g) of the 1938 Act, 16 U. S. C. § 590 (g). Section 8 (g) as enacted in 1938 and as it read in 1965 established an exception

BARLOW *v.* COLLINS

of the respondent Secretary of Agriculture in effect from
1938 to 1966 defined "making a crop" to exclude assignments to secure "the payment of the whole or any part
of a cash . . . rent for a farm." 20 Fed. Reg. 6511
(1955).[2] Following enactment of the 1965 Act, however, and before any payments were made under it, the
Secretary deleted the exclusion and amended the regulations expressly to define "making a crop" to include
assignments to secure ". . . the payment of cash rent

to the general prohibition against assignment in the Anti-Assignment Act, 31 U. S. C. § 203. Section 8 (g) provided:

"A payment which may be made to a farmer under this section,
may be assigned, without discount, by him in writing as security
for cash or advances *to finance making a crop.* Such assignment
shall be signed by the farmer and witnessed by a member of the
county committee . . . . Such assignment shall include the statement that the assignment is not made to pay or secure any pre-
existing indebtedness. This provision shall not authorize any suit
against or impose any liability upon the Secretary . . . if payment
to the farmer is made without regard to the existence of any such
assignment, . . ." 52 Stat. 35 and 205 (1938), 16 U. S. C.
§ 590h (g). (Emphasis added.)

Section 8 (g) was amended by 80 Stat. 1167 (1966) to permit
assignments not only to finance "making a crop" but also to fund
"handling or marketing an agricultural commodity, or performing
a conservation practice."

[2] 20 Fed. Reg. 6511, 6512 (Sept. 3, 1955) provided:

"*Payment may be assigned to finance making a crop.* A payment
which may be made to a farmer . . . under section 8 of the Soil
Conservation and Domestic Allotment Act as amended, may be
assigned only as security for cash or advances to finance making
a crop for the current crop year. To finance making a crop means
(a) to finance the planting, cultivating, or harvesting of a crop,
including the purchase of equipment required therefor; (b) to
provide food, clothing, and other necessities required by the assignor
or persons dependent upon the assignor; or (c) to finance the
carrying out of soil or water conservation practices. Nothing contained herein shall be construed to authorize an assignment given
to secure the payment of the whole or any part of the purchase
price of a farm or the payment of the whole or any part of a cash
or fixed commodity for rent for a farm."

BARLOW *v.* COLLINS

for land used (for planting, cultivating or harvesting)."
31 F. 2815 (1966).[3]

Petitioners, tenant farmers suing on behalf of themselves and other tenant farmers similarly situated, filed this action in the District Court for the Middle District of Alabama, Northern District. They sought a declaratory judgment that the amended regulations are invalid and unauthorized by statute, and an injunction enjoining the respondent federal officials from permitting assignments pursuant to the amended regulations.[4] Their

---

[3] 32 Fed. Reg. 14921 (Oct. 28, 1967), 7 CFR 709.3 (1968) now provides:

"Purposes for which a payment may be assigned.

"(a) A payment which may be made to a producer under any program to which this part is applicable may be assigned only as security for cash or advances to finance making a crop, handling or marketing an agricultural commodity, or performing a conservation practice, for the current crop year. No assignment may be made to secure or pay any preexisting indebtedness of any nature whatsoever.

"(b) To finance making a crop means (1) to finance the planting, cultivating, or harvesting of a crop, including the purchase of equipment required therefor and the payment of cash rent for land used therefor, or (2) to provide food, clothing, and other necessities required by the producer or persons dependent upon him.

"(c) Nothing contained herein shall be construed to authorize an assignment given to secure the payment of the whole or any part of the purchase price of a farm or the payment of the whole or any part of a fixed commodity rent for a farm."

[4] The respondents, in addition to the Secretary of Agriculture, are the State Executive Director of the Agricultural and Conservation Services in Alabama, and the administrator of that service in the U. S. Department of Agriculture. The complaint also included counts against petitioners' landlord alleging that he acted improperly to deprive them of their right to receive subsidy payments, and, further, that some of the petitioners had been illegally evicted because of their participation in litigation with respect to the cotton program, and in the case of one petitioner, because of his candidacy for A. S. C. S. county committeeman. The District Court held that there was jurisdiction of those counts and denied the landlord's motion to dismiss them. That ruling is not before us.

BARLOW *v.* COLLINS

complaint alleged that the petitioners were suffering
irreparable injury under the amended regulations because
they "were each year required [by their landlord] to
execute a rent note as security for the cash rent" pay-
able at the end of the crop year, and were therefore
forced to obtain from their landlord, at high prices and
high interest rates, because of lack of funds and credit,
the food and supplies needed to make a crop, thus being
deprived of the opportunity to use the authority to
assign payments as a bargaining tool to negotiate better
arrangements directly with one of the various merchants
engaged in selling food and supplies. Thus, petitioners
alleged that they suffered injury in fact from the operation of the amended regulations.[5]

The District Court, in an unreported opinion, held
that the petitioners "lack standing to maintain this action
against these [respondent] governmental officials," because those officials "have not taken any action which
invades any legally protected interest of the plaintiffs."
The Court of Appeals for the Fifth Circuit affirmed, one
judge dissenting. 398 F. 2d 398 (1968). The Court of
Appeals held that petitioners lacked standing not only
because they alleged no invasion of a legally protected
interest but also because petitioners "have not shown
us, nor have we found any provision of the Food and
Agriculture Act of 1965 which expressly or impliedly
gives plaintiffs standing to challenge this administrative
regulation or gives the courts authority to review such
administrative action." *Id.*, at 402. We granted certiorari. 395 U. S. 958 (1969). We reverse.

---

[5] The complaint alleged that some of the petitioners "were denied
the right to work the land" when they refused to execute assignments to their landlord. The complaint also alleged that "plaintiffs
have been tenant farmers on this land from eleven to sixty one
years . . . and [Williams Chas] been on this land [all his life]."

BARLOW *v.* COLLINS

I

Flast v. *Cohen*, 392 U. S. 83 (1968), recently reviewed the criteria governing the determination of standing in the absence of statutory aids. We there held that "The fundamental aspect of standing is that it focuses *on the party* seeking to get before a federal court and *not on the issues* he wishes to have adjudicated." *Id.*, at ——. (Italics supplied.) We confirmed what we said in *Baker* v. *Carr*, 369 U. S. 186, 204 (1962), that the "gist of the question of standing" is whether the party seeking relief has "alleged such a personal stake in the outcome of the controversy as to assure that concrete adverseness which sharpens the presentation of issues upon which the court so largely depends. . . ." "In other words," we said in *Flast*, "when standing is placed in issue in a case, the question is whether the person whose standing is challenged is a proper party to request an adjudication of a particular issue and not whether the issue itself is justiciable . . . . Thus, in terms of Article III limitations on federal court jurisdiction, the question of standing is related only to whether the dispute sought to be adjudicated will be presented in an adversary context and in a form historically viewed as capable of judicial resolution." 392 U. S., at ——. See also *Association of Data Processing, etc. Assn.* v. *Camp,* decided today, and *Chicago* v. *Atchison, T. & S. F. R. Co.,* 357 U. S. 77, 83 (1957).

This test is satisfied when the plaintiff alleges, as petitioners complaint alleged here, that the challenged action has caused him substantial injury in fact. We may reasonably expect that a person so harmed will frame the relevant questions with the necessary specificity, contest the issues with the necessary adverseness, and pursue the litigation vigorously. Such a plaintiff may therefore "be deemed to have the personal stake and

BARLOW *v.* COLLINS

interest that imparts the concrete adverseness to such
litigation . . . ." 392 U. S., at ——.[6] Recognition of
his standing is then consistent with the constitutional
limitations of Article III.

Accordingly, the District Court and the Court of
Appeals erred in holding fatal to petitioners' standing
their failure also to allege that respondents' action invaded their legally protected interests. Insofar as *Associated Industries* v. *Ickes,* 134 F. 2d 694 (1943), relied
upon by the District Court, supports that holding, it is
disapproved. That holding confuses the merits of the
controversy with the standing of the party to litigate
them. Standing is a question apart from other aspects
of justiciability and from the substantive merits of a
controversy. We said in *Flast* that "in deciding the
question of standing, it is not relevant that the substantive issues in the litigation might be nonjusticiable."
392 U. S. ——. Similarly, it is not relevant that, without
proof of the invasion of a legally protected interest, it
may be that no claim will be established upon which
relief can be granted.[7] It is true that the inquiry for
allegations of injury in fact often explores the same

---

[6] See Davis, 3 Administrative Law Treatise § 22.02, at 211–213
(1958); Jaffe, Judicial Control of Administrative Action 336 (1965).
Injury has generally been economic in nature, but it need not be.
See, e. g., *Scenic Hudson Preservation Conf.* v. *FPC,* 354 F. 2d 608
(C. A. 2d Cir.), cert. denied, 384 U. S. 941 (1965); *Office of Com-
munication of United Church of Christ* v. *FCC,* 359 F. 2d 944
(C. A. D. C. Cir. 1966).

[7] However, although injury in fact may be slight, it may suffice
for standing if the claimant can show that the pertinent legal
interest is so precious that even the slightest invasion of it constitutes significant injury. See *Flast, supra,* at 103–104. Similarly,
modest injury in fact may be sufficient for standing if the claimant
can show that he is a member of the only class likely to challenge
the administrative acts in question. Cf. *FCC* v. *Sanders Bros.
Radio Station,* 309 U. S. 470, 477 (1940).

BARLOW *v.* COLLINS

ground as the inquiry into whether a claim has been alleged upon which relief may be granted. But "[i]t is enough for purposes of standing that we have an actual controversy before us in which [petitioners have] a direct and substantial personal interest in the outcome." *Chicago v. Atchison, T. & S. F. R. Co., supra,* at 83. Respondents' argument that the amended regulation is a valid interpretation of the statutory phrase "making a crop," and is neither internally inconsistent with nor prohibited by the Secretary's statutory obligation to provide adequate safeguards to protect the interests of tenants and sharecroppers, 7 U. S. C. § 1444 (d)(10), "confuses the merits of the controversy with the standing of [petitioners] to litigate them." *Ibid.* See also *FCC v. Sanders Bros. Radio Station,* 309 U. S. 470, 476–477 (1940); *Scripps-Howard Radio, Inc. v. FCC,* 316 U. S. 4 (1942).

II

We also disagree with the Court of Appeals that judicial review of the Secretary's action at the instance of petitioners is in any event precluded. The Court of Appeals rested that holding on the view that no provision of the Food and Agriculture Act of 1965 "expressly or impliedly . . . gives the courts authority to review such administrative action." 398 F. 2d, at ——. This holding pertains, of course, not to the issue of standing but to the question whether Congress has precluded judicial review of the Secretary's action. Although the Court of Appeals, improperly we think, seems to have treated that question as an element of petitioners' standing,⁸ reviewability is a separate question governed by

---

⁸ In other cases, also, attention has centered on search for a "statutory aid" to standing, either explicit language granting members of claimants' class a right to challenge the agency action, *e. g., FCC v. Sanders Bros. Radio Station,* 309 U. S. 470 (1940);

BARLOW *v.* COLLINS

its own criteria. Reviewability of agency action poses difficult questions of congressional intent and public policy: the Court must inquire whether Congress has in express or implied terms precluded judicial review or committed the challenged action entirely to administrative discretion. No light is shed on those questions by the limited inquiry which determines standing, namely, whether the litigant has alleged substantial injury in fact.

Section 10 of the Administrative Procedure Act, 60 Stat. 243, 5 U. S. C. § 1009, provides for judicial review of agency action "[e]xcept so far as (1) statutes preclude judicial review or (2) agency action is by law committed to agency discretion." The amended regulation here under challenge was promulgated under 16 U. S. C. § 590 (d)(3) which authorizes the Secretary to "prescribe such regulations, as he may deem proper, to carry out the provisions of this chapter." Plainly this is not an express provision precluding judicial review, nor is there such a provision elsewhere in either the 1938 or 1965 Acts. Cf. *Schilling* v. *Rogers*, 363 U. S. 666, 670 (1966), construing § 7 (c) of the Trading with the Enemy Act. Nor does the permissive term "as he may deem proper" in § 590 (d)(3) "persuasively indicate that their administration [in defining 'making a crop'] was committed entirely to the discretionary judgment of the Executive branch 'without the intervention of the courts.' " *Schilling* v. *Rogers, supra,* at 674. On the contrary, this is an instance "where the only or principal dispute relates to the meaning of the statutory term" ["making a crop"], *NLRB* v. *Marcus Trucking Co.,* 286 F. 2d 583, 591 (19—), and that is a question of law

---

Scripps-Howard Radio, Inc. v. *FCC,* 316 U. S. 4 (1942), or "implied beneficiary" indicia that one of the statutory purposes was to protect the claimants' class, *e. g., The Chicago Junction Case,* 264 U. S. 258 (1924); *Hardin* v. *Kentucky Utilities,* 390 U. S. 1 (1968).

BARLOW *v.* COLLINS

traditionally decided by the courts. See *Texas Gas Corp. v. Shell Oil Co.*, 363 U. S. 263, 269–270 (1960).

The question then becomes whether the preclusion of judicial review can fairly be inferred. This Court has gone far toward establishing the proposition that preclusion of judicial review of administrative action adjudicating private rights is not lightly to be inferred. See *Leedom v. Kyne*, 358 U. S. 184 (1958); *Harrison v. Brucker*, 355 U. S. 579 (1958); *Stark v. Wickard*, 321 U. S. 288 (1944); *American School of Magnetic Healing v. McAnnulty*, 187 U. S. 94 (1902). Indeed, judicial review of such administrative action is the rule, and nonreviewability an exception which must be demonstrated. In *Abbott Laboratories v. Gardiner*, 387 U. S. 136, 140 (1967), we held that "judicial review of final agency action by an aggrieved person will not cut off unless there is persuasive reason to believe that such was the purpose of Congress." A clear command of the statute will preclude review; and such a command of the statute may be inferred from its purpose. However, "only upon a showing of 'clear and convincing evidence' of a contrary legislative intent should the courts restrict access to judicial review." *Id.*, at 141. Application of the principle is especially appropriate when the merits involve questions ordinarily resolved by courts. "The role of the courts should, in particular, be viewed hospitably where . . . the question sought to be reviewed does not significantly engage the agency's expertise . . . 'where the only principal dispute relates to the meaning of the statutory term' . . . presents issues on which courts, and not [administrators], are relatively more expert." *Hardin v. Kentucky Utilities Co.*, 390 U. S. 1, 14 (1968) (HARLAN, J.). Moreover, the right of judicial review is ordinarily inferred where congressional intent to protect the interests of the class of which the claimant is a member can be found; in such cases, unless members of the

BARLOW *v.* COLLINS

protected class may have judicial review the statutory
objectives might not be realized. See the *Chicago Junc-
tion Case,* 264 U. S. 258 (1924); *Hardin* v. *Kentucky
Utilities, supra; Norwalk Redevelopment Agency,* 395
F. 2d 920 (C. A. 2d Cir. 1968); *Curran* v. *Clifford,* No.
21040 (D. C. D. C. Cir. Dec. 22, 1968); *Western
Addition Community Organization* v. *Weaver,* 294 F.
Supp. 433 (D. C. N. D. Cal. 1968); *Powelton Civic Home
Owners Association* v. *HUD,* 284 F. Supp. 809 (1968).

Applying these principles. we think. contrary to the
Court of Appeals. that the statutory scheme is not to
be read as precluding judicial review but rather as authorizing the courts to review the action of the Secretary at
the instance of these petitioners. The class which they
represent—cash rent tenant farmers—is the group among
the farmers affected by the regulation which has been
most directly injured by it. Although nothing in the
relevant statutory language speaks directly to whether
cash rent tenant farmers may challenge the Secretary's
action. compare *Scripps-Howard Radio* v. *FCC, supra,*
implicit in the pertinent statutory provisions and their
legislative history is a congressional intent that the
Secretary protect the interests of tenant farmers. Both
of the relevant statutes expressly enjoin the Secretary
to do so. Section 1444 (d)(10) of the Food and Agriculture Act of 1965 states that "[t]he Secretary shall
provide adequate safeguards to protect the interests of
tenants . . . ." * Section 1444 (d)(13) of this Act. as

---

* In connection with the amended regulation, the Secretary invoked
§ 1444 (d)(10) to provide [32 Fed. Reg. 2935 (Feb. 16, 1967), as
amended, 32 Fed. Reg. 6127 (April 19, 1967)] that diversion and
price support payments assigned to a landlord

"shall not be approved for payment by the county committee if
the county committee determines that any of the following conditions exist . . . .

"(1) The landlord . . . has not afforded his tenants and sharecroppers an opportunity to participate in the program;

BARLOW *v.* COLLINS

noted earlier, incorporates by reference § 8 (g), as amended, of the Soil Conservation and Domestic Allotment Act. Section 590 (h)(b) of that Act, in turn, provides that "the Secretary shall, as far as practicable, protect the interests of tenants. . . ."

The legislative history, though sparse, indicates a congressional intent to benefit the tenants. At the time of § 8 (g)'s initial adoption in 1937, an attempt to state in the provision that assignments might be freely made was defeated in the Senate, the principal objection being that "the poor farmer may need protection against [merchants, doctors, bankers] who may go to him and induce him to make the assignment of an amount not yet due him . . . ." (Remarks of Senator Adams.) 82 Cong. Rec. 1755–1756, 1766 (1937). The House had previously voted to permit assignments to landlords only, despite some fear that " 'this may give the landlord an opportunity to gyp his tenant . . . .' " The sponsor of the amendment permitting such assignments, however, felt that landlords would guard the interests of their tenants, who might otherwise be at the mercy of "merchants and

---

"(2) The landlord . . . has, in anticipation of or because of participating in the program, reduced the number of tenants and sharecroppers on the farm . . . .

"(3) There exists between the . . . landlord and any tenant or sharecropper, any lease, contract, agreement or understanding unfairly exacted or acquired by the . . . landlord which was entered into in anticipation of participating in the program, the effect of which is:

"(i) To force the tenant or sharecropper to pay over to the landlord . . . any payment earned by him under the program;

"(ii) To change the status of any tenant or sharecropper so as to deprive him of any payment or right which he would otherwise have had under the program;

.   .   .   .   .

"(iv) To increase the rent to be paid by the tenant or decrease the share of the crop or its proceeds to be received by the sharecropper . . . ."

BARLOW *v.* COLLINS

speculators." (Remarks of Rep. Fulmer.) *Id.*, at 844.
As finally adopted, § 8 (g) enabled the farmers to make
assignments subject to three limitations: the assignment
had "to finance making a crop"; it could not pay or secure
a pre-existing debt; and it had to be made without discount. The report of the House managers of the measure
stressed these limitations. See H. R. Rep. No. 1767,
75th Cong., 2d Sess., 60 (1938). The fact that assignments could be made at all indicated a congressional
concern for the farmers' welfare, in the light of the general statutory prohibition on assignment of federal claims
enacted in the Anti-Assignment Act, 31 U. S. C. § 203.
This concern was noted in a letter from the Secretary
of the Department of Agriculture to the President of the
Senate in January 1952, in which the Secretary stated
that § 8 (g) "was enacted for the purpose of creating
additional credit to farmers to assist them in financing
farming operations." S. Rep. No. 1305 (1952). This
evidence of congressional concern for the well-being of
tenant farmers suffices to justify the inference that Congress meant that they should be entitled to judicial
review of the Secretary's action.

III

The judgments of the Court of Appeals and of the
District Court are therefore vacated and the case is
remanded to the District Court for a hearing on the
merits.

It is so ordered.

Justice Brennan's draft opinion of the Court in *Barlow* v. *Collins* would have liberalized the federal law of standing in two important respects: It would have (1) abolished the requirement that there had been a "legal wrong"[8] and (2) would have substituted for that requirement and other standing tests the single requirement of "injury in fact."

The first part of this proposed change was written into the final opinions in *Data Processing* and *Barlow*. The Brennan "might have been" turned into the Douglas "was"; it is, therefore, not necessary to discuss this aspect of the Brennan draft further.

The same is not true of the Brennan effort to state a simple injury-in-fact test as the sole standing criterion. The Brennan effort here was frustrated by the assignment of the other standing case before the Court to Justice Douglas. It will be recalled that Justice Brennan had sent an uncirculated copy of his draft (supra p. 32) to Douglas. The latter similarly sent his draft *Data Processing* opinion to Brennan before circulating it.

When Justice Brennan received the Douglas draft, he saw immediately that it differed from his *Barlow* draft on the standing issue. As Brennan put it in a January 20 *MEMORANDUM TO THE CONFERENCE*, "Bill Douglas' circulation in No. 85 [*Data Processing*] and mine in No. 249 [*Barlow*] differ on a very narrow but important question concerning how judges are to determine the standing of plaintiffs who challenge administrative action."

The memo explained the difference:

> Bill's approach has two stages: (1) Since Article III restricts judicial power to cases or controversies, the starting point is to ascertain whether "the plaintiff alleges that the challenged action has caused him injury in fact" (*Data Processing* at page 2); (2) if injury in fact is alleged, the judge then ascertains "whether the interest sought to be protected by the complainant is arguably within the zone of interests to be protected or regulated by the statute or constitutional guarantee in question" (*Id.*, at page 3). Only if both appear may standing be found. On the other hand, my approach restricts standing to inquiry (1), the constitutional requirement. At page 7 of *Barlow*, I conclude: "Recognition of his standing is then consistent with the Constitution, *and no further inquiry is pertinent to its existence.*"

After he had read the Brennan *Barlow* draft, Justice Douglas wrote him on January 8, "The only suggestion I have to make in your draft" was to change the sentence on satisfaction of the standing test (supra p. 32) to read, "This test is satisfied when the plaintiff alleges that the challenged action either touches a zone to which the law has already applied sanctions or causes harm, economic or otherwise, within the purview of the federal statute whose application is in question."

This change would, of course, have meant the adoption by Justice Brennan of the more restrictive Douglas two-prong standing test. This Brennan refused to do. Soon after receiving the Douglas note, Brennan replied with a January 8 letter stating that he accepted "your 'economic or otherwise'" suggestion because

> I fully agree, as you know, that the injury need not be economic. . . . [I]t occurs to me that this should be the extent of the revision. I'm afraid that the rest suggests the requirement of a showing of invasion of a legal interest. Although the thrust of the opinion is that this is not necessary for standing purposes, wouldn't that be the effect of requiring that the "challenged action either touches a zone to which the law has already applied sanctions or causes harm . . . within the purview of the federal statute whose application is in question?" In other words, wouldn't that require the *Barlow* plaintiffs to prove the merits in order to get standing—that is, to prove that "making a crop" forbids assignments for cash rent?

On January 13, Brennan again wrote Douglas to the same effect. During the next week the two Justices tried to work out a compromise that would produce a united Douglas–Brennan front. Both tried to reach an agreement because they feared that the other Justices might take a less liberal view of standing than either of them; the conference might well resolve the Douglas–Brennan disagreement by taking a harder line than either of them desired.

A penciled note in Justice Brennan's writing on three small memo pages bears out this interpretation of the compromise effort. Referring to Justice Douglas, the note states, "He's afraid that an open fight between us in conference might result in both of us losing out—and he thinks that would be more unfortunate because either opinion represents an advance."

Justice Brennan tried to rewrite *Barlow* to eliminate the conflict with *Data Processing*, but the attempt proved fruitless. A new draft of *Barlow* has the following in the writing of a Brennan clerk at its beginning: "Draft begun in attempt to bring Barlow into line with Douglas' approach—abandoned as hopeless."

The more Justice Brennan tried to bring *Barlow* into line with Douglas's *Data Processing* approach, the more he became convinced of the soundness of his own standing position. Finally, both Justices circulated their drafts as well as memoranda to the conference explaining their divergent approaches. The Brennan January 20 memo has already been quoted. It consisted of seven typed pages and retailed the Justice's view that the Douglas approach confused standing and the merits. It stated that such a confusion had prevailed in *Barlow* itself: "By confusing the merits with the tenant farmers' standing and their entitlement to judicial review, both the District Court and the Court of Appeals denied the farmers the focused and careful decision on the merits to which they are clearly entitled."

The difficulty could be avoided by the Brennan standing test. "The serious risk of injustice inherent in merging the inquiry into standing with the inquiries into reviewability and the merits, can be avoided, I submit, if the determination of standing is made to depend solely on whether plaintiff has alleged injury in fact."

The one question that must be asked to determine standing is that of harm to plaintiff. "More fundamentally," the Brennan memo declared, "in terms of the desirability of separating distinct questions from one another lest each one not be squarely faced and decided on its own merits, it is important to restrict standing to an inquiry into injury in fact. The search for so-called 'statutory aid to standing' is a distinct issue concerning the congressional plan for reviewability of the agency's action."

Justice Douglas replied with a two-page January 21 *MEMORAN-DUM TO THE CONFERENCE*. Taking direct issue with the Brennan view, Douglas wrote, "I do not think that the matter of standing can rest solely on the Article III inquiry." Douglas then explained why he would require more than injury in fact:

> [w]hen we deal with standing to attack the action of an agency operating under a statute, we have at least to look to the statute to determine whether there is any explicit barrier to the particular type of plaintiff making the claim. I think that the courts must go further and look at the statute to see if the claimant is at least arguably within the zone of interests protected by the statute.

In his January 20 memo, Justice Brennan had asserted about his split with Justice Douglas on the matter, "The Conference must decide the issue before either case can come down." And in concluding his memo Brennan noted, "Perhaps we can give some time at the conference on January 23 to resolving this difference in approach."

At the conference itself, the Justices supported the Douglas approach. Justice Brennan received only Justice White's support. After some further effort to rewrite *Barlow*, Justice Brennan decided to give up the case. In a January 26 "Dear Chief" letter, he wrote:

> I find that I can't rewrite my proposed opinion in the above to bring it into line with the Conference acceptance of Bill Douglas' approach to the determination of standing in No. 85—*Data Processing v. Camp*. I, therefore, suggest that this opinion be reassigned to another Justice. I'll then file a concurring opinion dissenting from his approach.

Barlow was then reassigned by the Chief Justice to Justice Douglas, who wrote the final opinion of the Court, resolving the standing issue on his own terms. *Data Processing* and *Barlow* were decided as companion cases, with the Douglas opinions in both issued with the decision announcements on March 3.

The Brennan memo had declared that the difference on the matter had reached the point where "I don't think our difference is 'much ado about nothing.'" Did it really matter, however, that the Douglas rather than the Brennan view on standing ultimately prevailed in *Data Processing* and *Barlow*?

Justice Douglas, for one, indicated at the time that it did. In his January 21 memo, he conceded, "Limiting standing to an Article III 'injury-in-fact' test would in some eyes have the advantage of giving many claimants an opportunity to obtain a ruling on the merits of their claims, when otherwise the statutory scheme reasonably interpreted might preclude them and all like them from any standing to be heard at all."

The test used for standing has a direct relationship to the right of access to the courts. Under the Brennan approach, all that would be needed to secure such access is to show injury in fact—some adverse effect from the governmental act that plaintiff challenges. The bipartite injury test adopted by the Court in *Data Processing* and *Barlow* adds an additional requirement. To satisfy the second prong of the Douglas test, plaintiffs must show that the relevant statutes were meant to protect them from the specific type of action they were challenging.[9]

The bipartite injury test laid down by the Douglas opinions is needlessly complex; despite the Court's disclaimer, it is a backward step toward the discredited "legal wrong" requirement. There is much to be said for state decisions rejecting the bipartite injury test in favor of a single "injury-in-fact" test.[10] If a challenged act does, in fact, cause injury to plaintiff, that should be enough to give him standing to challenge the act unless the injury itself is too remote. A person who has suffered injury in fact meets both the Article III requirement and the need to ensure that plaintiff has a personal interest in the act that he challenges. The required interest exists when plaintiff alleges that he has suffered harm as a result of defendant's action, that is, the test that would have been adopted had the Brennan draft opinion (supra p. 33) come down as the final opinion of the Court.

Notes

1. *Muskrat* v. *United States*, 219 U.S. 346, 361 (1911).
2. *Valley Forge Christian College* v. *Americans United*, 454 U.S. 464, 471 (1982).
3. Id. at 472.
4. Id. at 471.
5. E.g., *Valley Forge Christian College* v. *Americans United*, 454 U.S. 464 (1982).
6. 397 U.S. 159 (1970).
7. Id. at 150.
8. See Schwartz, *Administrative Law* § 8.15 (2d ed. 1984).
9. *Marshall & Ilsley Corp.* v. *Heimann*, 652 F.2d 685, 693 (7th Cir. 1981).
10. See *New Hampshire Bankers Assn.* v. *Nelson*, 302 A.2d 810, 811 (N.H. 1973).

2

Kirby v. *Illinois* (1972): Counsel, Lineups, and Defendants' Rights

A principal accomplishment of the Warren Court was its work in the area of criminal law. Any listing of the important cases decided by that Court would certainly include *Mapp* v. *Ohio*,[1] *Miranda* v. *Arizona*,[2] and *Gideon* v. *Wainwright*[3]—all decisions that expanded the rights of those accused of crimes. The essentials of the Warren legacy in this respect were not impaired under Chief Justice Burger. Thus, those principles defined in *Mapp*, *Miranda*, and *Gideon* remain settled law. But modifications were made in the Warren jurisprudence that limited some of the protections afforded criminal defendants.

The first such modification occurred in *Kirby* v. *Illinois*, which drastically restricted the right recognized in *United States* v. *Wade*[4] and a companion case, *Gilbert* v. *California*,[5] decided by the Warren Court in 1967. The Justices themselves referred to *Wade* and *Gilbert* as the Lineup Cases. Wade had been indicted for bank robbery. Without any notice to his lawyer, he was placed in a lineup and identified as the robber. He was convicted despite his claim that the conduct of the lineup violated his privilege against self-incrimination and his right to counsel. The court of appeals reversed. All the Justices voted to grant certiorari.

Gilbert had also been convicted after identification at a postindictment lineup without notice to his counsel. In addition, during an FBI interrogation, he had given handwriting exemplars to an agent. The state courts rejected his contention that the handwriting samples had been obtained in violation of his Fifth and Sixth Amendment rights. Certiorari was granted in the *Gilbert* case by a five-to-four vote, with Justices Clark, Harlan, Stewart, and White voting to deny.

At the February 17, 1967, conference, Justice Hugo L. Black took the strongest position in favor of the defendants. "These cases," he asserted, "represent a violation of the right to counsel and the privilege against self-incrimination." Black asserted that, "as soon as you utilize a man's person to get evidence from him, or take him to a place to get someone else's evidence by having him act out a crime, you must give him a lawyer because you can't compel him to be a witness against himself."

Chief Justice Warren's conference statement did not go that far. He expressed the view that "you can't take voice or writing exemplars, dress [defendant] a certain way, or act out anything. Doing these things is the equivalent of interrogation and, therefore, *Miranda*[6] would apply." On the other hand, when he presented the cases, Warren said, "If none of these things were done and it was a pure line-up, counsel can be excluded."

After extensive discussion, which centered on the Fifth Amendment privilege, the conference was closely divided. The vote was five to four to reverse in *Wade* and affirm in *Gilbert*. The bare majority consisted of Justices Clark, Harlan, Brennan, Stewart, and White. Justice Brennan had expressed the view (reflected the previous term in his *Schmerber* v. *California* opinion)[7] that no Fifth Amendment rights were violated by placing the suspect in a lineup and asking him to speak for identification. On considering the case after the conference, however, Brennan became convinced that the lineup was a "critical stage" requiring the presence of counsel under the Sixth Amendment. Brennan informed the others in an April 17 *Memorandum to the Conference* that he had switched his votes and enclosed draft opinions that vacated the convictions in *Wade* and *Gilbert* and remanded for further proceedings.

Justice Brennan's *Wade* draft rejected the Fifth Amendment claim but held that Wade had a Sixth Amendment right to counsel at the lineup. As Brennan explained it in an April 24 memorandum to the Chief Justice and Justices Black, Douglas, and Fortas, the draft's conclusion was "that the lineup was a critical stage of the prosecution at which Wade was as much entitled to the aid of counsel as at the trial itself." Brennan then stated a "fruits" rule for in-court identification—that is, that defendant had to show that the identification in the courtroom was the "fruits" of the lineup.

The *Gilbert* draft followed Brennan's *Schmerber* approach and held that the taking of the handwriting exemplars was valid. However, it vacated and remanded on the basis of *Wade* because of the lineup identification without counsel.

The most important aspect of the decisions in the Lineup Cases was the holding in Justice Brennan's *Wade* opinion that there was a Sixth Amendment right to counsel at the lineup. As already seen, Brennan circulated his draft to that effect on April 17. The next development was a meeting on April 21 of Justices Stewart, Clark, Harlan, and White. What happened there was described in an April 24 memorandum from Justice Brennan to the other four Justices. Brennan wrote:

> [Y]ou may be interested in something Potter told me this morning. He, Tom, John and Byron had a meeting on Friday to exchange views. Potter tells me that the four of them agree with Part I and where I concluded that neither the lineup itself nor anything shown by the record that Wade

was required to do in the lineup violated his privilege against self-incrimination.

However, all four reject Part IV [the section of Brennan's draft that extended the right to counsel to Wade]. Potter tells me that since this is a federal case, he would be willing to put the right to counsel on the basis of our supervisory power and that he believes Tom would do likewise. He is uncertain whether that would be acceptable to John and Byron, but does not rule out the possibility.

Brennan indicated in his memo that he was not willing to go along with Stewart's making the right to counsel at a lineup a federal rule issue rather than a constitutional issue.

I personally am convinced that the right to counsel should be declared a constitutional right for the reasons I have stated in the opinion. But apparently there can be a Court for that disposition only if you are of that view.

Douglas immediately sent back Brennan's memo with a written comment at the bottom, "I am [of your view]—but I'm not yet sure of the grounds."

After intensive discussion, Justice Brennan was able to secure the agreement of the Chief Justice and Justices Douglas, Clark, and Fortas to his right-to-counsel holding. Their ultimate agreement was pungently summarized in a May 9 Fortas memorandum to Brennan: "Needless to say, on the central point I agree, I agree. I totally agree. This is a critical stage. There is a right to counsel—Amendment V [sic], Amendment XIV. Federal. State."

Surprisingly, the last to join Justice Brennan on his holding was Chief Justice Warren. At the February 17 conference, he had expressed the view that counsel might be excluded from a lineup that required defendant only to stand and be identified. The Chief Justice continued to express difficulty with an automatic right to counsel at all lineups. What if, Warren asked, counsel was an obstructionist or was unavailable and his presence would require a delay in the identification? In the end, however, Warren went along and on June 5—a week before the decision was announced—informed Brennan that he was going to join his opinion in *Wade* except for Part I, the Fifth Amendment privilege discussion.

The result was that—as stated in Justice Brennan's companion *Gilbert* opinion—with reference to *Wade*

[W]e there held that a post-indictment pretrial lineup at which the accused is exhibited to identifying witnesses is a critical stage of the criminal prosecution; that police conduct of such a lineup without notice to, and in the absence of, his counsel denies the accused his Sixth Amendment right to counsel and calls in question the admissibility at trial of the in-court identifications of the accused by witnesses who attended the lineup.[8]

Though *Wade* itself involved a postindictment lineup, that was not a crucial factor in the Court's decision. As Justice Brennan, the author of the *Wade* opinion points out in his *Kirby* draft opinion, reprinted on p. 54, the same "hazards to a fair trial that inhere in a post-indictment" lineup are also present in a lineup after arrest and before indictment.

Kirby v. *Illinois*[9] involved just such a preindictment situation. The case arose out of the robbery of a man named Shard on a Chicago street. Shard's wallet, containing traveler's checks and a social security card, was taken from him. The next day Kirby and a companion were stopped by a police officer and asked for identification. Kirby produced a wallet with traveler's checks and a social security card bearing Shard's name. The two were arrested and taken to a police station. Shard was then brought to the station and positively identified them as the men who had robbed him. At Kirby's trial, Shard testified that he had identified Kirby at the station house showup. The Illinois Supreme Court held that the admission of this testimony was not error because the *Wade* holding was not applicable to preindictment identifications.

Kirby was first argued on November 11, 1971. At the conference the next day only seven Justices were present (Justices Black and Harlan had resigned just before the 1971 Term, and successors had not yet been appointed). Chief Justice Burger started the conference by indicating that he favored affirmance. "I don't have trouble," he declared, "with a preindictment and postindictment dichotomy" and *Wade* should be ruled applicable only to lineup-type identifications after indictment. Chief Justice Burger was supported by Justices Stewart and Blackmun (though the latter did say, "This leaves me with a bad taste").

The other four Justices at the conference (Douglas, Brennan, White, and Marshall) favored a reversal. They were led by Justice Brennan, who strongly urged that the *Wade* reasoning applied equally to pre- and postindictment identifications. There was agreement among the four-man majority that the opinion should be written by Justice Brennan because he had also authored the *Wade* opinion. Three days later, on November 15, Justice Douglas—authorized to make the assignment because he was the senior member of the majority—sent the following "Dear Chief" letter: "You ask about No. 70-5061—*Kirby* v. *Illinois*, I suggest Bill Brennan write that. In fact, as I recall that seemed to be the consensus at Friday's conference."

The next day, November 16, Justice Brennan circulated the draft opinion of the Court reprinted on p. 54. The Brennan opinion contains a simple and straightforward rejection of the pre- and postindictment dichotomy as the criterion on which the *Wade* lineup right to counsel turns. The draft asserts, "Our holdings in *Gilbert* and *Wade* did not turn on the circumstance that the lineups conducted were post-indictment without notice to counsel who represented the accused." Instead, says Brennan, the test for *any* pretrial confrontation of the accused is "whether the presence of his counsel is necessary to preserve the defendant's basic right to a fair trial."

Such a test, according to Brennan, requires a decision in Kirby's favor. "There plainly inheres in a showup after arrest and before indictment the hazards to a fair trial that inhere in a post-indictment confrontation." In this respect, "the confrontation after arrest differs not at all from the confrontation after indictment."

The conclusion is "that the principles of *Gilbert* and *Wade* apply to showups conducted after arrest." Hence, Kirby's conviction must be reversed because he "had not been advised that he had the right to have counsel present at the showup."

Justice Stewart had supported the Burger minority view at the conference. The *Wade* right to counsel, he said then, "is limited to postindictment. . . . This was investigative stage and I'd draw the line at that point." On November 22, less than a week after receiving the Brennan draft opinion of the Court, Stewart circulated the draft dissent reprinted on p. 60. This draft is not the same as the final Stewart opinion in the case. It is shorter and simpler in its approach.

Like the final Stewart opinion, the draft dissent starts by stressing that *Wade* and *Gilbert* involved only "a *post-indictment* pretrial lineup" (the emphasis is omitted in the final opinion). The draft then points to "[T]he significance of the moment when the suspect is formally charged . . . ; the institution of meaningful judicial proceedings marks the point at which the criminal investigation has ended and adversary proceedings have commenced."

The draft concedes that counsel may be required at other stages. "This Court, however, has never held in a pre-indictment case bottomed on the constitutional right to counsel that the failure to provide a lawyer will result in a broad, *per se* exclusion at trial of evidence obtained before the suspect was formally charged or allowed to plead." In particular, no prior decision "announced a *per se* exclusionary rule of the type the Court promulgates today in extending *Gilbert* to pre-indictment lineups."

Nor, the Stewart draft dissent concludes, should such a rule be pronounced in this case. Hence, "I would not extend the *Wade-Gilbert* rule to pre-indictment lineups, and would, accordingly, affirm the judgment before us."

1st DRAFT

SUPREME COURT OF THE UNITED STATES

No. 70–5061

Thomas Kirby, Etc., Petitioner, *v.* State of Illinois.	On Writ of Certiorari to the Appellate Court of Illinois. First District.

[November —. 1971]

MR. JUSTICE BRENNAN delivered the opinion of the Court.

Petitioner and Ralph Bean were convicted in Illinois Circuit Court of robbing Willie Shard. Before they were indicted but after their arrest the Chicago police conducted a police station showup without advising them that they might have counsel present.[1] Shard testified at trial that he identified the pair at the showup. The question is whether under *Gilbert* v. *California*, 388 U. S. 263 (1967), the admission of testimony concerning identification at a preindictment showup was constitutional error. *Gilbert* held, in the context of a post-indictment lineup conducted without notice to counsel, that, unless harmless error, "[o]nly a *per se* exclusionary rule as to such testimony can be effective sanction to assure that law enforcement authorities will respect the accused's constitutional right to the presence of his counsel at the critical lineup." *Id.,* at 273.

On February 21, 1968, Shard reported to the Chicago police that the previous day two men robbed him on a Chicago street of a wallet containing traveler's checks to his order and a social security card in his name. On February 22, Chicago police officers arrested petitioner

---

[1] Counsel was not appointed to represent petitioner until after the indictment was returned.

KIRBY *v.* ILLINOIS

and Ralph Bean when, in response to a request for identification, petitioner produced a wallet that contained three of Shard's traveler's checks and his social security card.[2] Shard was permitted to testify at petitioner's trial[3] that on February 22 a police officer drove him to the Maxwell police station. He was then brought to a large squad room where petitioner and Bean were seated at a desk or table with two police officers. Shard said that the officers asked him if petitioner and Bean were the robbers and that he answered that they were. The prosecution at trial then asked him, "And you positively identified them at the police station, is that correct?" Shard answered "Yes." The Appellate Court of Illinois, First District affirmed petitioner's conviction. 121 Ill. App. 2d 323, 257 N. E. 2d 589 (1970).[4] The Appellate Court held that the admission of Shard's testimony was proper under the decision of the Illinois Supreme Court in *People v. Palmer*, 41 Ill. 2d 571, 244 N. E. 2d 173 (1969), that *Gilbert* and the principles of the companion case of *United States v. Wade*, 388 U. S. 218 (1967), were to be applied only to post-indictment confrontations.[5] The Illinois

---

[2] The officers were not aware that Shard had been robbed. They stopped petitioner and Bean and demanded identification because they mistakenly thought petitioner might be another person who was being sought for another crime. They arrested petitioner and Bean because petitioner gave conflicting explanations of their possession of Shard's belongings. The Appellate Court held that this was sufficient to establish probable cause for petitioner's arrest. 121 Ill. App. 2d —, 257 N. E. 2d —. The correctness of that holding is not before us.

[3] Petitioner's pretrial motion to suppress Shard's identification testimony had been denied.

[4] Bean was also convicted but won reversal on appeal. The Appellate Court held that his identification resulted from his unlawful arrest, thus requiring suppression of Shard's identification testimony as to him. *People v. Bean*, 121 Ill. App. 2d 332, 257 N. E. 2d 562 (1st Dist. 1970).

[5] Accord: *State v. Fields*, 104 Ariz. 486, 455 P. 2d 964 (1969); *Perkins v. State*, 228 S. 2d 382 (Fla. 1969); *Buchanan v. Common-*

KIRBY *v.* ILLINOIS

Supreme Court denied leave to appeal. We granted certiorari limited to Question 2 presented in the petition,[6] 402 U. S. 995 (1971). We reverse.

Our holdings in *Gilbert* and *Wade* did not turn on the circumstance that the lineups conducted were post-indictment without notice to counsel who represented the accused. Rather the crux of the holdings was stated in *Wade,* 388 U. S., at 227:

> "In sum, the principle of *Powell* v. *Alabama* [287 U. S. 45] and succeeding cases requires that we scrutinize *any* pretrial confrontation of the accused to determine whether the presence of his counsel is necessary to preserve the defendant's basic right to a fair trial as affected by his right meaningfully to cross-examine the witnesses against him and to have

---

wealth, 210 Va. 664, 173 S. E. 2d 792 (1970); and *State* v. *Walters,* 457 S. W. 2d 817 (Sup. Ct. Mo., Div. 2, 1970).

Contra: *United States* v. *Greene,* 429 F. 2d 193 (CADC 1970); *Rivers* v. *United States,* 400 F. 2d 935 (CA5 1968); *United States* v. *Phillips,* 427 F. 2d 1035 (CA9 1970); *United States* v. *Clark,* 289 F. Supp. 610 (ED Pa. 1968); *United States* v. *Guillery,* 254 N. E. 2d 427 (Mass. 1970); *People* v. *Fowler,* 1 Cal. 3d 335, 82 Cal. Rptr. 363, 461 P. 2d 643 (1969); *Palmer* v. *State,* 5 Md. App. 691, 249 A. 2d 482 (1969); *People* v. *Hutton,* 21 Mich. App. 312, 175 N. W. 2d 860 (1970); *Commonwealth* v. *Whiting,* 439 Pa. 205, 266 A. 2d 738 (1970); *State* v. *Isaacs,* 24 Ohio App. 2d 115, 265 N. E. 2d 327 (1970); *In re Holley,* 268 A. 2d 723 (R. I. Sup. Ct. 1970); *Hayes* v. *State,* 46 Wis. 2d 93, 175 N. W. 2d 625 (1970); see also *Government of Virgin Islands* v. *Callwood,* 440 F. 2d 1206 (CA3 1971); *Cooper* v. *Picard,* 428 F. 2d 1351 (CA1 1970); *United States* v. *Ayers,* 426 F. 2d 524 (CA2 1970); *United States* v. *Broadhead,* 413 F. 2d 1351 (CA7 1969); *Martinez* v. *State,* 437 S. W. 2d 842 (Tex. Ct. Crim. App. 1969); *State* v. *Singleton,* 253 La. 18, 215 So. 2d 838 (1968); *State* v. *Wright,* 274 N. C. 84, 161 S. E. 2d 581 (1968); *State* v. *Hicks,* 76 Wash. 2d 80, 455 P. 2d 943 (1969); *Thompson* v. *State,* 451 P. 2d 704 (Nev. 1969).

[6] Question 2 is: "Whether due process requires that an accused be advised of his right to counsel prior to a pre-indictment identification which occurred at a police station several hours after his arrest and forty-eight hours after the alleged crime occurred."

KIRBY *v.* ILLINOIS

effective assistance of counsel at the trial itself. It calls upon us to analyze whether potential substantial prejudice to defendant's rights inheres in the particular confrontation and the ability of counsel to help avoid that prejudice." (Emphasis in original.)

There plainly inheres in a showup after arrest[*] and before indictment the hazards to a fair trial that inhere in a post-indictment confrontation. A showup after arrest is more than a mere step in the investigation of the crime. The arrest evidences the belief of the police that the perpetrator of the crime has been caught. A significant purpose of the showup at that stage is to accumulate proof to buttress that conclusion. Thus the confrontation after arrest differs not at all from the confrontation after indictment, which, in *Wade*, 388 U. S., at 228, we found to be ". . . peculiarly riddled with innumerable dangers and variable factors which might seriously, even crucially, derogate from a fair trial." It is a critical confrontation "where the results might well settle the accused's fate and reduce the trial itself to a mere formality." *Id.*, at 224. We see no distinction in the showup after arrest from custodial interrogation where the right to the presence of counsel is recognized. *Miranda v. Arizona*, 384 U. S. 436 (1966); see also *Escobedo v. Illinois*, 378 U. S. 478 (1964).

The State makes no claim that exigent circumstances justified the use of the highly suggestive form of showup

---

[*] This case does not require us to consider whether the right to counsel applies to showups that occur before custody, and we intimate no view concerning that question. Decisions involving the question include: *United States v. Cox*, 428 F. 2d 683 (CA7 1970); *Bratton v. Delaware*, 307 F. Supp. 643 (Del. 1969); *Bradford v. State*, 118 Ga. App. 457, 164 S. E. 2d 264; *People v. Cezarz*, 44 Ill. 2d 180, 255 N. E. 2d 1 (1969); *State v. Bibbs*, 461 S. W. 2d 755 (Mo. 1970); *State v. Moore*, 111 N. J. Super. 528, 269 A. 2d 534 (1970); *State v. Clark*, 2 Wash. App. 2d 45, 467 P. 2d 369 (1970).

KIRBY *v.* ILLINOIS

employed in this case. Cf. *Stovall* v. *Denno*, 388 U. S.
293 (1967). It was a form particularly fraught with the
peril of mistaken identification. In the setting of a police station squad room where all present except petitioner and Bean were police officers, the danger was quite
real that Shard's understandable resentment might lead
him too readily to agree with the police that the pair under
arrest, and the only persons exhibited to him were indeed
the robbers. The State had no case without Shard's
testimony, and safeguards against such consesquences
were therefore of critical importance: Bean took the
stand and testified that the pair found the checks and
social security card two hours before that arrest strewn
upon the ground in an alley. Indeed, Shard's testimony
underscores the necessity for such safeguards. For on
direct examination, Shard identified petitioner and Bean
not as the alleged robbers on trial in the courtroom but
as the pair he saw at the police station sitting with two
officers.[8] Such testimony lends strong support to the

---

[8] Only the following colloquy on redirect examination suggests
an in-court identification by Shard:

"Q. All right. Now, when they grabbed you and took your money,
did you see them then?

"A. Yes, I did.

"Q. Did you get a good look at them then?

"A. Yes.

"Q. Both of them?

"A. Correct.

"Q. When they walked away did you see them then?

"A. Yes.

"Q. Did you look at them, Willie?

"A. Yes.

"Q. Are those the same two fellows? Look at them, Willie.

"A. Correct.

"Q. Are those the same two that robbed you?

"A. Yes.

"Q. You are sure, Willie?

"A. Yes."

KIRBY *v.* ILLINOIS

observation that "[i]t is a matter of common experience that, once a witness has picked out the accused at the line-up, he is not likely to go back on his word later on, so that in practice the issue of identity may (in the absence of other relevant evidence) for all practical purposes be determined then and there, before the trial." Williams and Hammelmann, Identification Parades, Part I (1963), Crim. L. Rev. 479, 482.

We therefore held, contrary to the view of the Illinois Supreme Court in *People* v. *Palmer,* that the principles of *Gilbert* and *Wade* apply to showups conducted after arrest.[9] The admission of Shard's testimony was constitutional error because petitioner had not been advised that he had the right to have counsel present at the showup. In the circumstances of this case, we see no basis for the application of the doctrine of harmless error. The judgment affirming petitioner's conviction is therefore

Reversed.

---

[9] "The rule applies to any lineup, to any other techniques employed to produce an identification and *a fortiori* to a face-to-face encounter between the witness and the suspect alone, regardless of when the identification occurs, in time or place, and whether before or after indictment or information." *United States* v. *Wade,* 338 U. S., at 251 (WHITE, J., joined by Harlan, J., and STEWART, J.).

"The establishment of the date of formal accusation as the time wherein the right to counsel at lineup attaches could only lead to a situation wherein substantially all lineups would be conducted prior to indictment or information." *People* v. *Fowler,* 1 Cal. 3d 335, —, 82 Cal. Rptr. 363, —, 461 P. ed. 643, 650.

1st DRAFT

SUPREME COURT OF THE UNITED STATES

No. 70–5061

Thomas Kirby, Etc., Petitioner,
v.
State of Illinois.

On Writ of Certiorari to the Appellate Court of Illinois, First District.

[November —, 1971]

Mr. Justice Stewart, dissenting.

In *United States* v. *Wade*, 388 U. S. 218, this Court held that the presence of counsel was required at lineups that took place after the suspect had been indicted. As ▮▮▮▮▮▮▮▮▮▮ said in the companion case of *Gilbert* v. *California*, 388 U. S. 263:

> "We . . . held [in *Wade*] that a *post-indictment* pretrial lineup at which the accused is exhibited to identifying witnesses is a critical stage of the criminal prosecution . . . ." *Id.*, at 272 (emphasis supplied).

The importance of the institution of a formal accusatory charge, for Sixth Amendment purposes, was established in *Powell* v. *Alabama*, 277 U. S. 45, the seminal case involving the constitutional right to counsel. There the Court said that the "most critical" period for criminal defendants was "from the time of their arraignment until the beginning of their trial, when consultation, thoroughgoing investigation and preparation [are] vitally important." *Id.*, at 57. See also *Gideon* v. *Wainwright*, 372 U. S. 335. Recent decisions have emphasized the need for counsel after indictment or at arraignment. *Hamilton* v. *Alabama*, 368 U. S. 52; *Massiah* v. *United States*, 377 U. S. 201. See also *Spano* v. *New York*, 360 U. S. 315 (concurring opinion).

KIRBY *v.* ILLINOIS

The significance of the moment when the suspect is formally charged stems from the nature of our criminal justice system; the institution of meaningful judicial proceedings marks the point at which the criminal investigation has ended and adversary proceedings have commenced. *Escobedo* v. *Illinois,* 378 U. S. 478, 495 (dissenting opinion); *Massiah* v. *New York,* 377 U. S. 201. To be sure, recent cases have held that counsel may sometimes be constitutionally required at earlier stages of the criminal process. *Escobedo, supra; Coleman* v. *Alabama,* 399 U. S. 1. This Court, however, has never held in a pre-indictment case bottomed on the constitutional right to counsel that the failure to provide a lawyer will result in a broad, *per se* exclusion at trial of evidence obtained before the suspect was formally charged or allowed to plead.[1] Neither *Escobedo* nor *Coleman* announced a *per se* exclusionary rule of the type the Court promulgates today in extending *Gilbert* to pre-indictment lineups.[2]

---

[1] This Court held in *Gilbert, supra,* that only "a *per se* exclusionary rule as to such testimony [testimony relating to events at a lineup] can be an effective sanction to assure that law enforcement authorities will respect the accused's constitutional right to the presence of his counsel at the critical lineup." 388 U. S. 263, 273. In contrast to *Gilbert's per se* exclusionary rule, the exclusionary rule of *Miranda* v. *Arizona,* 384 U. S. 436, was based squarely on the need to protect the suspect's right against compulsory self-incrimination during a custodial interrogation. *White* v. *Maryland,* 373 U. S. 59, like *Hamilton* v. *Alabama,* 368 U. S. 52, involved a suspect who was brought before a judge and allowed to plead, although the state procedure was styled as "preliminary" and an indictment had not been brought. We found that this procedure was, in essence, like an arraignment, and that counsel's aid was required.

[2] The holding of *Escobedo* was limited to the relatively narrow facts of that case, 378 U. S. 478, 490–491, and under its rule evidence is only to be excluded if obtained during custodial interrogation, under like circumstances. See *Johnson* v. *New Jersey,* 384 U. S. 719. By contrast, the exclusionary rule of *Gilbert* applies across

KIRBY *v.* ILLINOIS

When the police attempt to place a suspect in a lineup after indictment, the accused will almost certainly have counsel (as did the defendants in both *Wade* and *Gilbert*). Thus, compliance with the right to counsel requirement at a post-indictment lineup should occasion little delay in the administration of justice, since a lawyer in the post-indictment setting is more likely to be familiar with his client's case and to be able to appear promptly. More important, after an indictment has been brought, the State is committed to prosecute and is, therefore, more likely to abuse identification procedures to secure a conviction than would be the case before the suspect is charged.

Obviously, there may be pre-indictment situations in which the police do abuse lineup procedures. Such abuses are not beyond the reach of the Constitution. The Due Process Clause of the Fifth and Fourteenth Amendments forbids a lineup which is unnecessarily suggestive and conducive to irreparable mistaken identification. *Stovall* v. *Denno,* 388 U. S. 293; *Foster* v. *California,* 394 U. S. 440. When the accused has not been formally charged, *Stovall* strikes the proper balance between the right of a suspect to be protected from prejudicial procedures and the need of the State to investigate an unsolved crime.

For these reasons, I would not extend the *Wade-Gilbert* rule to pre-indictment lineups, and would, accordingly, affirm the judgment before us.

---

the board. In *Coleman,* the Court held that counsel is required at preliminary hearings. Failure to provide counsel could be cured, however, if there was no substantial prejudice to the accused. In any event, *Coleman* does not involve a rule mandating the *per se* exclusion of evidence under the right to counsel guarantee. Testimony adverse to the accused is excluded under the Confrontation Clause. Cf. *Pointer* v. *Texas,* 380 U. S. 400.

As already seen, the conference vote in favor of Kirby had been taken when the Court consisted of only seven members. The same was true when the Brennan draft opinion of the Court (supra p. 54) and the Stewart draft dissent (supra p. 60) had been circulated. However, the situation in this respect changed when Justices Lewis F. Powell and William H. Rehnquist were sworn in on January 6, 1972. Now there was a full Court, and it was desirable to have *Kirby* decided by a majority rather than only a four-Justice plurality.

Reflecting the new situation, the Chief Justice sent around the following January 17, *Memorandum to the Conference:*

> I propose that this case be set for reargument this Term.
>
> I had been working on a dissent pursuing some of the same lines as are covered in Justice Stewart's circulation, but I see no point in circulating these views now. If the dissent circulated by Justice Stewart does not persuade any of the four who would reverse, my observations are not likely to achieve that objective.

On January 24, the Court issued an order restoring the *Kirby* case to the calendar for reargument.[10] The reargument took place on March 20 and 21. At the conference later that week, the seven who had participated in the November 12 conference on the case took the same positions they had taken in the earlier discussion. The Chief Justice again urged affirmance. "Does *Wade-Gilbert* apply to a preindictment confrontation?" he asked. "No and we don't have to overrule *Wade* and *Gilbert*." He went further and said, "I'd overrule if it were the only way to decide." But that was unnecessary here if the Court simply refused to "extend" *Wade* and *Gilbert* to this case.

The seven who had previously sat on the case again voted to reverse, four to three, but the two new Justices were for affirmance. Justice Powell indicated that he "would not apply *Wade* and *Gilbert* to preindictment. Per se exclusionary rules should be developed with great restraint. . . . So I won't extend *Wade* and *Gilbert*." Justice Rehnquist agreed. "On the basis of no extension to preindictment and that only," he said, "I'd affirm."

The four-to-three decision in Kirby's favor was thus changed to a five-to-four decision the other way. Justice Stewart converted his draft dissent into an opinion of the Court, which he circulated May 2. It went through three further drafts before being issued as the final *Kirby* opinion. On May 8, Justice Brennan circulated a dissent, based upon his draft opinion (supra p. 54), which was essentially the dissent ultimately issued by him.

Had the original Brennan draft (supra p. 54) come down as the final *Kirby* opinion, it would have made a substantial difference to the rights of criminal defendants. Identification of suspects through confrontation with their victims is most often a part—and a vital part—of the investigative stage. It usually occurs after the suspect is arrested and brought in for questioning. Postindictment lineups are relatively rare. To guarantee the right to counsel only for them, as the final *Kirby* decision does, is, in effect, to take away that right in most lineups.

Notes

 1. 367 U.S. 643 (1961).
 2. 384 U.S. 436 (1966).
 3. 372 U.S. 335 (1963).
 4. 388 U.S. 218 (1967).
 5. 388 U.S. 263 (1967).
 6. Supra note 2.
 7. 384 U.S. 757 (1966).
 8. Supra note 5 at 272.
 9. 406 U.S. 682 (1972).
10. 404 U.S. 105 (1972).

3

Frontiero v. Richardson (1973): Sexual Discrimination and the Standard of Review

The present century has seen a virtual transformation of the law in the field of women's rights. According to the famous Maitland epigram, "A woman can never be outlawed, for a woman is never in law."[1] Until the present day, American law displayed a similar attitude. The first case under the Fourteenth Amendment denied the right of women to practice law. "The paramount destiny and mission of woman," said Justice Bradley in his opinion, "are to fulfill the noble and benign offices of wife and mother. This is the law of the Creator."[2]

A century later, the law of the Creator was being construed differently. The common law jeremiad against women had been abandoned; virtually all legal disabilities based on sex were being eliminated, either by statute or judicial decision. Political rights, economic rights, the right to share in public services and benefactions—these were almost all placed beyond governmental power to make sexual classifications.

The removal of sexual disabilities was, however, not the work of the Warren Court, but of its successor. The sex discrimination issue was raised in only one case while Earl Warren sat in the Court's central chair. That case was *Hoyt* v. *Florida*,[3] decided in 1961. Mrs. Hoyt had been convicted in a Florida court of murdering her husband with a baseball bat. The jury was selected under a statute permitting women to decline to serve on juries. She claimed that her trial before an all-male jury worked an unconstitutional exclusion of women from jury service. The Florida Supreme Court affirmed the conviction.

Chief Justice Warren spoke strongly in favor of reversal at the conference on the case. "I would do this," he said, "on the narrow ground that, in this case, this statute has been limited to ten [women] a year out of 223 eligibles. This is a particularly flagrant case where a woman needs the help of a woman."

Justice Frankfurter, by then the Chief Justice's principal antagonist, took the opposite view, saying, "[H]ow can we say there has been a systematic exclusion here?" Warren was supported only by Justices Black and Douglas, and they decided ultimately to go along with an affirmance. Justice Harlan delivered the opinion, holding that the Florida exemption did not work an arbitrary exclusion of women from jury service. The Chief Justice and his supporters did not dissent, but they set the stage for future challenges to sexual classifications when they issued a one-paragraph concurrence that stressed the need for a state to make "a good faith effort to have women perform jury duty without discrimination on the ground of sex."[4]

The first case striking down a sexual classification was the Burger Court decision in *Reed* v. *Reed*.[5] At issue there was a state statute that provided that between persons equally qualified to administer estates, males must be preferred to females. All the Justices agreed that this law was based on an invalid discrimination and had to fall. The Chief Justice wrote a unanimous opinion holding that the statutory classification could not pass the test of reasonableness because "a difference in the sex of competing applicants for letters of administration" does not bear "a rational relationship to a state objective that is sought to be advanced by the operation of" the statute.[6] "By providing dissimilar treatment for men and women who are thus similarly situated, the challenged section violates the Equal Protection Clause."[7]

In *Reed*, the Court reviewed the sex-based classification under the same rational-basis test that it used in reviewing economic classifications. That test is, however, an extremely deferential one. All it requires is that the classification at issue has a reasonable basis in fact and that it "rest upon some ground of difference having a fair and substantial relation to [the] object of the legislation."[8] The court need determine only that the particular classification had been the product of a rational legislative choice.[9] Under the rational-basis test, "it is only the invidious discrimination, the wholly arbitrary act, which cannot stand."[10] Virtually all laws emerge untouched from mere rationality scrutiny: "that test . . . , when applied as articulated, leaves little doubt about the outcome; the challenged legislation is always upheld."[11]

Over the years, however, the Court developed a stricter level of scrutiny that was applied in certain cases. In such instances, the mere showing that a law was rationally related to a legitimate governmental objective was not enough to sustain a challenged classification. In those cases, the test of mere rationality gave way to one of strict scrutiny under which the classification was held to be denial of equal protection unless justified by a "compelling" governmental interest.[12]

In particular, strict scrutiny was required unnder the compelling-interest test when the classification operated to the peculiar disadvantage of a suspect class. This rule was first stated in a 1944 case, "It should be noted, to begin with, that all legal restrictions which curtail the civil rights of a single racial group are immediately suspect. This is not to say that all such restrictions are unconstitutional. It is to say that courts must subject them to the most rigid scrutiny."[13] Starting with the *Brown* school segregation case,[14] the Court has uniformly subjected racial classifications to the strict-scrutiny requirement.

The suspect-classification concept is based on the proposition that the Equal Protection Clause's "assertion of human equality is closely associated with the proposition that differences in color or creed, birth or status, are neither significant nor relevant to the way in which persons should be treated."[15] These differences should all be constitutionally irrelevant—mere accidents of birth or condition that fade into insignificance in the face of our common humanity. To such differences, the law should remain blind, not distinguishing on the basis of who a person is or what he is or what he possesses. From this point of view, all classifications based on race, ancestry, alienage[16] or indigency,[17] involve suspect classifications.

Should classification based on sex be treated as a suspect classification and, hence, one subject to strict scrutiny under the compelling-interest test? *Reed* v. *Reed*[18] answered in the negative. The Court there, we saw, invalidated the sexual classification at issue, but it did so on the ground that it violated the rational-basis test without any indication in the opinion that any other standard of review might be appropriate. So far as we know, indeed, the propriety of a stricter review standard was not considered by the conference.

Two years after *Reed*, the validity of a sexual classification was again presented to the Court in *Frontiero* v. *Richardson*.[19] This time, however, the issue of the proper standard of review was discussed among the Justices and reflected in the opinions ultimately issued. As we shall see, however, the original draft opinion of the Court circulated by Justice Brennan, reprinted on p. 70, merely followed the *Reed* approach and did not refer to the propriety of any other review test. Had this draft come down as the final *Frontiero* opinion, the law on sexual classifications might well be different from what it has since become. For, as will be seen, later cases have built on the Brennan opinion that was finally issued in *Frontiero* and have moved away from the *Reed* rational-basis test toward a standard that requires stricter scrutiny.

The question before the Court in *Frontiero* concerned the right of a female member of the armed services to claim her spouse as a dependent for the purpose of obtaining increased quarters' allowances on an equal footing with those obtained automatically by male members. Sharron Frontiero was an Air Force lieutenant who had asked for larger quarters and benefits after she had married. Under the relevant statutes, married men were automatically granted such benefits. But women had to prove that their husbands received more than half their support from them before they could qualify.

At the conference following argument, Chief Justice Burger declared, "*Reed* v. *Reed* has nothing to do with this," because, in Burger's view, there was no invidious discrimination here under the *Reed* test. The Chief Justice was supported only by Justice Rehnquist. The others found the law invalid, with the consensus being stated by Justice Stewart, who said that the statute was "on its face grossly discriminatory against a readily identifiable class in a basically fundamental role of life." The statute, like that in *Reed*, had to fall under the rational-basis test applied in that case.[20]

Justice Brennan, to whom the case was assigned, drafted an opinion of the Court that reflected the conference consensus. It was circulated on February 14, 1973, and is reprinted on p. 70. The Brennan covering memorandum began:

> As you will note, I have structured this opinion along the lines which reflect what I understood was our agreement at conference. That is, without reaching the question whether sex constitutes a "suspect criterion" calling for "strict scrutiny," the challenged provisions must fall for the reasons stated in *Reed*.

The Brennan memo went on to state:

> I do feel however that this case would provide an appropriate vehicle for us to recognize sex as a "suspect criterion." And . . . perhaps there is a Court for such an approach. If so, I'd have no difficulty in writing the opinion along those lines.

As indicated in his memo, Justice Brennan's draft opinion of the Court (infra p. 70) follows the *Reed* v. *Reed* approach standard of review. It notes appellant's contention "that sex, like race, alienage, and national origin, constitutes a 'suspect criterion,' and that a classification based upon sex must therefore be deemed unconstitutional unless necessary to promote a compelling governmental interest." Use of the *Reed* standard of review makes it unnecessary to deal with this contention. "We need not, and therefore do not, decide this question, however, for we conclude that the instant statutes cannot pass constitutional muster under even the more 'lenient' standard of review implicit in our unanimous decision only last term in *Reed* v. *Reed*."

The Brennan draft then goes on to show how, under the *Reed* test, the *Frontiero* statutes must be ruled invalid. "In terms of the constitutional challenge," says the draft, "the situation here is virtually identical to *Reed*. Here, as in *Reed*, the sole basis of the classification established in the challenged statutes is the sex of the individuals involved." Here too, "and again as in *Reed*, the Government concedes that the differential treatment accorded men and women under these statutes serves no purpose other than mere 'administrative convenience.' "

Even under *Reed*, however, efficacious administration is not enough to justify a law. "*Reed* itself stands for the proposition that, in cases such as these, 'administrative convenience' is not a shibboleth, the mere recitation of which dictates constitutionality. On the contrary, *Reed* establishes that any statutory scheme which draws a sharp line between the sexes, solely for the purpose of achieving administrative convenience" is based on arbitrary choice. "We therefore hold that, by according differential treatment to male and female members of the uniformed services for the sole purpose of achieving administrative convenience, the challenged statutes" are unconstitutional.

1st DRAFT

SUPREME COURT OF THE UNITED STATES

No. 71–1694

Sharron A. Frontiero and Joseph Frontiero, Appellants, *v.* Melvin R. Laird, Secretary of Defense, et al.	On Appeal from the United States District Court for the Middle District of Alabama.

[February —, 1973]

MR. JUSTICE BRENNAN delivered the opinion of the Court.

The question before us concerns the right of a female member of the uniformed services [1] to claim her spouse as a "dependent" for the purposes of obtaining increased quarters allowances and medical and dental benefits under 37 U. S. C. §§ 401, 403, and 10 U. S. C. §§ 1072, 1076, on an equal footing with male members. Under these statutes, a serviceman may claim his wife as a "dependent" without regard to whether she is in fact dependent upon him for any part of her support. 37 U. S. C. § 401 (1); 10 U. S. C. § 1072 (A). A servicewoman, on the other hand, may not claim her husband as a "dependent" under these programs unless he is in fact dependent upon her for over one-half of his sup-

---

[1] The "uniformed services" include the Army, Navy, Air Force, Marine Corps, Coast Guard, Environmental Science Services Administration, and Public Health Service. 37 U. S. C. § 101 (3); 10 U. S. C. § 1072 (1).

FRONTIERO *v.* LAIRD

port. 37 U. S. C. § 401; 10 U. S. C. § 1072 (2)(C).[2] Thus, the question for decision is whether this difference in treatment constitutes an unconstitutional discrimination against servicewomen in violation of the Due Process Clause of the Fifth Amendment. A three-judge District Court for the Middle District of Alabama, one judge dissenting, rejected this contention and sustained the constitutionality of the provisions of the statutes making this distinction. 341 F. Supp. 201 (1972). We noted probable jurisdiction. 409 U. S. —— (1972). We reverse.

I

In an effort to attract career personnel through re-enlistment, Congress established, in 37 U. S. C. § 401 *et seq.*, and 10 U. S. C. § 1071 *et seq.*, a scheme for the provision of fringe benefits to members of the uniformed services on a competitive basis with business and industry.[3] Thus, under 37 U. S. C. § 403, a member of the uniformed services with dependents is entitled to an

---

[2] 37 U. S. C. § 401 provides in pertinent part:

"In this chapter, 'dependent,' with respect to a member of a uniformed service, means—

"(1) his spouse;

. . . . .

"However, a person is not a dependent of a female member unless he is in fact dependent on her for over one-half of his support. . . ."
10 U. S. C. § 1072 (2) provides in pertinent part:

" 'Dependent,' with respect to a member . . . of a uniformed service, means—

"(A) the wife;

. . . . .

"(C) the husband, if he is in fact dependent on the member . . . for over one-half of his support. . . ."

[3] See 102 Cong. Rec., 84th Cong., 2d Sess., 3849–3850 (Cong. Kilday), 8043 (Sen. Saltonstall); 95 Cong. Rec., 81st Cong., 1st Sess., 7662 (Cong. Kilday), 7664 (Cong. Short), 7666 (Cong. Havenner), 7667 (Cong. Bates), 7671 (Cong. Price). See also 10 U. S. C. § 1071.

FRONTIERO *v.* LAIRD

increased "basic allowance for quarters" and, under 10 U. S. C. § 1076, a member's dependents are provided comprehensive medical and dental care.

Appellant Sharron Frontiero, a lieutenant in the United States Air Force, sought increased quarters allowances, and housing and medical benefits for her husband, appellant Joseph Frontiero, on the ground that he was her "dependent." Although such benefits would automatically have been granted with respect to the wife of a male member of the uniformed services, appellant's application was denied because she failed to demonstrate that her husband was dependent on her for more than one-half of his support.[1] Appellants then commenced this suit, contending that, by making this distinction, the statutes unreasonably discriminate on the basis of sex in violation of the Due Process Clause of the Fifth Amendment.[2] In essence, appellants asserted that the discriminatory impact of the statutes is two-fold: first, as a procedural matter, a female member is required to demonstrate her spouse's dependency, while no such burden is imposed upon male members; and second, as a substantive matter, a male member who does not provide more than one-half of his wife's support receives benefits, while a similarly situated female member is denied such benefits. Appellants therefore sought a permanent in-

---

[1] Appellant Joseph Frontiero is a full-time student at Huntingdon College in Montgomery, Alabama. According to the agreed stipulation of facts, his living expenses, including his share of the household expenses, total approximately $354 per month. Since he receives $205 per month in veterans' benefits, it is clear that he is not dependent upon appellant Sharron Frontiero for more than one-half of his support.

[2] "[W]hile the Fifth Amendment contains no equal protection clause, it does forbid discrimination that is 'so unjustifiable as to be violative of due process.'" *Schneider* v. *Rusk*, 377 U. S. 163, 168 (1964); see *Shapiro* v. *Thompson*, 394 U. S. 618, 641–642 (1969); *Bolling* v. *Sharpe*, 347 U. S. 497 (1954).

FRONTIERO *v.* LAIRD

junction against the continued enforcement of these statutes and an order directing the appellees to provide Lieutenant Frontiero with the same housing and medical benefits that a similarly situated male member would receive.

Although the legislative history of these statutes sheds virtually no light on the purposes underlying the differential treatment accorded male and female members,[6] a majority of the three-judge District Court surmised that Congress might reasonably have concluded that, since the husband in our society is generally the "breadwinner" in the family—and the wife typically the "dependent" partner—"it would be more economical to require married female members claiming husbands to prove actual dependency than to extend the presumption of dependency to such members." 341 F. Supp., at 207. Indeed, given the fact that approximately 99% of all members of the uniformed services are male, the District

---

[6] The housing provisions, set set forth in 37 U. S. C. § 701 *et seq.*, were enacted as part of the Career Compensation Act of 1949, which established a uniform pattern of military pay and allowances, consolidating and revising the piecemeal legislation that had been developed over the previous 40 years. See H. R. Rep. No. 779, 81st Cong., 1st Sess.; S. Rep. No. 733, 81st Cong., 1st Sess. The Act apparently retained in substance the dependency definitions of § 4 of the Pay Readjustment Act of 1942 (56 Stat. 361), as amended by § 6 of the Act of September 7, 1944 (58 Stat. 730), which required a female member of the service to demonstrate her spouse's dependency. It appears that this provision was itself derived from unspecified earlier enactments. See S. Rep. No. 917, 78th Cong., 2d Sess., 4.

The medical benefits legislation, 47 U. S. C. § 401 *et seq.*, was enacted as the Dependents' Medical Care Act of 1956. As such, it was designed to revise and make uniform the existing law relating to medical services for military personnel. It, too, appears to have carried forward, without explanation, the dependency provisions found in other military pay and allowance legislation. See H. R. Rep. No. 1805, 84th Cong., 2d Sess.; S. Rep. No. 1878, 84th Cong., 2d Sess.

FRONTIERO *v.* LAIRD

Court speculated that such differential treatment might conceivably lead to a "considerable saving of administrative expense and manpower." *Ibid.*

II

At the outset, appellants contend that sex, like race,[7] alienage,[8] and national origin,[9] constitutes a "suspect criterion," and that a classification based upon sex must therefore be deemed unconstitutional unless necessary to promote a compelling governmental interest. We need not, and therefore do not, decide this question, however, for we conclude that the instant statutes cannot pass constitutional muster under even the more "lenient" standard of review implicit in our unanimous decision only last Term in *Reed* v. *Reed*, 404 U. S. 71 (1971).

In *Reed*, we considered the constitutionality of an Idaho statute providing that, when two individuals are otherwise equally entitled to appointment as administratrix of an estate, the male applicant must be preferred to the female. Appellant, the mother of the deceased, and appellee, the father, filed competing petitions for appointment as administratrix of their son's estate. Since the parties, as parents of the deceased, were members of the same entitlement class, the statutory preference was invoked and the father's petition was therefore granted. Appellant claimed that this statute, by giving a mandatory preference to males over females without regard to their individual qualifications, violated the Equal Protection Clause of the Fourteenth Amendment.

---

[7] See *Loving* v. *Virginia*, 388 U. S. 1, 11 (1967); *McLaughlin* v. *Florida*, 379 U. S. 184, 191–192 (1964); *Bolling* v. *Sharpe*, 347 U. S. 497, 499 (1954).

[8] See *Graham* v. *Richardson*, 403 U. S. 365, 372 (1971).

[9] See *Oyama* v. *California*, 332 U. S. 633, 644–646 (1948); *Korematsu* v. *United States*, 323 U. S. 214, 216 (1944); *Hirabayashi* v. *United States*, 320 U. S. 81, 100 (1943).

FRONTIERO *v.* LAIRD

At the outset, we noted that the Idaho statute "provides that different treatment be accorded to the applicants on the basis of their sex; it thus establishes a classification subject to scrutiny under the Equal Protection Clause." 404 U. S., at 75. We then explained that, in order to satisfy the demands of the Constitution, "[a] classification 'must be reasonable, not arbitrary, and must rest upon some ground of difference having a fair and substantial relation to the object of the legislation, so that all persons similarly circumstanced shall be treated alike.' *Royster Guano Co.* v. *Virginia*, 253 U. S. 412, 415 (1920)." *Id.*, at 76.

In an effort to meet this standard, appellee contended that the statutory scheme was a reasonable measure designed to reduce the workload on probate courts by eliminating one class of contests. Moreover, appellee argued that the mandatory preference for male applicants was in itself reasonable since "men [are] as a rule more conversant with business affairs than . . . women." [10] Indeed, appellee maintained that "it is a matter of common knowledge, that women still are not engaged in politics, the professions, business or industry to the extent that men are." [11] And the Idaho Supreme Court, in upholding the constitutionality of this statute, suggested that the Idaho Legislature might reasonably have "concluded that in general men are better qualified to act as an administrator than are women." [12]

Although recognizing that the State's interest in achieving administrative efficiency "is not without some legitimacy," we held that, by ignoring the individual qualifications of particular applicants, the challenged statute necessarily provided "dissimilar treatment for men and women who are . . . similarly situated." *Id.*,

[10] Brief of Appellee, at 12, *Reed* v. *Reed*, 404 U. S. 71 (1971).
[11] *Id.*, at 12-13.
[12] *Reed* v. *Reed*, 93 Idaho 511, 514, 465 P. 2d 635, 638 (1970).

FRONTIERO *v.* LAIRD

at 76, 77. Indeed, "[t]o give a mandatory preference
to members of either sex over members of the other,
merely to accomplish the elimination of hearings on the
merits is to make the very kind of arbitrary legislative
choice forbidden by the [Constitution]. . . ." *Id.,* at 76.

In terms of the constitutional challenge, the situation
here is virtually identical to *Reed.* Here, as in *Reed,*
the sole basis of the classification established in the challenged statutes is the sex of the individuals involved.
Thus, under 37 U. S. C. §§ 401, 403, and 10 U. S. C.
§§ 1072, 1076, a female member of the uniformed services
seeking to obtain housing and medical benefits for her
spouse must prove his dependency in fact, whereas no
such burden is imposed upon male members. In addition, the statutes operate so as to deny benefits to a
female member, such as appellant Sharron Frontiero,
who provides less than one-half of her spouse's support,
while at the same time granting such benefits to a male
member who likewise provides less than one-half of his
spouse's support. Thus, to this extent at least, it may
fairly be said that these statutes command "dissimilar
treatment for men and women who are . . . similarly
situated." *Reed* v. *Reed, supra,* at 77.

Moreover, and again as in *Reed,* the Government
concedes that the differential treatment accorded men
and women under these statutes serves no purpose other
than mere "administrative convenience." In essence,
the Government maintains that, as an empirical matter,
wives in our society frequently are dependent upon their
husbands, while husbands rarely are dependent upon their
wives. With these considerations in mind, and given
the fact that approximately 99% of all members of the
uniformed services are male, the Government contends
that Congress might reasonably have concluded that it
would be both cheaper and easier simply conclusively to
presume that wives of male members are financially

FRONTIERO *v.* LAIRD

dependent upon their husbands, while burdening female members with the task of establishing dependency in fact.

Our prior decisions make clear, however, that although efficacious administration of governmental programs is not without some importance, "the Constitution recognizes higher values than speed and efficiency." *Stanley* v. *Illinois,* 405 U. S. 645, 656 (1972); cf. *Carrington* v. *Rash,* 380 U. S. 89, 96 (1965). And *Reed* itself stands for the proposition that, in cases such as these, "administrative convenience" is not a shibboleth, the mere recitation of which dictates constitutionality. On the contrary, *Reed* establishes that any statutory scheme which draws a sharp line between the sexes, solely for the purpose of achieving administrative convenience, necessarily involves "the very kind of arbitrary legislative choice forbidden by the [Constitution]. . . ." *Reed* v. *Reed, supra,* at 76. We therefore hold that, by according differential treatment to male and female members of the uniformed services for the sole purpose of achieving administrative convenience, the challenged statutes violate the Due Process Clause of the Fifth Amendment insofar as they require a female member to prove the dependency of her husband.[13] See *Reed* v. *Reed, supra;* cf. *Stanley* v. *Illinois, supra.*

Reversed.

---

[13] As noted earlier, the basic purpose of these statutes was to provide fringe benefits to members of the uniformed services in order to establish a compensation pattern which would attract career personnel through re-enlistment. See n. 3, *supra,* and accompanying text. Our holding in no wise invalidates the statutory schemes except insofar as they require a female member to prove the dependency of her spouse. See *Weber* v. *Aetna Casualty & Surety Co.,* 406 U. S. 164 (1972); *Levy* v. *Louisiana,* 391 U. S. 68 (1968); *Moritz* v. *Commissioner of Internal Revenue.* — F. 2d — (CA10 1972). See also 1 U. S. C. § 1.

Had the Brennan draft (supra p. 70) come down as the *Frontiero* opinion of the Court, it would have aborted the substantial development in sex discrimination law that has since occurred. The use of the rational-basis test in both *Reed* and *Frontiero* would probably have meant its adoption for all cases that involve sexual classifications. That would, in turn, have meant the same narrow scope of review for such classifications as is available in the review of economic classifications.

Soon after he circulated his draft, however, Justice Brennan received indications that some of the Justices were not satisfied with only the *Reed* test as the governing criterion in sex discrimination cases. On February 15, Justice White wrote to Brennan, "I would think that sex is a suspect classification, if for no other reason than the fact that Congress has submitted a constitutional amendment making sex discrimination unconstitutional. I would remain of the same view whether the amendment is adopted or not."

Interestingly, the White letter pointed out what opponents of strict scrutiny had urged—that it meant a return to the substantive due process approach used by the pre-1937 Court to invalidate economic regulation with which the Justices disagreed. "Of course," White's letter conceded, "the more of this we do on the basis of suspect classifications not rooted in the Constitution, the more we approximate the old substantive due process approach."

The next day, February 16, Justice Douglas sent a "Dear Bill" note to Justice Brennan, which was written at the bottom of the Brennan February 14 memo. Douglas wrote that he preferred the " 'suspect criterion' [approach] calling for strict scrutiny."

Two Justices, however, wrote opposing the suspect classification approach. In a February 15 letter joining the Brennan draft, Justice Powell stated, "I see no reason to consider whether sex is a 'suspect' classification in this case. Perhaps we can avoid confronting that issue until we know the outcome of the Equal Rights Amendment."

Justice Stewart, who turned out to be the key vote in the *Frontiero* decision, went even further. "I see no need," he wrote to Brennan on February 16, "to decide in this case whether sex is a 'suspect' criterion, and I would not mention the question in the opinion." Instead, he suggested to Brennan that he eliminate the paragraphs at the beginning of Part II of the draft that refer to the "suspect criterion" issue. In its place, Stewart wrote that he would "substitute a statement that we find that the classification effected by the statute is invidiously discriminatory." Stewart commented on this suggestion, "I should suppose that 'invidious discrimination' is an equal protection *standard* to which all could repair"—though, as it turned out, that was not to be true in this case.

If Justice Brennan could not obtain the votes of Justices Stewart and Powell, it was most unlikely that he could secure a Court for a stricter standard of review than that applied in his draft opinion. Despite this, Justice Brennan decided to rewrite his opinion to provide for strict scrutiny in cases involving sexual classifications. On February 28, he circulated a redraft opinion of the Court substantially similar to the final Brennan *Frontiero* opinion. It agreed with the contention "that classifications based upon sex, like classifications based upon race, alienage, and national origin, are inherently suspect and must therefore be subjected to close judicial scrutiny." The *Frontiero* statutes were ruled invalid, not under the *Reed* rational-basis test, but under the strict-scrutiny requirement of compelling interest.

The Brennan redraft called forth a March 2 two-page letter from Justice Powell that characterized the redraft as one "in which you have now gone all the way in holding that sex is a 'suspect classification.' " It will be recalled that Justice White's February 15 letter favored the suspect classification approach because of the Equal Rights Amendment. The Powell letter opposed that approach because of the proposed amendment. Powell wrote that he was concerned "about going this far at this time" because "it places the Court in the position of preempting the amendatory process initiated by the Congress."

If the Equal Rights Amendment were to be adopted, Powell explained, that would represent "the will of the people" expressed through the amending process.

> If, on the other hand, this Court puts "sex" in the same category as "race" we will have assumed a decisional responsibility (not within the democratic process) unnecessary to the decision of this case, and at the very time that legislatures around the country are debating the genuine pros and cons of how far it is wise, fair and prudent to subject both sexes to identical responsibilities as well as rights.

Justice Powell urged that the original Brennan draft was "as far as we need to go" in *Frontiero*. On the other hand, his letter concluded:

> If and when it becomes necessary to consider whether sex is a suspect classification, I will find the issue a difficult one. Women certainly have not been treated as being fungible with men (thank God!). Yet, the reasons for different treatment have in no way resembled the purposeful and invidious discrimination directed against blacks and aliens. Nor may it be said any longer that, as a class, women are a discrete minority barred from effective participation in the political process.

The Powell letter informed Justice Brennan that its author could not join his new opinion. A similar indication was given in a March 5 "Dear Bill" letter from Justice Blackmun:

> I have now concluded that it is not advisable, and certainly not necessary, for us to reach out in this case to hold that sex, like race and national origin and alienage, is a suspect classification. It seems to me that *Reed* v. *Reed* is ample precedent here and is all we need and that we should not, by this case, enter the arena of the proposed Equal Rights Amendment.

On March 3, Justice Brennan had received a letter from Justice Douglas agreeing with the *Frontiero* redraft. "For purposes of employment," wrote Douglas, "I think the discrimination is as invidious and purposeful as that directed against blacks and aliens. I always thought our 1874 decision[21] which gave rise to the 19th Amendment was invidious discrimination against women which should have been invalidated under the Equal Protection Clause." Justices White and Marshall also agreed to join the Brennan redraft.

At the end of his letter, Justice Douglas suggested, "There may be a way for you to sail between *Scylla* and *Charibdis* [*sic*]." Justice Brennan was, however, unwilling to try to steer between the two opposing positions, because he had become firmly convinced of the correctness of the suspect classification approach. He replied to Justice Powell's letter on March 6, writing that, though he had given much thought to Powell's argument, "I come out however still of the view that the 'suspect' approach is the proper one and, further, that now is the time, and this is the case, to make that clear."

The Brennan letter answered the Powell Equal Rights Amendment contention with the assertion, "[w]e cannot count on the Equal Rights Amendment to make the Equal Protection issue go away." Brennan noted that eleven states had voted against ratification and several more were expected to do so shortly. "Since rejection in 13 states is sufficient to kill the Amendment it looks like a lost cause. . . . I therefore don't see that we gain anything by awaiting what is at best an uncertain outcome." In addition Brennan wrote, "whether or not the Equal Rights Amendment eventually is ratified, we cannot ignore the fact that Congress and the legislatures of more than half the States have already determined that classifications based upon sex are inherently suspect."

The Brennan letter also raised a new contention, intended to suggest that the suspect-classification approach was not as radical as it seemed to Justice Powell and its other opponents. Brennan now asserted that the key step in applying that approach in sex discrimination cases had really been taken in *Reed*. He was convinced, Brennan asserted, "that the only rational explication of *Reed* is that it rests upon the 'suspect' approach."

This Brennan statement led Chief Justice Burger to send the Justice a March 6 letter, which began, "I have watched the 'shuttlecock' memos on the subject of *Reed* v. *Reed* and the 'suspect' classification problem." As the writer of the *Reed* opinion, the Chief Justice noted, "Some may construe *Reed* as supporting the 'suspect' view but I do not. The author of *Reed* never remotely contemplated such a broad concept." The Burger letter concluded that he would "join someone who expresses the narrow view expressed by Potter, Harry and Lewis."

In early May, Justice Powell himself did circulate an opinion rejecting the suspect classification approach in favor of that followed in *Reed* which, he said, supported the decision invalidating the *Frontiero* statutes. He was joined by Chief Justice Burger and Justice Blackmun. In his

May 8 letter joining the Powell opinion, the Chief Justice suggested that Powell insert the word "every" or "all" before his statement that the Brennan opinion "would hold that classifications based upon sex . . . are 'inherently suspect and must therefore be subjected to close judicial scrutiny.'" However, Burger concluded his letter, "With or without my puny effort to mute the outrage of 'Womens Lib,' I will join."

The Brennan persistence in adhering to the suspect-classification approach was now to lose him his majority. Justice Stewart finally refused to join and instead issued his one-sentence concurrence in the judgment only, which agreed that the statute at issue worked an invidious discrimination under *Reed* v. *Reed*. Justice Brennan had to recirculate his opinion (which he did on May 9) as a plurality opinion only. Though his use of the suspect-classification approach was joined by Justices Douglas, White, and Marshall, it was rejected by Justice Powell (joined by the Chief Justice and Justice Blackmun) and Justice Stewart, who issued their separate opinions concurring in the judgment on the *Reed* rational-basis approach, as well as by Justice Rehnquist, who dissented.

As already stated, had Justice Brennan's original draft come down as the *Frontiero* opinion of the Court, it would have confirmed the rational-basis test as the appropriate standard of review in sex discrimination cases. Had that standard been applied in the first two cases on the subject, it is most unlikely that the Court would have rejected it in later cases. The Brennan plurality opinion in *Frontiero*, on the other hand, opened the way to the adoption of a stricter standard in *Craig* v. *Boren*,[22] which was decided in 1976.

The *Craig* decision struck down an Oklahoma law prohibiting the sale of "nonintoxicating" 3.2 percent beer to males under the age of twenty-one and to females under the age of eighteen. Such a law was held a denial of equal protection to males eighteen to twenty years of age. Justice Brennan once again wrote the opinion. This time he realized that he could not secure a Court for a *Frontiero*-type opinion that treated sex as a suspect classification subject to the compelling interest requirement. Instead, the *Craig* opinion enunciates an in-between standard—stricter than the rational-basis test, but not as strict as the compelling interest requirement. "To withstand constitutional challenge, . . ." states the Brennan *Craig* opinion, "classifications by gender must serve important governmental objectives and must be substantially related to attainment of those objectives."[23] This test has enabled the Court to apply a stricter standard of review in the more recent sex discrimination cases than would have been permitted under the narrow review provided for in the Brennan original-draft *Frontiero* opinion.

In his *Craig* opinion, Justice Brennan stated that the stricter standard enunciated by him was established by previous cases, particularly *Reed* and that he was only applying *Reed* in striking down the Oklahoma law. This led Chief Justice Burger to write to Brennan on November 15, 1976, "you read into *Reed* v. *Reed* what is not there. Every gender distinction does not need the strict scrutiny test applicable to a *criminal* case. *Reed* was the innocuous matter of who was to probate an estate." Once again, the author of *Reed* objected to what Justice Brennan had read into his opinion. "But then," as the Chief Justice himself had noted in his March 7, 1973, letter to Brennan, "a lot of people sire offspring unintended!"

Notes

1. *Frederic William Maitland Reader* 134 (Delaney ed. 1957).
2. *Bradwell* v. *Illinois*, 16 Wall. 130, 141 (U.S. 1873).
3. 368 U.S. 57 (1961).
4. Id. at 69.
5. 404 U.S. 71 (1971).
6. Id. at 76.
7. Id. at 77.
8. Id. at 76.
9. *Alexander* v. *Fioto*, 430 U.S. 634, 640 (1977).
10. *New Orleans* v. *Dukes*, 427 U.S. 298, 303–4 (1976).
11. Marshall, J., dissenting, in *Massachusetts Board of Retirement* v. *Murgia*, 427 U.S. 307, 319 (1976).
12. See Harlan, J., dissenting, in *Shapiro* v. *Thompson*, 394 U.S. 618, 658 (1969).
13. *Korematsu* v. *United States*, 323 U.S. 214, 216 (1944).
14. *Brown* v. *Board of Education*, 347 U.S. 483 (1954).
15. *Regents* v. *Bakke*, 438 U.S. 265, 355 (1978).
16. These three classifications are listed as suspect in *Massachusetts Board of Retirement* v. *Murgia*, 427 U.S. 307, 313 (1976).
17. *San Antonio School District* v. *Rodriguez*, 411 U.S. 1, 61 (1973).
18. Supra note 5.
19. 411 U.S. 677 (1973).
20. According to Woodward and Armstrong, *The Brethren: Inside the Supreme Court* 254 (1979), the Chief Justice voted with the majority, with only Justice Rehnquist dissenting. The tally sheet of a Justice present at the conference that I have used has both of them for upholding the law. The February 16 letter of Justice Stewart, quoted supra, also refers to "the dissenters."
21. Justice Douglas was probably referring to *Bradwell* v. *Illinois*, 16 Wall. 130 (U.S. 1873).
22. 429 U.S. 190 (1976).
23. Id. at 197.

4

Roe v. Wade (1973):
How a Legal Landmark Manqué
Became a Constitutional Cause Célèbre

Without a doubt, the most controversial Burger Court decision was that in *Roe* v. *Wade*.[1] Few decisions ever handed down were more bitterly attacked. "It is hard to think of any decision in the two hundred years of our history," declared Cardinal Krol, the president of the National Conference of Catholic Bishops, "which has had more disastrous implications for our stability as a civilized society."[2] Condemnatory letters were sent to the Justices in unprecedented volume, particularly to Justice Blackmun, the author of the opinion. Even today, says Blackmun, so many years after the decision, antiabortion pickets continue to show up at his speeches.[3]

Justice Blackmun himself recently termed *Roe* v. *Wade* "a landmark in the progress of the emancipation of women."[4] But that could hardly have been said had Justice Blackmun's original draft come down as the opinion of the Court. That draft did not go nearly as far as the final opinion. On the contrary, although the draft did strike down the abortion statute before the Court, it did so on the ground of vagueness and not because it restricted a woman's right to have an abortion. The draft expressly avoided the issue of the state's substantive right to prohibit abortions or "imply that a State has no legitimate interest in the subject of abortions or that abortion procedures may not be subject to control by the State."[5]

Had the original Blackmun draft come down as the Court opinion, the case would not have dealt with the constitutional merits of state abortion prohibitions, but would have been only a narrow decision striking down a state law for vagueness. The subsequent schism that has been a major factor in American life might have been postponed or avoided—or possibly mitigated by its relegation to political rather than legal resolution.

Roe v. *Wade* came before the Supreme Court together with a companion case, *Doe* v. *Bolton*. In both cases, pregnant women sought declaratory and injunctive relief against state abortion laws, contending they were unconstitutional. At issue in *Roe* was a Texas statute that prohibited abortions except on medical advice for the purpose of saving the mother's life. The statute in *Doe* was a Georgia law that proscribed an abortion except as performed by a physician when necessary in "his best clinical judgment" because continued pregnancy would endanger a pregnant woman's life or injure her health; the fetus would likely be born with a serious defect; or the pregnancy resulted from rape. In addition, the Georgia statutory scheme posed three procedural conditions: (1) that the abortion be performed in an accredited hospital, (2) that the procedure be approved by the hospital staff abortion committee, and (3) that the performing physician's judgment be confirmed by independent examinations of the patient by two other physicians.

The final *Roe* v. *Wade* opinion contrasted the Texas and Georgia statutes as follows: "The Texas statutes under attack here are typical of those that have been in effect in many States for approximately a century. The Georgia statutes, in contrast, have a modern cast and are a legislative product that, to an extent at least, obviously reflects the influences of recent attitudinal change, of advancing medical knowledge and techniques, and of new thinking about an old issue."[6]

Nevertheless, as noted, both statutes were attacked as unconstitutional in the two cases before the Supreme Court. The lower courts had held that both laws were invalid—in *Roe* because the statute infringed upon the plaintiff's "fundamental right . . . to choose whether to have children [which] is protected by the Ninth Amendment" and in *Doe* because the reasons listed in the statute improperly restricted plaintiff's right of privacy and of personal liberty. The lower court, however, had refused to strike down the other provisions of the Georgia statute.

Roe v. *Wade* and *Doe* v. *Bolton* were both discussed at the same postargument conference in December 1971. The Chief Justice devoted much of his *Roe* v. *Wade* discussion to the question of standing. Referring to the lead plaintiff, he said, "Jane Roe is unmarried and pregnant. She doesn't claim health; just doesn't want the baby." In the Burger view, "The unmarried girl has standing. She didn't lose standing through mootness." This meant, the Chief Justice went on, that "she's entitled to an injunction if the statute is [un]constitutional." On the merits, Burger said, "The balance here is between the state's interest in protecting fetal life and the woman's interest in not having children." In weighing these interests, the Chief Justice concluded, "I can't find the Texas statute unconstitutional, although it's certainly archaic and obsolete."

Justice Douglas, who spoke next, declared categorically, "The abortion statute is unconstitutional. This is basically a medical and psychiatric problem"—and not one to be dealt with by prohibitory legislation. Douglas also criticized the statute's failure to give "a licensed physician an immunity for good faith abortions." He also was of the opinion that "all have standing" in the case. Justice Brennan, who followed, expressed a similar view, though he stressed more strongly than any of the others that the right to an abortion should be given a constitutional basis by the Court's decision.

Justice Stewart, next in order of seniority, also argued in favor of standing. "The issue of standing," he urged, "ought not to confuse this, if we agree that the unmarried girl has standing to get a judgment on the merits. She clearly has standing." On the merits, Stewart stated, "I agree with Bill Douglas." Stewart did, however, indicate that there might be some state power in the matter. "The state," he said, "can legislate, to the extent of requiring a doctor and that, after a certain period of pregnancy, [she] can't have an abortion."

Justice White began his presentation, "I agree with Potter on all preliminaries, but on the merits I am on the other side. They want us to say that women have a choice under the Ninth Amendment." But White said that he refused to accept this "privacy argument."

Justice Marshall declared, "I go with Bill Douglas, but the time problem concerns me." He thought that the state could not prevent abortions "in the early stage [of pregnancy]. But why can't the state prohibit after a certain stage?" In addition, Marshall said that he would use " 'liberty' under the Fourteenth Amendment as the constitutional base."

Justice Blackmun, then the junior Justice, spoke last. He agreed that "the girl has standing." On the merits, Blackmun's presentation displayed an ambivalence that was to be reflected in his draft *Roe* v. *Wade* opinion. "Can a state properly outlaw all abortions?" he asked. "If we accept fetal life, there's a strong argument that it can. But there are opposing interests: the right of the mother to life and mental and physical health, the right of parents in case of rape, the right of the state in case of incest. I don't think there's an absolute right to do what you will with [your] body." Blackmun did, however, say flatly, "This statute is a poor statute that . . . impinges too far on her."

The discussion of *Doe v. Bolton* paralleled that in *Roe v. Wade*. The Chief Justice had no doubt that "there was standing as to the pregnant girl." However, he asserted, "I do not agree with this carving up of the statute by the three-judge court." As Burger saw it, "The state has a duty to protect fetal life at some stage, but we are not confronted with that question here." The Chief Justice concluded, "I would hold this statute constitutional."

The Georgia statute received a more favorable review than its Texas counterpart from Justice Douglas. "This is a much better statute than Texas," he declared. But Douglas had doubts on the statute's practical effects. "We don't know," he stated, "how this statute operates. Is it weighted on the side of only those who can afford this? What about the poor?" Douglas said that he was inclined "to remand to the district court to find out."

Justice Brennan, on the other hand, had no doubts. He said that he would affirm the decision below "as far as it goes" but would also "go further to strike down the three-doctor thing as too restrictive." Justice Stewart agreed with the last point. But Justice White again spoke in favor of the state. As he saw it, "The state has power to protect the unborn child. This plaintiff didn't have trouble [taking][7] advantage of procedures. I think the state has struck the right balance here."

Once again, Justice Blackmun's position was ambivalent. "Medically," he pointed out, "this statute is perfectly workable." Blackmun emphasized the competing interests at stake. "I would like," he said "to see an opinion that recognizes the opposing interests in fetal life and the mother's interest in health and happiness." Blackmun indicated interest in the approach stated by Douglas earlier in the conference. "I would be perfectly willing," he stated, "to paint some standards and remand for findings as to how it operates: does it operate to deny equal protection by discriminating against the poor?"

The conference outcome was not entirely clear because the tally sheets of different Justices do not coincide on the votes.[8] What was clear, however, was that a majority were in favor of invalidating the laws: in *Roe* v. *Wade*, five (Justices Douglas, Brennan, Stewart, Marshall, and Blackmun) to two (the Chief Justice and Justice White) in the tally sheet made available to me—but four to three (with Blackmun added to the dissenters) according to Douglas's "Dear Chief" letter to Burger. Despite the fact that he was not part of the majority, the Chief Justice assigned the opinions in the two abortion cases to Justice Blackmun. Thus, on December 18, 1971, two days after the conference, Justice Douglas (whose tally sheet showed four votes for invalidating the laws, with himself as senior Justice in the majority) sent his "Dear Chief" missive, "As respects your assignment in this case, my notes show there were four votes to hold parts of the . . . Act unconstitutional. . . . There were three to sustain the law as written." Douglas concluded, "I would think, therefore, that to save future time and trouble, one of the four, rather than one of the three, should write the opinion."

The Chief Justice replied with a December 20 "Dear Bill" letter. "At the close of discussion of this case, I remarked to the Conference that there were, literally, not enough columns to mark up an accurate reflection of the voting in either the Georgia or the Texas cases. I therefore marked down no votes and said this was a case that would have to stand or fall on the writing, when it was done."

According to the Burger letter, "That is still my view of how to handle these two . . . sensitive cases, which, I might add, are quite probable candidates for reargument."

A few months later, the *Washington Post* reported the Burger–Douglas exchange. According to the *Post* story, Douglas sent his letter "asserting his prerogative to assign the case, but Burger held fast to his position."[9] Justices Douglas and Brennan, who had led the proabortion bloc at the conference then decided to wait to see the Blackmun drafts before doing anything further in the matter. Though Douglas had, as seen, tallied Blackmun with the minority, others had noted his vote as one with the majority. This might well mean Blackmun opinions that would reach the result favored by Douglas and Brennan.

That Justices Douglas and Brennan did reach the conclusion, just indicated is shown by a letter sent by Brennan to Douglas on December 30: "I gathered from our conversation yesterday that you too think we might better await Harry Blackmun's circulation in the *Texas* abortion case before circulating one." After all, when Justice Blackmun did circulate, it might make either a confrontation with the Chief Justice or a separate majority draft unnecessary.

The Brennan letter was called forth by an uncirculated Douglas draft in the Georgia case, which its author had sent to Justice Brennan soon after the assignment to Justice Blackmun. This printed draft is presumably what Justice Douglas would have circulated as his draft opinion of the Court had he been able to assign the abortion opinions. As such, it is reprinted on p. 93, and may serve as the first of our unpublished opinions in the abortion cases.

The Douglas draft, headed *Memorandum from MR. JUSTICE DOUGLAS*, is a typical Douglas product. Written personally at breakneck speed—almost six months before the Blackmun first draft was circulated—it was finished before the others had even had a chance to reflect seriously on what had happened at the argument and conference. Unlike the situation with other Douglas drafts, however, this first effort was not to be the only or final Douglas product. The Justice spent considerable effort in refining his opinion; there would be seven drafts of the Douglas opinion (the last on May 22, 1972) before it was replaced by Justice Blackmun's draft opinions in the two abortion cases. Probably, up until the Blackmun drafts were circulated, Douglas still hoped that he would be able to author the Court's abortion opinions—which would explain the unusual Douglas effort to improve his opinion through so many separate drafts. Ultimately, the Douglas seventh draft became the concurrence that the Justice issued in *Roe* v. *Wade*.

As already stated, it is the first Douglas draft that is reprinted on p. 93. In form, it is an opinion in the Georgia case, *Doe* v. *Bolton*. But its broad reasoning on the merits—grounding the right to an abortion on the constitutional right of privacy—is equally applicable to the Texas case, *Roe* v. *Wade*. "The right of privacy . . . ," Douglas declares, "is a species of 'liberty' of the person as that word is used in the Fourteenth Amendment. It is a concept that acquires substance, not from the predilections of judges, but from the emanations of the various provisions of the Bill of Rights, including the Ninth Amendment."

The heart of the Douglas draft is its holding that the abortion right is protected by the right of privacy. That right, says Douglas, "covers a wide range" and is "broad enough to encompass the right of a woman to terminate an unwanted pregnancy in its early stages, by obtaining an abortion." This does not mean that "the 'liberty' of the mother, though rooted as it is in the Constitution, may [not] be qualified by the State." But where fundamental rights are involved, "this Court has required that the statute be narrowly and precisely drawn and that a 'compelling state interest' be shown in support of the limitation." This requirement is of cardinal significance. "Unless regulatory measures are so confined and are addressed to the specific areas of compelling legislative concern, the police-power would become the great leveller of constitutional rights and liberties."

As the Douglas draft sees it, the statute at issue fails the constitutional test. That is true because, as Justice Brennan summarized the draft in his already-quoted December 30 letter, "The statute infringes the right of privacy by refusing abortions where the mother's mental, but not physical health is in jeopardy." The Douglas draft noted that "the vicissitudes of life produce pregnancies which may be unwanted or which may impair the 'health' in the broad . . . sense of the term or which may imperil the life of the mother or which in the full setting of the case may create such suffering, dislocations, misery, or tragedy as to make an early abortion the only civilized step to take. The suffering, dislocations, misery or tragedy just mentioned may be properly embraced in the 'health' factor of the mother as appraised by a person of insight." But the abortion statute did not embrace other than physical health and was therefore too narrow to meet constitutional requirements.

Justice Brennan sent his December 30 letter after reading the Douglas draft. The letter consisted of a ten-page analysis of the draft and suggestions for improvements. Brennan wrote, "I guess my most significant departure from your approach is in the development of the right-of-privacy argument." Brennan noted his agreement "that the right is a species of 'liberty' (although, as I mentioned yesterday, I think the Ninth Amendment . . . should be brought into this problem at greater length), but I would identify three groups of fundamental freedoms that, 'liberty' encompasses: *first,* freedom from bodily restraint or inspection, freedom to do with one's body as one likes, and freedom to care for one's health and person; *second,* freedom of choice in the basic decisions of life, such as marriage, divorce, procreation, contraception, and the education and upbringing of children; and, *third,* autonomous control over the development and expression of one's intellect and personality."

Brennan stressed that "The decision whether to abort a pregnancy obviously fits directly within each of the categories of fundamental freedoms I've identified and, therefore, should be held to involve a basic individual right." This meant "that the crucial question is whether the State has a compelling interest in regulating abortion that is achieved without unnecessarily intruding upon the individual's right. But here I would deal at length not only with the health concern for the well-being of the mother, but with the material interest in the life of the fetus and the moral interest in sanctifying life in general."

Brennan wrote that, "although I would, of course, find a compelling State interest in requiring abortions to be performed by doctors, I would deny any such interest in the life of the fetus in the early stages of pregnancy." It follows "there is a right to an abortion in the early part of the term," and that the right of privacy in the matter of abortions means that the decision is that of the woman and her alone.

"In sum," the Brennan letter concluded, "I would affirm the district court's conclusion that the reasons for an abortion may not be prescribed. I would further hold that the only restraint a State may constitutionally impose upon the woman's individual decision is that the abortion must be performed by a licensed physician."

The later Douglas drafts as well as the ultimate Douglas concurrence adopted many of the Brennan suggestions. The Douglas draft also had an influence on Justice Blackmun's drafting process. There is a note in Douglas's hand, dated March 6, 1972, indicating that a copy of the Douglas draft had been "sent . . . to HB several weeks ago."

In his December 30 letter, Justice Brennan had written, "I appreciate that some time may pass before we hear from Harry." Justice Blackmun was known as the slowest worker on the Court. The abortion cases were his first major assignment, and he worked at them during the next few months, mostly alone and unassisted in the Court library; he was still working on his draft as the Court term wore on. It was mid-May before he felt able to circulate anything.

Finally, on May 18, 1972, Justice Blackmun sent around the draft *Roe* v. *Wade* opinion reprinted on p. 103. "Herewith," began the covering memo, "is a first and tentative draft for this case." Blackmun wrote that "it may be somewhat difficult to obtain a consensus on all aspects. My notes indicate, however, that we were generally in agreement to affirm on the merits. That is where I come out on the theory that the Texas statute, despite its narrowness, is unconstitutionally vague."

The memo went on, "I think that this would be all that is necessary for disposition of the case, and that we need not get into the more complex Ninth Amendment issue. This may or may not appeal to you."

However, Blackmun informed his colleagues, "I am still flexible as to results, and I shall do my best to arrive at something which would command a court."

The Blackmun draft, headed *Memorandum of MR. JUSTICE BLACKMUN*, is the first draft of the *Roe* v. *Wade* opinion. As the covering memo explained, it avoids the broader constitutional issue and strikes down the Texas statute on the ground of vagueness. The draft starts by dealing with the issues of standing and mootness. It finds that Roe had standing and that the termination of her pregnancy did not render the case moot.

On the merits, the Blackmun draft holds that the Texas statute is unconstitutionally vague. The difficulty here was that, in *United States* v. *Vuitch*,[10] decided the year before, the Court had upheld a similar

District of Columbia abortion law against a vagueness attack. The Blackmun draft distinguishes *Vuitch* on the ground that the statute there prohibited abortion unless "necessary for the preservation of the mother's life or health," whereas the Texas statute only permitted abortions "for the purpose of saving the life of the mother." Consequently, the draft concluded, *Vuitch* "provides no answer to the constitutional challenge to the Texas statute."

In the Texas statute, "Saving the mother's life is the sole standard." According to the Blackmun draft, this standard is too vague to guide physicians' conduct in abortion cases. "Does it mean that he may procure an abortion only when, without it, the patient will surely die? Or only when the odds are greater than even that she will die? Or when there is a mere possibility that she will not survive?"

After posing other questions which, in Blackmun's view, are not definitely answered, the draft reaches its conclusion: "We conclude that Art. 1196, with its sole criterion for exemption as 'saving the life of the mother,' is insufficiently informative to the physician to whom it purports to afford a measure of professional protection but who must measure its indefinite meaning at the risk of his liberty, and that the statute cannot withstand constitutional challenge on vagueness grounds."

It must be conceded that the Blackmun draft's vagueness analysis is far from impressive. If anything, the "life-saving" standard in the *Roe* v. *Wade* statute is more definite than the "health" standard upheld in *Vuitch*. But the draft's disposition of the case on the vagueness ground enabled the draft to avoid addressing what Justice Brennan, in a May 18 "Dear Harry" letter—after he had read the draft—called "the core constitutional question." Hence, as the Blackmun draft stated, "There is no need in Roe's case to pass upon her contention that under the Ninth Amendment a pregnant woman has an absolute right to an abortion, or even to consider the opposing rights of the embryo or fetus during the respective prenatal trimesters."

Indeed, so far as the draft contains intimations on the matter, they tend to support state substantive power over abortions. "Our holding today," the draft is careful to note, "does not imply that a State has no legitimate interest in the subject of abortions or that abortion procedures may not be subjected to control by the State." On the contrary, "We do not accept the argument of the appellants and of some of the *amici* that a pregnant woman has an unlimited right to do with her body as she pleases. The long acceptance of statutes regulating the possession of certain drugs and other harmful substances, and making criminal indecent exposure in public, or an attempt at suicide, clearly indicate the contrary." This is, of course, completely different from the approach ultimately followed in the *Roe* v. *Wade* opinion of the Court.

In his covering memo transmitting his *Roe* v. *Wade* draft, Justice Blackmun also referred to the companion case, *Doe* v. *Bolton*. "The Georgia case, yet to come," he wrote, "is more complex. I am still tentatively of the view, as I have been all along, that the Georgia case merits reargument before a full bench. I shall try to produce something, however, so that we may look at it before any decision as to that is made."

On May 25, a week after he had sent around his *Roe* v. *Wade* draft, Justice Blackmun circulated his draft *Doe* v. *Bolton* opinion, which is reprinted on p. 120. "Here, for your consideration," the covering memo began, "is a memorandum on the second abortion case." As summarized in the memo, his opinion "would accomplish . . . the striking of the Georgia statutory requirements as to (1) residence, (2) confirmation by two physicians, (3) advance approval by the hospital abortion committee, and (4) performance of the procedure only in [an] accredited hospital."

The Blackmun *Doe* draft, like that in *Roe*, is headed *Memorandum of MR. JUSTICE BLACKMUN*. Though it strikes down the Georgia statute on the grounds noted in the covering memo, it also deals with the claim that the law is an "invalid restriction of absolute fundamental right to personal and marital privacy." Here Blackmun was substantially influenced by the treatment in the Douglas draft (infra p. 93), particularly the later redrafts, which Justice Douglas noted in a May 19 letter, "I believe I gave you, some time back."

Blackmun's *Doe* draft begins its privacy discussion by stating, "The Court, in varying contexts, has recognized a right of personal privacy and has rooted it in the Fourteenth Amendment, or in the Bill of Rights, or in the latter's penumbras." The draft refers to the assertion "that the scope of this right of personal privacy includes, for a woman, the right to decide unilaterally to terminate an existing but *unwanted* pregnancy without any state interference or control whatsoever." This assertion is flatly rejected. "Appellants' contention, however, that the woman's right to make the decision is absolute—that Georgia has either no valid interest in regulating it, or no interest strong enough to support any limitation upon the woman's sole determination—is unpersuasive."

In particular, the draft rejects as "illogical and unfair" the argument that "the State's present professed interest in the protection of embryonic and fetal 'life' is somehow to be downgraded. That argument condemns the State for past 'wrongs' and also denies it the right to readjust its views and emphases in the light of the more advanced knowledge and techniques of today."

The *Doe* draft, in a manner utterly unlike that in the final Blackmun opinions, stresses the countervailing interest in fetal life. "The heart of the matter is that somewhere, either forthwith at conception, or at 'quickening,' or at birth, or at some other point in between, another being becomes involved and the privacy the woman possessed has become dual rather than sole. The woman's right of privacy must be measured accordingly." That being the case, "The woman's personal right . . . , is not unlimited. It must be balanced against the State's interest."

This means that "we cannot automatically strike down the remaining features of the Georgia statute simply because they restrict any right on the part of the woman to have an abortion at will." The remainder of the draft balances "the impact of the statute upon the right, as it relates to the state interest being asserted." The balancing process leads, as the covering memo summarized it, to invalidation of the residence, accreditation, approval, and confirmation requirements.

The invalidation of the two-physician confirmation requirement was a difficult step for Justice Blackmun to take. "I might say," he wrote in his covering memo, "that this was not the easiest conclusion for me to reach." Blackmun then referred to his own experience as counsel to the Mayo Clinic. "I have worked closely with supervisory hospital committees set up by the medical profession itself, and I have seen them operate over extensive periods. I can state with complete conviction that they serve a high purpose in maintaining standards and in keeping the overzealous surgeon's knife sheathed. There is a lot of unnecessary surgery done in this country, and intraprofessional restraints of this kind have accomplished much that is unnoticed and certainly is unappreciated by people generally."

On the other side, the memo states, "I have also seen abortion mills in operation and the general misery they have caused despite their being run by otherwise 'competent' technicians." Despite this, the *Doe* draft comes down against the Georgia physician-review requirement.

The Blackmun *Doe* draft is certainly an improvement over his first *Roe v. Wade* effort. Like the latter, however, it did not deal directly with Justice Brennan's "core constitutional question." Indeed, the implication here, too, was that substantial state power over abortion did exist. Under the *Doe* draft, as the Blackmun covering memo pointed out, the state may provide "that an abortion may be performed only if the attending physician deems it necessary 'based upon his best clinical judgment,' if his judgment is reduced to writing, and if the abortion is performed in a hospital licensed by the State through its Board of Health." This is, of course, wholly inconsistent with the Court's final decision in *Roe v. Wade*.

Justice Blackmun ends his *Doe* covering memo by again explaining his approach in the *Roe v. Wade* draft. "I should observe," he points out, "that, according to information contained in some of the briefs, knocking out the Texas statute in *Roe v. Wade* will invalidate the abortion laws in a *majority* of our States. Most States focus only on the preservation of the life of the mother. *Vuitch*, of course, is on the books, and I had assumed that the Conference, at this point, has no intention to overrule it. It is because of *Vuitch's* vagueness emphasis and a hope, perhaps forlorn, that we might have a unanimous court in the Texas case, that I took the vagueness route."

1st DRAFT

SUPREME COURT OF THE UNITED STATES

No. 70-40

Mary Doe et al., Appellants, *v.* Arthur K. Bolton, as Attorney General of the State of Georgia, et al.	On Appeal from the United States District Court for the Northern District of Georgia.

[January —, 1972]

Memorandum from MR. JUSTICE DOUGLAS.

This is a suit in a three-judge District Court to declare Georgia's abortion law [1] unconstitutional. It is a class action raising numerous constitutional claims including the denial of Equal Protection guaranteed by the Fourteenth Amendment. Original plaintiffs also included doctors, nurses, social workers, ministers, and counsellors. But they were dsmissed by the District Court which proceeded to hold that portions of the Georgia abortion law were unconstitutional. 319 F. Supp. 1048, 1057. The case is here by direct appeal. 28 U. S. C. § 1253.

I

Mary Doe is 22 years old and was about 11 weeks pregnant at the time the complaint was filed. She and her husband were unemployed; their marriage had been unstable; during the pendency of the suit, her husband abandoned her. She desired an abortion because she was emotionally and economically unable to care for and support another child. She and her husband have three other children, the third being placed at birth with adoptive parents and the other two being removed from their

[1] Ga. Code Ann. § 26-1201 *et seq.* Set forth in the Appendix.

DOE *v.* BOLTON

custody by state authorities since the parents were unable
to care for them.

Mary Doe applied for an abortion at the Grady Memorial Hospital in Atlanta and after a period of 25 days
was notified that her application was denied by the hospital's abortion committee because she did not come
within any of the three reasons stated in § 26–1202 (a)
giving the permissible statutory bases of the physicians
belief "based upon his best clinical judgment that an
abortion is necessary because:

> "(1) A continuation of the pregnancy would
> endanger the life of the pregnant woman or would
> seriously and permanently injure her health; or
>
> "(2) The fetus would very likely be born with a
> grave, permanent, and irremediable mental or physi-
> cal defect; or
>
> "(3) The pregnancy resulted from forcible or stat-
> utory rape."

We hold that Mary Doe—concededly a real, not a
fictitious person—is an aggrieved person having standing
to sue. Her suit is adequate to raise all the constitutional questions tendered. Hence we need not determine
whether the doctors, nurses, social workers, ministers,
and counsellors, whom the District Court dismissed,
would also have standing to sue.

II

In *United States* v. *Vuitch*, 402 U. S. 62, 68, a majority
of the Court upheld against the charge of unconstitutional vagueness an abortion statute of the District of
Columbia which made an abortion a criminal offense
unless it was "necessary for the preservation of the
mother's life or health and under the direction of a
competent licensed practitioner of medicine." Prior to
that statute the District had allowed abortions only for

DOE *v.* BOLTON

the purpose of preserving the life of the mother. *Id.*, 70, n. 5. The addition of the word "health" broadened the statute, enabling the majority to hold that "health" now "includes psychological as well as physical well-being." *Id.*, 72. The majority disposed of the unconstitutional-for-vagueness argument by saying, ". . . whether a particular operation is necessary for a patient's physical or mental health is a judgment that physicians are obviously called upon to make routinely whenever surgery is considered." *Ibid.*

The questions presented in the present case go far beyond the issue of vagueness. They involve the right of privacy, one aspect of which we considered in *Griswold* v. *Connecticut*, 381 U. S. 479. The right of privacy in the family circle covers a wide range: liberty to marry a person of one's own choosing, *Loving* v. *Virginia*, 388 U. S. 1, the right of procreation, *Skinner* v. *Oklahoma*, 316 U. S. 535, the liberty to direct the education of one's children, *Pierce* v. *Society of Sisters*, 268 U. S. 510.

We said in Griswold:

". . . Various guarantees create zones of privacy. The right of association contained in the penumbra of the First Amendment is one, as we have seen. The Third Amendment in its prohibition against the quartering of soldiers 'in any house' in time of peace without the consent of the owner is another facet of that privacy. The Fourth Amendment explicitly affirms the 'right of the people to be secure in their persons, houses, papers, and effects, against unreasonable searches and seizures.' The Fifth Amendment in its Self-Incrimination Clause enables the citizen to create a zone of privacy which government may not force him to surrender to his detriment. The Ninth Amendment provides: 'The enumeration in the Constitution, of certain rights, shall

DOE *r.* BOLTON

not be construed to deny or disparage others retained
by the people.'" 381 U. S. 484.

The *Griswold* case involved a law forbidding the use of
contraceptives. We held that law as applied to married
people unconstitutional. We said:

> "We deal with a right of privacy older than the
> Bill of Rights—older than our political parties,
> older than our school system. Marriage is a coming
> together for better or for worse, hopefully enduring,
> and intimate to the decree of being sacred." *Id.*, 486.

We agree with the District Court that *Griswold* and
related cases "establish a constitutional right to privacy
broad enough to encompass the right of a woman to
terminate an unwanted pregnancy in its early stages, by
obtaining an abortion." 319 F. Supp. ——.

That was the view of the Supreme Court of California
in *People* v. *Belous*,[2] 71 Cal. 2d 954, 963.

Such a holding is, however, only the beginning of the
problem. The State has interests to protect. While
there are the dangers of childbirth to the lives of some
women, voluntary abortion at any time and place regardless of medical standards is a rightful concern of society.
The woman's health is part of that concern; and the life
of the fetus after quickening is another concern. These
concerns justify the State in treating the problem as a
medical one. The reply here is that Georgia so treated
it by allowing an abortion when otherwise the condition
would "endanger" the life of the woman or "seriously and
permanently injure her health."

The difficulty is that the statute as construed and applied does not give full sweep to the "psychological as

---

[2] The California abortion statute, held unconstitutional in the
Belous case made it a crime to perform or help perform an abortion
"unless the same is necessary to preserve [the mother's] life." 71
Cal. 2d, at 959.

DOE *v.* BOLTON

well as physical well-being" which saved the concept "health" from being void for vagueness in *United States v. Vuitch, supra,* at 72.

The right of privacy described in *Griswold* is a species of "liberty" of the person as that word is used in the Fourteenth Amendment. It is a concept that acquires substance, not from the predilections of judges, but from the emanations of the various provisions of the Bill of Rights, including the Ninth Amendment. There is no "liberty," in the absolute sense, to do with one's body as one likes. See *Jacobson* v. *Massachusetts,* 197 U. S. 11, 29. But the vicissitudes of life produce pregnancies which may be unwanted, or which may impair the "health" in the broad *Vuitch* sense of the term or which may imperil the life of the mother or which in the full setting of the case may create such suffering, dislocations, misery, or tragedy as to make an early abortion the only civilized step to take. The suffering, dislocations, misery or tragedy just mentioned may be properly embraced in the "health" factor of the mother as appraised by a person of insight. Or they may be part of a broader medical judgment based on what is "appropriate" in a given case, though perhaps not "necessary" in a strict sense.

The "liberty" of the mother, though rooted as it is in the Constitution, may be qualified by the State for the reasons we have stated. But where fundamental personal rights and liberties are involved, the corrective legislation must be "narrowly drawn to prevent the supposed evil," *Cantwell* v. *Connecticut,* 310 U. S. 296, 307, and not be dealt with in an "unlimited and indiscriminate" manner. *Shelton* v. *Tucker,* 364 U. S. 479, 490. And see *Talley* v. *California,* 362 U. S. 60. Unless regulatory measures are so confined and are addressed to the specific areas of compelling legislative concern, the police

DOE *v.* BOLTON

power would become the great leveller of constitutional
rights and liberties.[3]

We agree with the District Court that Georgia's statute
by its narrow application of the term "health" does not
meet constitutional requirements.

III

There are procedural problems of constitutional dignity
involved in Georgia's law which were not reached by the
District Court.

In the first place, the abortion patient has no opportunity to be heard, to know the reasons why she is denied an abortion, or to appeal an adverse decision.

State action adversely affecting liberties of the people
can be done only in accordance with procedural due
process, not be arbitrary fiat.

We held in *Goldberg* v. *Kelly,* 397 U. S. 254, 264, that
before welfare is discontinued "only a pre-termination
evidentiary hearing provides the recipient with procedural due process." Not all governmental benefits, we
said, need be so terminated. Welfare benefits were dif-

---

[3] In order to uphold legislative action which touches upon or limits
a fundamental right, this Court has required that the statute be
narrowly and precisely drawn and that a "compelling state interest"
be shown in support of the limitation. *E. g., Kramer* v. *Union Free
School Dist.,* 395 U. S. 621 (1969); *Shapiro* v. *Thompson,* 394 U. S.
618 (1969); *Carrington* v. *Rash,* 380 U. S. 89 (1965); *Sherbert* v.
Verner, 374 U. S. 398 (1963); *NAACP* v. *Alabama ex rel. Patterson,*
357 U. S. 449 (1958). On the other hand, where no more than
economic interests are touched upon, this Court has upheld legislative action upon a showing of only a "rational basis" for the classification or limitation. *E. g., Schilb* v. *Keubel,* 404 U. S. —— (1971);
Richardson v. *Belcher,* 404 U. S. —— (1971); *United States* v.
Maryland Savings-Share Ins. Corp., 400 U. S. 4 (1970); *McDonald*
v. *Board of Election Commissioners,* 394 U. S. 802 (1969); *McGowan*
v. *Maryland,* 366 U. S. 420 (1961); *Williamson* v. *Lee Optical Co.,*
348 U. S. 483 (1955).

DOE *v.* BOLTON

ferent, we concluded, because termination "may deprive
an eligible recipient of the very means by which to live
while he waits." *Ibid.* We added that important governmental interests were served by a pre-termination
hearing, since this Nation's long-term commitment has
been "to foster the dignity and well-being of all persons
within its borders," as protection "against the societal
malaise that may flow from a widespread sense of unjustified frustration and insecurity." *Id.,* at 265.

In *Bell* v. *Burson,* 402 U. S. 535, we held a motor vehicle registration and a driver's license so critical to one's
livelihood or profession in these modern days may not
be revoked by a State, even following an accident where
the licensee carries no automobile liability insurance,
unless there is first a hearing that puts in issue the
"reasonable possibility of a judgment being rendered
against him as a result of the accident. *Id.,* at 544.

Procedural due process is the requirement when wages
are garnished, *Sniadach* v. *Family Finance Corp.,* 395
U. S. 337; when one is disqualified for unemployment
compensation, *Sherbert* v. *Verner,* 374 U. S. 398; when
one is discharged from public employment, *Slochower* v.
Board of Education, 350 U. S. 551; when tax exemptions
are denied, *Speiser* v. *Randall,* 357 U. S. 513. As we said
in *Wisconsin* v. *Constantineau,* 400 U. S. 433, 437, "Where
a person's good name, reputation, honor or integrity are
at stake because of what the government is doing to him,
notice and an opportunity to be heard are essential."
The examples need not be enlarged. We have at times
disagreed as to whether the "private interest" at stake
had that dignity and dimension which brought into play
the requirements of procedural due process. *Cafeteria
Workers* v. *McElroy,* 367 U. S. 886, was such a case.

But we have no doubt that the "liberty" of the mother
involved in a negative ruling on her application for an

DOE *v.* BOLTON

abortion has constitutional dimensions and accordingly
she should have been granted a hearing.

IV

Under the Georgia Act the mother's physician is not
the sole judge as to whether the abortion should be performed. Two other licensed physicians must concur in
his judgment.[1] Moreover, the abortion must be performed in a licensed hospital;[2] and the abortion must be
approved in advance by a committee of the medical staff
of that hospital.[3]

Physicians, who speak to us in this case through an
amicus brief, complain of the Georgia Act's interference
with their practice of their profession.

We have spoken often of First and Fourteenth Amendment rights of freedom of association in various frames
of reference. See e. g., *NAACP* v. *Alabama*, 357 U. S.
449, 462. The lawyer-client relation has that constitutional protection, as we held in *NAACP* v. *Button*, 371
U. S. 415. Freedom to associate and privacy in one's
associations have no more conspicuous place than in the
physician-patient relationship, unless it be in the priest-
parishioner relation.

It is one thing for a patient to agree that her physician
may consult with another physician about her case. It
is quite a different matter for the State compulsorily to
impose on that physician-patient relationship another
layer or, as in this case, still a third layer of physicians.
Then the freedom of association protected by the First
and Fourteenth Amendments becomes only a matter of
theory not a reality, for a multiple physician approval
system is mandated by the State.

The State licenses a physician. If he is derelict or
faithless, the procedures available to punish him or to

[1] See § 26–1202 (b)(3) in the Appendix.
[2] See § 26–1202 (b)(4).
[3] Section 26–1202 (b)(5).

DOE *v.* BOLTON

deprive him of his license are well known. He is entitled to procedural due process before professional disciplinary sanctions may be imposed. See *In re Ruffalo*, 390 U. S. 544. Crucial here, however, is state-imposed control over the medical decision whether pregnancy should be interrupted. The good-faith decision of the patient's chosen physician is overridden and the final decision passed on to others in whose selection the patient has no part. This is a total destruction of the freedom of association between physician and patient and the privacy which that entails.

The right to seek advice on one's health and the right to place his reliance on the physician of his choice are basic to First and Fourteenth Amendment values. It may be that reasons can be conjured up for some invasion of that "liberty" of the mother. But here again, we deal with fundamental rights and liberties, which can be contained or controlled only by discretely drawn legislation that preserves the "liberty" but regulates only those phases of the problem of compelling legislative concern. The imposition by the State of group controls over the physician-patient relation is not made on any medical procedure apart from abortion, no matter how dangerous the medical step may be. The oversight imposed on the physician and patient in abortion cases denies them their "liberty," that is their freedom of association, without any compelling, discernible state interest.

Since Georgia treats the problem as a medical problem, the control must be through the physician of the mother's choice and the standards set for his performance.

V

Mary Doe for herself and other members of her class alleges in her first cause of action that the Georgia Act violates the Equal Protection Clause of the Fourteenth Amendment. The argument is that three physicians are required and only those who can afford to pay the fees

DOE *v.* BOLTON

of three physicians have as a practical matter recourse to an abortion. Moreover. the hospital committee of three doctors must also approve; and the operation must take place in a licensed hospital. The costs of a private hospital bar the indigents. it is said. who should be allowed to use public health facilities. Moreover. even wage earners—not indigents alone—cannot afford three doctors and the hospital costs. It is further argued that 105 of Georgia's 159 counties have no accredited hospital at all. It is said that a HEW study [7] shows that the Georgia system has had a racially discriminatory application.

In this connection it is represented that not all counties have even five doctors and that in some there are no Blacks licensed to practice. The District Court made no findings on this phase of the case. Therefore the cause must be remanded to it.

On remand we add only one more word. If the rights which a pregnant woman has are to be meaningful. the time space within which she must move is quite limited. These special circumstances. it is urged. warrant injunctive relief against future applications of the Act to deny women in the class represented by Mary Doe abortions performed by qualified physicians.

There may be other facets of the case which will also warrant additional findings.

We accordingly remand the cause for proceedings consistent with this opinion.

So ordered.

[7] See Rochat. Tyler. and Schoenbucher. An Epidemiological Analysis of Abortion in Georgia, 61 Am. J. of Public Health 541 (1971).

1st DRAFT

SUPREME COURT OF THE UNITED STATES

No. 70–18

From: Blackmun,

Recirculated: ___

| Jane Roe et al.. Appellants. *v.* Henry Wade. | On Appeal from the United States District Court for the Northern District of Texas. |

[May —. 1972]

Memorandum of MR. JUSTICE BLACKMUN.

Under constitutional attack here are abortion laws of the State of Texas.[1] 2A Texas Penal Code. Arts.

---

[1] "Article 1191. Abortion

"If any person shall designedly administer to a pregnant woman or knowingly procure to be administered with her consent any drug or medicine, or shall use towards her any violence or means whatever externally or internally applied. and thereby procure an abortion, he shall be confined in the penitentiary not less than two nor more than five years; if it be done without her consent, the punishment shall be doubled. By 'abortion' is meant that the life of the fetus or embryo shall be destroyed in the woman's womb or that a premature birth thereof be caused.

"Art. 1192. Furnishing the means

"Whoever furnishes the means for procuring an abortion knowing the purpose intended is guilty as an accomplice.

"Art. 1193. Attempt at abortion

"If the means used shall fail to produce an abortion, the offender is nevertheless guilty of an attempt to produce abortion, provided it be shown that such means were calculated to produce that result, and shall be fined not less than one hundred nor more than one thousand dollars.

"Art. 1194. Murder in producing abortion

"If the death of the mother is occasioned by an abortion so produced or by an attempt to effect the same it is murder.

"Art. 1196. By medical advice

"Nothing in this chapter applies to an abortion procured or at-

ROE *v.* WADE

1191–1194 and 1196 (1961). These statutes make it
a crime to "procure an abortion," as therein defined, or
to attempt one, except with respect to "an abortion
procured or attempted by medical advice for the purpose
of saving the life of the mother."

I

Jane Roe,[2] a single woman residing in Dallas County,
Texas, in March 1970 instituted this federal suit against
the District Attorney of the county. The plaintiff
sought (1) a declaratory judgment that the Texas abortion laws are unconstitutional on their face and (2) an
injunction restraining the defendant from enforcing the
challenged statutes.

Roe alleged that she was unmarried and pregnant;
that she wished to terminate her pregnancy by an abortion "performed by a competent, licensed physician,
under safe, clinical conditions"; that her life did not
appear to be threatened by the continuation of her
pregnancy; and that she could not afford to travel to
another jurisdiction in order to secure there a legal
abortion under safe conditions. By an amendment to
her complaint, Roe purported to sue "on behalf of herself
and all other women" similarly situated. She claimed
a deprival of rights protected by the First, Fourth, Fifth,
Eighth, Ninth, and Fourteenth Amendments.

tempted by medical advice for the purpose of saving the life of the
mother."

The foregoing Articles, together with Art. 1195, comprise Chapter
9 of Title 15 of the Penal Code. Article 1195, not attacked here,
reads:

"Art. 195. Destroying unborn child

"Whoever shall during parturition of the mother destroy the
vitality or life in a child in a state of being born and before actual
birth, which child would otherwise have been born alive, shall be
confined in the penitentiary for life or for not less than five years."

[2] The name is a pseudonym.

ROE *v.* WADE

James Hubert Hallford, a physician licensed under Texas law, sought, and was granted, leave to intervene in the Roe suit. In his complaint in intervention the doctor specified types of conditions he saw in pregnant women who came to him as patients.

John and Mary Doe,[3] a married couple, filed a companion complaint to that of Roe. This also names the District Attorney as defendant, claimed like constitutional deprivations, and sought declaratory and injunctive relief. The Does alleged that they were a childless couple; that Mrs. Doe was suffering from a "neural-chemical" disorder; that her physician had "advised her to avoid pregnancy until such time as her condition was materially improved, although a pregnancy at the present time would not present a serious risk" to her life; that pursuant to medical advice she had discontinued use of birth control pills; and that if she should become pregnant, she would want to terminate the pregnancy by an abortion performed by a competent, licensed physician under safe, clinical conditions. By an amendment to their complaint, the Does purported to sue "on behalf of themselves and all couples similarly situated."

The two actions were consolidated and heard together by a duly convened three-judge district court. The suits thus presented the situations of the pregnant single woman, the childless and nonpregnant married couple, and the licensed practicing physician, all joining in the attack upon the Texas abortion laws. Upon the filing of affidavits, motions were made to dismiss and for summary judgment. The court found that Roe and Dr. Hallford, and members of their respective classes, had standing, but that the Does had failed to allege facts sufficient to state a present controversy and therefore

---

[3] These names also are pseudonyms.

ROE *v.* WADE

did not have standing. It concluded that, on the declaratory judgment request, abstention was not warranted; that the "fundamental right of single women
and married persons to choose whether to have children is protected by the Ninth Amendment, through
the Fourteenth Amendment"; that the Texas abortion
laws were void on their face because they were both overbroad and vague; and that abstention was warranted
with respect to the request for an injunction. The court
then dismissed the Doe complaint, declared the abortion
laws void, and dismissed the application for an injunction. 314 F. Supp. 1217 (ND Tex. 1970).

The plaintiffs Roe and Doe and the intervenor, pursuant to 28 U. S. C. § 1253, appealed to this Court from
that part of the District Court's judgment denying injunctive relief. The defendant District Attorney filed
a notice of appeal, pursuant to the same statute, from
the District Court's grant of declaratory relief to Roe
and Dr. Hallford. Both sides also have taken protective appeals to the United States Court of Appeals for
the Fifth Circuit; that court ordered those appeals held
in abeyance pending decision here.

We postponed the decision on jurisdiction to the hearing on the merits. 402 U. S. 941 (1971).

II

It might have been preferable if the defendant, pursuant to our Rule 20, had presented to us a petition
for certiorari before judgment in the Court of Appeals
with respect to the granting, adverse to him, of declaratory relief. Furthermore, we are aware that, under
Mitchell v. *Donovan,* 398 U. S. 427 (1970), and *Gunn* v.
University Committee, 399 U. S. 383 (1970), § 1253
does not authorize an appeal to this Court from the
grant or the denial of declaratory relief alone. We conclude, nevertheless, that those decisions do not prevent

ROE *v.* WADE

our review of both the injunctive and the declaratory
aspects of a case of this kind when it is properly here,
as this one is, on appeal under § 1253 from specific denial
of injunctive relief, and the arguments as to both aspects
are necessarily identical. See *Carter* v. *Jury Commission*, 396 U. S. 320 (1970), and *Florida Lime and Avocado Growers, Inc.* v. *Jacobsen,* 362 U. S. 73, 80–81
(1960). It would be destructive of time and energy for
all concerned were we to rule otherwise.

III

We are next confronted with issues of justiciability,
standing and abstention. Do Roe and the Does have
that "personal stake in the outcome of the controversy,"
Baker v. *Carr,* 369 U. S. 186, 204 (1962), that insures
that "the dispute sought to be adjudicated will be presented in an adversary context and in a form historically
viewed as capable of judicial resolution," *Flast* v. *Cohen,*
392 U. S. 83, 101 (1968), and *Sierra Club* v. *Morton,* ——
U. S. —— (1972)? And what effect does the pendency
of criminal charges against Dr. Hallford in state court,
for violating the same Texas abortion laws, have upon
the propriety of the federal court's granting relief to
him as a plaintiff-intervenor?

A. Jane Roe. Despite the use of the pseudonym, it
is not suggested that Roe is a fictitious person. For
purposes of her case, we accept as true her existence,
her pregnant state as of the time of the inception of
her suit in March 1970 and as late as May 21 of that
year when she filed an alias affidavit with the District
Court, and her inability to secure a legal abortion in
Texas.

Viewing Roe's case as of the time of its filing and
as late as May 21, there can be little dispute that it
then presented a case or controversy and that, wholly
apart from the class aspects, she, as a pregnant single

ROE *v.* WADE

woman thwarted by the State's abortion laws, had standing to challenge them. Indeed, we do not read the
appellee's brief as really asserting anything to the contrary. The "logical nexus between the status asserted
and the claim sought to be adjudicated," *Flast v. Cohen,*
392 U. S., at 102, and the necessary degree of conten-
tiousness, *Golden v. Zwickler,* 394 U. S. 103 (1969), are
both present.

The appellee notes, however, that the record does not
disclose that Roe was pregnant at the time of the District Court hearing on May 22, 1970,[4] or on June 17
when the court's opinion and judgment were filed. He
therefore suggests that Roe's case is now moot because
she and all others like her are no longer subject to any
1970 pregnancy.

The usual rule in federal cases is that the existence
of an actual controversy is necessary at all stages of
appellate or certiorari review and not only at the date
the action is initiated. *United States v. Munsingwear,
Inc.,* 340 U. S. 36, 39–41 (1950); *Golden v. Zwickler,*
394 U. S., at 108; *SEC v. Medical Committee for Human
Rights,* 404 U. S. 403, 405 (1972). But if, as here,
pregnancy is a significant fact in litigation, the 266-day
human gestation period is so short that the pregnancy
will have terminated before the usual appellate process
is complete. If that termination makes a case moot,
pregnancy litigation seldom, if ever, will survive beyond
the trial stage, if then, and appellate review will be
effectively denied. Our law is not that rigid. Pregnancy often comes more than once to the same woman

---

[4] The appellee's brief, p. 13, twice states that the hearing before
the District Court was held on July 22, 1970. The docket entries,
Appendix 2, and the transcript, Appendix 76, disclose this to be an
error. The July date apparently is the time of the reporter's transcription. Appendix 77.

ROE *v.* WADE

and in the general population, if man is to survive, it is always with us.

Pregnancy provides almost a classic justification for a conclusion of nonmootness. Otherwise, it is "capable of repetition, yet evading review." See *Southern Pacific Terminal Co. v. Interstate Commerce Commission,* 219 U. S. 498, 515 (1911); *Moore v. Ogilvie,* 394 U. S. 814, 816 (1969); *Carroll v. President and Commissioners,* 393 U. S. 175, 178–179 (1968); *Sibron v. New York,* 392 U. S. 40, 50–53 (1968); *United States v. W. T. Grant Co.,* 345 U. S. 629, 632–633 (1953).

We therefore agree with the District Court that Jane Roe had standing to undertake this litigation and that the termination of her 1970 pregnancy did not render the case moot.

B. Dr. Hallford. The doctor's position is different from that of Roe and from that of the Does. He came into Roe's litigation as a plaintiff-intervenor alleging in his complaint that he:

> "in the past has been arrested for violating the Texas Abortion Laws and at the present time stands charged by indictment with violating said laws in the Criminal District Court of Dallas County, Texas to-wit: (1) The State of Texas vs. James H. Hallford, No. C–69–5307–IH, and (2) The State of Texas vs. James H. Hallford, No. C–69–2524–H. In both cases the defendant is charged with abortion . . . ."

In his immediately preceding application for leave to intervene the doctor made like representations as to the abortion charges pending in the state court. These representations were also repeated in the affidavit he executed and filed in support of his motion for summary judgment.

ROE *v.* WADE

Dr. Hallford is therefore in the situation of seeking, in a federal court, declaratory and injunctive relief with respect to the same state statutes under which he is charged in criminal prosecutions simultaneously pending in state court. Although he stated that he has been arrested in the past for violating the State's abortion laws, he makes no allegation of any extraordinary circumstance, where the danger of irreparable loss is great and immediate in posing a threat to any federally protected right, that cannot be eliminated by his defense against the state prosecutions. Neither is there any allegation of harassment or bad faith prosecution. He seeks now, for purposes of standing, to draw a distinction between pending prosecutions and possible future ones. We see no merit in that distinction. Under the circumstances, therefore, our decision last Term in *Samuels* v. *Mackell,* 401 U. S. 66 (1971), compels the conclusion that the District Court erred when it granted declaratory relief to Dr. Hallford and failed to refrain from doing so. The court, of course, was correct in refusing to grant injunctive relief to the doctor; the reasons supportive of that action, however, are those expressed in *Samuels* v. *Mackell, supra,* and in *Younger* v. *Harris,* 401 U. S. 37 (1971); *Boyle* v. *Landry,* 401 U. S. 77 (1971); *Perez* v. *Ledesma,* 401 U. S. 82 (1971); and *Byrne* v. *Karalexis,* 401 U. S. 216 (1971). See also *Dombrowski* v. *Pfister,* 380 U. S. 479 (1965). We note, in passing, that *Younger* and its companion cases were decided after the three-judge District Court's decision here.

Dr. Hallford's complaint in intervention, therefore, is to be dismissed.[5] He is remitted to his defenses in

_____

[5] We need not consider what different result, if any, would follow if Dr. Hallford's intervention were on behalf of a class. His complaint in intervention does not purport to assert a class suit and makes no reference to any class apart from an allegation that he "and others similarly situated" must necessarily guess at the mean-

ROE *v.* WADE

the state criminal proceedings against him. We therefore reverse the judgment of the District Court to the extent that it granted Dr. Hallford relief and failed to dismiss his complaint in intervention.

C. The Does. In view of our ruling as to Roe's standing in her case, the issue of the Does' standing in their case has little significance. The claims they assert are essentially the same as those of Roe, and the statutes they attack are the same. Nevertheless, we briefly refer to the Does' posture.

Their pleadings present them as a childless married couple, the female not being pregnant, who have no desire to have children at this time because of their having received medical advice that Mrs. Doe should avoid pregnancy, and for "other highly personal reasons." But they "fear . . . they may face the prospect of becoming parents." And if pregnancy ensues, they "would want to terminate" it by an abortion. They then assert the inability to obtain an abortion legally in Texas and, consequently, their facing the alternatives of an illegal abortion there or of going outside Texas to some place where the procedure could be obtained legally and competently.

We thus have a married couple as plaintiffs who have, as their asserted immediate and present injury, only an alleged "detrimental effect upon [their] marital happiness' because they are forced to "the choice of refraining from normal sexual relations or of endangering

---

ing of Art. 1196. His application for leave to intervene goes a little further for it asserts that plaintiff Roe does not adequately protect the interest of the doctor "and the class of people who are physicians . . . and the class of people who are . . . patients . . . ." The leave application, however, is not the complaint. Despite the District Court's statement to the contrary. 314 F. Supp., at 1225, we fail to perceive the bare essentials of a class suit in the Hallford complaint.

ROE *v.* WADE

Mary Doe's health through a possible pregnancy." But they are a couple who, in the future, might develop a condition on Mrs. Doe's part brought about by future intercourse and the future failure of those contraceptive measures they feel they might safely employ, and who thereupon, at that time in the future, might want an abortion that might then be unavailable to them legally under the Texas statute.

This very phrasing of the Doe's position reveals the speculative basis of their alleged injury. It is well settled in Texas that Mrs. Doe may not be a principal or an accomplice under Art. 1191 with respect to any abortion upon her and thus is not herself subject to prosecution under the Texas abortion laws. *Watson* v. *State,* 9 Tex. App. 237, 244–245 (1880); *Moore* v. *State,* 37 Tex. Cr. Rep. 552, 561, 40 S. W. 287, 290 (1897); *Shaw* v. *State,* 73 Tex. Cr. Rep. 337, 339, 165 S. W. 930, 931 (1914); *Fondren* v. *State,* 74 Tex. Cr. Rep. 552, 557, 169 S. W. 411, 414 (1914); *Gray* v. *State,* 77 Tex. Cr. Rep. 221, 229, 178 S. W. 337, 341 (1915)." And their alleged injury rests on possible future contraceptive failure, possible future pregnancy, possible future unpreparedness for parenthood, and possible future impairment of health. Any one or more of these several possibilities may not take place and all may not combine. These possibilities, in the Does' estimation, might have some real or imagined impact upon their marital

---

⁶ There is no immunity in Texas for the father who is not married to the mother. *Hammett* v. *State,* 84 Tex. Cr. Rep. 635, 209 S. E. 661 (1919). But we have found no case that determines the issue as to the husband of the aborted mother. Since the appellants do not claim or demonstrate that the statute has been used against husbands, and since prosecution is dependent upon the further contingency that Mrs. Doe's husband aid in obtaining an abortion, if one becomes necessary or desirable, we conclude that Doe's status in this case is not materially different from his wife's.

ROE *v.* WADE

happiness. But we are not prepared to say that the bare allegation of so indirect an injury is sufficient for their case to present an actual case or controversy. We conclude, as a consequence, that they have no standing to pursue the lawsuit they have initiated. *Golden* v. *Zwickler, supra*, 394 U. S., at 109–110 (1969); *Younger* v. *Harris*, 401 U. S., at 41–42. Their purported case falls far short factually of those resolved otherwise in the cases. *Investment Company Institute* v. *Camp*, 401 U. S. 617 (1971), *Data Processing Service* v. *Camp*, 397 U. S. 150 (1970), and *Epperson* v. *Arkansas*, 393 U. S. 97 (1968), that the Does urge upon us.

The Does, therefore, are not appropriate plaintiffs in this litigation. Their complaint was properly dismissed by the District Court and we affirm that dismissal.

IV

We turn to the merits. The Texas abortion laws are not new. They appeared in essentially their present form as Arts. 1071–1076 of Texas Revised Criminal Statutes, 1911. And they read substantially the same as Arts. 536–541 of Revised Statutes of Texas, 1879, and as Arts. 2192–2197 of Paschal's Laws of Texas, 1866. The final article in each of these compilations made reference, as does the present Art. 1196, to "medical advice for the purpose of saving the life of the mother."

A. Long ago a suggestion apparently was made that the Texas statutes were unconstitutionally vague because of definitional deficiencies. The Texas Court of Criminal Appeals had little difficulty with that suggestion for it disposed of it peremptorily:

> "It is also insisted in the motion in arrest of judgment that the statute is unconstitutional and void in that it does not sufficiently define or describe the offense of abortion. We do not concur [with

ROE *v.* WADE

counsel] in respect to this question." *Jackson* v.
State, 55 Tex. Cr. Rep. 79, 89; 115 S. W. 262, 268
(1908).

We are advised, however, that the same court, on
November 2, 1971, in *Thompson* v. *State*, No. 44,071,
an opinion apparently not yet published, held, against
constitutional challenge, that the Texas abortion laws
are not vague or overbroad. The copy of the opinion
with which we have been furnished indicates that the
court held "that the State of Texas has a compelling
interest to protect fetal life"; that Art. 1191 "is designed
to protect fetal life," citing *Mayberry* v. *State*, 271 S. W.
2d 635 (Tex. Crim. App. 1954); that the Texas homicide
statutes, particularly 2A Texas Penal Code Art. 1205,
are intended to protect a person "in existence by actual
birth" and thereby implicitly recognize other human
life that is not "in existence by actual birth"; that the
definition of human life is for the legislature and not
the courts; that Art. 1196 "is more definite than the
District of Columbia statute upheld in *Vuitch*"; and
that the Texas statute "is not vague and indefinite or
overbroad." A physician's abortion conviction was
therefore affirmed.[7] The *Thompson* case thus appears
to be a flat and recent holding by the Texas court that
the State's abortion laws are not unconstitutional for
vagueness.

Elsewhere, decisions on constitutional challenges, on
various grounds, to other state abortion statutes do not
appear to be fully consistent. See *Babbitz* v. *McCann*,
310 F. Supp. 293, 297–298 (ED Wis. 1970), appeal
dismissed, 400 U. S. 1 (1970); *Rosen* v. *Louisiana State*

---

[7] In a footnote the Texas court observed that any issue as to the
burden of proof under the exemption of Art. 1196 "is not before us."
See *Veevers* v. *State*, 354 S. W. 2d 161, 166 (Tex. Cr. App. 1962).
Cf. *United States* v. *Vuitch*, 402 U. S. 62, 69–71 (1971).

ROE *v.* WADE

Board of Medical Examiners, 318 F. Supp. 1217 (ED
La. 1970), appeal pending; *Steinberg* v. *Brown,* 321
F. Supp. 741 (ND Ohio 1970); *Doe* v. *Scott,* 321
F. Supp. 1385 (ND Ill. 1971), appeal pending; *Corkey*
v. *Edwards,* 322 F. Supp. 1248 (WDNC 1971), appeal
pending; *Doe* v. *Rampton,* —— F. Supp. —— (Utah
1971), appeal pending; *People* v. *Belous,* 71 Cal. 2d 954,
458 P. 2d 194 (1969), cert. denied, 397 U. S. 915 (1970).

B. Last Term, in *United States* v. *Vuitch,* 402 U. S.
62 (1971), decided after the District Court's ruling in
the present cases was handed down, we had under consideration a District of Columbia statute that made
the procuring of an abortion a crime unless it "were
done as necessary for the preservation of the mother's
life or health and under the direction of a competent
licensed practitioner of medicine." The District Court
had dismissed a physician's indictment under that statute
on the ground that it was unconstitutionally vague.
This Court reversed that dismissal and remanded the
case. MR. JUSTICE DOUGLAS was of the view that the
statute failed to meet the requirements of procedural
due process, 402 U. S., at 74, and dissented in part. MR.
JUSTICE STEWART, also dissenting in part, 402 U. S., at 96,
was of the opinion that a "competent licensed practitioner of medicine" was wholly immune from being
charged with the commission of a criminal offense under
the District of Columbia statute.

The vagueness claim in *Vuitch* focused only on the
word "health" in the District statute and on its application to mental as well as to physical well-being. The
Texas statute, Art. 1196, with which we are here concerned, exempts from criminal abortion, described in
Art. 1191, only an abortion procured "by medical advice
for the purpose of saving the life of the mother." No
reference whatsoever is made to health. Saving the
mother's life is the sole standard. *Vuitch's* analysis was

ROE *v.* WADE

that the word "health" in the statute was employed
in accord with general usage and modern understanding
and included psychological as well as physical well-
being, and thus presented no problem of vagueness, because this "is a judgment that physicians are obviously
called upon to make routinely," 402 U. S., at 72, and
is of little assistance here. Certainly it provides no
answer to the constitutional challenge to the Texas
statute.

C. We are not here concerned with broad areas of
medical judgment as to health generally. We are concerned, in contrast, with a procedure that is exempt from
criminality only if it is "for the purpose of saving the
life of the mother." So viewed, we encounter difficulties
of great consequence under the vagueness challenge.

The exempting Art. 1196, of course, has application
only to one rendering "medical advice." Although even
this is by no means certain or clear, we assume, for purposes of simplifying the issue, that this protective provision is available only to the licensed physician, and is
not available to the unlicensed physician or particularly
to the nonphysician who would procure the abortion
under the guise of rendering "medical advice," whatever
that may mean as applied to him. But what does the
statute say even for the licensed physician? Does it
mean that he may procure an abortion only when, without it, the patient will surely die? Or only when the
odds are greater than even that she will die? Or when
there is a mere possibility that she will not survive? So
far as we can determine, the Texas courts have not limited
the statute and have only repeated its phrasing. See
Ex parte Vick, 292 S. W. 889, 890 (Tex. Crim. App.
1927). Further, who is to exercise that judgment—the
physician alone in the light of his training and experience, or a group or committee of his peers, or a medical
association, or a hospital review committee? And when
is the saving of a life to be measured in the time scale?

ROE *v.* WADE

Must death be imminent?   Or is it enough if life is prolonged for a year, a month, a few days, overnight? Is a mother's life "saved" if a post-rape or post-incest or "fourteenth-child" abortion preserves, or tends to preserve, her mental health?   If the procedure is generally favorable to the mother's health, is her life thereby "saved" within the meaning of the statute?   One's well-being and the very continuance of life depends sometimes on slender differences in medical treatment, in body chemistry, in exposure to infection, and in medical knowledge.

The applicable standard is whether the statute is "so vague that men of common intelligence must necessarily guess at its meaning and differ as to its application," *Connally* v. *General Construction Co.,* 269 U. S. 385, 391 (1926); *Cameron* v. *Johnson,* 390 U. S. 611, 616 (1968), or, phrased another way:

> "It is established that a law fails to meet the requirements of the Due Process Clause if it is so vague and standardless that it leaves the public uncertain as to the conduct it prohibits or leaves judges and jurors free to decide, without any legally fixed standards, what is prohibited and what is not in each particular case." *Giaccio* v. *Pennsylvania,* 382 U. S. 399, 402–403 (1966).

We conclude that Art. 1196, with its sole criterion for exemption as "saving the life of the mother," is insufficiently informative to the physician to whom it purports to afford a measure of professional protection but who must measure its indefinite meaning at the risk of his liberty, and that the statute cannot withstand constitutional challenge on vagueness grounds.

V

This conclusion that Art. 1196 is unconstitutionally vague means, of course, that the Texas abortion laws,

ROE *v.* WADE

as a unit, must fall. The medical exception of Art. 1196
does not go out alone for then the State would be left
with a statute proscribing all abortion procedures no
matter how medically urgent the cause. Then, too, the
physician's professional obligation and duty would be
improperly thwarted.

Our holding today does not imply that a State has no
legitimate interest in the subject of abortions or that
abortion procedures may not be subjected to control by
the State. The nub of the matter is the appropriate-
ness of the control when criminal sanctions are imposed.
We do not accept the argument of the appellants and
of some of the *amici* that a pregnant woman has an unlimited right to do with her body as she pleases. The
long acceptance of statutes regulating the possession of
certain drugs and other harmful substances, and making
criminal indecent exposure in public, or an attempt at
suicide, clearly indicate the contrary.

There is no need in Roe's case to pass upon her contention that under the Ninth Amendment a pregnant
woman has an absolute right to an abortion, or even to
consider the opposing rights of the embryo or fetus
during the respective prenatal trimesters. We are literally showered with briefs—with physicians and para-
medical and other knowledgeable people on both sides—
but this case, as it comes to us, does not require the
resolution of those issues.

VI

Although the District Court granted plaintiff Roe and
intervenor Hallford declaratory relief, it stopped short
of issuing an injunction against enforcement of the Texas
abortion laws. The Court has recognized that different
considerations enter into a federal court's determination
of declaratory relief, on the one hand, and injunctive
relief, on the other. *Zwickler* v. *Koota,* 389 U. S. 241,

ROE *v.* WADE

252–255 (1967); *Dombrowski* v. *Pfister,* 380 U. S. 479
(1965). We are not dealing here with a statute that,
on its face, appears to abridge free expression, an area
of particular concern under *Dombrowski* and refined in
Younger v. *Harris,* 401 U. S., at 50.

We find it unnecessary to decide whether the District
Court erred in withholding injunctive relief for we assume that the Texas prosecutorial authorities will give
full credence to the decision of this Court relative to the
constitutional invalidity of the Texas abortion laws.

The judgment of the District Court as to intervenor
Hallford is reversed and Dr. Hallford's complaint in intervention is dismissed. In all other respects, the judgment of the District Court is affirmed. Costs are allowed
to the appellee.

MR. JUSTICE POWELL and MR. JUSTICE REHNQUIST
took no part in the consideration or decision of this case.

1st DRAFT   From: Blackmun

SUPREME COURT OF THE UNITED STATES

Circulated:

No. 70–40

Recirculated:

Mary Doe et al., Appellants,	On Appeal from the
v.	United States District
Arthur K. Bolton, as Attorney General of the State of Georgia, et al.	Court for the Northern District of Georgia.

[May —, 1972]

Memorandum of MR. JUSTICE BLACKMUN.

In this appeal the Georgia criminal abortion statutes are under constitutional attack. The statutes, §§ 26–1201 to 26–1203 of the State's Criminal Code, formulated by Georgia Laws 1968, 1249, 1277, are set forth in the Appendix.[1] They have not been tested constitutionally in the Georgia courts.

Section 26–1201 defines criminal abortion. Section 26–1202, however, removes from that definition abortions "performed by a physician duly licensed" in Georgia when, "based upon his best clinical judgment . . . an abortion is necessary because"

"(1) A continuation of the pregnancy would endanger the life of the pregnant woman or would seriously and permanently injure her health," or

"(2) The fetus would very likely be born with a grave, permanent, and irremediable mental or physical defect," or

"(3) The pregnancy resulted from forcible or statutory rape."

---

[1] The italicized portions of the statutes in the Appendix are those held unconstitutional by the District Court.

DOE *v.* BOLTON

Section 26–1202 then specifies a number of prerequisites for the abortion if it is to qualify under the exception. These are (1) and (2) residence of the woman in Georgia, (3) reduction to writing of the performing physician's medical judgment and written concurrence in that judgment by at least two other Georgia licensed physicians, (4) performance of the abortion in a licensed and "accredited" hospital, (5) approval in advance by a hospital abortion committee, (6) certification in a rape situation, and (7), (8), and (9) maintenance and confidentiality of records. There is a provision for judicial determination of the legality of a proposed abortion on petition of the circuit law officer or of a close relative, as therein defined, of the woman, and for expeditious hearing of that petition. There is also a provision giving a hospital the right not to admit an abortion patient, and giving any physician and any hospital employee or staff member the right not to participate in the procedure because of moral or religious grounds.

Section 26–1203 provides that a person convicted of criminal abortion shall be punished by imprisonment for not less than one nor more than 10 years.

As appellants acknowledge,[2] the 1968 Georgia statute is patterned after the American Law Institute's Model Penal Code § 230.3 (Proposed Official Draft, 1962). Other States have legislation based upon the Model Penal Code. See Ark. Stats. §§ 41–303 to 41–310 (Supp. 1971); Cal. Health & Safety Code §§ 25950–55.5 (West Supp. 1972); Colo. Rev. Stats. 40–2–50 to 40–2–53 (Perm. Cum. Supp. 1967); Del. Code §§ 1790–1793 (Supp. 1970); Kan. Stat. § 21–3407 (Supp. 1971); Md. Code, Art. 43, §§ 137–139 (Repl. 1971); N. Mex. Stat. §§ 40A–5–1 to 40A–5–3 (Supp. 1971); N. C. Gen. Stat.

---

[2] Brief, at 25, n. 5; Tr. of Oral Arg. 9.

DOE *v.* BOLTON

§ 14–45.1 (Supp. 1971); Ore. Rev. Stat. §§ 435.405 to
435.495; S. C. Code §§ 16–87 to 16–89 (Supp. 1971);
Va. Code §§ 18.1–62 to 18.1–62.3 (Supp. 1971). Mr.
Justice Clark has described some of these States as having "led the way." Religion, Morality, and Abortion:
A Constitutional Appraisal, 2 Loyola U. (L. A.) L. Rev.
1, 11 (1969).

I

On April 16, 1970, Mary Doe,[3] 23 other individuals
(nine described as Georgia-licensed physicians, seven as
nurses registered in Georgia, five as Georgia clergymen,
and two as Georgia social workers), and two nonprofit
Georgia corporations, instituted this action in the Northern District of Georgia against the State's Attorney General, the District Attorney of Fulton County, and the
Chief of Police of the city of Atlanta. The plaintiffs
sought a declaratory judgment that the Georgia abortion
statutes were unconstitutional in their entirety. They
also sought injunctive relief restraining the defendants
and their successors from enforcing the challenged
statutes.

Mary Doe alleged:

(1) She was a 22-year-old Georgia citizen, married,
and nine weeks pregnant. She had three living children.
The two older ones had been placed in a foster home
because of Doe's poverty and inability to care for them.
The youngest, born July 19, 1969, was with adoptive
parents. Doe's husband had recently abandoned her
and she was forced to live with her indigent parents
and their eight children. She and her husband, however,
had become reconciled. He was a construction worker
and only sporadically employed. She had been a mental
patient at the State Hospital. She had been advised
that an abortion could be performed on her with less
danger to her health than if she gave birth to the child

---

[3] The name is a pseudonym. Complaint, Appendix 7.

DOE *v.* BOLTON

she was carrying. She would be unable to support or care for the new child.

(2) On March 25, 1970, Doe made application to the Abortion Committee of Grady Memorial Hospital, Atlanta, to be considered for a therapeutic abortion under § 26–1202 of the Georgia Code. Her application was denied 16 days later, on April 10, when she was eight weeks pregnant, on the ground that her situation was not one within the reach of § 26–1202 (a).[4]

(3) Because of this denial of her application, Doe was faced with the alternatives of either relinquishing "her right to decide when and how many children she will bear" or seeking an abortion illegal under the Georgia statutes. This was a violation of rights guaranteed her by the First, Fourth, Fifth, Ninth, and Fourteenth Amendments. She sued "on her own behalf and on behalf of all others similarly situated."

The other plaintiffs claimed the Georgia statutes "chilled and deterred" them from practicing their respective professions and, thus, deprived them of their constitutional rights. Those plaintiffs also purported to sue on their own behalf and on behalf of others similarly situated.

A three-judge District Court was convened. An offer of proof as to Doe's identity was made but the court felt it unnecessary to receive that proof. The case was tried on the pleadings and interrogatories.

By its *per curiam* opinion the District Court held that all the plaintiffs had standing, but that only Doe presented a justiciable controversy. On the merits, the court held unconstitutional those portions of § 26–

---

[4] Mary Doe, by her answers to interrogatories, stated that her application for an abortion was approved at Georgia Baptist Hospital on May 5, 1970, but that she was not approved as a charity patient there and had no money to pay for an abortion. Appendix 64.

DOE *v.* BOLTON

1202 (a) and (b)(3) that would limit legal abortions
to the three situations specified; § 26–1202 (b)(6) relating to certification in a rape situation; and
§ 26–1202 (c) authorizing the court proceeding upon
the petition of the circuit law officer or a designated
relative of the woman. Declaratory relief, accordingly,
was granted. The court, however, upheld the other
parts of the statute and denied altogether the request
for an injunction. 319 F. Supp. 1048 (ND Ga. 1970).

Claiming that they are entitled to broader relief, the
plaintiffs have taken a direct appeal pursuant to 28
U. S. C. § 1253. The decision on jurisdiction was postponed to the hearing on the merits. 402 U. S. 941
(1971).

The defendants filed a direct cross appeal but this
was dismissed for want of jurisdiction. 402 U. S. 936
(1971). We are advised by the appellees, Brief, at 42,
that an alternative appeal on their part is pending in
the United States Court of Appeals for the Fifth Circuit.
The extent, therefore, to which the decision below is adverse to the appellees, that is, the extent to which
portions of the Georgia statute were held to be unconstitutional, technically is not now before us.[5] *Swarb*
v. *Lennox,* 405 U. S. 191, 201 (1972).

II

Our decision today in *Roe* v. *Wade, ante,* at ——,
establishes (1) that the case is properly here on direct
appeal under 28 U. S. C. § 1253, for the three-judge District Court specifically denied the injunctive relief the
plaintiff-appellants requested; (2) that, despite her
pseudonym, we may accept as true Mary Doe's existence
and her pregnant state on April 16, 1970; (3) that the

---

[5] What we decide today, however, may well have implications for
the issues raised by the appellees' appeal pending in the Fifth
Circuit.

DOE *v.* BOLTON

constitutional issue is substantial; (4) that the termination of Doe's and all other Georgia pregnancies existing in 1970 has not rendered the case moot; and (5) that Doe and her class, that is, pregnant Georgia women, do have standing to maintain the action and do present a justiciable controversy.

The standing-justiciable controversy status of the other plaintiff-appellants—physicians, nurses, clergymen, social workers, and corporations—is less certain but, inasmuch as Doe and her class are recognized, is perhaps a matter of no great significance. We conclude, however, that the physician-appellants, who are Georgia-licensed doctors consulted by women about pregnancies, also present a justiciable controversy despite the fact that the record does not disclose that any one of them has been prosecuted, or threatened, for violation of the State's abortion statutes. The physician is the person against whom these criminal statutes directly operate in the event he procures an abortion that does not qualify under the statutes' exception and with respect to which all the statutorily prescribed conditions are not met.

In holding that the physicians, while theoretically having standing, did not present a justiciable controversy, the District Court seems to have relied primarily on *Poe* v. *Ullman,* 367 U. S. 497 (1961). There a sharply divided court dismissed an appeal from a state court on the ground that it presented no real controversy justifying the adjudication of a constitutional issue. But the challenged Connecticut statute, deemed to prohibit the giving of medical advice on the use of contraceptives, had been enacted in 1879 and, with only one apparent exception, no one had ever been prosecuted under it. Georgia's statute, in contrast, is recent and not moribund. Furthermore, it is the successor to other Georgia abortion statutes under which,

DOE *v.* BOLTON

we are told,[6] physicians have been prosecuted. The
present case, in our view, is closer to *Epperson v. Arkansas*, 393 U. S. 97 (1968), where the Court recognized
the right of a schoolteacher, though not charged criminally, to challenge her State's anti-evolution statute.
See also *Griswold v. Connecticut*, 381 U. S. 479, 481
(1965).

The parallel claims of the nurse, clergy, social worker,
and corporate appellants are another step removed. As
to them, the Georgia statutes operate less directly. Not
being licensed physicians, the nurses and the others are
in no position to render medical advice. They would
be reached by the abortion statutes only in their capacity as accessories or counsellor-conspirators. We
conclude that we need not pass upon the status of
these additional appellants in this suit for the issues
are sufficiently and adequately presented by Mary Doe
and by the physician-appellants, and nothing is gained
or lost by the presence or absence of the nurses, the
clergymen, the social workers, and the corporations. See
Roe v. Wade, ante, at ——.

III

The appellants attack the Georgia abortion statutes
on several grounds: (A) invalid restriction of an absolute fundamental right to personal and marital privacy; (B) vagueness; (C) deprivation of procedural
and substantive due process; (D) improper limitation
to Georgia residents; and (E) denial of equal protection.
We consider these claims in turn.

A. The Court, in varying contexts, has recognized a
right of personal privacy and has rooted it in the Fourteenth Amendment, or in the Bill of Rights, or in
the latter's penumbras. See *Eisenstadt v. Baird*, ——
U. S. ——. —— (1972); *Griswold v. Connecticut*, 381

---

[6] Tr. of Oral Arg. 21–22.

DOE *v.* BOLTON

U. S., at 484; *Stanley* v. *Georgia,* 394 U. S. 557, 564
(1969); *Loving* v. *Virginia,* 388 U. S. 1, 12 (1967);
Skinner v. *Oklahoma,* 316 U. S. 535, 541–542 (1942);
Pierce v. *Society of Sisters,* 268 U. S. 510 (1925); *Meyer*
v. *Nebraska,* 262 U. S. 390 (1923).

The appellants assert that the scope of this right of
personal privacy includes, for a woman, the right to
decide unilaterally to terminate an existing but *unwanted*
pregnancy without any state interference or control
whatsoever. They argue that if, by *Griswold,* one
is protected in deciding to limit the size of her family
by the use of contraceptives, she deserves to have that
right equally protected by having a choice to terminate
an unwanted pregnancy due to contraceptive failure.
See Mr. Justice Clark's article, cited above, Religion,
Morality and Abortion: A Constitutional Approach, 2
Loyola U. (L. A.) L. Rev. 1, 8–9 (1969).

They further argue that the present Georgia statutes
must be viewed historically, that is, from the fact that
prior to the 1968 Act an abortion in Georgia was not
criminal if performed to "preserve the life" of the mother.
See the 1933 Georgia Criminal Code, § 26–1102, which
was the codification of Acts 1876, No. 130, § 2, p. 113.
And when so viewed, they contend, Georgia heretofore
has given little, and certainly not first, consideration
to the unborn child.

Finally, it is argued that the statute does not adequately protect the woman's right. This is so, it is
said, because it would be physically and emotionally
damaging to Doe to bring a child into her poor, "father-
less" [7] family, and because advances in medicine and in
medical techniques have made it safer for a woman to
have a medically induced abortion than to bear a child.
Thus a statute "which requires a woman to carry an
unwanted pregnancy to term infringes not only on a

---

[7] Appellants' Brief 25.

DOE *v.* BOLTON

fundamental right of privacy but on the right to life itself."

We agree that a woman's interest in making the fundamental personal decision whether or not to bear an unwanted child is within the scope of personal rights protected by the Ninth and Fourteenth Amendments, as articulated in the decisions cited above. Appellants' contention, however, that the woman's right to make the decision is absolute—that Georgia has either no valid interest in regulating it, or no interest strong enough to support any limitation upon the woman's sole determination—is unpersuasive.

The appellants themselves recognize that a century ago medical knowledge was not so advanced as it is today, the techniques of antisepsis were not known, and any abortion procedure was dangerous for the pregnant woman. To restrict the legality of the abortion to the situation where it was deemed necessary, in medical judgment, for the preservation of the woman's life was only a natural and expected line drawing in the exercise of the legislative judgment of that time. A State is not to be reproached for a past judgmental determination of this kind made in the light of then existing medical knowledge. It is therefore illogical and unfair to argue, as the appellants do, that, because the earlier emphasis was on the preservation of the woman's life, the State's present professed interest in the protection of embryonic and fetal "life" is somehow to be downgraded. That argument condemns the State for past "wrongs" and also denies it the right to readjust its views and emphases in the light of the more advanced knowledge and techniques of today.

In any event, it is clear that Georgia's concern historically has not been for the mother alone. The cases decided under the 1876 Act have given recognition in various ways to the unborn. See *Taylor* v. *State,* 105.

DOE *v.* BOLTON

Ga. 846, 33 S. E. 190 (1899); *Sullivan v. State,* 121 Ga. 183, 48 S. E. 949 (1904); *Barrow v. State,* 121 Ga. 187, 48 S. E. 950 (1904); *Passley v. State,* 194 Ga. 327, 21 S. E. 2d 230 (1942); *Tucker v. Howard L. Carmichael & Sons,* 208 Ga. 201, 65 S. E. 2d 909 (1951); *Hornbuckle v. Plantation Pipe Line Co.,* 212 Ga. 504, 93 S. E. 2d 727 (1956); *Fallaw v. Hobbs,* 113 Ga. App. 181, 147 S. E. 2d 517 (1966).

The pregnant woman cannot be isolated in her privacy. She carries an embryo and, later, a fetus, if one is to accept the medical definitions of the developing young in the human uterus. See Dorland's Illustrated Medical Dictionary, pp. 478–479 and 547 (24th Edition, 1965). The situation, therefore, is inherently different from marital intimacy, or bedroom possession of obscene material, or marriage, or the right to procreate, or private education, with which *Eisenstadt, Griswold, Stanley, Loving, Skinner, Pierce,* and *Meyer* were respectively concerned.

The heart of the matter is that somewhere, either forthwith at conception, or at "quickening," or at birth, or at some other point in between, another being becomes involved and the privacy the woman possessed has become dual rather than sole. The woman's right of privacy must be measured accordingly. It is not for us of the judiciary, especially at this point in the development of man's knowledge, to speculate or to specify when life begins. On this question there is no consensus even among those trained in the respective disciplines of medicine, or philosophy, or theology.

In related contexts we have rejected the claim that an individual has an unlimited right to do as he pleases with his body. See, for example, *Jacobson v. Massachusetts,* 197 U. S. 11 (1905) (compulsory vaccination), and *Buck v. Bell,* 274 U. S. 200 (1927) (compulsory

DOE *v.* BOLTON

sterilization). Except to note that the State's interest
grows stronger as the woman approaches term, we need'
not delineate that interest with greater detail in order
to recognize that it is a "compelling" state interest. As
such, it may constitutionally be asserted when the State
does so with appropriate regard for fundamental individual rights. *Cantwell* v. *Connecticut,* 310 U. S. 296,
307 (1940). The woman's personal right, therefore, is
not unlimited. It must be balanced against the State's
interest.

Consequently, we cannot automatically strike down
the remaining features of the Georgia statute simply
because they restrict any right on the part of the
woman to have an abortion at will. The inquiry must
be one that examines with particularity the impact
of the statute upon the right, as it relates to the state
interest being asserted. We turn to this inquiry in
Part C, *infra.* First, however, we consider the appellants' alternative theory that the statute as a whole must
fall because it is unconstitutionally vague.

B. The vagueness argument centers in the proposition
that, with the District Court's having stricken the statutorily stated reasons, it still remains a crime for a physician to perform an abortion except when, as § 26–1202 (a)
reads, it is "based upon his best clinical judgment that
an abortion is necessary." It is said that the word
"necessary" is so vague that it does not warn the physician of what conduct is proscribed; that the statute is
wholly without objective standards and is subject to
diverse interpretations; and that doctors will choose
to err on the side of caution and will be arbitrary.

One answer to this, of course, is that this state of
affairs, if it is unfortunate, has been brought about
by the appellants' success in the District Court. Before
portions of the statute were stricken, it possessed the

DOE *v.* BOLTON

objective standards specifically stated. Now that those standards have been removed, it is the appellants who complain that the statute has become vague.

Be that as it may, the net result of the District Court's decision is that the abortion determination, so far as the physician is concerned, is made in the exercise of his professional, that is, his "best clinical judgment" in the light of all the attendant circumstances. He is not now restricted to the three situations specified. Instead, he may range farther afield wherever his medical judgment, properly and professionally exercised, so dictates and directs him.

The vagueness argument is set at rest, we feel, by the decision only last Term in *United States* v. *Vuitch*, 402 U. S. 62, 71–73 (1971), when it was raised with respect to a District of Columbia statute outlawing abortions "unless the same were done as necessary for the preservation of the mother's life or health and under the direction of a competent licensed practitioner of medicine. . . ." The Court interpreted the statute to bear upon psychological as well as physical well-being, and, having done so, concluded that the term "health" presented no problem of vagueness. "Indeed, whether a particular operation is necessary for a patient's physical or mental health is a judgment that physicians are obviously called upon to make routinely whenever surgery is considered." 402 U. S., at 72. So here, whether, in the words of the Georgia statute, "an abortion is necessary," is a judgment that a Georgia physician will be called upon to make routinely.

We agree with the District Court, 319 F. Supp., at 1058, that the medical judgment may be exercised in the light of *all* factors—emotional, economic, psychological, familial, physical—relevant to the well-being of the patient. Despite the appellants' seeming protestation to the contrary, all these factors have a bearing

DOE *v.* BOLTON

upon health. This, of course, allows the attending
physician the room he needs to make his medical judgment. And it is room that operates for the benefit,
not the disadvantage, of the pregnant woman.

C. Mary Doe's due process attack on the statute
focuses on (1) the restriction of abortions to accredited
hospitals, (2) the pregnant woman's asserted inability
to make a presentation to the hospital abortion committee, and (3) the allegedly cumbersome and time-
consuming features of the confirming process. Appellant
physicians argue that by subjecting their individual medical judgments whether a patient should have an abortion to additional consultation and committee approval
unduly restricts their right to practice their profession,
and thus deprives them of due process.

Resolution of these issues, as has been noted, requires
an inquiry into the adequacy of the State's justifications
for encroaching upon the fundamental personal privacy
right of Mary Doe recognized in Part A, *supra.*

The first aspect concerns accreditation by the Joint
Commission on the Accreditation of Hospitals. This
Commission is a nonprofit corporation without governmental sponsorship or overtones. No question is raised
about the integrity of the organization or about the
high purpose of the accreditation process.[s] That proc-

---

[s] Since its founding, JCAH has pursued the "elusive goal" of
defining the "optimal setting" for "quality of services in hospitals."
JCAH, Accreditation Manual for Hospitals, Foreward (Dec. 1970).
The Manual's Introduction states the organization's purpose to
establish standards and conduct accreditation programs that will
afford quality medical care "to give patients the optimal benefits
that medical science has to offer." This ambitious and admirable
goal is illustrated by JCAH's decision in 1966 "to raise and strengthen
the standards from their present level of minimum essential to the
level of optimum achievable. . . ." Some of these "optimum
achievable" standards required are: disclosure of hospital ownership and control; a dietetic service and written dietetic policies;

DOE *v.* BOLTON

ess, however, has to do with hospital standards generally and has no present particularized concern with abortion as a medical or surgical procedure.⁹ Indeed, in Georgia there is no restriction on surgery being performed in a hospital not yet accredited by the JCAH so long as other requirements imposed by the State, such as that the hospital and the operating surgeon be licensed, are met. See Georgia Code §§ 88–1901 and 88–1905 and § 84–907 (Supp. 1971). Furthermore, accreditation by the Commission is not granted until a hospital is in operation at least one year. Accreditation is also dependent upon the hospital's having, among other things, a radiology department, a mass casualty program, and nuclear medicine facilities. These requirements do bear upon general hospital quality and status, but they impress us as having little bearing on a hospital's qualification as a place where an abortion—or any other particular medical or surgical procedure—may be safely performed. The Model Penal Code § 230.3 does not, for example, include this requirement. And see Commissioners on Uniform State Laws, Uniform Abortion Act (Second Tentative Draft, August 1970), containing no accredited hospital limitation.¹⁰

a written disaster plan for mass emergencies; a nuclear medical services program; facilities for hematology, chemistry, microbiology, clinical microscopy, and sero-immunology; a professional library and document delivery service; a radiology program; a social services plan administered by a qualified social worker; and a special care unit.

⁹ "The Joint Commission neither advocates nor opposes any particular position with respect to elective abortions." Letter dated July 9, 1971, from John I. Brewer, M. D., Commissioner, JCAH, to the Rockefeller Foundation. Brief for *amici*, American College of Obstetricians and Gynecologists, *et al.*, p. A–3.

¹⁰ Some statutes do not have the JCAH accredited hospital requirement. Alas. Stat. § 11.15.060 (1970); Haw. Sess. Laws, 1970,

DOE *v.* BOLTON

We therefore hold that the JCAH accreditation requirement does not withstand constitutional scrutiny
in the present context. It is a requirement that simply
is not "based on differences that are reasonably related
to the purposes of the Act in which it is found." *Morey
v. Doud,* 354 U. S. 457, 465 (1957). That is not to
say, as the appellants themselves concede, Brief, at 40,
that Georgia may not or should not adopt standards
for licensing all facilities where abortions may be performed so long as those standards have a reasonable
relationship to the objective the State seeks to
accomplish.

The second aspect of the attack, relating to the hospital abortion committee and the pregnant woman's
access to it, is based primarily on *Goldberg v. Kelly,*
397 U. S. 254 (1970), concerning the termination of
welfare benefits, and *Wisconsin v. Constantineau,* 400
U. S. 433 (1971), concerning the posting of an alcoholic's
name. It is suggested that it is still a badge of infamy
"in many minds" to bear an illegitimate child, and that
the Georgia system enables the committee members'
personal views as to extramarital sex relations, and
punishment therefor, to govern their decisions.

This approach obviously is one founded on suspicion
and one that discloses a lack of confidence in the integrity of physicians. It appears also to place undue
emphasis on the abortion committee and on its seeming
isolation. The pregnant woman's principal counsel in
the abortion decision is her personal physician. It is
he who makes the initial recommendation. Presumably, and hopefully—if she has been candid with him—

Act 1; N. Y. Penal Law § 125.05.3 (McKinney 1971–1972 Supp.).
Washington's statute has the requirement but couples it with the
alternative of "a medical facility approved . . . by the state board
of health." Wash. Rev. Code § 9.02.070 (1971 Supp.).

DOE *v.* BOLTON

he knows all aspects of her case. He serves her essentially as the family physician so esteemed in memory. Following accepted medical procedure, his recommendations would be conveyed with underlying reasons to the two other physicians who, pursuant to § 26–1202 (b)(3), must separately examine and confirm. At that point the medical judgment is complete. To each and all of these physicians the woman has full access.

We see nothing in the Georgia statute that denies access to the hospital abortion committee by or on behalf of the pregnant woman. If the access point alone were involved, we would not be persuaded to strike down the committee provision on the unsupported assumption that access is not provided. It is perhaps worth noting, also, that the abortion committee has a function of its own. It is a committee of the hospital and its members are members of the hospital's medical staff. The committee's composition usually is a changing one. In this way its work burden is more readily accepted and is shared. The committee's function is protective of the hospital. It enables the hospital appropriately to be advised that its posture and activities are in accord with legal requirements. It is to be remembered that the hospital is an entity and that it, too, has legal rights and legal obligations. The committee's focus is on it, and not on the pregnant woman.

To say also that physicians will be guided in their hospital committee decisions by their predilections on extramarital sex unduly narrows the issue to pregnancy outside marriage. This case involves more than extramarital sex and its product. In addition, the suggestion is necessarily somewhat degrading to the conscientious physician, particularly the obstetrician, whose professional activity is concerned with the physical and mental welfare, the woes, the emotions and the concern of his feminine patients. He, more than anyone else, is

DOE *v.* BOLTON

knowledgeable in this area of patient care, and is aware
of human frailty, so-called "error," and needs. And
the good physician—despite the presence of rascals in
the medical profession, as in all others, we trust that
most physicians are "good"—will have a sympathy and
an understanding for the pregnant woman patient that
probably is not exceeded by any of those who participate in other areas of professional counseling.

Saying all this, however, does not settle the issue
of the constitutional propriety of the presence of the
hospital abortion committee in the Georgia statutory
system. Viewing the statutes as a whole, we see no
pertinence in the system for the advance approval by
the abortion committee. Under § 26–1202 (e) a hospital is free not to admit a patient for an abortion and
not to have an abortion committee. Furthermore, a
physician or any other employee is free to refrain, for
moral or religious reasons, from participating in the
abortion procedure. These provisions obviously are
in the statute in order to afford some protection to
the individual and to the denominational hospital in
the observance of religiously dictated precepts, and in
business decisions. From this point of view, § 26–
1202 (e) affords adequate protection to the hospital and
little additional protection is provided by the abortion
committee prescribed by § 26–1202 (b)(5).

We conclude that the interposition of the hospital
abortion committee is unnecessary and is unduly restrictive of the patient's rights and needs that, at this
point, have already been medically delineated and sub-
stantiated by her personal physician. To ask more
serves neither the hospital nor the State.

The third aspect of the attack focuses on the "time
and availability of adequate medical facilities and personnel." It is said that the system imposes substantial
and irrational roadblocks and "is patently unsuited"

DOE *v.* BOLTON

to prompt determination and "makes a mockery of Georgia's attempt to justify its statute."

Time, of course, is critical in the abortion process. Risks during the first trimester of pregnancy are admittedly lower than during later months.

The appellants purport to show by a local study [11] of Grady Memorial Hospital (serving indigent residents in Fulton and DeKalb Counties) that the "mechanics of the system itself forced . . . discontinuation of the abortive process" because the medium time for the workup was 15 days. The same study shows, however, that 27% of the candidates for abortion were already 13 or more weeks pregnant at the time of application, that is, they were at the end of or beyond the first trimester when they made their request. It is too much to say, as the appellants do, that these persons "were victims of the system over which they had no control." If higher risk was incurred because of abortions in the second rather than the first trimester, much of that risk was due to delay in application, and not to the alleged cumbersomeness of any system. We note, in passing, that appellant Doe had no delay problem herself; the decision in her case was made well within the first trimester.

It should be manifest that our rejection of the accredited hospital requirement and, more important, of the hospital abortion committee's advance approval eliminates the major grounds of the attack based on the system's delay and the lack of facilities. There remains, however, the required confirmation by two Georgia licensed physicians in the recommendation of the pregnant woman's own consultant. We conclude that this, too, must fall.

---

[11] L. Baker and M. Freeman, Abortion Surveillance at Grady Memorial Hospital, Center for Disease Control (U. S. Department of HEW, PHS), June and July 1971.

DOE *v.* BOLTON

The statute's emphasis, as has been repetitively noted, is on the attending physician's "best clinical judgment that an abortion is necessary." That should be sufficient. The reasons for the presence of the confirmation step in the statute are perhaps apparent, but they are insufficient to withstand constitutional challenge. We are cited to no other voluntary medical or surgical procedure—not even childbirth—for which Georgia requires confirmation by two other physicians. If a physician is licensed by the State, he is recognized by the State as capable of exercising acceptable clinical judgment. If he fails in this, professional censure or deprivation of his license are available remedies. Required acquiescence by co-practitioners has no rational connection with the patient's needs and unduly infringes on the physician's right to practice. The attendant physician will know when a consultation is advisable—the doubtful situation, the need for assurance when the medical decision is a delicate one, and the like. Physicians have followed this routine for decades and know its usefulness and benefit. It is still true today that "Reliance must be placed upon the assurance given by his license, issued by an authority competent to judge in that respect, that he [the physician] possesses the requisite qualifications." *Dent* v. *West Virginia,* 129 U. S. 114, 122–123 (1889). That is the measure. See *United States* v. *Vuitch,* 402 U. S., at 71.

D. The Georgia residence requirement is said to be violative of the right to travel stressed in *Shapiro* v. *Thompson,* 394 U. S. 618, 629 (1969), and other cases. We see no restriction in the statute on the travel right. One is no less free, because of the statute, to come to or to depart from the State of Georgia. And it can be said that the residence requirement is not without some relationship to the availability of post-procedure medical care for the aborted patient.

DOE *v.* BOLTON

Nevertheless, we cannot approve the constitutionality of the residence requirement. It is not based on a policy of preserving state-supported facilities for Georgia residents, for the bar applies as well to private hospitals and to privately retained physicians. There is no intimation, either, that Georgia facilities are utilized to capacity in caring for Georgia residents. Just as the Privileges and Immunities Clause, Const., Art. IV, § 2, protects persons who enter other States to ply their trade, *Ward* v. *Maryland,* 79 U. S. (12 Wall.) 418, 430 (1870); *Blake* v. *McClung,* 172 U. S. 239, 248–256 (1898), so must it protect persons who enter Georgia seeking the medical services available there. A contrary holding would mean that a State may limit to its own residents the general medical care available within its borders. This we cannot approve.

~~E. The~~ last argument on this phase of the case is (the usual one) namely, that the Georgia system is ~~violative of equal~~ protection because it discriminates against the poor. The appellants do not urge that abortion should be performed by others than licensed physicians, so we have no argument that because the wealthy can better afford physicians, the poor should have non-physicians made available to them. The appellants acknowledge that the procedures are "non-discriminatory in . . . express terms," but they suggest that they have produced invidious discriminations. The District Court rejected this approach out of hand. 319 F. Supp., at 1056. It rests primarily on the accreditation and approval and confirmation requirements, discussed above, and on the assertion that 105 of the 159 counties in Georgia have no accredited hospital. Appellants' Jurisdictional Statement 18, Appendix G. We have set aside the accreditation approval and confirmation requirements, however, and, with that, the discrimination argument necessarily collapses in all significant aspects.

DOE v. BOLTON

IV

The appellants complain, finally, of the District
Court's denial of injunctive relief. A like claim was
made in *Roe* v. *Wade, ante,* at ——. We declined decision there insofar as injunctive relief was concerned,
and we decline it here. We assume that Georgia's
prosecutorial authorities will give full recognition to the
judgment of this Court.

In summary, we hold that the JCAH accredited hospital provision and the requirements as to approval by
the hospital abortion committee, as to confirmation by
two additional physicians, and as to residence in Georgia
are all unconstitutional. Specifically, the following portions of § 26–1202 (b) are stricken:

(1) Subsections (1), (2), and (5).

(2) That portion of Subsection (3) following the
words, "Such physician's judgment is reduced to writing."

(3) That portion of Subsection (4) following the
words, "Such abortion is performed in a hospital recognized by the State Board of Health."

The judgment of the District Court is therefore modified and, as so modified, is

Affirmed.

MR. JUSTICE POWELL and MR. JUSTICE REHNQUIST
took no part in the consideration or decision of this
case.

1st DRAFT

From: White

SUPREME COURT OF THE UNITED STATES

Circulated:

No. 70–18

Recirculate

Jane Roe et al., Appellants, *v.* Henry Wade.	On Appeal from the United States District Court for the Northern District of Texas.

[May —, 1972]

MR. JUSTICE WHITE, dissenting.

I dissent from the Court's decision that the Texas abortion statute, which allows abortions only when they are "procured or attempted by medical advice for the purpose of saving the life of the mother," 2A Texas Penal Code Art. 1196, is unconstitutionally vague.

This decision necessarily overrules *United States* v. *Vuitch*, 402 U. S. 62 (1971), decided only last Term, which upheld against vagueness attack D. C. Code Ann. § 22–201 which allowed abortion only when "necessary for the preservation of the mother's life or health and under the direction of a competent licensed practitioner of medicine." In that case, a district court had dismissed an indictment on the ground that the statutory standard was unconstitutionally vague, 305 F. Supp. 1032, and the Government appealed directly to this Court, which reversed the District Court's decision. The vagueness discussion in *Vuitch* did not, as the majority asserts, "focus . . . only on the word 'health,'" although the greater part of the discussion in this Court's opinion and in that of the District Court was devoted to parsing that phrase. The lower court had treated the statutory standard as the "preservation-of-life-or-health standard," 305 F. Supp., at 1035, as did this Court, 402 U. S., at 70, 71. Furthermore, the decision that the "preservation-of-life" standard is not impermissibly vague was a necessary part

ROE *v.* WADE

of the Court's holding. since it would otherwise have been
forced to affirm the District Court's decision voiding the
statute, despite the fact that it had overruled that court's
decision regarding the vagueness of the "preservation-
of-health" standard. Instead, the Court upheld the
D. C. statute in its entirety.

If called upon to reconsider this Court's decision in
Vuitch, I would reaffirm it and would not. therefore,
void the Texas statute on vagueness grounds. If a
standard which refers to the "health" of the mother, a
referent which necessarily entails the resolution of perplexing questions about the interrelationship of physical,
emotional, and mental well-being, is not impermissibly
vague, a statutory standard which focuses only on "saving
the life" of the mother would appear to be *a fortiori*
acceptable. The Court's observation that "whether a
particular operation is necessary for a patient's physical
or mental health is a judgment that physicians are obviously called upon to make routinely whenever surgery
is considered," 402 U. S., at 72 (footnote omitted), is
particuarly applicable to medical decisions as to when
the life of a mother is endangered, since the relevant
factors in the latter situation are less numerous and are
primarily physiological.

Finally, the vagueness claim is not properly presented
in appellant Roe's attack on the Texas statute. There
is no question that Art. 1196 does not authorize abor-
tions-by-request and that it instead articulates a standard which a woman seeking an abortion would recognize
as relevant to her case. Any Texas doctor would similarly realize that an abortion could not be performed
unless the requirements of Art. 1196, whatever they might
be, were met. On its face, therefore, the statute divides
women seeking abortions into two classes: those who
make some claim that an abortion is necessary to save
their life and those who do not. Assuming that the stat-

ROE *v.* WADE

utory standard is impermissibly vague, confusion and uncertainty will be created among women in the former group. Appellant Roe, however, falls into the latter group, since her complaint asserts that she desires an abortion "[b]ecause of the economic hardships and social stigmas involved in bearing an illegitimate child." and admits that her "life does not appear to be threatened by the continuation of her pregnancy." (R., at 11.) Indeed, appellant Roe argues at length that the right to terminate an unwanted pregnancy, for whatever reason, is an integral part of constitutionally protected rights of privacy. (Brief of Appellants, at 99–109.) For such women, who make no claim that an abortion is necessary for the purpose of saving their life, the possible vagueness of the statutory standard is irrelevant since, however, the class of women is defined who qualify for an abortion because their life is somehow endangered, they are *ipso facto* outside of this class. "The underlying principle [of the void for vagueness doctrine] is that no man shall be held criminally responsible for conduct which he could not reasonably understand to be proscribed." *United States v. Harriss*, 347 U. S. 612, 617 (1954). See also: *United States v. National Dairy Corp.*, 372 U. S. 29, 32–33 (1963); *Jordan v. De George*, 341 U. S. 223, 231 (1951); *United States v. Petrillo*, 332 U. S. 1, 7 (1947). Whatever merit appellant's Ninth Amendment and related claims may have, it cannot be rationally contended that it is not perfectly apparent that the abortion she desires is clearly prohibited by the Texas statute. This is not a case involving "the transcendent value to all society of constitutionally protected expression," *Gooding v. Wilson*, 405 U. S. —, — (1972), in which appellant might have standing to attack the possible infirmity of the statute as applied to members of another class. Cf. *Baggett v. Bullitt*, 377 U. S. 360, 366 (1964); *NAACP v. Button*, 371 U. S. 415, 433 (1963).

Had the Blackmun first drafts in the abortion cases come down as the final decisions, the last fifteen years in American life and politics might have been quite different. It soon became apparent, however, that the Blackmun drafts were not going to receive the five-Justice imprimatur needed to transform them into Court opinions.

First came indications that the drafts were not satisfactory to the leaders of the conference majority. On May 18, soon after he had received the drafts, Justice Brennan sent a "Dear Harry" letter, headed, "RE: *No. 70-18—Roe* v. *Wade*."

"My recollection of the voting on this and the *Georgia* case," Brennan wrote, "was that a majority of us felt that the Constitution required the invalidation of abortion statutes save to the extent they required that an abortion be performed by a licensed physician within some limited time after conception. I think essentially this was the view shared by Bill, Potter, Thurgood and me. My notes also indicate that you might support this view at least in this *Texas* case."

This led Brennan to urge a decision on the constitutional merits. "In the circumstances, I would prefer a disposition of the core constitutional question. Your circulation, however, invalidates the Texas statute only on the vagueness ground. . . . I think we should dispose of both cases on the ground supported by the majority."

The Brennan letter closed with an attempt to mollify Blackmun, who was, after all, the least firm of those willing to invalidate the laws. "This does not mean, however, that I disagree with your conclusion as to the vagueness of the Texas statute." But such deference did not indicate a Brennan inclination to allow the case to be decided narrowly. "I only feel that there is no point in delaying longer our confrontation with the core issue on which there appears to be a majority and which would make reaching the vagueness issue unnecessary."

The next day, May 19, Justice Douglas wrote to Blackmun, "[M]y notes confirm what Bill Brennan wrote yesterday in his memo to you—that abortion statutes were invalid save as they required that an abortion be performed by a licensed physician within a limited time after conception." "That," according to Douglas, "was the clear view of a majority of the seven who heard the argument. . . . So I think we should meet what Bill Brennan calls the 'core issue.' " Justice Douglas also referred to the fact that, at the conference, "the Chief had the opposed view, which made it puzzling as to why he made the assignment at all."

The Brennan and Douglas letters indicated opposition to the Blackmun attempt to avoid the "core [constitutional] issue" in *Roe* v. *Wade*. But soon, for a reason unrelated to legal analysis, moves on the part of the conference minority led the proaffirmance majority to change their position and support the Blackmun drafts as they were written.

The abortion cases had come before a seven-Justice Court. The two vacancies were filled when Justices Powell and Rehnquist took their seats on January 6, 1972. After the Blackmun drafts, supra pages 103 and

120, were circulated, the Chief Justice directed his efforts to securing a reargument in the cases, arguing that the decisions in such important cases should be made by a full Court. To blunt the reargument effort, Justice Douglas sent a May 25 letter expressly joining the Blackmun *Roe* draft. Douglas wrote that he had previously thought otherwise, "But I now think it best to hand it down as you have written it."

At this point Justice White issued his brief draft dissent, which is reprinted on p. 141. It was circulated May 29 and effectively demonstrated the weakness of the Blackmun vagueness approach in striking down the Texas law. Referring to the *Vuitch* decision that a statute that permitted abortion on "health" grounds was not unconstitutionally vague, the White draft declared, "If a standard which refers to the 'health' of the mother, a referent which necessarily entails the resolution of perplexing questions about the interrelationship of physical, emotional, and mental well-being, is not impermissibly vague, a statutory standard which focuses only on 'saving the life' of the mother would appear to be *a fortiori* acceptable." Surely, "the relevant factors in the latter situation are less numerous and are primarily physiological."

On May 31, Chief Justice Burger sent around a *MEMORANDUM TO THE CONFERENCE* favoring reargument. The Chief Justice wrote, "[T]hese cases . . . are not as simple for me as they appear to be for others. The states have, I should think, as much concern in this area as in any within their province; federal power has only that which can be traced to a specific provision of the Constitution." Moreover, the Burger memo went on, "This is as sensitive and difficult an issue as any in this Court in my time and I want to hear more and think more when I am not trying to sort out several dozen other difficult cases." Because of these factors, the memo concluded, "I vote to reargue early in the next Term."

The Burger move to secure reargument was opposed by the Justices in favor of striking down the abortion laws. They feared that, after the reargument, the two new Justices would vote for the laws. In addition, the White draft dissent might lead another Justice to withdraw his support from the Blackmun *Roe* draft—maybe even Blackmun himself whose position had been none too firm in the matter. At the least, the draft was subject to further erosion simply because it was based on the vulnerable vagueness argument.

On May 31, Justice Brennan wrote to Justice Blackmun, "I see no reason to put these cases over for reargument. I say that since, as I understand it, there are five of us (Bill Douglas, Potter, Thurgood, you and I) in substantial agreement with both opinions and in that circumstance I question that reargument would change things." Later that day, Blackmun received a similar note from Justice Marshall, "Like Bill Brennan, I, too, am opposed to reargument of these cases."

By now, however, Justice Blackmun was ready to break the five-man majority for immediate issuance of his opinions. He himself had become convinced that the cases should be reargued and circulated a May 31 *MEMORANDUM TO THE CONFERENCE* to that effect:

> Although it would prove costly to me personally, in the light of energy and hours expended, I have now concluded, somewhat reluctantly, that re-argument in *both* cases at an early date in the next term, would perhaps be advisable.

He gave two reasons for his position:

> 1. I believe, on an issue so sensitive and so emotional as this one, the country deserves the conclusion of a nine-man, not a seven-man court, whatever the ultimate decision may be.
> 2. Although I have worked on these cases with some concentration, I am not yet certain about all the details. Should we make the Georgia case the primary opinion and recast Texas in its light? Should we refrain from emasculation of the Georgia statute and, instead, hold it unconstitutional in its entirety and let the state legislature reconstruct from the beginning? Should we spell out—although it would then necessarily be largely dictum—just what aspects are controllable by the State and to what extent? For example, it has been suggested that . . . Georgia's provision as to a licensed hospital should be held unconstitutional, and the Court should approve performance of an abortion in a "licensed medical facility." These are some of the suggestions that have been made and that prompt me to think about a summer's delay.

The Blackmun memo concluded with a vote supporting the Chief Justice, "I therefore conclude, and move, that both cases go over the Term."

Justice Douglas replied to Justice Blackmun with a letter the same day. "I feel quite strongly," Douglas wrote, "that they should not be re-argued." He also had two reasons. "In the first place, these cases which were argued last October have been as thoroughly worked over and con-sidered as any cases ever before the Court in my time."

Here, the Douglas letter went out of its way to praise Blackmun's work, "[T]hose two opinions of yours in *Texas* and *Georgia* are credit-able jobs of craftsmanship and will, I think, stand the test of time. While we could sit around and make pages of suggestions, I really don't think that is important. The important thing is to get them down."

The second reason given by Douglas was that reargument was not proper where an opinion was supported by a majority of the full Court. "I have a feeling," Douglas wrote, "that where the Court is split 4–4 or 4–2–1 or even in an important constitutional case 4–3, reargument may be desirable. But you have a firm 5 and the firm 5 will be behind you in these two opinions until they come down. It is a difficult field and a dif-ficult subject. But where there is that solid agreement of the majority I think it is important to announce the cases, and let the result be known so that the legislatures can go to work and draft their new laws."

The Douglas letter concluded with another kudo to Blackmun,

"Again, congratulations on a fine job. I hope the 5 can agree to get the cases down this Term, so that we can spend our energies next Term on other matters."

The next day, June 1, an angry Douglas letter was sent to the Chief Justice:

> Dear Chief:
> I have your memo to the Conference dated May 31, 1972 re *Abortion Cases.*
> If the vote of the Conference is to reargue, then I will file a statement telling what is happening to us and the tragedy it entails.

The threatened Douglas statement was never issued, even though the Justices did vote to have *Roe* and *Doe* reargued. The Douglas attempt to defeat reargument was doomed when the two new Justices voted in favor of reargument. On June 1, Justice Powell circulated a *MEMORANDUM TO THE CONFERENCE*, which began, "The question is whether the abortion cases should be reargued." Powell noted that he had not until then participated in the vote on reargument motions. This case, he wrote, was different. "I have been on the Court for more than half a term. It may be that I now have a duty to participate in this decision, although from a purely personal viewpoint I would be more than happy to leave this one to others."

The Powell memo went on, "I have concluded that it is appropriate for me to participate in the pending question. . . . I am persuaded to favor reargument primarily by the fact that Harry Blackmun, the author of the opinions, thinks the cases should be carried over and reargued next fall. His position, based on months of study, suggests enough doubt on an issue of large national importance to justify the few months delay."

Justice Rehnquist also sent around a June 1 memo voting in favor of reargument, as did Justice White on June 5. That gave the motion for reargument five votes. When, on June 29, the last day of the 1971 Term, the Court issued its order setting the abortion cases for reargument, only Justice Douglas was listed as dissenting.[11]

In one of those tricks legal history sometimes plays, it was Justice Douglas and the others who favored invalidating the abortion laws who gained the most from the order for reargument. Had Douglas won his battle to prevent reargument, the original Blackmun drafts would have remained the final *Roe* and *Doe* opinions. They would have dealt narrowly with the issues before the Court and, as he predicted in his note to Blackmun, sent legislatures to work drafting new abortion laws, for these opinions were clearly not ringing affirmations of the right to abortion. By moving for reargument, Chief Justice Burger hoped to secure the votes of the two new Justices and then persuade Justice Blackmun himself to switch to an opinion upholding the abortion laws. From his point of view, the Chief Justice would have been better off had the weak original *Roe* draft come down. As it turned out, he got a split vote from the new Justices and a vastly improved *Roe* opinion, with its broadside confirmation of the constitutional right to an abortion.

The abortion cases themselves were reargued on October 11, 1972. At the conference following reargument, the Justices who had participated in the earlier conference took the same positions as before. The two new Justices took opposing positions. Justice Powell said that he was "basically in accord with Harry's position," whereas Justice Rehnquist stated, "I agree with Byron [White]"—who had declared, "I'm not going to second guess state legislatures in striking the balance in favor of abortion laws."

Several Justices expressed dissatisfaction with the approach of the Blackmun *Roe* draft (supra p. 103), agreeing with Justice Stewart's statement that "I can't join in holding that the Texas statute is vague." Stewart was for striking that law but urged a different approach. He said that he would "follow John Harlan's reasoning in the Connecticut case[12] and can't rest there on the Ninth Amendment. It's a Fourteenth Amendment right, as John Harlan said in *Griswold.*"[13]

Justice Stewart thought that the Court should deal specifically with the query raised by the Chief Justice, "Is there a fetal life that's entitled to protection?" As Stewart saw it, "[I]t seems essential that we deal with the claim that the fetus is not a person under the Fourteenth Amendment."

Justice Blackmun informed the conference, "I am where I was last Spring." However, this time he made a much firmer statement in favor of invalidating the abortion laws. He also said, "I'd make Georgia the lead case." But he was opposed on this by several others, particularly Justice Powell, who stated, "I think Texas should be the lead case."

Most important of all, Justice Blackmun announced to the conference, "I've revised both the Texas and Georgia opinions of the last term." During the past summer, Blackmun had devoted his time to the abortion opinions and had completely rewritten them. On November 21, he circulated a completely revised draft of his *Roe v. Wade* opinion. "Herewith," began the covering memo, "is a memorandum (1972 fall edition) on the Texas abortion case."

Justice Blackmun's second *Roe* draft expressly abandoned the vagueness holding on which his first draft had turned. The holding on the constitutional merits, the new draft states, "makes it unnecessary for us to consider the attack made on the Texas statute on grounds of vagueness." The covering memo explains, "I have attempted to preserve *Vuitch* in its entirety. You will recall that the attack on the Vuitch statute was restricted to the issue of vagueness. 420 U.S. at 73. I would dislike to have to undergo another assault on the District of Columbia statute based, this time, on privacy grounds."

The new Blackmun draft contains the essentials of the final *Roe v. Wade* opinion, including its lengthy historical analysis. In a separate November 21 note to Justice Brennan, Blackmun wrote, "In that portion of this proposed opinion that deals with abortion history I have referred to the development of the canon law and to the position of the Catholic Church. I personally would very much appreciate your paying particular attention to these passages. I believe they are accurate factually, but I do not want them to be offensive or capable of being regarded as unduly critical by any reader. Your judgment as to this will be most helpful."

The new draft was similar to the final opinion in its treatment of the right to privacy, concluding "that the right of personal privacy includes the abortion decision, but that this right is not unqualified and must be considered against important state interests in regulation." It also states that abortion statutes are to be judged by the compelling-interest standard, as well as stating that the word *person* in the Fourteenth Amendment does not include a fetus—a point that was once thought to have been added in a later draft at Justice Stewart's insistence.[14]

The second draft also adopts the time approach followed in the final opinion. However, it uses the end of the first trimester of pregnancy alone as the line between invalid and valid state power. "You will observe," Justice Blackmun explains in his covering memo, "that I have concluded that the end of the first trimester is critical. This is arbitrary, but perhaps any other selected point, such as quickening or viability, is equally arbitrary."

The draft states that before the end of the first trimester, the state "must do no more than to leave the abortion decision to the best medical judgment of the pregnant woman's attending physician." However, "For the stage subsequent to the first trimester, the State may, if it chooses, determine a point beyond which it restricts legal abortions to stated reasonable therapeutic categories."

Later drafts refined this bipartite time test to the tripartite approach followed in the final *Roe* opinion. In large part, this was in response to the suggestion in a December 12 letter from Justice Marshall. "I am inclined," Marshall wrote, "to agree that drawing the line at viability accommodates the interests at stake better than drawing it at the end of the first trimester. Given the difficulties which many women may have in believing that they are pregnant and in deciding to seek an abortion, I fear that the earlier date may not in practice serve the interests of those women, which your opinion does seek to serve."

The Marshall letter stated that his concern would be met "If the opinion stated explicitly that, between the end of the first trimester and viability, state regulations directed at health and safety alone were permissible."

Marshall recognized "that at some point the State's interest in preserving the potential life of the unborn child overrides any individual interests of the women." However, he concluded, "I would be disturbed if that point were set before viability, and I am afraid that the opinion's present focus on the end of the first trimester would lead states to prohibit abortions completely at any later date."

Justice Blackmun adopted the Marshall suggestion, even though Justice Douglas sent him a December 11 letter: "I favor the first trimester, rather than viability."

In addition, Justice Brennan sent a December 13 "Dear Harry" letter. "While as you know," the letter began, "I am in basic agreement with your opinions in these cases, I too welcome your giving second thoughts to the choice of the end of the first trimester as the point beyond which a state may appropriately regulate abortion practices." The Justice, however, questioned whether "viability" was the appropriate point.

Brennan summarized the latest Blackmun drafts: "I read your proposed opinions as saying, and I agree, that a woman's right of personal privacy includes the abortion decision, subject only to limited regulation necessitated by the compelling state interests you identify. Moreover, I read the opinions to say that the state's initial interests (at least in point of time if not also in terms of importance) are in safeguarding the health of the woman and in maintaining medical standards."

The Brennan letter then asked, "[I]s the choice of 'viability' as the point where a state may begin to regulate abortions appropriate? For if we identify the state's initial interests as the health of the woman and the maintenance of medical standards, the selection of 'viability' (i.e., the point in time where the fetus is capable of living outside of the woman) as the point where a state may begin to regulate in consequence of these interests seems to me to be technically inconsistent."

As Justice Brennan saw it, " 'Viability,' I have thought, is a concept that focuses upon the fetus rather than the woman." Brennan preferred an approach that he said corresponded more with the medical factors that gave rise to the "cut-off" point. "For example," Brennan wrote, "rather than using a somewhat arbitrary point such as the end of the first trimester or a somewhat imprecise and technically inconsistent point such as 'viability,' could we not simply say that at that point in time where abortions become medically more complex, state regulation—reasonably calculated to protect the asserted state interests of safeguarding the health of the woman and of maintaining medical standards—becomes permissible[?]"

Despite the Douglas and Brennan letters, Justice Blackmun continued to use the "viability" approach, though he did modify it in later drafts to meet the Marshall suggestion. At this point, Justice Stewart delivered a more fundamental criticism of the Blackmun approach in a December 14 letter. "One of my concerns with your opinion as presently written is the specificity of its dictum—particularly in its fixing of the end of the first trimester as the critical point for valid state action. I appreciate the inevitability and indeed wisdom of dicta in the Court's opinion, but I wonder about the desirability of the dicta being quite so inflexibly 'legislative.' " This is, of course, the common criticism that has since been directed at *Roe v. Wade*—that the high bench was acting more like a legislature than a court; its drawing of lines at trimesters and viability was, in the Stewart letter's phrase, "to make policy judgments" that were more "legislative" than "judicial." Justice Stewart worked on a lengthy opinion giving voice to this criticism. In a December 27 letter, however, he informed Justice Blackmun, "I have now decided to discard the rather lengthy concurring opinion on which I have been working, and to file instead a brief monograph on substantive due process, joining your opinions."

In early December, Justice Blackmun had sent around a revised draft of his *Doe* v. *Bolton* opinion as well. This was substantially very close to the final opinion in the Georgia case. On December 21, the Justice circulated further drafts and then, on January 17, 1973, the final versions that came down as the Court opinions in the two cases on January 22.

According to Justice Blackmun's November 22 covering memo transmitting his second *Roe* v. *Wade* draft, "As I stated in conference, the decision, however made, will probably result in the Court's being severely criticized." Just before he circulated the final *Roe* v. *Wade* draft, Blackmun sent around a January 16 *MEMORANDUM TO THE CONFERENCE*, which began, "I anticipate the headlines that will be produced over the country when the abortion decisions are announced." Because of this, the Justice was enclosing the announcement from the bench that he proposed to read when the two cases were made public. With this announcement, the memo expressed the hope that "there should be at least some reason for the press not going all the way off the deep end."

The Blackmun announcement did not, of course, have the calming effect for which its author hoped. On the contrary, the scare headlines and controversy were, if anything, far greater than anything anticipated by the Justice and his colleagues. All that would have been avoided had the original Blackmun *Roe* v. *Wade* draft come down as the final Court opinion. Instead of a *cause célèbre*, *Roe* might then have been a mere constitutional footnote used by law professors to illustrate how the Court can evade important legal issues.

Notes

1. 410 U.S. 113 (1973).
2. Woodward and Armstrong, *The Brethren: Inside the Supreme Court* 238 (1979).
3. *Washington Post National Weekly Edition*, October 1, 1984, p. 33.
4. *New York Times*, March 8, 1976, p. 7.
5. Infra p. 90.
6. 410 U.S. at 116.
7. The conference notes I used read "getting" but this seems an error.
8. See Woodward and Armstrong, op. cit. supra note 2, at 170.
9. *Washington Post*, July 4, 1972, p. 1.
10. 402 U.S. 62 (1971).
11. 408 U.S. 919 (1972).
12. *Poe* v. *Ullman*, 367 U.S. 497 (1961).
13. *Griswold* v. *Connecticut*, 381 U.S. 479 (1967).
14. Woodward and Armstrong, op. cit. supra note 2, at 233.

5

United States v. Nixon (1974): Bad Presidents Make Hard Law

Just after five o'clock on a hot July day in 1974, William J. Brennan, Jr., left his chambers in the nation's ornate marble temple to justice that one predecessor, Harlan F. Stone, had called "bombastically pretentious,"[1] and climbed into his red VW square-back sedan.

Driving from the Supreme Court, he turned west on Constitution Avenue and headed to Georgetown University Hospital, where his old comrade-in-the-law Earl Warren was being treated for a heart attack that had felled him a week earlier.

Justice Brennan found Warren, then eighty-three, surprisingly alert and in good spirits. The man Brennan fondly called "Super Chief" had avidly followed politics and the law since his retirement as Chief Justice five years before. He was eager to hear the latest on the *Nixon* case,[2] then before the Supreme Court.

Justice Brennan had a lot to confide. Earlier that afternoon, Tuesday, July 9, the Justices had concluded their conference on whether President Nixon must surrender his potentially incriminating Watergate tapes to the U.S. District Court.

Those tapes, it was widely believed, contained the smoking gun evidence sought by the special prosecutor and by congressional investigators of Richard Nixon's participation in a felonious coverup of illegal acts committed on behalf of his administration. The President had maneuvered politically and had fought legally to maintain possession of the tapes—and the primacy of executive privilege. He even had indicated that if the Supreme Court ordered him to give them up, he might refuse.[3]

The eight Justices participating in the conference, Brennan told Warren, had decided unanimously that Nixon must turn over the crucial tapes to the court. It was a decision that, one month later, would force the removal from office of a President for the first time in the nation's history.

The case had provoked a "lively discussion" at the conference, Brennan said. "It was very quickly apparent," he told Warren, "that the President would be treated like any other person."

When the Justice told Warren the news, the old Chief lifted himself from the pillows.

"Thank God, thank God, thank God!" Warren declared fervently. "If you don't do it this way, Bill, it's the end of the country as we have known it."

Earl Warren sank back on the bed. The judiciary had again wielded ultimate political power in the United States, this time in a very special area of the law. It had made a decision in a dispute between one of the branches of government and the other two.

Yet, though the decision may have led to Richard Nixon's forced relegation to political limbo, it was far from an unqualified defeat for presidential power. The presidency, as distinguished from Mr. Nixon, may have gained at least as much as it lost from the Supreme Court decision.

According to one of Justice Holmes's most celebrated aphorisms, "Great cases like hard cases make bad law."[4] This occurs because the "immediate interests exercise a kind of hydraulic pressure which makes what previously was clear seem doubtful, and before which even well settled principles of law will bend."[5] The Holmes aphorism is particularly applicable to the Supreme Court case involving President Nixon.

It is as difficult for Supreme Court Justices as for ordinary mortals to consider any matter involving Richard Nixon with the "cold neutrality of an impartial judge" of which Burke speaks.[6] Nixon's presence as a litigant may have exerted the kind of "hydraulic pressure" that results in distorted decision with baneful precedential effects. If hard cases and great cases make bad law, the same may be true of a case involving Nixon, particularly when it arises out of his misstewardship of the highest office.

United States v. *Nixon*[7] itself was, in many ways, the culmination of the Watergate scandal that dominated the news during Nixon's shortened second term. The case itself arose from a motion filed by the Watergate special prosecutor for a subpoena *duces tecum** that directed President Nixon to produce certain tape recordings and documents relating to his conversations with aides and advisers. Following the return of an indictment against top White House aides and others for crimes arising out of the Watergate scandal, the special prosecutor determined that the tapes and documents in the President's possession were relevant evidence in the criminal trial and sought their production through the subpoena. The President moved to quash the subpoena, asserting that conversations between a President and his close advisers were privileged and that the doctrine of separation of powers precluded judicial review of his privilege claim. This view, if accepted, would have meant an absolute, unqualified presidential immunity from judicial process under all circumstances.

If Karl Marx was correct when he said, "The general ethos of bu-

_____

* *Duces tecum* literally means "carry with you."

reaucracy is secrecy,"[8] then the Nixon administration was among our most bureaucratic. The Nixon years witnessed not only an increased frequency of executive privilege claims, but also an expansion of their scope. In the face of congressional investigation, Nixon went so far as to assert a complete immunity for the White House from disclosure requirements. On March 12, 1973, for example, he directed that no "member or former member" of the White House staff appear before Congress.[9] A month later, Attorney General Richard G. Kleindienst made the extraordinary claim that the President "is empowered to forbid federal employees from testifying before congressional committees under any circumstances and to block congressional demands for *any* document within the executive branch."[10] Internal White House conversations, however, suggest that these extreme assertions were tactical moves to frustrate the Watergate investigations.

The extent to which the White House was willing to use executive privilege as a coverup tactic may be seen from a discussion of whether two former White House staff members implicated in Watergate misdeeds should be made "consultants" in order to shield them with executive privilege:

> HALDEMAN: Say, did you raise the question with the President on Colson as a consultant . . . ?
>
> DEAN: The thought was as a consultant, without doing any consulting, he wants it for continued protection on—
>
> HALDEMAN: Solely for the purpose of executive privilege protections, I take it. . . .
>
> PRESIDENT: What happens to Chapin?
>
> DEAN: Well, Chapin doesn't have quite the same problem in appearing as Colson will.
>
> HALDEMAN: Yeah—you have the same problem of Chapin appearing as Colson.
>
> PRESIDENT: Well, can't—that would [be] such an obvious fraud to have both of them as consultants, that that won't work.[11]

The President's claim in the *Nixon* case—later characterized by the Court as "a claim of absolute Presidential privilege against inquiry by the coordinate Judicial Branch"[12]—would have immunized even such patent misuses of executive privilege from all judicial scrutiny. The claim was, however, rejected by the district court. On May 20, 1974, Judge John J. Sirica (who had earlier played such a significant part in frustrating the White House attempt to end the entire investigation by having the burglars themselves plead guilty and take short first-offender sentences) denied the motion to quash the subpoena and ordered the President to deliver the tapes and other subpoenaed items to the court. An appeal was filed in the U.S. Court of Appeals, but before that court could act, the Supreme Court, on June 15, granted the special prosecutor's petition asking the highest tribunal to hear the case on an expedited basis before the Court of Appeals decision.

The news about Watergate, of course, had fully penetrated to Olympus. From the beginning, in fact, the Justices had followed the unfolding scandal with increasing fascination. Even before oral argument, the Justices had begun circulating memoranda that dealt with the merits of the case. This was done, as Justice Powell indicated in a July 6 *MEMORANDUM TO THE CONFERENCE,* in accordance "with the indications by several Justices at our last Conference that exchanges of memoranda would be welcomed."

Characteristically, the first member of the Court to circulate a memo was Justice Douglas. On July 5, three days before argument, he sent around a twenty-nine-page printed "Memorandum from MR. JUSTICE DOUGLAS." It was accompanied by a covering letter explaining that it was only a memorandum. Despite this, the Douglas memo was really the first draft of an opinion in the case and, as such, is reprinted on p. 163.

The draft was a typical Douglas product. It exemplified the Justice's ability to turn out drafts far more quickly than any of the others. Once when Douglas had said that he needed more time for an opinion, Justice Black, who opposed delay, had waspishly replied, "Brother Douglas says he 'would like time to work further on [his opinion] beyond this week.' But he does not say that he wants or needs an extra month, and it is inconceivable that he does, in view of his well-known speed in writing all his opinions."[13]

The Douglas draft did deal with three of the important issues before the Court: appealability, standing, and privilege. On the first two, the Douglas presentation played a direct part in the final *Nixon* opinion. But, like so many Douglas products, the draft was unpolished, as though it had been all-too-facilely written at a single sitting (even though it had undergone three drafts before the oral argument). In addition, it raised matters that were better left unsaid by the Supreme Court. Thus, it referred to the controversial dismissal of the first Watergate prosecutor, Archibald Cox, as "the illegal firing of the previous Special Prosecutor"—deciding an issue not before the Court and one on which the Justices have never given their opinion.

Even more distressing was the Douglas discussion of whether the grand jury might name the President as an unindicted coconspirator. The record in the case had been sealed. However, after it was reported in the press that Nixon had been named, the Court made public the following extract from the sealed record:

> On February 25, 1974, in the course of its consideration of the indictment in the instant case, the . . . Grand Jury, by a vote of 19–0, determined that there is probable cause to believe that Richard M. Nixon (among others) was a member of the conspiracy to defraud the United States and to obstruct justice charged in Count 1 of the instant indictment, and the Grand Jury authorized the Special Prosecutor to identify Richard M. Nixon (among others) as an unindicted co-conspirator in connection with subsequent legal proceedings in this case.[14]

In addition, Nixon's counsel petitioned the Court to decide whether the grand jury had the right "under the Constitution" to charge an incumbent President as an unindicted coconspirator.

Part IV of the Douglas draft dealt with "[t]he argument that we should examine *the evidence* before the grand jury with a view of determining that the grand jury was not justified in naming Richard M. Nixon as a co-conspirator." Douglas asserted "that that finding was made for the benefit of the House Judiciary Committee which now has before it the impeachment question." This meant that the Court was being asked to rule that the grand jury finding "is not competent evidence in impeachment proceedings." This, said Douglas, is a "political" question because "all the matters pertaining to the process of impeachment are beyond the reach of judicial power. They rest exclusively in the political branch."

It is fortunate that the Court did not follow the Douglas lead and deal with the grand jury issue in the *Nixon* opinion. It was really irrelevant to the overriding issue in the case—that of executive privilege. More than that, the Douglas disposition of the issue could only have given comfort to the White House. By not confirming the grand jury's authority, it might enable the President to discredit both its action and that of the special prosecutor who had relied on its work. It would be preferable to avoid the question and keep the Court entirely out of the grand jury issue.

On the principal issue in the case—that of executive privilege—the Douglas draft was categorical in its denial of the President's claim. And, unlike the final *Nixon* opinion, it did so without recognizing any presidential privilege to withhold information. As Douglas saw it, "Whether in some circumstances the executive power carries with it an 'executive privilege' to be immune from process running either from the Congress or the federal courts is a question we need not reach in this case." Despite this statement, the Douglas draft specifically repudiates the notion "which permits a President to say that his 'executive privilege' can withhold those documents or which says that the President, rather than the court, will pass on the materiality or relevance of the withheld material in the trial of the defendants." Such an unreviewable presidential power would be contrary to the basic presuppositions of our system. "The President is, for constitutional purposes, the chief law enforcement and prosecutorial officer in the Nation; to allow him to conceal from a court information which may be critical to the fairness of a trial of named defendants would be a monstrous affront to the rule of law under which we live."

The Douglas draft was much stronger in its flat statement "that there is no Executive privilege of the President which justifies withholding these materials from the District Court" than either Chief Justice Burger's later *Nixon* drafts or the memorandum on the subject circulated by Justice Powell on July 6, two days before the oral argument. The Powell memo was accompanied by a covering note that informed the others, "the attached memorandum reflects my thinking after rather intensive study for the past two weeks." Powell also noted, "I submit this to you with all the obvious caveats: the views and conclusions stated are tentative and subject, of course, to oral argument and our discussion at Conference."

The Powell memo began by stating, "This memorandum is intended to serve as a tentative proposal for portions of a draft opinion." Powell then listed the different parts that should make up the Court's opinion:

> As I envision it, an appropriate opinion would consist of five parts:
> Part I   statement of facts;
> Part II   jurisdiction and justiciability;
> Part III   the merits of the President's assertion of absolute and unre-
>   viewable authority to withhold the tapes from *in camera* in-
>   spection;
> Part IV   standards and procedures governing the exercise of judicial
>   authority to order the President to comply with a subpoena
>   *duces tecum;* and
> Part V   application of Parts III and IV to the facts of this case and
>   disposition.

The Powell memo summarized briefly Parts I, II, and V. The Justice dealt with Parts III and IV in attached tentative drafts. As explained in the memo, the Part III draft was intended to "address in general terms whether the President's decision to withhold confidential conversations subpoenaed for use in criminal proceedings is final and binding on the courts. The constitutional underpinnings of this question seem to me to deserve from this Court a more searching explication than they have yet received." With regard to the Part IV draft, Powell wrote, "My suggested resolution of the constitutional issue posed in Part III would vest in the Federal Judiciary a power over the office of the President that is plainly susceptible of abuse. Standards and procedures to govern the exercise of such power are obviously important. I have addressed this subject in the attached tentative draft of Part IV."

The Powell drafts of his proposed Part III and Part IV are found on page 190. They constitute a tentative draft of the most important parts of the *Nixon* opinion and served as the foundation for Part IV of the final opinion, headed "The Claim of Privilege."

The Powell draft of his "Proposed Part III," like the final *Nixon* opinion, rejects the President's assertion "that the decision whether to reveal such confidential conversations for use in a criminal proceeding is his alone to make." It does recognize a "principle of confidentiality" for executive communications, yet notes that it need not "always prevail over competing societal interests." The key question, Powell writes, is "not whether in this or any other case we find some greater public good outweighing the generalized need for confidentiality, but rather who is empowered under our Constitution to make that decision."

In answering this question, Powell states that executive privilege has a constitutional foundation (a principle also stated in the final opinion and one which, in the long run, may turn out the most important laid down by the *Nixon* case). But Powell also finds that "because the production of all material evidence in a criminal trial furthers the judiciary's constitutional mandate to do justice, it too is a matter of constitutional import." This means that "Both Article II and Article III are involved here."

Who is to balance the claims of one against those of the other? The Powell answer is that "the ultimate authority to decide whether in a particular case confidentiality must give way to some greater public interest resides in that branch whose constitutional responsibilities are more gravely affected."

This was the most unfortunate part of the Powell draft. Had it been agreed to by the others, it would have meant a virtual acceptance of the President's claim of unreviewable executive privilege in all cases except those involving "the Judiciary's need for evidence material to criminal trials," which Powell himself refers to as "rare and isolated instances." In all other cases, it could be argued, it is the executive branch "whose constitutional responsibilities are more gravely affected," and in them, under the Powell approach, the President has "the ultimate authority to decide whether in a particular case confidentiality must give way."

The Powell draft of "Proposed Part IV" was equally disturbing. Here the draft dealt with the standard for enforcement of the special prosecutor's subpoena. Rule 17(c) of the *Federal Rules of Criminal Procedure* provides that subpoenas are to be enforced unless "compliance would be unreasonable or oppressive." Further, subpoenas are to be enforced only where the material sought is relevant and admissible. In the ordinary case, as Justice Brennan pointed out in a July 8 *Memorandum to the Conference*, a subpoena is to be enforced "when the District Court can conclude that the application is made in good faith; that the material sought is evidentiary in character and relevant to issues likely to be raised at trial; and that the material will assist in pre-trial preparation and is not otherwise obtainable prior to trial by reasonable efforts."

Powell, however, urged in his draft that the normal Rule 17(c) standard was not enough to protect the President. Instead, he declared, when a President invokes executive privilege, "the court must require a special showing from the moving party." The Rule 17(c) standard must give way to one of "compelling justification." As the draft sums up the Powell view, "The standard, then, is necessity. The movant must show by extrinsic evidence that the subpoenaed materials are essential to the ends of justice." This was a standard that went far toward adopting the position asserted by the President's counsel. In this case itself, the special prosecutor might well not have been able to meet the Powell standard.

On the morning of July 8, just before oral argument began, Justice Brennan circulated a four-page substitute for the Powell "Proposed Part IV." It applied what it termed the normal "exacting standards of Rule

17(c)" to the case and concluded "that the standards of Rule 17(c) have been correctly applied."

The day after the oral argument, on Tuesday, July 9, the Justices met in conference. Eight of them were present in the Court's ornate conference room—Justice Rehnquist having disqualified himself from the case. As Justice Brennan told former Chief Justice Warren later that day, the Justices were united in holding that the President must turn over the subpoenaed tapes and other documents. On the other hand, none disputed the existence of some executive privilege. The conference discussion in this respect was summarized in a July 12 "Dear Chief" letter circulated by Justice Powell, "[w]e were all in accord that there is a privilege of confidentiality with respect to presidential conversations and papers. We also agreed that it is a qualified privilege and not absolute or unreviewable; and, in this case, that the Special Prosecutor has made a showing which overcomes the privilege and justifies *in camera* review."

There was, however, some disagreement on the Rule 17(c) issue. According to the Powell letter, "We were not entirely in agreement as to the standard to be met in overcoming the privilege." Powell himself urged the view taken in his draft. As his letter put it, "[S]ome of us emphasized that a President of the United States (and it must be remembered that we are speaking not just of the present incumbent) must be entitled to a higher level of protection against disclosure than a citizen possessing no privilege who is charged with crime or who may be a witness in a criminal case." The opposing view was stated by Justice White, who, we shall see, wrote the draft on Rule 17(c) that formed the basis for the *Nixon* opinion's treatment of the point.

Another matter on which there was some difference at the conference was that of the authorship of the opinion. Justice Brennan said that the Court should emphasize its decision ordering the President to turn over the tapes by issuing the strongest opinion possible. This could be done if the Court delivered a joint opinion in the name of each of the participating Justices. The Court had done so only once before, in its decision in the 1958 Little Rock school-desegregation case, where the joint opinion of the Justices dramatically underlined the unanimity of their rebuff to Governor Orval Faubus's defiance of desegregation orders. Brennan urged the same approach here.

Chief Justice Burger, however, refused to go along with the Brennan suggestion. "The responsibility is on my shoulders," declared the Chief Justice. He said that he would prepare the opinion and would circulate its different parts as he finished them.

On July 10, the day after the conference, Chief Justice Burger began to send around the different sections of his draft *Nixon* opinion. The first two sections, headed "Statement of Facts" and "Jurisdiction," were accompanied by the following *MEMORANDUM TO THE CONFERENCE*, "As I stated at the Conference yesterday I will not await a complete draft but will send sections as they are ready.

"The enclosed material is not intended to be final, and I will welcome—indeed I invite—your suggestions." At the bottom the Chief Justice had written, "More later!"

The following day, July 11, two further sections were circulated. The Chief Justice's covering memorandum read: "Enclosed are proposed sections on Justiciability and Rule 17(c). Bear in mind the titles and numbering and sequence of parts will await the final treatment of substance.

"I believe we have encountered no insoluble problems to this point."

This left the most important part of the opinion—that on executive privilege—still to be done. Its preparation was slightly delayed by Earl Warren's death on July 9, shortly after Justice Brennan's visit to his former Chief. In a *MEMORANDUM TO THE CONFERENCE*, sent later on July 11, Chief Justice Burger wrote:

> With the sad intervention of Chief Justice Warren's death, the schedules of all of us have been altered. I intend to work without interruption (except for some sleep) until I have the "privilege" section complete and the final honing complete on all parts.
>
> I think it is unrealistic to consider a Monday, July 15, announcement. This case is too important to "rush" unduly although it is in fact receiving priority treatment.
>
> I would hope we could meet an end-of-the-week announcement, i.e., July 19 or thereabouts.

Almost a week later, on July 17, the Chief Justice circulated his draft of the privilege section. His accompanying *MEMORANDUM TO THE CONFERENCE* stated:

> This morning I gave a copy of the working draft of the part dealing with the claim of privilege to Mr. Justice Brennan to enable him to have it before going to Nantucket. Although it is still in rough form it is more nearly final than any of the other material previously circulated, and it may expedite our undertaking to have it in your hands now.
>
> I hope to circulate a full opinion draft by the week's end.

Though, as just seen, Chief Justic Burger prepared and circulated his draft *Nixon* opinion in installments, his five sections are reprinted together starting on p. 202. Taken as such, they constitute the first draft of the Burger *Nixon* opinion. This draft differs drastically from the opinion ultimately delivered. Substantial changes, we shall see, had to be made—both by the Chief Justice and, even more so, by the other Justices—before the opinion could come down as the final *Nixon* opinion.

The Burger draft contains the same five sections as the final *Nixon* opinion. The draft begins with a brief statement giving the factual background of the case. Then there is a section headed "Jurisdiction"—essentially similar to that in the final opinion—holding that the order below was an appealable order. The next section, on Justiciability, was based substantially on the Douglas June 6 draft. It, too, was similar to the comparable section in the final opinion.

The Burger section headed "The Rule 17(c) Question" did not deal with the Powell–White dispute over the proper standard to be applied in a subpoena enforcement proceeding against the President. The draft upheld the district court's enforcement order as Judge Sirica's assessment of the relevancy and evidentiary value of the items sought was not clearly erroneous.

The heart of the Burger draft, as of the final *Nixon* opinion, was its section on "The Claim of Executive Privilege." Here, the Burger draft was more favorable to the presidential claims than the opinion ultimately delivered. The draft, like the final opinion, found a constitutional base for executive privilege. But the draft supported this finding by casting a gratuitous doubt on the doctrine of judicial review itself, "Like the power of judicial review first announced by this Court under the authority of Article III in *Marbury, supra,*[15] certain powers and privileges flow from the nature of enumerated powers; the protection of the confidentiality of presidential communications has similar constitutional underpinnings."

In the footnote supporting this statement, the Chief Justice cast a similar doubt on the *Nixon* subpoena itself. To the special prosecutor's claim that there was no constitutional provision for a presidential privilege, the note stated, "But the silence of the Constitution on this score is not dispositive. There is similarly nothing said in the Constitution authorizing the very subpoena at issue in this case. The only express provision in the Constitution for compulsory process [is] found in the 6th Amendment guarantee that an accused shall have such process to secure evidence in his favor. It could be argued from this express provision that no other compulsory process was contemplated but it takes little reflection to see that without coercive power to produce witnesses and evidence the Article III functions of courts could not be performed."

The draft, like the final opinion, rejected the presidential claim of "an absolute privilege as against a subpoena essential to enforcement of criminal statutes." But the draft went on to say, "Since we conclude that the legitimate needs of the judicial process may outweigh presidential privilege when the privilege is based solely on the generalized need for confidentiality, it is necessary, in a given case to resolve these competing interests in a manner that preserves the essential functions of each branch."

The implication is that, where an "essential" function of the President is involved, the privilege claim may prevail even over the needs of the judicial process. This implication is strengthened by the draft's later development of the notion of presidential "core functions," which would also prevail in any privilege case. "Under Article II" states the Burger draft, "a president, for example, exercising certain of his enumerated war powers, as in repelling a hostile attack, or exercising the veto power, or conducting foreign relations is exercising powers at the very core of his constitutional role. The courts have shown the utmost deference to presidential actions in the performance of these core functions."

The draft discussed two cases involving foreign relations and military secrets. According to the Chief Justice, "each dealt with a presidential function lying at the core of Article II authority. In the present case, however, the generalized claim of confidentiality relates to none of the kinds of activities for which courts have traditionally shown the utmost deference, but on the contrary the claim is somewhat removed from the central or core function of the chief executive."

In this case, "the need for relevant evidence in the conduct of a criminal trial lies at the very core of the Article III function of a federal court." In such a situation, the Article III function prevails. "Thus here the core function of Article III is pitted against a generalized need for presidential confidentiality without a showing that such confidentiality is necessary to protect a core function of Article II. Under these circumstances the generalized assertion of privilege must yield to the demonstrated specific need for evidence in a pending criminal trial."

The difficulty with this Burger "core function" approach is indicated by the following queries written by a Justice on his copy of the draft next to the passage just quoted: "What does this mean? May St. Clair[16] argue other core functions at stake? What is a core function?"

In the first place, there was the question of what was meant by a "core function." As already seen, the Burger draft recognizes foreign relations and military secrets as involving "core functions" of the President. But the draft itself recognizes that the "core function" concept is not necessarily limited to these matters. Instead, it states that, "by referring to the deference due to all discussions of military and foreign policy secrets, we intend to intimate no view that discussion of highly sensitive domestic policies, for example, devaluation of the currency, imposition or lifting of wage and price controls, would not be entitled to a very high order of privilege, since the economic consequences of disclosure of such discussions could well be as pervasive and momentous as the disclosure of military secrets."

If that was true of "highly sensitive domestic policies," the same might be true of other domestic acts involving presidential duties "lying at the core of Article II authority." The "core function" concept has what Justice Black once termed "accordion-like qualities."[17] It is capable of expansion or contraction in each individual case because it is without any defined limits to ensure that it will be kept within proper bounds. As the Justice indicated in his written queries noted above, counsel for the President could easily argue in the given case that "*core* functions [are] at stake." If that argument is accepted, the implication of the Burger draft is that the President's claim of privilege is conclusive. As the draft puts it, "The courts have shown the utmost deference to presidential actions in the performance of . . . core functions." If a court finds that a "core function" is involved, under the Burger approach, the President's prerogative in the matter become dispositive.

SUPREME COURT OF THE UNITED STATES

Nos. 73–1766 AND 73–1834

United States, Petitioner,
73–1766   *v.*
Richard M. Nixon, President
of the United States,
et al.

Richard M. Nixon, President
of the United States,
Petitioner,
73–1834   *v.*
United States.

On Writs of Certiorari to
the United States Court
of Appeals for the District of Columbia Circuit.

[July —, 1974]

Memorandum from MR. JUSTICE DOUGLAS.

On April 18, 1974, at the request of the Special Prosecutor, the District Court issued a subpoena *duces tecum* to respondent Richard M. Nixon, President of the United States, directing him to produce tape recordings and documents relating to 64 conversations between the President and his advisors. These materials were sought by the Special Prosecutor for use at the impending trial in *United States v. Mitchell et al.,* Cr. No. 74–110 (D. D. C.); the subpoena was issued pursuant to Rule 17 (c) of the Federal Rules of Criminal Procedure.

On May 1, 1974, respondent filed a Special Appearance and Motion to Quash the subpoena, claiming that the materials sought "are within the constitutional privilege of the President to refuse to disclose confidential information when disclosure would be contrary to the public interest." On May 13, 1974, respondent further moved for an order expunging the grand jury's naming of respondent as an unindicted co-conspirator in *United States* v. *Mitchell.*

On May 20, 1974, the District Court denied both the motion to quash and the motion to expunge, and ordered respondent to produce the subpoenaed materials.

On May 24, 1974, respondent filed a notice of appeal in the District Court, docketed the appeal in the Court of Appeals for the District of Columbia Circuit, and filed a petition for a writ of mandamus in that same Court of Appeals.

On that same date, petitioner requested that this Court issue a writ of certiorari before judgment to the Court of Appeals, as authorized by 28 U. S. C. § 1254 (1) and by Rule 20 of the Rules of this Court. In view of the public importance of the issues presented and of the desirability of a prompt resolution of those issues by this Court, the petition was granted and the case set for oral argument. — U. S. — (May 31, 1974).

On June 6, 1974, a cross-petition for certiorari before judgment was filed by respondent; for the same reasons set forth above, the cross-petition was likewise granted, — U. S. — (June 15, 1974).

On June 19, 1974, respondent filed with this Court a motion seeking disclosure to respondent and his counsel and transmittal to this Court of all evidence presented to the grand jury relating to the grand jury's action in naming respondent as an unindicted co-conspirator. Disposition of the motion was deferred pending oral argument of the case.

Respondents Strachan and Ehrlichman, named defendants in *United States* v. *Mitchell et al.*, subsequently sought to present certain additional questions concerning the availability to them, as defendants, of any potentially exculpatory materials in the President's possession. Disposition of these issues was likewise deferred pending oral argument.

I

One of the questions presented is whether the District Court's order of May 20, 1974, was an appealable order.

By the express terms of 28 U. S. C. § 1291, the courts of appeals are given jurisdiction over appeals from *"final decisions of the district courts"* (emphasis added). This requirement of finality as a precondition of review is designed to promote judicial efficiency in the administration of justice; it embodies a strong congressional policy against piecemeal review and against the obstruction or impediment of ongoing judicial proceedings by interlocutory appeals. See, *e. g., Cobbledick* v. *United States,* 309 U. S. 323, 324-326 (1940).

In applying this policy to the appealability of orders concerning the production of documents or other information before a grand jury or at trial, this Court has

> "Consistently held that the necessity for expedition in the administration of the criminal law justifies putting one who seeks to resist the production of desired information to a choice between compliance with a trial court's order to produce prior to any review of that order, and resistance to that order with the concomitant possibility of an adjudication of contempt if his claims are rejected on appeal."

United States v. *Ryan,* 402 U. S. 530, 533 (1971), and cases cited therein. Only upon an adjudication of contempt does "the witness' situation [become] so severed from the main proceeding as to permit an appeal," *Cobbledick* v. *United States, supra,* 309 U. S., at 328; prior to that point, any challenge to the production of information is regarded as an integral part of the initial proceedings, and a denial of such a challenge is merely interlocutory in nature *Ibid.; Alexander* v. *United States,* 201 U. S. 117, 121-122 (1906).

Exceptions to this principle have been recognized in
a "limited class of cases where denial of immediate
review would render impossible any review whatsoever
of an individual's claims." *United States* v. *Ryan, supra.*
Thus in *Perlman* v. *United States,* 247 U. S. 7 (1918),
where the appellant sought to raise a claim of privilege
against the production of exhibits belonging to him but
in the custody of a third party, the Court permitted
immediate review of an order compelling production of
the exhibits; in so doing, the Court noted that denial
of immediate review would preclude appellant from ever
obtaining effective review of his claim of privilege, since
the custodian of the property could not have been expected to undergo contempt proceedings in order to
preserve appellant's right to judicial review of his claims.
247 U. S., at 12–13. The instant case, however, presents no such danger, the subpoenaed materials are
within respondent's personal custody, and respondent
would undoubtedly have full opportunity to obtain
prompt appellate review of his claim of privilege subsequent to any adjudication of contempt for his refusal
to comply with the subpoena in question.

Nevertheless, a requirement that the President personally place himself in contempt of a court ruling in
order to secure review of that ruling would present an
unfortunate and unnecessary risk of constitutional confrontation between two branches of the Government.
As was recognized by the court in *Nixon* v. *Sirica,* ——
U. S. App. D. C. ——, 487 F. 2d 700 (1973),

> "In the case of the President, contempt of a judi-
> cial order—even for the purpose of enabling a con-
> stitutional test of the order—would be a course
> unseemly at best." 487 F. 2d, at 707 n. 21.

Moreover, it is clear that the interests protected by the
final order principle, namely, judicial efficiency and the
expeditious conduct of ongoing proceedings, would be
frustrated rather than served by a requirement in this

case that the President place himself in contempt of the court in order to obtain review of his constitutional claims of privilege. Such a requirement would be likely to engender protracted litigation over the contempt power and unduly delay any opportunity for a review on the merits of the underlying claim of privilege.

For these reasons, I would hold that in the unique circumstances, presented by the case, the order entered by the District Court was an appealable order, and that respondent's appeal from that order is therefore properly before this Court under a writ of certiorari before final judgment.

There is also jurisdiction in the mandamus suit. Under the All Writs Act, 28 U. S. C. § 1651 (a), the Court of Appeals, like this Court, is authorized to "issue all writs necessary or appropriate in aid of [its] respective jurisdiction and agreeable to the usages and principles of law." The proper function of these writs was set forth in *Ex parte Peru*, 318 U. S. 578, 583 (1934):

> "The historic use of writs of prohibition and mandamus directed by an appellate to an inferior court has been to exert the revisory appellate power over the inferior court. The writs thus afford an expeditious and effective means of confining the inferior court to a lawful exercise of its prescribed jurisdiction, or of compelling it to exercise its authority when it is its duty to do so."

"Jurisdiction" in this sense is not to be narrowly or technically defined, see *Will* v. *United States*, 389 U. S. 90, 95 (1967), but neither does it encompass the full range of reversible errors; thus writs are not available to correct mere errors "made in the course of the exercise of the court's jurisdiction to decide issues properly brought before it." *Bankers Life & Casualty Co.* v. *Holland*, 346 U. S. 379, 382 (1953). The extraordinary writs are not to be used to circumvent the principle of finality embodied in 28 U. S. C. § 1291, thus "thwart-

[ing] the Congressional policy against piecemeal appeals . . . ." *Roche* v. *Evaporated Milk Association,* 319
U. S. 21, 30 (1943);

> "[t]he supplementary review power conferred on
> the courts by Congress in the All Writs Act is meant
> to be used only in the exceptional case where there
> is clear abuse of discretion or 'usurpation of judicial
> power' of the sort held to justify the writ in *De Beers
> Consolidated Mines* v. *United States,* 325 U. S. 212,
> 217 (1945)."

Bankers Life & Casualty Co. v. *Holland, supra,* 346 U. S.,
at 383. See also *Will* v. *United States, supra,* 389 U. S.,
at 95–96; *Roche* v. *Evaporated Milk Assn., supra,* 319
U. S., at 26–31.

Nevertheless, the granting or withholding of a common law writ is within "the sound discretion of the
Court," *Ex parte Peru, supra,* 318 U. S., at 584; and this
Court has recognized that where a petitioner presents
substantial issues of first impression concerning the
power of the lower court to grant the relief in question,
mandamus may be an appropriate vehicle for interlocutory review of those issues. See *Schlagenhauf* v. *Holder,*
379 U. S. 104, 110–111 (1964).

In *Nixon* v. *Sirica, supra,* the Court of Appeals for the
District of Columbia Circuit was asked to review a district court order directing the President to produce certain materials for *in camera* inspection and possible disclosure to a grand jury; the President, respondent herein,
claimed a constitutional privilege to withhold the requested materials. Citing *Schlagenhauf,* the Court of
Appeals held that the executive privilege issue was "a
jurisdictional problem of 'first impression' involving a
'basic, undecided question,'" 487 F. 2d, at 707, and that
exercise of the review power granted by the All Writs
Act was therefore appropriate.

In the instant case, respondent's petition presented
substantial allegations of usurpation of power by the Dis-

trict Court in ordering compliance by the President with a trial subpoena in the face of his assertions of privilege to withhold the materials in question. Technically, of course, these allegations might be said to have lost their status as issues of first impression within the District of Columbia Circuit by virtue of that circuit's earlier ruling in *Nixon* v. *Sirica, supra;* therefore it might be said that there would have been no basis for consideration of the mandamus petition in the instant case by the Court of Appeals, and that there is thus no basis for transfer of the petition to this Court by writ of certiorari before judgment.

Nevertheless, the instant case differs from *Nixon* v. *Sirica* in at least one possibly significant respect, namely, that the underlying subpoena in the former case sought production of materials before a grand jury, while the subpoena in the instant case seeks production of materials for trial. In any event, it was certainly proper for respondent to file his petition with the Court of Appeals and to seek a determination by that court as to whether the issues raised by the petition had been foreclosed by the opinion in *Nixon* v. *Sirica.* Pending such a determination by the Court of Appeals, § 1254 (1) and Rule 20 clearly permit this Court to issue a writ of certiorari before judgment and thereby to assert jurisdiction over the petition; and since the issues raised by the petition are issues of first impression before this Court and are unquestionably issues of considerable public importance, the rationale of *Schlagenhauf* permits the Court to consider the merits.

II

It was argued by the President in the District Court that the Special Prosecutor has no standing to bring this action, and that the court has no jurisdiction over it, because it is an "intra-executive" dispute. There are essentially two elements to this argument: first, that as an inferior officer in the Executive Branch the Special Prosecutor may not sue his superior over a matter of Executive

Branch policy, and second, that in effect this is a suit in which the government is suing itself, and must necessarily fail to present a case or controversy under the well established proposition that no man may sue himself.

Although the very title of the case may seem anomalous, this would certainly not be the first time that this Court has decided a case which on the surface appeared to be one in which the government was on both sides. Thus, in *Secretary of Agriculture* v. *United States,* 347 U. S. 645, the Secretary intervened in Interstate Commerce Commission proceedings on behalf of various agricultural interests, and when the case ultimately came to court the United States was required to be named as a defendant under 28 U. S. C. § 2322. The Court did not even pause to consider whether any difficulty was presented by the apparent anomaly of the United States appearing on both sides of the case, for there was no question but that a concrete controversy between the parties was presented by the Secretary's challenge to various Commission orders. The issue, it would seem, had been decided by the earlier case of *United States* v. *Interstate Commerce Commission,* 337 U. S. 426, in which the government, as a shipper, sought review of the Commission's determination that various railroads need not make reparations to the government for charges allegedly in violation of the Interstate Commerce Act. Again the United States was required to be named as a defendant in the suit, so that it literally appeared on both sides of the case. The Attorney General was required to appear for the United States as defendant, under 28 U. S. C. § 2322, yet the Attorney General also brought this suit on the government's behalf. Thus the Attorney General was also quite literally the attorney for parties on either side of the action. On this basis the three-judge District Court had dismissed the action without reaching the merits, on the theory that the Government could not maintain a suit against itself. This Court reversed.

The opinion for the Court by Justice Black is instructive, and is based upon the proposition that "courts must look behind the names that symbolize the parties to determine whether a justiciable case or controversy is presented." 337 U. S., at 430. It was clear that the basic question presented, whether the railroads had illegally extracted sums of money from the United States, "was a question of the type which are traditionally justiciable," *ibid.*, and the formal appearance of the Attorney General for the Government as a statutory defendant was held no bar because in reality the Commission and the Railroads, as the real parties in interest, "vigorously defended." *Id.*, at 432. The Court rejected the notion that Congress, by making the Government a statutory defendant in all cases brought against the I. C. C., "intended to make it impossible for the Government to press a just claim which could be vindicated only by a court challenge of a Commission order." *Id.*, at 431.

Considered in this light it would seem that there is the requisite "adversity" here between the parties presenting a genuine case or controversy, and the underlying issue, whether a trial subpoena under Rule 17 (c) of the Federal Rules of Criminal Procedure ought to be quashed, is clearly "a question of the type which are traditionally justiciable." There is certainly no doubt that each party is vigorously represented. If this case is different, therefore, it must be because the Special Prosecutor somehow stands on a different footing than the Interstate Commerce Commission, an independent agency. Close examination of this point, however, compels the contrary conclusion.

The Special Prosecutor is not an appointee of the President, but of the Attorney General, and the Attorney General's authority to create and fill this position derives directly from Congress rather than the President. See 28 U. S. C. §§ 509, 510, 515, 533, and 535. This is in accord with the Congress' constitutional authority under Art. II, § 2, "to vest the appointment of such inferior officers, as they think proper, in the President alone, in

the Courts of Law, or in the Heads of Departments."
Congressional power over these "inferior officers" is rather
complete, and this Court has held that when exercising
its power under this clause the Congress may, for example,
provide restraints on the Department Head's power to
remove the officer. *United States* v. *Perkins,* 116 U. S.
483. Additionally, because the power to appoint has
been placed in the Department Head, he only has the
power to remove absent any contrary rule established by
Congress. *Myers* v. *United States,* 272 U. S. 52, 161–162,
disapproved on other grounds, *Humphrey's Executor* v,
United States, 295 U. S. 602, 626.

Thus, although the President has the constitutional
obligation to see that the laws are faithfully executed, he
does not have the power directly to remove an inferior
officer appointed by the Attorney General under his statutory authority; nor does he have the authority to direct
the course of any individual litigation, for Congress has
explicitly vested that authority in the Attorney General,
28 U. S. C. § 516. This reality was demonstrated in
rather practical terms when the President sought the
termination of Special Prosecutor Archibald Cox; his
only means of obtaining it was to secure an Attorney
General who would carry out his wishes. The famous
battle of President Jackson over the Bank of the United
States illustrates the same point; the President sought
withdrawal of deposits from the Bank, but Congress had
entrusted that function to the Secretary of the Treasury,
and Jackson went through three secretaries before finding
one who would follow his wishes. Van Deusen, The
Jacksonian Era, 1828–1848, at 80–82 (1959).

In the present case the Attorney General has explicitly
exercised his authority under 28 U. S. C. § 510, authorizing him to delegate any of his functions, to make a very
broad delegation to the Special Prosecutor. That delegation is spelled out in regulations issued by the Attorney
General pursuant to his authority under 5 U. S. C. § 501,
and vest in the Special Prosecutor virtually all of the
Attorney General's statutory authority to control the

course of investigations and litigation related to "all offenses arising out of the 1972 Presidential Election for which the Special Prosecutor deems it necessary and appropriate to assume responsibility, allegations involving the President, members of the White House staff, or Presidential appointees, and any other matters which he consents to have assigned to him by the Attorney-General." 38 Fed. Reg., at 30739. In particular, the Special Prosecutor was given full authority, *inter alia,* for "determining whether or not to contest the assertion of 'Executive Privilege' or any other testimonial privilege." *Ibid.* The regulations then go on to provide:

> "In exercising this authority, the Special Prosecutor will have the greatest degree of independence that is consistent with the Attorney-General's statutory accountability for all matters falling within the jurisdiction of the Department of Justice. The Attorney General will not countermand or interfere with the Special Prosecutor's decisions or actions. The Special Prosecutor will determine whether and to what extent he will inform or consult with the Attorney General about the conduct of his duties and responsibilities. In accordance with assurances given by the President to the Attorney General that the President will not exercise his Constitutional powers to effect the discharge of the Special Prosecutor or to limit the independence he is hereby given, the Special Prosecutor will not be removed from his duties except for extraordinary improprieties on his part and without the President's first consulting the Majority and Minority Leaders and Chairman and ranking Minority Members of the Judiciary Committees of the Senate and the House of Representatives and ascertaining that their consensus is in accord with his proposed action."

A subsequent amendment to the regulations added at the end of the above quoted paragraph that "the jurisdiction of the Special Prosecutor will not be limited without the President's first consulting with such members of Congress and ascertaining that their consensus is in accord with his proposed action." 38 Fed. Reg. 32,805. Thus not only has the Attorney General vested broad authority in his appointee, the Special Prosecutor, but he has provided by regulation, "in accordance with assurances given the Attorney General by the President," that the President will not direct him to terminate or limit the authority of the Special Prosecutor without first obtaining the approval of specified members of Congress.

There can be no question that the delegation of authority to the Special Prosecutor is lawful, and the regulations so providing have the force of law, *Accardi* v. *Shaughnessy*, 347 U. S. 260, 265. In *Accardi* the Attorney General had issued regulations creating three administrative levels below himself to consider, *inter alia*, applications to suspend the deportation of an alien, an exercise of discretion entrusted to the Attorney General by Congress. Although the regulations provided for the possibility of ultimate review by the Attorney General, the regulations clearly required that the initial decisions be made at a lower level, with appeal to a Board of Immigration Appeals which had been delegated by the Attorney General "such discretion and power conferred upon the Attorney General by law. . . ." *Id.*, at 266. The Board was appointed by the Attorney General and served at his pleasure, *ibid.*, and in Accardi he had in effect instructed the Board to deny the petitioner's application for suspension. The Court held that the Board's resulting denial was unlawful because it had been deprived of the discretion which the Attorney General had delegated to it. "[A]s long as the regulations remain operative, the Attorney General denies himself the right to sidestep the Board or dictate its decision in any manner." *Id.*, at 267.

Accardi is but one of a number of cases requiring a department to honor the regulations it has promulgated. In *Vitarelli* v. *Seaton*, 359 U. S. 535, the Secretary of State dismissed an employee without affording him certain procedural safeguards guaranteed by department regulations as to dismissals based upon grounds of national security. Although by statute the Secretary was authorized to dismiss employees in petitioner's class summarily, the Court held the dismissal unlawful, "Having chosen to proceed against petitioner on security grounds, the Secretary . . was bound by the regulations which he himself had promulgated for dealing with such cases, even though without such regulations he could have discharged petitioner summarily." *Id.,* at 539–540. And see *Service v. Dulles,* 354 U. S. 363; *Peters v. Hobby,* 349 U. S. 331.

The result is that the Attorney General is clearly bound by his own regulations regarding the Special Prosecutor, and by law the Attorney General is the only person with authority to either terminate or limit the Special Prosecutor's authority. It is on this basis that the termination of former Special Prosecutor Archibald Cox, to whom almost identical regulations applied, was held unlawful. *Nader v. Bork,* 366 F. Supp. 104 (D. D. C. 1973). So long as these regulations remain in effect, then the Watergate Special Prosecution Force is effectively a quasi-independent agency, and the Special Prosecutor is vested with the final and exclusive authority under 28 U. S. C. § 516 to secure evidence for a prosecution within his jurisdiction. His decisions in these matters is by law reviewable only by the Attorney General, and the Attorney General has by valid regulations delegated all his authority in the matter to the Special Prosecutor. Without doubt the President could cause the regulations to be revoked either by so directing the then incumbent Attorney General, or by finding a new Attorney General if the present incumbent refuses to follow such a directive. But of course the President has not chosen to follow such a course, and this case must be decided by reference to the law and regulations currently in force, not those which might at some future time be enacted or promulgated.

It therefore necessarily follows that the present case

presents a genuine controversy within the jurisdiction of
the court. The parties are truly adverse. The Special
Prosecutor, as the only party with authority to act on
behalf of the United States in this matter, seeks evidence
in connection with the trial in *United States v. Mitchell
et al.*, currently pending in the District Court for the District of Columbia, and the President is an adverse party
opposing the production of that evidence. The question
of whether the subpoena should be quashed is clearly a
justiciable one, and this Court therefore has jurisdiction.[1]

This is the only conclusion which comports with the
realities of the situation. The office of the Special Prosecutor was established explicitly to be an independent
agency in response to the public demand for a prosecutor
who was not subject to the direction of the President
whose activities are intertwined with the investigations
which need be conducted. Following the illegal firing
of the previous Special Prosecutor, *Nader v. Bork, supra,*
various bills were introduced in the Congress to re-estab-
lish the office as agency which by law would be wholly
independent of the President, see S. Rep. No. 93–595
and No. 93–596, 93d Cong., 1st Sess. That legislation
was dropped on the basis of assurances to the Congress
that the current regulations would provide the same result, and that this Special Prosecutor would be wholly
independent under them. See Hearings before the Senate
Committee on the Judiciary on the Special Prosecutor,
93d Cong., 1st Sess., pt. 2, at 571–573. On this basis the
regulations included the extraordinary provisions requiring the President to obtain the consent of specified Mem-

---

[1] As Justice Frankfurter once said, "So strongly were the framers
of the Constitution bent on securing a reign of law that they endowed
the judicial office with extraordinary safeguards and prestige. No
one, no matter how exalted his public office or how righteous his
private motive, can be judge in his own case. That is what courts
are for. And no type of controversy is more peculiarly fit for judicial determination than a controversy that calls into question the
power of a court to decide." *United States v. Mine Workers*, 330
U. S. 258, 308–309.

bers of Congress ² before exercising his authority to direct
the Attorney General to terminate or limit the Special
Prosecutor's authority.   See letter from Acting Attorney
General Bork to Special Prosecutor Leon Jaworski, November 21, 1973.   Indeed, the central concern was to
guarantee the Special Prosecutor's freedom to determine
on his own authority if there was evidence in the President's possession which was necessary to carry on his
duties and his right to seek judicial process if necessary
to secure that evidence.   See Hearings, *supra*.   The Attorney General has repeatedly given assurances that the
Special Prosecutor is wholly independent in this regard.³

The regulations were carefully drafted to ensure the
Special Prosecutor's independence in response to these
concerns, and they are unambiguous.   It would be inconsistent with the law, those regulations, and the facts
of this case to conclude anything other than that the
Special Prosecutor has standing to bring this action on
behalf of the United States, and that a justiciable case
or controversy is presented for the Court's decision.

III

The words "Executive Privilege" do not appear in the
Constitution.   Article II, § 1 vests "the executive power"
in the President.   Whether in some circumstances the
executive power carries with it an "executive privilege"
to be immune from process running either from the Congress or the federal courts is a question we need not reach

---

² Cf *Humphrey's Executor v United States*, 295 U. S. 602, and
Wiener v United States 357 U. S. 349, limiting the power of the
President to remove a commissioner who has been confirmed by the
Senate and performs adjudicatory function.

³ "Q. Mr. Bork, you may have stated in generally, but so it is
perfectly clear and specific, it is clearly understood by you and
by Mr. Jaworski that he is free to go to court to press for additional tapes or Presidential papers if he deems it necessary?

"THE ACTING ATTORNEY GENERAL.   That is absolutely
clear "

Press conference of Acting Attorney General Bork, November 1,
1973.

in this case. For this case in its starkest and simplest
terms involves a narrow and it would seem almost a
frivolous question. It is whether any part of the "judicial power of the United States" which Art. III, § 1
vests in the federal courts can by insistence of the President on "executive privilege" be shared by him.

That is the central issue in this case. There has been
an indictment against named individuals and an actual
trial of six of them underway for alleged violations of
federal laws. Article II, § 3 provides that the President
"shall take care that the laws be faithfully executed."
The "laws" of the United States plainly include not only
Acts of Congress but judgments of the federal courts.
His power of nomination of federal judges granted by
Art. II, § 2 gives him a nexus with the federal judicial
system. And the power bestowed by the same section
"to grant reprieves and pardons for offenses against the
United States, except in cases of impeachment" em-
powers him to act to relieve convicts of judgments
rendered against them. But there is nothing in the Constitution that allows him to shape, condition, or participate in the judicial process. Nor does it contain a
statement of any immunity that he has from the duty
to obey Acts of Congress or judgments of courts.

When the Fifth Amendment speaks of due process, it
speaks in terms of "any person." When the Sixth Amendment speaks of "criminal prosecutions," it speaks of "the
accused." The federal laws enacted by Congress customarily contain these generalities—excepting neither
judges, Senators, Congressmen, Ambassadors, cabinet officers, or any federal civil or military personnel. Income
tax evasion, smuggling of drugs into the country, acceptance of bribes to perform official duties, election frauds,
deprivation of civil rights of others—these theoretically
could all be committed by any person from the President
on down. The Speech or Debate Clause of § 6 of Art. I
gives Members of Congress protection for liability for
what they say "in either House." Moreover, a President
no more than a judge can be sued for action taken in good

faith but later found to have been erroneous as where a trial judge is overruled on appeal or a President who removes a commissioner from a bureau is later held to have acted beyond the scope of his authority. But any official—whether a President or one of a lowlier status—who conspires to violate a federal law stands on the same footing as any common criminal, so far as indictments by grand juries are concerned. Whether there are limitations on criminal prosecutions of a President are questions that need not be reached here. They need mention solely because of the possible rivalry between a common criminal prosecution of a President and the impeachment procedure prescribed by Art. I of the Constitution.

The President appoints with the advice and consent of the Senate an Attorney General. It was once assumed by virtue of *Myers* v. *United States*, 272 U. S. 52, that one nominated by the President could be removed by the President. But subsequent decisions have altered that doctrine. Humphrey, removed by Franklin D. Roosevelt from the Federal Trade Commission, was held to be lawfully entitled to the office, *Humphrey's Executor* v. *United States*, 295 U. S. 602, and later a War Claims Commissioner removed by Eisenhower was held to have been unlawfully removed. *Wiener* v. *United States*, 357 U. S. 349. In both the *Humphrey* and the *Wiener* cases, the person removed had not only been confirmed by the Senate but also was performing adjudicatory functions as commissioner, comparable to a judicial function. An Attorney General serves a different role. As chief law enforcement official, he operates to see to it that the laws are enforced equally and honestly against all. Whether if he moved to indict a President for violating a federal law the President could end the matter by removing the Attorney General is an unresolved question we need not reach. For here the person seeking aid of the "judicial power" of Art. III to obtain documents the President has is a Special Prosecutor, named by the President after the President had removed from that office Archibald Cox. The present Special Prosecutor was chosen by the President with a promise to the Congress that he would not be removed except with the concurrence of the Congress. No effort has been made to remove him. The source of the authority behind the present Special Prosecutor is relevant here only to emphasize the weight of his authority, there being nothing in the background of his designation to indicate that the procedures he follows are to be less pervasive than those which the law of the land both permits and requires.

As noted by the Court of Appeals in *Nixon v. Sirica*, 487 F. 2d 700, 708 *et seq.*, this Court has, on numerous occasions, found it appropriate to issue compulsory process against officials of the Executive Branch. See, *e. g., Youngstown Sheet & Tube Co. v. Sawyer*, 343 U. S. 579 (1952), *Kendall v. United States ex rel. Stokes*, 12 Pet. (37 U. S.) 524 (1838). This has been true even when the clear and explicit thrust of the Court's action has been to restrain the desires or commands of the President himself, as in *Youngstown Sheet & Tube Co. v. Sawyer*, *supra*. Of course, considerations of comity have normally resulted in process being directed to lower executive officials rather than to the President himself; nevertheless; where the President has taken personal custody of disputed property and thereby placed himself personally in the midst of the controversy, the interests of justice may require that comity give way and that process issue, if necessary, against the President himself.

Such was the result in *United States v. Burr*, 25 Fed. Cas. 30 (No. 14,692d) (C. C. D. Va. 1807), in which Chief Justice Marshall approved the issuance of a subpoena *duces tecum* to President Jefferson for the production of certain correspondence between the President and one General Wilkinson. The Chief Justice found no basis for any Presidential immunity to process:

"In the provisions of the constitution, and of the statute, which give to the accused a right to the compulsory process of the court, there is no exception whatever. The obligation, therefore, of those provisions is general; . . . if an exception to the general principle exist, it must be looked for in the law of evidence." *Id.,* at 34.

Any attempt to analogize the situation of the President to that of the king, to whom English law granted immunity from process, was rejected. The Chief Justice found the only possible objection to issuance of a subpoena against the President to be the practical consideration that compliance might interfere with his duties as chief executive; and even this consideration was found to be no bar to the *issuance* of a subpoena, since

"[t]he guard, furnished to this high officer, to protect him from being harassed by vexatious and unnecessary subpoenas, is to be looked for in the conduct of a court *after* those subpoenas have issued; not in any circumstance which is to precede their being issued." *Ibid.* (emphasis added).

He therefore concluded, with some reluctance, that a subpoena could and must issue:

"It cannot be denied that to issue a subpoena to a person filling the exalted position of the chief magistrate is a duty which would be dispensed with more cheerfully than it would be performed; but, if it be a duty, the court can have no choice in the case." *Ibid.*

As noted by the Chief Justice, *supra,* the Constitution makes no express mention of any Presidential immunities; this silence is in marked contrast to the specific immunities from arrest and inquiry granted to legislators by the "Speech and Debate" Clause, Art. I, § 6, cl. 1 of the Constitution. Nor can the principle of separation of powers be read to confer such immunity on the President; for his position as guardian and executor of the laws does not authorize him to flout or disregard those laws, but rather dictates that he be scrupulous in observing and abiding by them. As this Court stated in *United States v. Lee,* 106 U. S. 196, 220 (1882):

"No man in this country is so high that he is above the law. No officer of the law may set that law at defiance, with impunity.   All the officers of the Government, from the highest to the lowest, are creatures of the law and are bound to obey it.

"It is the only supreme power in our system of government, and every man who, by accepting office, participates in its functions, is only the more strongly bound to submit to that supremacy, and to observe the limitations which it imposes upon the exercise of the authority which it gives."

Respondent contends that, even if process may properly issue to him, he has an absolute privilege to withhold the subpoenaed information if he determines that disclosure would be contrary to the public interest.   He further contends that, by virtue of the absolute nature of that privilege, the courts have no power to review or question his decision to invoke the privilege.   Petitioner, on the other hand, contends that it is for the courts to assess the validity of a claim of privilege interposed to prevent disclosure of evidence for use in a criminal prosecution.

In support of their respective contentions, both parties have gathered and presented a considerable quantity of historical precedent and critical comment.   Nearly 200 years of disputes have produced a pattern marked by Executive assertions of absolute privilege to withhold information, rejection of such assertions by the Judicial and Legislative Branches, and a general reluctance of any of the branches to pursue the issue to an apocalyptic resolution.   The historical path is, for the most part, littered with practical compromises and practical retreats. Nevertheless, as far as the Judicial Branch is concerned, it is clear that the courts have neither recognized nor enforced an absolute privilege against disclosure by the Executive.

In *United States v. Burr,* 25 Fed. Cas. 187 (No. 14,694) (C. C. D. Va. 1807), Chief Justice Marshall was confronted with further proceedings concerning the correspondence between General Wilkinson and President Jefferson.   The United States Attorney, acting on behalf of the President, sought to withhold portions of one letter on the ground that the contents ought not to be made public. The Chief Justice was evidently troubled by the idea of second-guessing the President's determination that the matter should not be disclosed; nevertheless, he clearly indicated his belief that the President's claim of privilege was subject to review by the courts, and would be enforced only where the reasons asserted appeared sufficient to the court.

"The president, although subject to the general rules which apply to others, may have sufficient motives for declining to produce a particular paper, and those motives *may be* such as to restrain the court from enforcing its production. . . . I can readily conceive that the president might receive a letter which it would be improper to exhibit in public, because of the manifest inconvenience of its exposure. *The occasion for demanding it ought, it such a case, to be very strong, and to be fully shown to the court before its production could be insisted on. . . .*

". . . Perhaps the court ought to consider the reasons which would induce the president to refuse to exhibit such a letter as conclusive on it, *unless such letter could be shown to be absolutely necessary in the defence.* The president may himself state the particular reasons which may have induced him to withhold a paper, and the court would unquestionably allow their full force to those reasons. At the same time, the court could not refuse to pay proper attention to the affidavit of the accused. But on objections being made by the president to the production of a paper, the court would not proceed further in the case *without such an affidavit as would clearly shew the paper to be essential to the justice of the case. . . .*

". . . Had the president, when he transmitted it, subjected it to certain restrictions, and stated that in his judgment the public interest required certain parts of it to be kept secret, and had accordingly made a reservation of them, *all proper respect would*

have been paid to it . . . ." 25 Fed. Cas., at 191–
192 (emphasis added).

It is evident from the quoted passages that while the
Chief Justice was willing to give all due consideration
to the justifications advanced by the President for withholding the evidence in question, he fully recognized that
the ultimate determination as to the sufficiency of those
reasons, when balanced against the materiality of the
evidence to the defense, would have to be made by the
court.

That principle was followed by this Court in *United
States v. Reynolds*, 345 U. S. 1 (1953), in which the
Government sought to rely on a claimed Executive power
to withhold documents in order to bar production of
certain Air Force documents at the request of a private
tort plaintiff. While recognizing the existence of a privilege protecting military and state secrets, the Court stated
that "[j]udicial control over the evidence in a case cannot be abdicated to the caprice of executive officers."
Id., at 9–10.

In the instant case, of course, respondent does not contend that the subpoenaed materials contain military or
state secrets but claims a privilege for "intra-govern-
mental documents reflecting advisory opinions, recommendations and deliberations comprising part of a process
by which governmental decisions and policies are formulated." *Carl Zeiss Stiftung v. V. E. B. Carl Zeiss, Jena*,
40 F. R. D. 318, 324 (D. D. C. 1966), aff'd on opinion below, —— U. S. App. D. C. ——, 384 F. 2d 979 (1967).
Yet as we recently noted in *Environmental Protection
Agency v. Mink*, 410 U. S. 73 (1973), disputed memoranda have normally been required to be produced for
in camera inspection in order to determine whether they
should be disclosed or withheld on the basis of a claimed
privilege.[4] *Id.*, at 87–88 and n. 15.

---

[4] Such a procedure is, of course, impermissible where a privilege
holder relies upon his Fifth Amendment privilege against self-

In *Nixon v. Sirica, supra,* the Special Prosecutor sought to obtain specified tape recordings of presidential conversations for presentation to a grand jury. The Court of Appeals found that the Special Prosecutor had made a "uniquely powerful showing" that the requested tapes were essential to the performance of the grand jury's function; and the court further found that a particularly compelling public interest would be served by disclosure, in light of the grand jury's vital dual function of not only indicting those as to whom probable cause to believe that they engaged in criminal activity may be shown, but also refusing to indict persons as to whom probable cause cannot be shown and thereby sparing such persons the ordeal of an unwarranted trial. 487 F. 2d, at 717.

The instant case, of course, involves materials sought by the Special Prosecutor for use in impending criminal prosecutions. The bulk of the cases in which executive privilege has been discussed have been civil suits. In the context of a criminal prosecution, however, recent decisions of this Court seem clearly to compel the conclusion that no executive privilege can be recognized as a justification for the suppression of evidence material to the issues of guilt or innocence. Where the liberty of an accused is at stake, the Government's desire for secrecy cannot be permitted, in the name of executive privilege, to override the constitutional demands for a fair trial.[5]

Under our decision *Brady v. Maryland,* 373 U. S. 83, a prosecutor who has in his possession or available information of an exculpatory nature commits reversible error if he does not submit that evidence to the defense. The error is kin to allowing the trial to go forward on

---

incrimination. The President, however, apparently made no effort to introduce that particular privilege into these proceedings.

[5] See *Gravel v. United States,* 408 U. S. 606, 644–646 (DOUGLAS, J., dissenting).

evidence known to the prosecutor to be false. *Mooney v. Holohan,* 294 U. S. 103. In neither case is due process satisfied unless full disclosure is made.

If there is a doubt whether the undisclosed evidence is exculpatory and aids the defense or is incriminatory and aids the prosecution, the practice is to deliver the material *in camera* to the trial court who makes the necessary finding on materiality and relevance of the secret information or data. That was the procedure we adopted in *Alderman v. United States,* 394 U. S. 165, for examining the content of wiretaps which were alleged to have been unlawfully made

The present case is technically different from our earlier ones dealing with information in the possession of the prosecutor. He does not have the material sought. The President has it and refuses to turn it over to the Special Prosecutor or to Judge Sirica, who is presiding over the criminal cases against the six defendants. The *Brady* and *Alderman* procedures are protective of the rights of accused under the Fifth and Sixth Amendments. They help make sure that by executive tactics the right to a fair trial is not impaired. The President is the Chief Executive who is charged by Art. I, § 3 with taking "care that the laws be faithfully executed." It would be a travesty to twist or qualify that command by the addition of an "unless" clause which permits a President to say that his "executive privilege" can wtihhold those documents or which says that the President, rather than the court, will pass on the materiality or relevance of the withheld material in the trial of the defendants. In either case the grant of any such authority to the President would be to allow him to share the "judicial power" of Art. III. For then it would be an unreviewable *"in camera"* inspection by the President which would determine the relevance and materiality of the documents in his possession. The President is, for constitutional purposes, the chief law enforcement and prosecutorial officer in the Nation; to allow him to conceal from a court information which may be critical to the fairness of a trial of named defendants would be a monstrous affront to the rule of law under which we live.

There is another aspect of the requirements of a fair trial which delivery of the information in possession of the President to the trial court would serve.

We held in *Jencks* v. *United States*, 353 U. S. 657, that the defense in a federal criminal prosecution was entitled generally to obtain for impeachment purposes statements which had been made to government agents by government witnesses. These statements were to be turned over to the defense in time for cross-examination if their contents related to the subject matter of the witness' direct testimony. That decision was followed by an Act of Congress, 18 U. S. C. § 3500, which like the *Jencks* decision rested not on constitutional grounds but discovery procedures appropriate for federal criminal trials. Section 3500 applies not only to written statements of the witness but "mechanical, electrical, or other recording, or a transcription thereof . . . record contemporaneously with the making of such oral statements." Section 3500 permits a court to inspect the statements *in camera* where it contains matter not relevant to the case at bar. When we sustained § 3500 in *Palermo* v. *United States*, 360 U. S. 343, MR. JUSTICE BRENNAN pertinently observed:

> "This responsibility of the federal trial judge, it goes without saying, is not to be delegated to the prosecutor. Questions of production of statements are not to be solved through one party's determination that interview reports fall without the statute and hence that they are not to be produced to defense counsel or to the trial judge for his determination as to their coverage. I am confident that federal trial judges will devise procedural methods whereby their responsibility is not abdicated in favor of the unilateral determination of the prosecuting arm of the Government." *Id.*, at 361.

And see *Campbell* v. *United States,* 365 U. S. 85; 373 U. S. 487,

The reason for the Act may assure insofar as possible another aspect of the fairness of a trial. The federal agent or employee testifying as to events long past may have inaccurate recollections or may be confusing one episode with another, and the like. The Jencks Act is part of the arsenal of the law to help test the credibility and reliability of witnesses.

The six defendants in the case from Judge Sirica's court were federal agents in various capacities. They may well take the stand as witnesses. If so, the documents in possession of the President should be in possession of the trial judge, so that a trial need not be delayed while protracted collateral litigation is pursued to gain possession of those documents.

Much has been argued about the relevance or materiality of this information and we are asked to rule upon it. We, however, are far removed from the trial and not acquainted with the ramifications of the issues which are emerging. It is the part of wisdom only to hold that there is no Executive privilege of the President which justifies withholding these materials from the District Court and that they should be examined by the district judge *in camera* with power to release and make public during the trial of any portions exculpatory for the defendants or incriminating for use by the prosecution.

IV

The argument that we should examine *the evidence* before the grand jury with the view of determining that the grand jury was not justified in naming Richard M. Nixon as a co-conspirator is not, in my view, a justiciable question. It is obvious from the history of this grand jury that that finding was made for the benefit of the House Judiciary Committee which now has before it the impeachment question. So what in substance we are being asked to do is to rule that a certain bit of evidence produced by the grand jury and sent to the House Judiciary Committee is not competent evidence in impeachment proceedings. I think that beyond question that issue is a "political" issue not a justiciable one.

By Art. I, § 2 the House is given "the sole power of impeachment" and by Art. I, § 3 the Senate has "the sole power to try all impeachments." We held in *Baker v. Carr*, 369 U. S. 186, 217, that a question is "political" and not justiciable if there is found "a textually demonstrable constitutional commitment of the issue to a coordinate political department." It seems manifest that the grant of impeachment powers to the House and to the Senate is a clear demonstration of such a commitment. The rules of evidence, the standards to be applied, the weight of evidence, and all the matters pertaining to the process of impeachment are beyond the reach of judicial power. They rest exclusively in the political branch.⁶ We have no more business ruling that the grand jury had or did not have evidence which justified it in naming Nixon as a co-conspirator than we would in limiting the House to only certain categories of hearsay evidence or determining whether they should act only on the preponderance of evidence or on a showing of probable cause or on some other standard. The impeachment procedures have been left by the Congress entirely to the House and the Senate and are none of the business of this Court. So in my view we should decline to answer the fifth question presented in the cross-petition in 73–1834.

political

---

⁶ Whether the grand jury should be precluded from sending any report to the House Judiciary Committee because that committee deals solely with a ~~potential~~ issue is not pertinent here, because the naming of the President as a co-conspirator has no bearing on his duty to obey Judge Sirica's order.

JUSTICE POWELL'S DRAFT *

Proposed Part III

We are a nation governed by the rule of law. Nowhere is our commitment to this principle more profound than in the enforcement of the criminal law, "the twofold aim of which is that guilt shall not escape or innocence suffer." *Berger* v. *United States*, 295 U. S. 78, 88 (1935). Conviction of the guilty and exoneration of the innocent are matters of the greatest consequence for a people devoted to equal justice under law. Individuals are subject to criminal penalties for conduct proscribed by society. The imposition of such penalties turns on what was done and by whom and with what intent. Enforcement of the criminal law requires ascertainment of these facts. It is, in short, a search for truth.

We have committed that pursuit to an adversary system in which the parties contest all issues before a court of law. To develop their opposing contentions of fact, the parties are entitled to invoke the court's authority to compel production of relevant evidence. Because the adversary nature of our system is tempered by an overriding concern for fairness to the individual, the prosecutor has an obligation to reveal evidence that may be favorable to the defense. "The United States Attorney is the representative not of an ordinary party to a controversy, but of a sovereignty whose obligation to govern impartially is as compelling as its obligation to govern at all; and whose interest, therefore, in a criminal prosecution is not that it shall win a case, but that justice shall be done." *Berger* v. *United States, supra,* at 88. In addition, the accused has the right to a fair trial by making the best possible defense on the basis of all material evidence. And the court itself has the paramount duty to ensure that justice is done. Accordingly, the need to develop all relevant facts is both elemental and comprehensive, for the ends of the criminal law would

---

* Original in typescript.

be defeated if judgments were founded on a fragmentary or speculative presentation of the facts. To the extent that the search for truth is restrained, the integrity of the process of criminal justice is impaired. As a general proposition, therefore, the law is entitled to every man's evidence. See *Branzburg* v. *Hayes,* 408 U. S. 665, 688 (1972).

This rule, however, is not absolute. It admits of exceptions designed to protect weighty and legitimate competing interests. Thus, the Fifth Amendment to the Constitution provides that no man "shall be compelled in any criminal case to be a witness against himself." And an attorney may not be required to reveal what his client has told him in confidence. These and other interests are recognized at law by evidentiary privileges against forced disclosure. Such privileges may be established in the Constitution, by statute, or at common law. Whatever their origins, these exceptions to the demand for every man's evidence are not lightly created nor expansively construed, for they are in derogation of the search for truth.

> "The pertinent general principle, responding to the deepest needs of society, is that society is entitled to every man's evidence. As the underlying aim of judicial inquiry is ascertainable truth, everything rationally related to ascertaining the truth is presumptively admissible. Limitations are properly placed upon the operation of this general principle only to the very limited extent that permitting a refusal to testify or excluding relevant evidence has a public good transcending the normally predominant principle of utilizing all rational means for ascertaining truth." *Elkins* v. *United States,* 364 U. S. 206, 234 (1960) (dissenting opinion of Frankfurter, J.).

In this case the President challenges a subpoena requiring the production of materials for use in certain

criminal prosecutions.[1] He claims that he has a privilege against compliance with that subpoena and that his
decision not to comply is final and binding on the courts.
He does not contend that disclosure of the subpoenaed
material would compromise state secrets. There is no
claim that the conversations at issue involved matters
of military planning or intelligence, sensitive aspects of
foreign affairs, or any other data whose disclosure would
be contrary to the national interest. Rather, the President grounds his assertion of privilege in the generalized
interest in preserving the confidentiality of his discussions with his advisors. Because maintaining confidentiality for such discussions is essential to his high office,
he claims a privilege against forced disclosure. The
President further argues that only he can assess accurately the degree to which disclosure in a particular
case would impair the effective performance of his constitutional duties. Thus he asserts that the decision
whether to reveal such confidential conversations for use
in a criminal proceeding is his alone to make.

The President's argument rests in part on the nature
of government itself and in part on the tripartite division of sovereign powers within our government. All
nations find it necessary to shield from public scrutiny
some of the deliberations that constitute the process of
government. Those selected to conduct the affairs of
state must be free to speak plainly to one another and
to seek honest and forthright advice on matters of national policy. Yet human experience teaches that those
who expect public dissemination of their remarks may
temper candor with a concern for appearances. The
willingness to advance tentative ideas, to play the devil's

---

[1] In *Nixon* v. *Sirica*, 487 F. 2d 700, 708–712 (1973), there was
some question concerning the power of the courts to compel the
President to produce materials for *in camera* inspection. No such
inquiry need detain us here, for the *authority* of the courts to say
what the law is does not depend on their *power* to secure compliance. *Kendal* v. *United States ex rel. Stokes,* 12 Pet. (37 U. S.)
524, 613 (1838).

advocate, and to reveal the ultimate basis for a particular view may succumb to public posturing and a reticence born of the fear of appearing foolish. That consequence would distort and impair the search for sound public policy. Accordingly, a general expectation of confidentiality for deliberations among the officers of government and their advisors serves the public good.[2]

The Framers of our Constitution understood this point. When they undertook to draft the Charter for a fledgling nation, they chose not to hold their debates in public. Rather, they maintained the secrecy of their discussions until well after ratification of the Constitution by the States. Modern practice reflects continued appreciation of the insight of the Framers. For example, the House-Senate Conference Committees that meet to resolve differences in bills that have passed both Houses hold their proceedings in confidence. Similarly, the deliberations of this Court are conducted in utmost secrecy. In these and other instances, officers of government need to be able to rely on an expectation of confidentiality to facilitate plain talk.

That the need for confidentiality exists in any government does not mean, however, that it must always prevail over competing societal interests. See, *e. g., Conway* v. *Rimmer,* 1 A11 E. R. 874 (1968). Some greater public good may warrant occasional inroads into the principle of confidentiality. The President does not contest this proposition but contends that he has final and unreviewable authority to decide whether competing considerations outweigh the generalized need for confidentiality

---

[2] "Freedom of communication vital to fulfillment of wholesome relationships is obtained only by removing the specter of compelled disclosure. . . . [G]overnment . . . needs open but protected channels for the kind of plain talk that is essential to the quality of its functioning." *Carl Zeiss Stiftung* v. *V. E. B. Carl Zeiss, Jena,* 40 F.R.D. 318, 325 (DDC 1966). See *Nixon* v. *Sirica,* —— U. S. App. D. C. ——, ——, 487 F. 2d 700, 713 (1973) ; *Kaiser Aluminum & Chem. Corp.* v. *United States,* 157 F. Supp. 939 (Ct Cl 1958) (*per* Reed, J.) ; *The Federalist* No. 64 (S. F. Mittel ed. 1938).

in a particular instance. In a unitary government no serious question arises concerning who has authority to make this determination. There both the interest in confidentiality and whatever conflicting interests may be at stake reside in the government as a whole. In our system of limited government and diffuse powers, the inquiry is more complicated.

Under our Constitution the people have delegated their sovereignty to three coordinate but independent branches. To each the Constitution commits specified functions and lodges in each the powers essential to the effective performance of those duties. The three branches rest in a state of formal equilibrium, each restraining the capacity of the others to work harm, for the Framers feared tyranny by those who govern more than they valued efficiency in government. As James Madison made the point, "[t]he accumulation of all powers, legislative, executive, and judiciary, in the same hands, whether of one, a few, or many, and whether hereditary, self-appointed, or elective, may justly be pronounced the very definition of tyranny." *The Federalist,* No. 47, p. 313 (S. F. Mittel ed. 1938).[3] The Framers therefore structured our Constitution around the fundamental principle of separation of powers. Definition of the precise contours of that concept in a particular case is, of course, a task for the courts. The assignment of powers among the branches and the limitations on those powers are matters of fundamental law, and "[i]t is emphatically the province and duty of the judicial department to say what the law is." *Marbury* v. *Madison,* 1 Cranch 137, 177 (1803).

The principle of separation of powers requires us to determine at the outset not whether in this or any other case we find some greater public good outweighing the

---

[3] In the words of Mr. Justice Brandeis, "[t]he doctrine of separation of powers was adopted by the Convention of 1787 not to promote efficiency but to preclude the exercise of arbitrary power." *Myers* v. *United States,* 272 U. S. 52, 293 (1926). (dissenting opinion).

generalized need for confidentiality, but rather who is empowered under our Constitution to make that decision. That question—who has constitutional authority to balance the competing interests in a particular instance—is at base an issue of separation of powers.

The President contends that due regard for that concept requires us to hold that he and he alone may make that decision. Preserving confidentiality for discussions with his advisors assists him in the effective exercise of his executive powers. Article II vests those powers exclusively in him. Therefore, he argues, the decision whether to sacrifice confidentiality in a particular case is similarly committed exclusively to his discretion and cannot be reviewed or overridden by the judicial branch. With all respect, we find nothing in the concept of separation of powers that compels this conclusion.

The constitutional structure embodied in that phrase makes each of the three departments supreme in its sphere, but it also requires each to respect the authority of the others. Separation implies interaction as well as independence:

> "While the Constitution diffuses power the better to secure liberty, it also contemplates that practice will integrate the dispersed powers into a workable government. It enjoins upon its branches separateness but interdependence, autonomy but reciprocity." *Youngstown Sheet & Tube Co.* v. *Sawyer,* 343 U. S. 579, 635 (1952) (concurring opinion of Jackson, J.).

In many respects the interaction of the powers of the branches is expressly detailed in the Constitution. So, for example, the Congress may legislate and the President may veto, only to have his veto overridden by a two-thirds vote of both Houses. In other instances, the authority of one branch or another to make a particular decision is not expressly stated. It is determined by the relationship of the matter in question to the specifically enumerated powers. This is such a case.

The Constitution explicitly mentions neither the President's interest in confidentiality nor the judiciary's need for every man's evidence in the enforcement of the criminal laws. Nor does that document expressly declare the mode of interaction between those competing concerns. Yet to the extent that the interest in confidentiality pertains to the President's effective exercise of his executive powers, it is nevertheless constitutionally based. And because the production of all material evidence in a criminal trial furthers the judiciary's constitutional mandate to do justice, it is a matter of constitutional import. Both Article II and Article III are involved here. The defect in the President's argument in favor of unqualified and unreviewable discretion to withhold the subpoenaed materials is that it derives solely by inference from his enumerated powers; it ignores the countervailing demands of Article III. Far from compelling this approach, the concept of separated powers counsels against it, for preservation of the state of dynamic equilibrium implicit in our tripartite structure of government requires analysis of both aspects of the problem. It also requires that the resolution of the competing interests in this case be accomplished in a manner that accords maximum possible protection to the needs of each branch. As this analysis indicates, the ultimate authority to decide whether in a particular case confidentiality must give way to some greater public interest resides in that branch whose constitutional responsibilities are more gravely affected.

We must balance the essentiality of an unreviewable privilege to the President's performance of the responsibilities vested in him against the inroads of such a privilege on the duties committed to the Judiciary.[4] The

---

[4] We wish to emphasize the narrow scope of this inquiry. We are not here concerned with the balance between the President's generalized interest in confidentiality and the Judiciary's need for relevant evidence in civil litigation, nor with that between the confidentiality interest and Congressional demands for information, nor with that between the President's interest in preserving state se-

interest in confidentiality, as distinct from the preservation of state secrets, is a generalized concern. The goal is to promote candor by maintaining an expectation of confidentiality rather than to preserve secrecy for the substance of any particular communication. The asserted need for unreviewable presidential discretion to refuse to comply with a subpoena presumes that rare and isolated instances of disclosure would negate the general expectation of confidentiality and thus defeat the ability of the President to obtain candid advice. We think that this assumption is unfounded. The willingness to speak plainly is not so fragile that it would be undermined by some remote prospect of disclosure in narrowly defined and isolated circumstances. At least this is true where the prospect of disclosure is limited to demands for evidence demonstrably material to a criminal prosecution. It requires no clairvoyance to foresee that such demands will arise with the greatest infrequency nor any special insight to recognize that few advisors will be moved to temper the candor of their remarks by such an unlikely possibility.[5] Thus, while the

crets and any other concern, whether originating in Congress or the courts. We address only the conflict between the President's assertion of unreviewable authority to decide whether to divulge confidential conversations and the Judiciary's need for evidence material to criminal trials.

[5] Mr. Justice Cardozo made this point in an analogous context. Speaking for a unanimous Court in *Clark* v. *United States*, 289 U. S. 1 (1933), he emphasized the importance of maintaining the secrecy of the deliberations of a petit jury in a criminal case. "Freedom of debate might be stifled and independence of thought checked if jurors were made to feel that their arguments and ballots were to be freely published to the world." *Id.*, at 13. Nonetheless, the Court also recognized that isolated inroads on confidentiality designed to serve the paramount need of the criminal law would not vitiate the interests served by secrecy:

A juror of integrity and reasonable firmness will not fear to speak his mind if the confidences of debate are barred to the ears of mere impertinence or malice. He will not expect to be shielded against the disclosure of his conduct in the event that there is evidence reflecting upon his honor. The chance that general interest in confidentiality is weighty indeed, it is not significantly impaired by the demands of criminal justice.

On the other hand, an unqualified privilege against disclosure of evidence demonstrably relevant to a criminal trial would cut deeply into the role of the Judiciary under Article III. While the President's interest in confidentiality is general in nature, the courts' need for production of material evidence in a criminal proceeding is not. The enforcement of the criminal laws does not depend on an assessment of the broad sweep of events but on a limited number of specific historical facts concerning the conduct of identified individuals at given times. The President's broad interest in confidentiality would not be vitiated by disclosure of a limited number of confidential conversations, but nondisclosure of those same conversations could gravely impair the pursuit of truth in a criminal prosecution.

Thus where the President's ground for withholding subpoenaed materials from use in a criminal trial is only the generalized interest in confidentiality, his decision is not binding on the courts. He may be ordered, in a proper case, to produce the requested materials.[6] We do

---

now and then there may be found some timid soul who will take counsel of his fears and give way to their repressive power is too remote and shadowy to shape the course of justice. Id., at 16.

[6] No prior case from this or any other court resolves the precise issue before us. Earlier precedents cited by the parties have dealt with state secrets, *e. g., United States* v. *Reynolds,* 345 U. S. 1 (1953), with claims of executive privilege by subordinate executive officers in the context of civil trials, *e. g., ibid; Committee for Nuclear Responsibility, Inc.* v. *Seaborg,* —— App. D. C. ——, 463 F. 2d 788 (1971) ; *Kaiser Aluminum & Chemical Corp.* v. *United States,* 157 F. Supp. 939 (Ct. Cl. 1958) ; *Carl Zeiss Stiftung* v. *V. E. B. Carl Zeiss, Jena,* 40 F.R.D. 318 (CD 1966), aff'd on opinion below, 384 F. 2d 979 (CADC 1967), cert. denied, 389 U. S. 952 (1968), or with the unique responsibilities and powers of a grand jury. See *Nixon* v. *Sirica,* —— App. D. C. ——, 487 F. 2d 700 (1973). Nevertheless, our conclusion is in full accord with the principle underlying all of those cases—that in the final analysis it is the duty of a

not reach this conclusion lightly nor do we wish to suggest that courts may presume to order the President of the United States to produce confidential materials absent compelling justification. The avoidance of unnecessary harassment of our Chief Executive, the importance of the expectation of confidentiality for his discussions with his advisors, and proper deference to the head of a coordinate branch of government who is himself charged by the Constitution to "take Care that the Laws be faithfully executed" suggest that courts should be as reluctant to tread this ground as the sound discharge of their constitutional responsibilities will allow. Courts must follow certain standards and procedures to assure that the President's legitimate interests are adequately protected. It is to those requirements that we now turn.

Proposed Part IV

In determining whether to order the President to produce records of confidential communications for use in a criminal trial, a court should be guided by a solicitous concern for the effective discharge of his duties and the dignity of his high office. Of course, no citizen should be subjected to unwarranted inroads on his time or interruptions of his affairs, but the public interest in preserving the confidentiality of the Oval Office and in avoiding vexatious harassment of an incumbent President is of an entirely different order of importance. Consequently, we believe that "[i]n no case of this kind would a court be required to proceed against the President as against an ordinary individual." *United States* v. *Burr*, 25 Fed. Cas. 187, 191 (No. 14964), (CCD Va. 1807) (*per* Marshall, C. J.). Rather, courts should follow standards and procedures designed to afford the greatest possible protection for the legitimate interests of the presidency consistent with the overriding duty to ensure that justice is done.

---

court to determine whether a claim of executive privilege must give way in a particular instance.

Ordering the President to produce confidential records for use in a criminal proceeding involves three decisional stages: issuance of the subpoena, return of the subpoena, and *in camera* inspection. The decision whether to issue a subpoena *duces tecum* to the President is governed by the same standard applicable to citizens generally. "The guard, furnished to this high officer, is to be looked for in the conduct of the court after the subpoenas have issued; not in any circumstance which is to proceed their being issued." *United States* v. *Burr,* 25 Fed. Cas. 30, 34 (No. 14,692d) (CCD Va. 1807) (*per* Marshall, C. J.). The standard is stated in Rule 17 of the Federal Rules of Criminal Procedure. It requires a defined showing of relevance and forbids fishing expeditions. Faced with a judicial determination that Rule 17 has been satisfied, the President may well forego any claim of executive privilege. After all, he is charged by the Constitution with the duty to "take Care that the Laws be faithfully executed" and will doubtless be aware of the needs of the criminal justice system. If, however, the President decides that release of the subpoenaed materials would prove injurious to the public interest, he may invoke executive privilege for his confidential communications and so indicate on the return of the subpoena.

It is at this stage that the court must require a special showing from the moving party. As Chief Justice Marshall stated, "on objections being made by the president to the production of a paper, the court would not proceed further in the case without such an affidavit as would clearly shew the paper to be *essential to the justice of the case*". *United States v. Burr* (No. 14,-694), *supra,* at 192 (emphasis added). The standard, then, is necessity. The movant must show by extrinsic evidence that the subpoenaed materials are essential to the ends of justice. They must be not merely cumulative or duplicative of other evidence but central to the resolution of the issue at hand. This standard of necessity has been employed by other courts dealing with claims of privilege by subordinate executive officials in civil cases, *Carl Zeiss Stiftung* v. *V. E. B. Zeiss, Jena,* 40 F.R.D. 318, 321 (DDC 1966), *Kaiser Aluminum & Chemical Corp.* v. *United States,* 157 F. Supp. 939 (Ct Cl 1958) (*per* Reed, J.). It is not less appropriate as the test for determining whether an assertion by the President himself of a privilege based on the legitimate interest in confidentiality must yield to requirements of criminal justice.

If the requisite showing has been made, the court should order production of the subpoenaed materials for *in camera* inspection. As the preceding discussion makes plain, *in camera* proceedings are not a substitute for a showing that production is essential to the ends of justice. Rather, "the party seeking discovery must make a preliminary showing of necessity to warrant even *in camera* disclosure. . . ." *Committee for Nuclear Responsibility, Inc.* v. *Seaborg,* —— U. S. App. D. C. ——, ——, 463 F. 2d 788, 792 (1971). See *Carl Zeiss Stiftung, supra,* 40 F.R.D., at 331. When *in camera* proceedings are warranted, identification and excision will then be the court's primary function. It must identify those statements material and necessary to the criminal trial and release them for introduction in evidence. This inquiry may have to occur in stages, for instances may arise when this determination can be made intelligently only after the issues have crystallized during the course of the trial. The court must also excise all other material and provide whatever summaries and abstracts are needed to render the whole comprehensible. Due care must be exercised to avoid release of excised material or its contents.

Finally, a court should stay any order of disclosure for a reasonable time to allow the President to appeal that decision if he so chooses. The Courts of Appeal and ultimately this Court stand ready to enter such further orders as are required to prevent unwarranted disclosure of subpoenaed materials.

* * * * * * * *

CHIEF JUSTICE BURGER'S FIRST DRAFT *

STATEMENT OF FACTS

On March 1, 1974, a grand jury of the United States District Court for the District of Columbia returned an indictment charging John N. Mitchell, H. R. Haldeman, John D. Ehrlichman, Charles W. Colson, Robert C. Mardian, Kenneth W. Parkinson, and Gordon Strachan, with various offenses, including a conspiracy to defraud the United States and to obstruct justice. At some or all of the times pertinent to the indictment, Mr. Mitchell was Chairman of the Committee for the Re-Election of the President; Mr. Haldeman and Mr. Ehrlichman were Assistants to the President. Mr. Colson was Special Counsel to the President. Mr. Mardian was employed by the President's re-election campaign; Mr. Parkinson was an attorney for that committee. Mr. Strachan was a White House Staff Assistant. The grand jury also named the President—among others—as an unindicted member of the conspiracy charged in the indictment. The grand jury lodged with District Court, at the time it returned the indictment, a sealed report. An accompanying memorandum recommended that the materials be submitted to the Committee on the Judiciary of the House of Representatives. The grand jury stated that it had heard evidence which, in the words of the District Court, had "a material bearing on matters within the primary jurisdiction of the Committee in its current inquiry. . . ." 370 F. Supp. 1219, 1221 (1974). At that time it was not disclosed to the District Judge or to the President's counsel that the President had been named as a co-conspirator. On March 18, 1974, the District Court, without objection from the President, held that delivery of the Report to the House Committee could be made.

On April 18, 1974, upon motion of the Special Prosecutor, a subpoena *duces tecum* was issued to the Presi-

---

* Original in typescript.

dent by the United States District Court and made returnable on May 2, 1974. This subpoena required the production, in advance of the September 9 trial date, of certain tapes, memoranda, papers, transcripts, or other writings relating to certain precisely identified meetings between the President and others. The specific meetings are enumerated in a schedule appearing at pages 42a-46a of the appx. The Special Prosecutor was able to be precise because the daily White House logs had been made available to the Special Prosecutor. Defendants Colson, Mardian and Strachan formally joined in the Special Prosecutor's motion for issuance of the subpoena. Defendant Strachan also filed a motion for issuance of the subpoena. Defendant Strachan also filed a motion for issuance of a subpoena identical to that of the Special Prosecutor in the event that enforcement of the Special Prosecutor's subpoena was abandoned.

On April 30, the President voluntarily made public edited transcripts of forty-three conversations; portions of twenty conversations subject to subpoena in the present case were included. On May 1, 1974, the President filed a "special appearance" and motion to quash the subpoena, as permitted under Rule 17 (c), F. R. Crim. Proc. At the joint suggestion of the Special Prosecutor and Counsel for the President, and with the approval of counsel for the defendants, further proceedings in the District Court were held *in camera* because some material submitted to the District Court by the Special Prosecutor in opposition to the motion to quash was considered especially sensitive. This material was submitted under seal with the Special Prosecutor's petition for writ of certiorari in this case. All seven defendants argued in opposition to the motion to quash at the hearing in the District Court. At that hearing, further motions to expunge the grand jury's finding that the President was a co-conspirator and for protective orders against the disclosure of that information were filed or raised orally by Counsel for the President.

On May 20, 1974, the District Court denied the motion

to quash and the motions to expunge and for protective orders. It further ordered "the President or any subordinate officer, official or employee with custody or control of the documents or objects subpoenaed" to deliver to the Court, on or before May 31, 1974, the originals of all subpoenaed items, as well as an index and analysis of those items, together with tape copies of those portions of the subpoenaed recordings for which transcripts had been released to the public by the President on April 30. The District Court stayed its order pending appellate review on condition that appellate review was sought before 4:00 p.m., May 24. The court further provided that matters filed under seal remain under seal when transmitted as part of the record.

On May 24, 1974, the President filed a timely notice of appeal from that order. The certified record from the District Court was also docketed in the United States Court of Appeals for the District of Columbia Circuit. On the same day, the President also filed a petition for writ of mandamus in the Court of Appeals seeking review of the District Court's order in this additional way.

On the same day, May 24, the Special Prosecutor filed, in this Court, a petition for a writ of certiorari before judgment. On May 31, the petition was granted with an expedited briefing schedule. On June 6, the President filed, under seal, a cross-petition for writ of certiorari before judgment. This cross-petition was granted by order of June 15.

On June 6—the same day on which he filed his cross-petition here—the President entered a special appearance in the District Court and requested that the court lift its protective order regarding the naming of certain individuals as co-conspirators and to any additional extent deemed appropriate by the court. This motion of the President was based on the ground that the disclosures in the news media made the reasons for continuance of the protective order no longer meaningful. On June 7, the District Court removed its protective order and, on June 10, both counsel jointly moved this Court to unseal those parts of the record which related to the action of the grand jury regarding the President. After receiving a statement in opposition from the defendants, this Court denied that motion on June 15, 1974, except for the grand jury's immediate finding relating to the status of the President as an unindicted co-conspirator.

On June 10—the same day on which he filed the above motion here—the President's counsel again entered a special appearance on behalf of the President and moved the District Court to disclose all matters and evidence before the grand jury which pertained to its action in naming or authorizing the Special Prosecutor to identify the President as an unindicted co-conspirator. The President's counsel also requested that this material be transmitted to this Court. The District Court denied the motion on June 18; the motion was renewed in this Court the following day. On June 24, this Court, by order, deferred ruling until hearing on the merits.

> To: Mr. Justice Douglas
> Mr. Justice Brennan
> Mr. Justice Stewart
> Mr. Justice White
> Mr. Justice Marshall
> Mr. Justice Blackmun
> Mr. Justice Powell
> Mr. Justice Rehnquist
> From: The Chief Justice
> Circulated: Jul 10 1974

JURISDICTION

Jurisdiction here is posited on 28 U. S. C. § 1254 (1). A case must be "in" the Court of Appeals for us to exercise our jurisdiction under 28 U. S. C. § 1254. Here there may be a question whether this case was properly in the United States Court of Appeals for the District of Columbia Circuit when we granted certiorari.* That

---

* We granted expedited hearing of this case, bypassing the Court of Appeals, but it is clear that before the petition for certiorari was

court's jurisdiction under 28 U. S. C. § 1291 encompasses only "final decisions of the district courts." The issue is whether the District Court's order was final, and thus properly appealable.

The finality requirement embodies a strong congressional policy against piecemeal reviews, and against the obstruction or impediment of ongoing judicial proceedings by interlocutory appeals. See, *e. g., Cobbledick* v. *United States,* 309 U. S. 323, 324–26 (1940). It promotes judicial efficiency and hastens the ultimate termination of litigation.

In applying this principle to an order denying a motion to quash and requiring the production of evidence pursuant to a subpoena *duces tecum* it has been repeatedly held that the order is not final and hence not appealable. *United States* v. *Ryan,* 402 U. S. 530, 532 (1971); *Cobbledick* v. *United States,* 309 U. S. 322 (1940); *Alexander* v. *United States,* 201 U. S. 117 (1906). This Court has

> "Consistently held that the necessity for expedition in the administration of the criminal law justifies putting one who seeks to resist the production of desired information to a choice between compliance with a trial court's order to produce prior to any review of that order, and resistance to that order with the concomitant possibility of an adjudication of contempt if his claims are rejected on appeal." *United States* v. *Ryan,* 402 U. S. 530, 533 (1971), and cases cited therein.

The requirement of risking contempt, however, is not without exception. In some instances the purposes underlying the finality rule require a different result. For example, in *Perlman* v. *United States,* a subpoena had been directed to a third party requesting certain exhibits. The appellant, who owned the exhibits, sought to raise a

---

filed in this Court, a notice of appeal had been docketed by the President in the District Court and the certified record had been docketed in the Court of Appeals. These actions all occurred on May 24, 1974.

claim of privilege. The Court held an order compelling production appealable because it was unlikely the third party would risk a contempt citation in order to allow immediate review of the appellant's claim of privilege. 247 U. S. at 12–13. That case fell within the "limited class of cases where denial of immediate review would render impossible any review whatsoever of an individual's claims. *United States* v. *Ryan, supra,* 402 U. S. at 533.

Here too the contempt avenue to immediate appeal is peculiarly inappropriate, although for different reasons than in *Perlman*. To require a President to personally place himself in contempt of a court merely to trigger the administrative mechanisms for review of the ruling would be unseemly, and present an unnecessary risk of constitutional confrontation between two branches of the Government. Similarly, a federal judge should not be placed in the posture of issuing a citation in order to invoke review. The issue of whether a President can be cited for contempt could itself engender protracted litigation, and would further delay both review on the merits of his claim of privilege, and the ultimate termination of the underlying criminal action. The likelihood that this would occur and thereby avoid the purposes behind the finality rule leads us to conclude that the order of the District Court was an appealable order. Therefore, the President's appeal from that order was properly in the Court of Appeals, and is now properly before this Court under a writ of certiorari before judgment. 28 U. S. C. 1254; 28 U. S. C. 2101 (e). *Gay* v. *Ruff,* 292 U. S. 25, 30 (1934).

JUSTICIABILITY

In the District Court, the President's counsel argued that the court lacked jurisdiction to issue the subpoena on the ground that the matter was an intra-branch dispute not subject to judicial resolution. The argument has been renewed in this Court with emphasis on the contention that the dispute does not present a "case" or "controversy" which can be adjudicated in the federal courts. *Flast* v. *Cohen,* 392 83, 94–95 (1968). At the outset, the President makes clear that he does not question the jurisdiction of the Court to resolve *inter-*branch conflicts. *Marbury* v. *Madison,* 1 Cranch (5 U. S.) 137 (1803). Nor does he question the right of the Court to check an unconstitutional or illegal assumption of power by the Executive Branch as in *Youngstown Sheet & Tube Co.* v. *Sawyer,* 343 U.S. 579 (1952). However, he argues, "the federal courts will not intrude into areas committed to the other branches of government." *Flast, supra,* at 5. He views the present dispute as essentially a jurisdictional dispute within the Executive Branch which he analogizes to a dispute between two Congressional committees. Since the Executive Branch has exclusive authority and absolute discretion to decide whether to prosecute a case, *Confiscation Cases,* 7 Wall (74 U. S.) 454 (1869), he argues that it follows an executive decision is final in determining what evidence is to be used in the case. Although counsel concedes the President has delegated certain specific powers to the Special Prosecutor (President's brief, p. 42), he has not "waived or delegated to the Special Prosecutor the President's duty to claim privilege as to all materials . . . which fall within the President's inherent authority to refuse to disclose to any executive officer." *Ibid.* Therefore, the Special Prosecutor's demand for the items presents, in his view, a political question since it involves a textually demonstrable grant of power under Article II. *Gilligan* v. *Morgan,* 413 U. S. 1 (1972) ; *Baker* v. *Carr,* 369 U. S. 186 (1962).

The mere assertion of "intra-branch dispute," without more, has never operated to defeat federal court jurisdiction. Justiciability does not turn on such a surface inquiry. In *United States* v. *Interstate Commerce Commission,* 337 U. S. 426 (1949), the Court observed "courts must look behind the names that symbolize the parties to determine whether a justiciable case or controversy is presented." 337 U. S. at 430. See also: *Powell* v. *Mc-*

Cormack, 395 U. S. 486 (1969) ; *ICC* v. *Jersey City,* 322 U. S. 503 (1944) ; *ex rel. Chapman* v. *FPC,* 345 U. S. 153 (1953) (Secretary of Interior against FPC) ; *Secretary of Agriculture* v. *United States,* 347 U. S. 645 (1954) (Secretary of Agriculture against the ICC) ; *Federal Maritime Board* v. *Isbrandsten Co.,* 356 U. S. 481, 482 n. 2 (1958) (FMB against the Justice Department and Secretary of Agriculture). As recently as this term the Court resolved disputes between Anti-trust Division of the Justice Department and the Comptroller of the Currency in *United States* v. *Marine Bank,* — U. S. (1974), and *United States* v. *Connecticut National Bank,* — U. S. — (1974).

In resolving this question, an essential starting point is the nature of the proceeding for which the evidence is sought—a pending criminal prosecution. It is a judicial proceeding in a federal court for the alleged violation of federal laws; such criminal actions are brought in the name of the United States. *Berger* v. *United States,* 295 U. S. 78 (1935). Under the authority of Article II, section 2, Congress has vested in the Attorney General the power to conduct the government's criminal litigation. 28 U. S. C. 516. It has also vested in him the power to appoint subordinate officers to assist him in the discharge of his duties. 28 U. S. C. 509, 510, 515, 533. Acting pursuant to that authority, the Attorney General has delegated the authority to represent the United States in these particular matters to a special prosecutor with unique authority and tenure.[1] The regulations of

---

[1] Regulations issued by the Attorney General pursuant to his authority under 5 U. S. C. § 501, vest in the Special Prosecutor plenary authority to control the course of investigations and litigation related to "all offenses arising out of the 1972 Presidential Election for which the Special Prosecutor deems it necessary and appropriate to assume responsibility, allegations involving the President, members of the White House staff, or Presidential appointees, and any other matters which he consents to have assigned to him by the Attorney General." 38 Fed. Reg., at 30739. In particular, the Special Prosecutor was given full authority, *inter alia,* "to contest the assertion of 'Executive Privilege' . . . and handl[e] all aspects

the Attorney General specifically give him the power to
contest the invocation of executive privilege in his attempt to procure material deemed relevant to the performance of these duties.[2]   38 Fed. Reg., at 30739.   So long

---

of any cases within his jurisdiction." *Ibid.*   The regulations then
go on to provide:

> "In exercising this authority, the Special Prosecutor will have
> the greatest degree of independence that is consistent with the
> Attorney-General's statutory accountability for all matters
> falling within the jurisdiction of the Department of Justice.
> The Attorney General will not countermand or interfere with
> the Special Prosecutor's decisions or actions.   The Special
> Prosecutor will determine whether and to what extent he will
> inform or consult with the Attorney General about the conduct
> of his duties and responsibilities.   In accordance with assur-
> ances given by the President to the Attorney General that the
> President will not exercise his Constitutional powers to effect
> the discharge of the Special Prosecutor or to limit the indepen-
> dence he is hereby given, the Special Prosecutor will not be re-
> moved from his duties except for extraordinary improprieties
> on his part and without the President's first consulting the Ma-
> jority and Minority Leaders and Chairman and ranking Mi-
> nority Members of the Judiciary Committees of the Senate and
> House of Representatives and ascertaining that their consensus
> is in accord with his proposed action."

[2] That this was the understanding of Acting Attorney General
Robert Bork, the author of the regulations establishing the independence of the Special Prosecutor is shown by his testimony before
the Senate Judiciary Committee

> Although it is anticipated that Mr. Jaworski will receive co-
> operation from the White House in getting any evidence he
> feels he needs to conduct investigations and prosecutions, it is
> clear and understood on all sides that he has the power to use
> judicial processes to pursue evidence if disagreement should
> develop.

Hearings Before the Senate Judiciary Committee on the Special
Prosecutor, 93rd Cong., 1st Sess., pt. 2, at 470 (1973).   Acting Attorney General Bork gave similar assurances to the House Subcommittee on Criminal Justice.   Hearings Before the House Judiciary
Subcommittee on Criminal Justice on H. J. Res. 784 and H. R.
10937, 93rd Cong., 1st. Sess. 266 (1973).   At his confirmation hearings, Attorney General William Saxbe testified that he shared Acting Attorney General Bork's views concerning the Special Prosecu-

as these regulations are extant they have the force of law and as long as the President leaves the Attorney General in office and as long as the incumbent Attorney General leaves the current regulations in force, the Executive Branch is bound by them. *Accardi* v. *Shaughnessy,* 347 U. S., at 265–67 (1954) ; *Service* v. *Dulles,* 354 U. S. 363 (1957) ; *Vitarelli* v. *Seaton,* 359 U. S. 535 (1959). Here the President has explicitly shared with eight designated leaders of the Legislative Branch the power to alter the Special Prosecutor's authority or to dismiss him.

In moving to quash the subpoena for the material in his personal possession, the President is not acting simply as a participant in the prosecutorial function of the Executive Branch, but rather as a party with a particular, individual interest. See: *United States* v. *ICC,* 337 U. S. 426, 430 (1949) ; *Secretary of Agriculture* v. *United States,* 350 U. S. 1962 (1956). In short, for the narrow and limited purpose of determining the proper use of these materials in the particular criminal action now pending, the President's expressed legal position is realistically and concretely "adverse" to that of the Government as advanced by its specially constituted attorney. There is thus "that concrete adverseness which sharpens the presentation of issues upon which the court so largely depends for illumination of difficult constitutional question," *Baker* v. *Carr,* 369 U. S. 186, 204 (1962). Since it is a matter arising in the ordinary course of a federal criminal prosecution it is a matter within the traditional scope of Article III power. *Id.,* at 217. In light of that genuine adverseness, the mere formality that both parties are officers of the Executive Branch is not tube viewed as rising to the level of a jurisdictional bar. It would be inconsistent with the applicable law and regulations and the unique facts of this case to conclude other than that

tor's authority to test any claim of executive privilege in the courts. Hearings before the Senate Judiciary Committee on the Nomination of William B. Saxbe to be Attorney General, 93rd Cong., 1st Sess. 9 (1973).

the Special Prosecutor has standing to bring this action and that a justiciable case or controversy is presented for decision.

[Although the parties treat the 17 (c) issue last, it seems more appropriate to me to determine this matter before reaching the question of privilege. If the requirements of Rule 17 (c) are not met, the subpoena duces tecum should not have been issued and the President would never have been required to interpose the claim of presidential privilege to bar its enforcement. Therefore, if the Court finds that the requirements of the Rule have *not* been met, it would not be necessary to reach and decide the issue of executive or presidential privilege. Cf. *Arkansas-Louisiana Gas Co. v. Dept. of Public Utilities,* 304 U. S. 617, 64 (1938). This section will be re-examined to accord with treatment of "presidential privilege."]

THE RULE 17 (C) QUESTION

In essence, the President's counsel argues that the Special Prosecutor is attempting to use the subpoena as a discovery device, or to uncover material not yet known to him. He argues that the Special Prosecutor has requested the 64 conversations on the "bald assertion" that each "contains or is likely to contain evidence that will be relevant to the trial of this case." He also argues that the Special Prosecutor gave no factual support for his claim that some of the material may be relevant and has failed to show that each of the 64 items is evidentiary in nature. The President's counsel also notes that the Special Prosecutor contends that the statements made during the conversations may be useful to the Government for purposes of impeaching certain of the defendants should they elect to testify. In responding, counsel for the President correctly points out that the courts have generally held that materials useful to challenge the credibility of witnesses cannot be obtained in advance of trial and that discovery of such evidence must await the occasion when a defendant testifies.

The Special Prosecutor, emphasizing that the enforcement of a subpoena duces tecum is committed to the trial court's sound discretion, argues that the District Court's determination should not be disturbed in the absence of a decision on review that the District Court's action was arbitrary and unsupported in the record. This is especially true, he argues, where the assessment of the relevancy and of the evidentiary value of the items is primarily a determination of fact and the District Judge is intimately familiar with the grand jury's investigation. He argues that the material sought is relevant if it is related to the charges the indictment; it is evidentiary if it would be admissible in the party's direct case or can be used to impeach a witness. As to the majority of conversations involved in the subpoena, the Special Prosecutor argues the specificity standard is satisfied by consideration of the transcripts already made public by the White House, by uncontradicted testimony and other evidence. As to the remaining conversations, he argues that there is strong circumstantial evidence indicating the standard is met. Common sense dictates, he submits, that the parties seeking production cannot tell precisely the contents until the documents are examined.

Rule 17 (c) provides:

> "A subpoena may also command the person to whom it is directed to produce the books, papers, documents or other objects designated therein. The court on motion made promptly may quash or modify the subpoena if compliance would be unreasonable or oppressive. The court may direct that books, papers, documents or objects designated in the subpoena be produced before the court at a time prior to the trial or prior to the time when they are to be offered in evidence and may upon their production permit the books, papers, documents or objects or portions thereof to be inspected by the parties and their attorneys."

The leading case in this Court interpreting Rule 17 (c)

is *Bowman Dairy Co.* v. *United States,* 341 U. S. 214
(1950). This case established certain fundamental
characteristics of the subpoena duces tecum in criminal
cases: (1) it was not intended to provide additional
means of discovery in criminal cases. 341 U. S., at 220;
(2) its chief innovation was to expedite the trial by providing a time and place *before* trial for the inspection of
subpoenaed materials. *Id.,* at 220. The Court quoted
a statement of a member of the advisory committee that
the purpose of the Rule was to bring the documents into
court "in advance of the time that they are offered in
evidence, so that they may be inspected in advance, for
the purpose . . . of enabling the party to see whether
he can use it or whether he wants to use it." 341 U. S.,
at 220 n. 5. Both parties agree with the District Court
that the cases decided in the wake of *Bowman* have basically adopted Judge Weinfeld's formulation of the required showing in *United States* v. *Iozia,* 13 F. R. D. 335,
338 (D. C. N. Y. 1965). Under this test, in order to require production prior to trial, the moving party must
show: (1) that the documents are evidentiary and relevant; (2) that they are not otherwise procurable reasonably in advance of trial by exercise of due diligence; (3)
that the party cannot properly prepare for trial without
such production and inspection in advance of trial and
that the failure to obtain such inspection may tend unreasonably to delay the trial; (4) that the application is made
in good faith and is not intended as a general fishing expedition. Moreover, the District Court properly relied on
the fact that the materials were being sought from a third
party rather than from an opposing party, and thus the
subpoena could not be regarded as an impermissible attempt to circumvent the discovery limitations applied to
parties by Rule 16.

In reviewing the determination of the District Court
that the requirements of Rule 17 (c) are met in this case,
a good starting place is the purpose of the Rule as seem
by this Court, i.e., to expedite the trial by permitting advance access and selection of evidence to be proffered at

trial. *Bowman, supra* at p. 220.[1] It seems clear that the Special Prosecutor cannot obtain this particular evidence in any other way. Likewise, it seems reasonable to assume that the analysis and possible transcription of the tape recording, if obtained, would take a significant period of time.[2]

Against this backdrop, the Special Prosecutor must, in order to carry his burden, clear three hurdles: (1) relevancy; (2) admissibility; (3) specificity. Our own review of the record necessarily affords a less comprehensive view of the total situation available to a trial judge and we are unwilling to conclude that the District Court's evaluation of the Special Prosecutor's showing under the Rule 17 (c) was clearly erroneous.

It goes without saying that our holding that the District Court was not "clearly erroneous" in ordering *in camera* inspection does not dispose of all Rule 17 (c) problems. When the material is received by the District Judge he will be obliged to examine it to make his final appraisal under the Rule 17 (c) requirements of relevancy and admisability; and, of course, in this process a judge *must* be conscious of the sensitivity of publication of presidential confidences.[3]

---

[1] The Manual for Complex and Multi-district Litigation published by the Administrative Office of the United States Courts recommends that Rule 17 (c) be encouraged in complex criminal cases in order that each party may be compelled to produce its documentary evidence well in advance of trial in advance of the time it is to be offered. P. 142, CCH Ed.

[2] The Special Prosecutor estimates 2 months (brief p. 139). This factor seems especially relevant in determining whether the statements are admissible for impeachment purposes.

[3] See *United States* v. *Burr*, 25 Fed. Cus. 30 (Case No. 14,694) (C. C. D. Va. 1807), at 192:

> In regard to the secrecy of these parts which it is stated are improper to give out to the world, the Court will take any order that may be necessary.

The Claim of Executive Privilege

A

We turn now to the issue of whether a president, by virtue of that office, has a privilege against compliance with a judicial subpoena in a criminal case. By common law and statute various privileges against compelled testimony and compulsory production of tangible evidence have developed to protect the confidential communications, for example those between husband and wife, priest and penitent, lawyer and client, doctor and patient. The Fifth Amendment grants an absolute privilege against being required to give self incriminatory testimony. The Constitution contains an express privilege protecting members of Congress from being required "to answer in any other place" than Congress for acts and conversations in the performance of legitimate legislative duties.[1] The term "executive privilege" is a term of broad application and is asserted to be inherent in all systems of government to ensure the confidentiality of private communications among officials concerning governmental decision and policy making. It is urged that in our system of divided powers allocated to three separate coordinate branches, the independence of each requires that internal deliberations in decision making be protected from disclosure.

The effective functioning of the judicial system, however, requires that courts obtain evidence and only recently the Court restated an ancient proposition of the law, albeit in the context of a grand jury inquiry rather than a trial,

> " 'the public . . . has a right to every man's evidence' except for those persons protected by a constitutional, common law or statutory privilege, *United States* v. *Bryan*, 339 U. S. at 331 (1949) ; *Blackmer*

---

[1] U. S. Const. Art. I, Sec. 6; *cf.*, *United States* v. *Johnson*, 319 U. S. 503; *United States* v. *Brewster*, 408 U. S. 501; *Gravel* v. *United States*, 408 U. S. 606.

v. *United States,* 284 U. S. at 421, 438 (1932). . . ."
Branzburg v. *U. S.,* —— U. S. —— (1973).

The issues presented by this case revolve around the "exceptions" referred to by the Court in *Branzburg.*

Because of the key role of the testimony of witnesses in the judicial process, courts have been historically cautious about the privileges against being required to give evidence. Justice Frankfurter, dissenting in *Elkins* v. *United States,* 364 U. S. 206, 234 (1960) said of this:

> "Limitations are properly placed upon the operation of this general principle only to the very limited extent that permitting a refusal to testify or excluding relevant evidence has a public good transcending the nominally predominent principle of utilizing all rational means for ascertaining truth."

The issues before us are narrow and precise. We deal here with a *third party* subpoena issued to the President demanding material thought by the Special Prosecutor and held by the District Court to be relevant in a pending criminal trial. The President has not ignored the subpoena but has responded to it. In his response it is not contended that the subpoenaed material involves matters of military planning or intelligence or sensitive aspects of foreign affairs or national security, but rather the broad necessity of preserving the confidentiality of conversation between a chief executive and his advisers. Since we have already concluded in Part —— that the District Court did not err in authorizing the issuance of the subpoena duces tecum, two questions remain to be resolved: (a) whether a federal court can review the claim of presidential privilege [2] in the circumstances present,

---

[2] We employ the term "presidential privilege" to describe those communications to which a president himself is a party; this is part of the broader concept of "executive privilege" which includes an array of lesser executive branch officials and employees. See *Scheuer* v. *Rhodes,* —— U. S. —— (1974) ; *Barr* v. *Matteo,* 360 U. S. 564, 573–574 (1959).

and (b) assuming such a review is available, whether the District Court, on this record, correctly ordered an *in camera* inspection.

B

Although the President's counsel asserts that the privilege of confidentiality of presidential communications is absolute he does not challenge the authority of this Court to interpret the law.[3]   Each branch of the government in the performance of its assigned constitutional duties must interpret the Constitution and the interpretation of its powers by any branch is due the utmost respect by the others. Ultimately, however, "it is emphatically the province and duty of the judicial department to say what the law is." *Marbury* v. *Madison*.   No holding of the Court has defined the scope of judicial power to enforce a subpoena calling for confidential presidential papers, but recent examples are found where the exercise of powers by the Executive Branch, *Youngstown Sheet & Tube Co.*, *supra*,[4] and the Legislative Branch, *Powell* v. *McCormack*, *supra*, were found in conflict with the Constitution. However, in a civil suit for damages brought against the United States a claim of privilege as to military secrets was sustained without in camera examination by the district court. *Reynolds* v. *United States*, — U.S. — (1952).

The President's claim of absolute privilege rests on two grounds one of which is common to all governments and one of which is peculiar to our system of separation of powers.   The first ground is the valid need for protection of communications between high government officials and those who advise and assist them in the performance of their manifold duties; the importance of this confi-

---

[3] Implicit in the presidential grant of authority to the Special Prosecutor to contest a presidential claim of privilege was a reservation of a president's undoubted right to assert a privilege in the courts.

[4] *Youngstown Sheet & Tube Co.* is of limited relevance since that case involved a seizure of property, not a testimonial privilege.

dentiality is too plain to require extended discussion. Human experience teaches that those who expect public dissemination of their remarks may well temper candor with a concern for appearances and for their own interests to the detriment of the decision making process. To the extent the interest in confidentiality pertains to a president's effective exercise of his Article II executive powers it can be said to derive from the supremacy of each branch within its own assigned area of constitutional duties. Like the power of judicial review first announced by this Court under the authority of Article III in *Marbury, supra,* certain powers and privileges flow from the nature of enumerated powers;[5] the protection of the confidentiality of presidential communications has similar constitutional underpinnings.

The second ground asserted by the President's counsel in support of the claim of absolute privilege rests on the doctrine of separation of powers. As a generalization it is correct that under the Constitution each branch is supreme in its own sphere, free from intrusion by other branches. *Humphrey's Executor, supra,* at 629-30; *Kilbourn* v. *Thompson,* 103 U.S. 168, 190-191 (1880). It is also argued that this independence insulates a presi-

---

[5] The Special Prosecutor argues that there is no provision in the Constitution for a presidential privilege as to his communications corresponding to the privilege of members of Congress under the Speech or Debate Clause. Enumerated powers of the three branches do not invariably fix the limits of their authority:

> Let the end be legitimate, let it be within the scope of the constitution, and all means which are appropriate, which are plainly adapted to that end, which are not prohibited, but consistent with the letter and spirit of the constitution, are constitutional. *McCulloch* v. *Maryland*, 4 Wheat. (17 U. S.) 316, 421 (1819)

> The rule of constitutional interpretation announced in *McCulloch* v. *Maryland*, 4 Wheat. 316, that that which was reasonably appropriate and relevant to the exercise of a granted power was considered as accompanying the grant, has been so universally applied that it suffices merely to state it. *Marshall* v. *Gordon, et al.,* 234 U. S. 521, 537.

dent from a judicial subpoena in an ongoing criminal prosecution, and thereby protects the presidential interest in his confidential communications.

However, neither the doctrine of separation of powers, nor the need for confidentiality of high level communications, without more, can sustain an absolute, unqualified presidential privilege of immunity from judicial process under all circumstances. Given the unique circumstances shown by this record, the claim that compliance with a judicial subpoena will have far reaching and adverse effects on the general expectation of confidentiality and thus defeat the ability of a president to obtain candid and honest advice is not an argument to be dismissed lightly. To be sure, the President's need for complete candor and objectivity from advisers calls for great deference from the courts. However, when that privilege depends solely on the broad, undifferentiated claim of public interest in the confidentiality of such conversations, a confrontation with other values arises. Absent a claim of need to protect military, diplomatic or sensitive national security secrets, we find it difficult to accept the argument that even the very important interest in confidentiality of presidential communications is significantly diminished by production of such material for *in camera* inspection with all the protection that a district court will be obliged to provide. A district judge will doubtless enforce with particularly scrupulous care all necessary safeguards when he privately examines the personal and official conversations of a president.

The impediment that an absolute, unqualified privilege would place in the way of the primary constitutional duty of the Judicial Branch to do justice in criminal prosecutions would plainly conflict with the function of the courts under Article III. In designing the structure of our government and dividing and allocating the sovereign power among three coequal branches, the Framers of the Constitution sought to provide a comprehensive system, but the separate powers were not intended to operate with absolute independence. Rather the three branches were to "dovetail," leaving no vacuum or void, with each branch respecting the powers of the others:

> "While the Constitution diffuses power the better to secure liberty, it also contemplates that practice will integrate the dispersed powers into a workable government. It enjoins upon its branches separateness but interdependence, autonomy but reciprocity." *Youngstown Sheet & Tube Co.* v. *Sawyer,* 343 U. S. 579, 635 (1952) (concurring opinion of Jackson, J.).

To read the Article II powers of the President as providing an absolute privilege as against a subpoena essential to enforcement of criminal statues on no more than a generalized claim of the public interest in confidentiality of non-military and non-diplomatic discussions would upset the constitutional balance of "a workable government" and gravely impair the role of the courts under Article III.

C

Since we conclude that the legitimate needs of the judicial process may outweigh presidential privilege when the privilege is based solely on the generalized need for confidentiality, it is necessary, in a given case to resolve these competing interests in a manner that preserves the essential functions of each branch. The right and indeed the duty to resolve that question does not free the judiciary from according high respect to the representations made on behalf of the President. *United States* v. *Burr,* 257 Fed. Cas. pp. 187, 190, 191–2 (Case No. 14694) (1807)

The right of privacy of every citizen to the confidentiality of his conversations, private papers and records has been accorded a high place in our concept of liberty although it is not expressed in the Constitution. The right of a president to the confidentiality of his conversations and correspondence, like the claim of confidentiality of judicial deliberations, for example, has all the values to which we accord deference for the private citizen and added to that the necessity for protection of the public interest in candid, objective and even blunt or harsh opinions in presidential decision making. That such openness and candor requires assurance on the part of advisers and aides that their utterances will not be broadcast is beyond debate. A president and those who assist him must be free to explore alternatives in the process of shaping policies and making decisions and to do so in a way many would be unwilling to express except privately. Moreover, neither a president nor his advisers should be open to invasion of this privacy and confidentiality except for the most over-riding reasons. This is the predicate justifying a presumptive privilege for presidential communications, and the privilege is fundamental to the operation of government and inextricably rooted in the separation of powers under the Constitution. In *Nixon* v. *Sirica,* the Court of Appeals held that such conversations are "presumptively privileged" 487 F. 2d at 717 (D. C. Cir 1974) and this position is accepted by both parties in the present litigation. We agree with Chief Justice Marshall's observation, therefore, that "in no case of this kind would a court be required to proceed against the President as against an ordinary individual." *United States* v. *Burr,* 25 Fed. Cas. 187, 191 (No. 14964) (CCD Va. 1897). Rather the courts should follow standards and implement procedures that will adequately protect the undoubted need to preserve the legitimate confidentiality of that office, with due recognition of the Article III functions of the federal courts.

We come then to whether the presumptive privilege of presidential communications, when asserted on the limited basis of generalized confidentiality, can override a subpoena to secure evidence required in a pending criminal prosecution. The competing demands—the generalized privilege of confidentiality on the one hand, and the function of Article III courts on the other—must be examined to ascertain the relative importance of the presumptive privilege in the whole scheme of Article II, as compared with the importance which the need for relevant evidence occupies in the fulfillment of Article III duties of the Judicial Branch. Under Article II a president, for example, exercising certain of his enumerated war powers, as in repelling a hostile attack, or exercising the veto power, or conducting foreign relations is exercising powers at the very core of his constitutional role. The courts have shown the utmost deference to presidential actions in performance of these core functions. In *C. & S. Air Lines* v. *Waterman Steamship Corp.*, 333 U. S. 103, 111 dealing with presidential authority involving foreign policy considerations affecting international airline routes the Court said:

> "The President, both as Commander-in-Chief and as the Nation's organ for foreign affairs, has available intelligence services whose reports are not and ought not to be published to the world. It would be intolerable that courts, without the relevant information, should review and perhaps nullify actions of the Executive taken on information properly held secret." Id. at 111.

In *United States* v. *Reynolds,* 345 U. S. at 9, dealing with a claimant's demand for evidence in a damage case the Court said

> ". . . Judicial control over the evidence in a case cannot be abdicated to the caprice of executive officers. Yet we will not go so far as to say that the court may automatically require a complete disclosure to the judge before the claim of privilege will be accepted in any case. It may be possible to satisfy the court, from all the circumstances of the case, that there is a reasonable danger that compulsion of the evidence will expose military matters which, in the interest of national security, should not be divulged. When this is the case, the occasion for the privilege is appropriate, and the court should not jeopardize the security which the privilege is meant to protect by

insisting upon an examination of the evidence, even
by the judge alone, in chambers."

* * *

"Where there is a strong showing of necessity, the
claim of privilege should not be lightly accepted, but
even the most compelling necessity cannot overcome
the claim of privilege if the court is ultimately satisfied that military secrets are at stake. A *fortiori,*
where necessity is dubious, a formal claim of privilege, made under the circumstances of this case, will
have to prevail."   345 U. S. at 10–11.

We see therefore that *Waterman Steamship, supra* and
Reynolds, supra each dealt with a presidential function
lying at the core of Article II authority.   In the present
case, however, the generalized claim of confidentiality relates to none of the kinds of activities for which courts
have traditionally shown the utmost deference, but on the
contrary the claim is somewhat removed from the central
or core function of the chief executive.

In contrast the need for relevant evidence in the conduct of a criminal trial lies at the very core of the Article
III function of a federal court.   Although the administration of criminal justice is shared by the Executive and
Judicial branches in the sense that the former investigates and initiates prosecutions under standards prescribed by Congress, the adjudicatory function is vested
exclusively in the courts.[6]   Under our adversary system
of criminal justice not only do both sides have an interest
in securing all relevant evidence that is probative on the
issue of guilt, but the very integrity of the system and
public confidence in the system depends upon full disclosure of the facts within the framework of the rules of
evidence.   Without the power to compel the production

---

[6] The Congress defines crimes, fixes penalties and prescribes procedures for the administration of criminal justice to be applied by
the courts thus integrating "the dispersed powers into a workable
government."   343 U. S. at 635.

of evidence the basic function of the courts under Article III could not be performed.

Thus here the core function of Article III is pitted against a generalized need for presidential confidentiality without a showing that such confidentiality is necessary to protect a core function of Article II. Under these circumstances the generalized assertion of privilege must yield to the demonstrated, specific need for evidence in a pending criminal trial.[7]

D

The initial issuance of a subpoena is, as we have noted, governed by Rule 17 (c) which requires a showing of relevance, and admissibility and sufficient specificity to preclude "fishing expeditions." We have earlier determined that the District Court did not err in authorizing the issuance of the subpoena. If a president concludes that compliance with a subpoena would be injurious to the public interest, he may properly as was done here, invoke a claim of privilege on the return of the subpoena. The original return here was a motion to quash the subpoena. Upon receiving a claim of privilege from the Chief Executive, it was the duty of the District Court to treat the subpoenaed material as "presumptively privileged" and to require the Special Prosecutor to demonstrate, by extrinsic evidence, that the presidential material was required for the just resolution of the pending criminal case for which it is sought and that it is admissible and probative. The District Court treated the material as presumptively privileged and then proceeded to find that the

---

[7] We are not called on to decide what a district court should do if confronted by a categorical claim of privilege for military, foreign policy secrets or national security. However, by referring to the deference due to all discussions of military and foreign policy secrets, we intend to intimate no view that discussion of highly sensitive domestic policies, for example, devaluation of the currency, imposition or lifting of wage and price controls, would not be entitled to a very high order of privilege, since the economic consequences of disclosure of such discussions could well be as pervasive and momentous as the disclosure of military secrets.

Special Prosecutor had made a sufficient showing to rebut the presumptive privilege and had shown a sufficiently
compelling need justifying *in camera* judicial examination. On the basis of our examination of the material
submitted we are unable to conclude that the District
Court erred in ordering inspection of the subpoenaed materials. Accordingly the subpoenaed materials shall be
transmitted forthwith to the District Court for *in camera*
inspection. We therefore now turn to the important
question of the District Court's responsibilities in conducting the *in camera* examination of presidential materials or communications delivered under the compulsion
of the subpoena *dues tecum.*

E

Action to implement the subpoena duces tecum was
stayed until this Court's resolution of the issues raised
by the petitions for certiorari. Those issues now having
been resolved the matter of implementation will rest with
the District Court. "[T]he guard, furnished to [the
President] to protect him from being harassed by vexatious and unnecessary subpoenas, is to be looked for in
the conduct of the [district] court after the subpoenas
have issued; not in any circumstances which is to precede their being issued." *U. S.* v. *Burr, supra* at 25 Fed.
Cas. at 30 (1807) (Emphasis added). An *in camera* inspection imposes a heavy duty on the District Court.
Statements that meet the test of admissibility and relevance must be isolated; all other material must be excised. At this stage the District Court is not limited to
representations of the Special Prosecutor as to the evidence sought by the subpoena; now the recordings themselves will be available to the District Court for *in camera*
inspection. It is elementary that *in camera* inspection of
evidence is always a procedure calling for scrupulous protection against any release or publication of material not
found by the court, at that stage, to be both admissible in
evidence and relevant to the issues of the trial for which
it is sought. That being true of an ordinary situation, it

is obvious that the District Court has a very heavy responsibility to see to it that presidential conversations, which are either not admissible or not relevant to the case, are accorded that high degree of respect due to the private conversations of any high ranking government officer and particularly those of a president of the United States. Chief Justice Marshall sitting as District Judge in the *Burr* case, *supra* was extraordinarily careful to point out that:

> "[I]n no case of this kind would a Court be required to proceed against the President as against an ordinary individual." *U. S.* v. *Burr,* 25 Fed. Cases 187. 191 (No. 14694)

This was not because Marshall thought in any sense that a president was above the law but because a president's communication and activities dealt with a vastly wider range of sensitive material than would be true of the "ordinary individual" and that it was in the public interest to afford presidential confidentiality the greatest protection [8] consistent with the fair administration of justice. The need for confidentiality even as to idle conversations with associates in which casual reference might be made concerning political leaders within the country or foreign statesmen is too obvious to call for further discussion. If it should develop that digests of some parts of the excised material are essential to understanding or providing a connection with the material found relevant

---

[8] When the subpoenaed material is delivered to the District Judge *in camera* questions may arise as to the excising of parts and it lies within the discretion of that court to seek the aid of the Special Prosecutor and the President's counsel for *in camera* consideration on the validity of particular excisions whether the basis of excision is on relevancy or admissibility or under such cases as *Reynolds, supra* or *Waterman Steamship, supra.* Any order entered releasing material to the Special Prosecutor over objections of the President's counsel shall, of course, be stayed for a reasonable time to provide opportunity for appellate review; the record should be sealed for any review that may be sought.

and admissible, the District Judge may in his discretion resolve that problem.

At all times the District Court has a heavy responsibility to see to it that until released to the Special Prosecutor no *in camera* material is revealed to anyone. This burden applies with even greater force to excise material; once that decision is made, the excised material is restored to its privileged status and should be returned under seal to its lawful custodian.

JUSTICE WHITE'S DRAFT*

NOS. 73–1766 & 73–1834
UNITED STATES *v.* NIXON

The President challenges the subpoena *duces tecum* and the judgment of the District Court denying the motion to quash on two general grounds. First, it is urged that the Special Prosecutor has failed to satisfy the requirements of Rule 17 (c) governing the issuance of subpoenas *duces tecum* in criminal proceedings. Second, he insists that whether or not Rule 17 (c) has been satisfied, the subpoenaed materials may be withheld in his absolute discretion pursuant to an executive privilege, which is extended to him by the Constitution and is beyond review by the courts and which, if subject to judicial review, need not yield in the circumstances of this case.

Because a ruling favorable to the President under Rule 17 (c) would obviate our reaching major constitutional issues with respect to the existence and scope of the claimed executive privilege, we initially deal with whether the requirements of Rule 17 (c) have been satisfied. See *Ashwander* v. *Tennessee Valley Authority,* 297 U. S. 288, 346–347 (1936) (Brandeis, J., concurring).

The rule provides:

> "A subpoena may also command the person to whom it is directed to produce the books, papers, documents or other objects designated therein. The court on motion made promptly may quash or modify the subpoena if compliance would be unreasonable or oppressive. The court may direct that books, papers, documents or objects designated in the subpoena be produced before the court at a time prior to the trial or prior to the time when they are to be offered in evidence and may upon their production permit the books, papers, documents or objects or portions thereof to be inspected by the parties and their attorneys."

---

* Original in typescript.

A subpoena for documents may thus be quashed if their production would be "unreasonable or oppressive," but not otherwise.[1]

In applying that standard, it has been established that it is neither unreasonable nor oppressive to require the production of documents that to a rational mind would appear to contain or constitute relevant and admissible evidence with respect to the guilt or innocence of defendants charged with crime. Whether this is the entire reach of the subpoenas issuable under 17 (c), particularly where either prosecution or defense is seeking documents from a third party,[2] we need not decide; for we are convinced that the relevance and the evidentiary nature of the subpoenaed tapes were sufficiently shown as a preliminary matter to warrant the District Court's refusal to quash the subpoena.

Our conclusion is based on the record before us, much of which is under seal. Of course, the contents of the subpoenaed tapes cannot at this stage be accurately demonstrated by the Special Prosecutor, but there is a sufficient likelihood that each of the tapes contains conversations relevant [3] to the Watergate case and to the proof of, or defense against, the charges against the defendants in this case. With respect to many of the tapes, the Special Prosecutor offered the sworn testimony or statements of one or more of the participants in the conversations as to what was said at the time. As for the remainder of the tapes, the identity of the participants and timing of the conversations, taken in their total context, permit a rational inference that the so-called Watergate break-in or cover-up was one of the subjects discussed.

We also think it sufficiently likely that each of the subpoenaed tapes contains evidence that is not only relevant but also admissible with respect to the charges contained in the indictment. The most cogent objection to the admissibility of the taped conversations [4] here at issue is that they are a collection of out-of-court statements by declarants not subject to cross-examination and are therefore inadmissible hearsay. Plainly, however, the hearsay rule does not automatically bar from evidence any relevant out-of-court statements of a defendant in a criminal case. Such statements are not hearsay, but declarations by a party to the case. They "would surmount all objections based on the hearsay rule . . ." and, at least as against the declarant himself, "would be admissible for whatever inferences" might reasonably be drawn. *United States* v. *Matlock,* —— U. S. —— (1974).[5]

Here most of the tapes contain conversations to which one or more of the defendants were themselves party.

Declarations by one defendant would also be admissible against other defendants if there has been a sufficient preliminary showing, by independent evidence, of a conspiracy among the declarant and the other defendants, and if the declarations at issue were in furtherance of that conspiracy.[6] The same is true of declarations of co-conspirators who are not defendants in the case on trial. As a preliminary matter, there must be substantial, independent evidence of the conspiracy, at least enough to take the question to the jury. *United States* v. *Vaught,* 485 F. 2d 320, 323 (CA 4 1973); *United States* v. *Hoffa,* 349 F. 2d 20, 41–42 (CA 6 1965), *aff'd on other grounds,* 385 U. S. 293 (1966); *United States* v. *Santos,* 385 F. 2d 43, 45 (CA 7 1967), *cert. denied,* 390 U. S. 954 (1968); *United States* v. *Morton,* 483 F. 2d 573, 576 (CA 8 1973); *United States* v. *Spanos,* 462 F. 2d 1012, 1014 (CA 9 1972); *Carbo* v. *United States,* 314 F. 2d 718, 737 (CA 9 1963), *cert. denied,* 377 U. S. 953 (1964). Whether the standard has been satisfied is a question of admissibility of evidence to be decided by the trial judge.[7] Here the trial judge was quite satisfied as to the evidentiary nature of each of the tapes, at least for the purposes of justifying a subpoena for documents under Rule 17. On the basis of the record before us, we find no basis for disturbing this conclusion.

Enforcement of a pre-trial subpoena *duces tecum* must necessarily be committed to the sound discretion of the trial court, since the necessity for the subpoena most often turns upon a determination of factual issues. Therefore, in the absence of a finding of arbitrariness or a complete lack of support in the record, appellate courts will not normally disturb a District Court's determination that the applicant for a subpoena complied with the standards of Rule 17 (c). See, *e. g., Sue* v. *Chicago Transit Authority,* 279 F. 2d 416, 419 (CA 7 1960) ; *Shotkin* v. *Nelson,* 146 F. 2d 402 (CA 10 1944). In cases such as this, however, where a subpoena is directed to the President of the United States, appellate review, in deference to a coordinate branch of government, should be particularly meticulous to ensure that the standards of Rule 17 (c) have been correctly applied. From our close scrutiny of the supportive materials submitted by the Special Prosecutor to the District Court, we are fully persuaded that the District Court's denial of the President's motion to quash was consistent with Rule 17 (c).[8]

JUSTICE STEWART'S DRAFT †

IV

Having determined that the requirements of Rule 17 (c) have been satisfied in this case, we must confront the President's claim that he is nonetheless entitled to have the subpoena quashed because of a constitutional privilege to refuse to disclose confidential conversations with and among his aides and advisers. The President's first and broadest contention is that the judiciary is without power to review this claim of privilege once he has formally asserted it. He argues alternatively that, even if his claim of privilege is subject to judicial review, the courts should hold as a matter of constitutional law that the privilege he has asserted must prevail over the subpoena duces tecum in this case.

A

We unreservedly reject the claim that the President alone, by simple assertion of privilege, had the unreviewable power to decide not to deliver the subpoenaed materials to the District Court. Under our Constitution, it is only the Judicial Branch that is ultimately empowered to determine questions of law, even though those questions may involve the scope of the other branches' powers.*

This basic postulate of our constitutional system was strikingly confirmed a generation ago in *Youngstown Sheet & Tube Co.* v. *Sawyer*, 343 U. S. 579, where this Court held invalid the President's asserted power to seize the nation's steel mills. Perhaps even more relevantly, several recent decisions of this Court have made clear that it is for the judiciary alone to delineate the scope of

---

† Original in typescript.

* The only limiting principle is that expressed in *Mississippi* v. *Johnson*, 4 Wall. 475, which held that it is not for the judiciary to determine whether or not the President is faithfully executing the laws. The Court there noted that "the duty thus imposed [by Art. II] on the President is in no just sense ministerial. It is purely executive and political."

constitutional immunity or privilege, even the explicit immunity conferred upon members of the Legislative Branch by the Speech and Debate Clause, U. S. Const. Art I, sec. 6. *Doe* v. *McMillan*, 412 U. S. 306, 318, n. 12; *Gravel* v. *United States*, 408 U. S. 606; *United States* v. *Brewster*, 408 U. S. 501; *United States* v. *Johnson*, 329 U. S. 503.

As the Court stated in *Baker* v. *Carr*, 369 U. S. 186, 211, and reaffirmed in *Powell* v. *McCormack*, 395 U. S. 486, 521, "[d]eciding whether a matter has in any measure been committed by the Constitution to another branch of government, or whether the action of that branch exceeds whatever authority has been committed, is itself a delicate exercise in constitutional interpretation, and is a responsibility of this Court as ultimate interpreter of the Constitution. . . . Our system of government requires that federal courts on occasion interpret the Constitution in a manner at variance with the construction given the document by another branch. The alleged conflict that such an adjudication may cause cannot justify the courts' avoiding their constitutional responsibility." *Powell* v. *McCormack, supra,* at 549 (footnote omitted).

We hold, in short, that no part of the "judicial power of the United States" which Art. III, § 1, of the Constitution vests in the federal courts can by insistence of the President on "executive privilege" be shared by him. Any other view would be false to the basic concept of the separation of powers that lies at the very heart of our constitutional structure—a structure whose primary purpose was to insure against tyranny.* As James Madison made the point, "[t]he accumulation of all powers, legislative, executive, and judiciary, in the same hands, whether of one, a few, or many, and whether hereditary, appointed, or elective, may justly be pro-

---

* In the words of Mr. Justice Brandeis, "[t]he doctrine of separation of powers was adopted by the Convention of 1787 not to promote efficiency but to preclude the exercise of arbitrary power." *Myers* v. *United States*, 272 U. S. 42, 293.

nounced the very definition of tyranny." *The Federalist,*
No. 47, p. 313 (S. F. Mittel ed. 1938).

Under our Constitution, "no man can be judge in his
own case, however exalted his station, however righteous
his motives. . . ." *Walker* v. *City of Birmingham,* 388
U. S. 307, 320–321. As the Court put the matter in
United States v. *Lee,* 106 U. S. 196, 220:

> "No man in this country is so high that he is above
> the law.   No officer of the law may set that law at
> defiance with impunity.   All the officers of the gov-
> ernment, from the highest to the lowest, are crea-
> tures of the law, and are bound to obey it."

And, in the classic words of Chief Justice Marshall in
Marbury v. *Madison,* 1 Cranch 137, 177: "It is emphatically the province and the duty of the judicial department to say what the law is."   The existence and scope
of Presidential privilege is thus a judicial question for
the Judicial Branch alone to decide.   It is a question that
must, therefore, be decided here and now.

B

If, as we have held, it is for the judiciary alone to
determine the existence and scope of Presidential privilege in any given context, the President argues that we
should determine that the privilege must prevail over the
subpoena duces tecum issued in this case by the District
Court at the request of the Special Prosecutor in anticipation of a forthcoming criminal trial.

We are a nation governed by the rule of law.   Nowhere is our commitment to this principle more profound
than in the enforcement of the criminal law, "the two-
fold aim of which is that guilt shall not escape or innocence suffer." *Berger* v. *United States,* 295 U. S. 78, 88
(1935).   Conviction of the guilty and exoneration of the
innocent are matters of the greatest consequence for a
people devoted to equal justice under law.   Individuals
are subject to criminal penalties for conduct proscribed
by society.   The imposition of such penalties turns on

what was done and by whom and with what intent. Enforcement of the criminal law requires ascertainment of these facts. It is, in short, a search for truth.

We have committed that pursuit to an adversary system in which the parties contest all issues before a court of law. To develop their opposing contentions of fact, the parties are entitled to invoke the court's authority to compel production of relevant evidence. Because the adversary nature of our system is tempered by an overriding concern for fairness to the individual, the prosecutor has an obligation to reveal evidence that may be favorable to the defense. "The United States Attorney is the representative not of an ordinary party to a controversy, but of a sovereignty whose obligation to govern impartially is as compelling as its obligation to govern at all; and whose interest, therefore, in a criminal prosecution is not that it shall win a case, but that justice shall be done." *Berger* v. *United States, supra,* at 88. In addition, the accused has the right to a fair trial by making the best possible defense on the basis of all material evidence. And the court itself has the paramount duty to ensure that justice is done. Accordingly, the need to develop all relevant facts is both elemental and comprehensive, for the ends of the criminal law would be defeated if judgments were founded on a fragmentary or speculative presentation of the facts. To the extent that the search for truth is restrained, the integrity of the process of criminal justice is impaired. As a general proposition, therefore, the law is entitled to every man's evidence. See *Branzburg* v. *Hayes*, 408 U.S. 665, 688 (1972).

This rule, however, is not absolute. It admits of exceptions designed to protect weighty and legitimate competing interests. Thus, the Fifth Amendment to the Constitution provides that no man "shall be compelled in any criminal case to be a witness against himself." And an attorney may not be required to reveal what his client has told him in confidence. These and other interests are recognized at law by evidentiary privileges against forced disclosure. Such privileges may be established in the Constitution, by statute, or at common law. Whatever their origins, these exceptions to the demand for every man's evidence are not lightly created nor expansively construed, for they are in derogation of the search for truth.

In this case the President challenges a subpoena requiring the production of materials for use in certain criminal prosecutions. He claims that he has a privilege against compliance with that subpoena. He does not contend that disclosure of the subpoenaed material would compromise state secrets. There is no claim that the conversations at issue involved matters of military planning or intelligence, sensitive aspects of foreign affairs, or any other data whose disclosure would be contrary to the national interest. Rather, the President grounds his assertion of privilege in the generalized interest in preserving the confidentiality of his discussions with his advisers. Because maintaining confidentiality for such discussions is essential to high office, he claims a privilege against forced disclosure. The President further argues that only he can assess accurately the degree to which disclosure in a particular case would impair the effective performance of his constitutional duties.

The President's argument rests in part on the nature of government itself and in part on the tripartite division of sovereign powers within our government. All nations find it necessary to shield from public scrutiny some of the deliberations that constitute the process of government. Those selected to conduct the affairs of state must be free to speak plainly to one another and to seek honest and forthright advice on matters of national policy. Yet human experience teaches that those who expect public dissemination of their remarks may temper candor with a concern for appearances. The willingness to advance tentative ideas, to play the devil's advocate, and to reveal the ultimate basis for a particular view may succumb to public posturing and a reticence born of the fear of appearing foolish. That consequence would distort and impair the search for sound public policy. Accordingly, a general expectation of confidentiality for deliberations among the officers of government and their advisers serves the public good.*

The framers of our Constitution understood this point. When they undertook to draft the Charter for a fledgling nation, they chose not to hold their debates in public. Rather, they maintained the secrecy of their discussions until well after ratification of the Constitution by the States. Modern practice reflects continued appreciation of the insight of the framers. For example, the House-Senate Conference Committees that meet to resolve differences in bills that have passed both Houses hold their proceedings in confidence. Similarly, the deliberations of this Court are conducted in utmost secrecy. In these and other instances, officers of government need to be able to rely on an expectation of confidentiality to facilitate plain talk.

That the need for confidentiality exists in any government does not mean, however, that it must always prevail over competing societal interests. See, *e. g., Conway* v. *Rimmer,* 1 All E. R. 874 (1968). Some greater public good may warrant occasional inroads into the principle of confidentiality. The Constitution does not explicitly mention the President's interest in confidentiality. Yet to the extent that the interest in confidentiality pertains to the President's effective exercise of his executive powers, it is nevertheless constitutionally based. The Constitution does confer the right upon every defendant "to be confronted with the witnesses against him" and

---

* "Freedom of communication vital to fulfillment of wholesome relationships is obtained only by removing the specter of compelled disclosure. . . . [G]overnment . . . needs open but protected channels for the kind of plain talk that is essential to the quality of its functioning." *Carl Zeiss Stiftung* v. *V. E. B. Carl Zeiss, Jena,* 40 F.R.D. 318, 325 (DDC 1966). See *Nixon* v. *Sirica,* —— U. S. App. D. C. ——, ——, 487 F. 2d 700, 713 (1973); *Kaiser Aluminum & Chem. Corp.* v. *United States,* 157 F. Supp. 939 (Ct. Cl. 1958) (*per* Reed, J.); *The Federalist* No. 64 (S. F. Mittel ed. 1938).

"to have compulsory process for obtaining witnesses in his favor." (Am. VI)   And, of course, the Constitution also guarantees that no person shall be deprived of liberty without due process of law.   (Am. V)   Because the production of all material evidence in a criminal trial furthers those guarantees, it too is a matter of constitutional import.

We must balance the essentiality of the privilege to the President's performance of the responsibilities vested in him against the inroads of such a privilege on the fair administration of criminal justice.*   The interest in confidentiality, as distinct from the preservation of state secrets, is a generalized concern.   The goal is to promote candor by maintaining an expectation of confidentiality rather than to preserve secrecy for the substance of any particular communication.   The asserted need to refuse to comply with a subpoena presumes that rare and isolated instances of disclosure would negate the general expectation of confidentiality and thus defeat the ability of the President to obtain candid advice.   We think that this assumption is unfounded.   The willingness to speak plainly is not so fragile that it would be undermined by some remote prospect of disclosure in narrowly defined and isolated circumstances.   At least this is true where the prospect of disclosure is limited to demands for evidence demonstrably material to a criminal prosecution. It requires no clairvoyance to foresee that such demands will arise with the greatest infrequency nor any special insight to recognize that few advisers will be moved to temper the candor of their remarks by such an unlikely

---

* We wish to emphasize the narrow scope of this inquiry. We are not here concerned with the balance between the President's generalized interest in confidentiality and the need for relevant evidence in civil litigation, nor with that between the confidentiality interest and Congressional demands for information, nor with that between the President's interest in preserving state secrets and any other concern, whether originating in Congress or the courts. We address only the conflict between the President's assertion of a privilege not to divulge confidential conversations and the constitutional need for evidence material to criminal trials.

possibility.*   Thus, while the general interest in confidentiality is weighty indeed, it is not significantly impaired by the demands of criminal justice.

On the other hand, an unqualified privilege against disclosure of evidence demonstrably relevant to a criminal trial would cut deeply into the guarantee of due process of law.   While the President's interest in confidentiality is general in nature, the constitutional need for production of material evidence in a criminal proceeding is not. The enforcement of the criminal laws does not depend on an assessment of the broad sweep of events but on a limited number of specific historical facts concerning the conduct of identified individuals at given times.   The President's broad interest in confidentiality would not be vitiated by disclosure of a limited number of confidential conversations, but nondisclosure of those same conversations could gravely impair the pursuit of truth in a criminal prosecution.

Thus where the President's ground for withholding subpoenaed materials from use in a criminal trial is only the generalized interest in confidentiality, it cannot prevail over the needs of due process of law in a federal

---

* Mr. Justice Cardozo made this point in an analogous context. Speaking for a unanimous Court in *Clark* v. *United States*, 289 U. S. 1 (1933), he emphasized the importance of maintaining the secrecy of the deliberations of a petit jury in a criminal case. "Freedom of debate might be stifled and independence of thought checked if jurors were made to feel that their arguments and ballots were to be freely published to the world." *Id.*, at 13.   Nonetheless, the Court also recognized that isolated inroads on confidentiality designed to serve the paramount need of the criminal law would not vitiate the interests served by secrecy:

A juror of integity and reasonable firmness will not fear to speak his mind if the confidences of debate are barred to the ears of mere impertinence or malice.   He will not expect to be shielded against the disclosure of his conduct in the event that there is evidence reflecting upon his honor.   The chance that now and then there may be found some timid soul who will take counsel of his fears and give way to their repressive power is too remote and shadowy to shape the course of justice." *Id.*, at 16.

criminal trial. The privilege of his office, although of constitutional dimensions, is qualified in nature. He may be ordered, therefore, upon a proper showing, to produce the requested materials.* We do not reach this conclusion lightly nor do we wish to suggest that courts may presume to order the President of the United States to produce confidential materials absent sufficient justification. The avoidance of unnecessary harassment of our Chief Executive, the importance of the expectation of confidentiality for his discussions with his advisers, and proper deference to the head of a coordinate branch of government who is himself charged by the Constitution to "take Care that the Laws be faithfully executed" suggest that courts should be as reluctant to tread this ground as the sound discharge of their constitutional responsibilities will allow. Courts must follow certain standards and procedures to assure that the President's legitimate interests are adequately protected. It is to those requirements that we now turn.

---

* No prior case from this or any other court resolves the precise issue before us. Earlier precedents cited by the parties have dealt with state secrets, *e. g.*, *United States* v. *Reynolds*, 345 U. S. 1 (1953), with claims of executive privilege by subordinate executive officers in the context of civil trials, *e. g.*, *ibid; Committee for Nuclear Responsibility, Inc.* v. *Seaborg*, — App. D. C. —, 463 F. 2d 788 (1971) ; *Kaiser Aluminum & Chemical Corp.* v. *United States*, 157 F. Supp. 939 (Ct. Cl. 1958) ; *Carl Zeiss Stiftung* v. *V. E. B. Carl Zeiss, Jena*, 40 F. R. D. 318 (CD 1966), aff'd on opinion below, 384 F. 2d 979 (CADC 1967), cert. denied, 389 U. S. 952 (1968), or with the unique responsibilities and powers of a grand jury. See *Nixon* v. *Sirica*, — App. D. C. —, 487 F. 2d 700 (1973). Nevertheless, our conclusion is in full accord with the principle underlying all of those cases—that the privilege is far from absolute as a matter of constitutional law.

SUPREME COURT OF THE UNITED STATES

Nos. 73–1766 AND 73–1834

| United States, Petitioner, 73–1766 *v.* Richard M. Nixon, President of the United States, et al. | On Writs of Certiorari to the United States Court of Appeals for the District of Columbia Circuit. |
| Richard M. Nixon, President of the United States, Petitioner, 73–1834 *v.* United States. | |

[July —, 1974]

MR. CHIEF JUSTICE BURGER delivered the opinion of the Court.

This case presents for review the denial of a motion, filed on behalf of the President, to quash a third-party subpoena duces tecum issued by the United States District Court for the District of Columbia, pursuant to Fed. Rule Crim. Proc. 17 (c). The subpoena directed the President to produce certain tape recordings and documents relating to his conversations with aides and advisers. The court rejected the President's claims of absolute executive privilege, of lack of jurisdiction, and of failure to satisfy the requirements of Rule 17 (c). The President appealed to the Court of Appeals. We granted the United States' petition for certiorari before judgment,[1] and also the President's responsive cross-

---

[1] See 28 U. S. C. §§ 1254 (1) and 2101 (e) and our Rule 20. See, *e, g., Youngstown Sheet & Tube Co.* v. *Sawyer,* 343 U. S. 937, 579,

UNITED STATES *v.* NIXON

petition for certiorari before judgment,[2] because of the public importance of the issues presented and the need for their prompt resolution. — U. S. —, — (1974).

On March 1, 1974, a grand jury of the United States District Court for the District of Columbia returned an indictment charging seven named individuals[3] with various offenses, including conspiracy to defraud the United States and to obstruct justice. The grand jury also named the President, among others, as a co-conspirator. On April 18, 1974, upon motion of the Special Prosecutor, a subpoena duces tecum was issued pursuant to Rule 17(c) to the President by the United States District Court and made returnable on May 2, 1974. This subpoena required the production, in advance of the September 9 trial date, of certain tapes, memoranda, papers, transcripts, or other writings relating to certain precisely identified meetings between the President and others.[4] The Special Prosecutor was able to fix the time, place and persons present at these discussions because the

---

584 (1952); *United States v. United Mine Workers,* 329 U. S. 708, 709, 710 (1946); 330 U. S. 258, 269 (1947); *Carter v. Carter Coal Co.,* 298 U. S. 238 (1936); *Rickert Rice Mills v. Fontenot,* 297 U. S. 110 (1936); *Railroad Retirement Board v. Alton R. Co.,* 295 U. S. 330, 344 (1935); *United States v. Bankers Trust Co.,* 294 U. S. 240, 243 (1935).

[2] This cross-petition raised the issue whether the grand jury acted within its authority in naming the President as a co-conspirator. Since we find resolution of this issue unnecessary to the disposition of the case, the cross-petition for certiorari is denied as improvidently granted.

[3] The seven defendants are John N. Mitchell, H. R. Haldeman, John D. Ehrlichman, Charles W. Colson, Robert C. Mardian, Kenneth W. Parkinson, and Gordon Strachan. Each had occupied either a position of responsibility on the White House staff or the Committee for the Re-Election of the President.

[4] The specific meetings and conversations are enumerated in a schedule attached to the subpoena. 42a–46a of the App.

UNITED STATES *v.* NIXON

White House daily logs and appointment records had been delivered to him. On April 30, the President publicly released edited transcripts of 43 conversations; portions of 20 conversations subject to subpoena in the present case were included. On May 1, 1974, the President's counsel, filed a "special appearance" and a motion to quash the subpoena, under Rule 17 (c). This motion was accompanied by a formal claim of privilege. At a subsequent hearing,[5] further motions to expunge the grand jury's action naming the President as a co-conspirator and for protective orders against the disclosure of that information were filed or raised orally by counsel for the President.

On May 20, 1974, the District Court denied the motion to quash and the motions to expunge and for protective orders. —— F. Supp. —— (1974). It further ordered "the President or any subordinate officer, official or employee with custody or control of the documents or objects subpoenaed," *id.,* at ——, to deliver to the District Court, on or before May 31, 1974, the originals of all subpoenaed items, as well as an index and analysis of those items, together with tape copies of those portions of the subpoenaed recordings for which transcripts had been released to the public by the President on April 28. The District Court rejected jurisdictional challenges based on a contention that the dispute was nonjusticiable because it was between the Special Prosecutor and the Chief Executive and hence "intra-executive" in character; it also rejected the contention that the judiciary was without authority to review an assertion of executive privilege by the President. The rejection of the first challenge was based on the authority and powers vested

---

[5] At the joint suggestion of the Special Prosecutor and counsel for the President, and with the approval of counsel for the defendants, further proceedings in the District Court were held *in camera,*

UNITED STATES *v.* NIXON

in the Special Prosecutor by the regulation promulgated by the Attorney General; the court concluded that a justiciable controversy was presented. The second challenge was held to be foreclosed by the decision in *Nixon v. Sirica,* — U. S. App. D. C. —, 487 F. 2d 700 (1973). The District Court held that the judiciary, not the President, was the final arbiter of a claim of executive privilege. The court concluded that, under the circumstances of this case, the presumptive privilege was overcome by the Special Prosecutor's prima facie "demonstration of need sufficiently compelling to warrant judicial examination in chambers . . . ." — F. Supp. — (1974). The court held, finally, that the Special Prosecutor had satisfied the requirements of Rule 17 (c). The District Court stayed its order pending appellate review on condition that review was sought before 4 p. m., May 24. The court further provided that matters filed under seal remain under seal when transmitted as part of the record.

On May 24, 1974, the President filed a timely notice of appeal from the District Court order, and the certified record from the District Court was docketed in the United States Court of Appeals for the District of Columbia Circuit. On the same day, the President also filed a petition for writ of mandamus in the Court of Appeals seeking review of the District Court order.

On May 24, the Special Prosecutor also filed, in this Court, a petition for a writ of certiorari before judgment. On May 31, the petition was granted with an expedited briefing schedule. — U. S. — (1974). On June 6, the President filed, under seal, a cross-petition for writ of certiorari before judgment. This cross-petition was granted June 15, 1974, — U. S. — (1974)." and the case was set for argument on July 8, 1974.

" On June 19, 1974, the President's counsel moved for disclosure and transmittal to this Court of all evidence presented to the grand jury

UNITED STATES *v.* NIXON

I

JURISDICTION

The threshold question presented is whether the May 20, 1974, order of the District Court was an appealable order and whether this case was properly "in" the United States Court of Appeals when the petition for certiorari was filed in this Court.[*] That Court of Appeals' jurisdiction under 28 U. S. C. § 1291 encompasses only "final decisions of the district courts." Since the appeal was timely filed and all other procedural requirements were met, the petition was properly before this Court for consideration if the District Court order was final. 28 U. S. C. § 1254 (1); 28 U. S. C. § 2101 (e).

The finality requirement of 28 U. S. C. § 1291 embodies a strong congressional policy against piecemeal reviews, and against obstructing or impeding an ongoing judicial proceeding by interlocutory appeals. See, *e. g., Cobbledick v. United States,* 309 U. S. 323, 324–326 (1940). This requirement ordinarily promotes judicial efficiency and hastens the ultimate termination of litigation. In applying this principle to an order denying a motion to quash and requiring the production of evidence pursuant to a subpoena duces tecum, it has been repeatedly held that the order is not final and hence not appealable, *United States v. Ryan,* 402 U. S. 530, 532 (1971); *Cobbledick v. United States,* 309 U. S. 322 (1940); *Alexander v. United States,* 201 U. S. 117 (1906). This Court has

> "consistently held that the necessity for expedition

---

relating to its action in naming the President as an unindicted co-conspirator. Action on this motion was deferred pending oral argument of the case.

[*] We granted expedited hearing of this case, before judgment in the Court of Appeals; before the petition for certiorari was filed in this Court, a notice of appeal had been docketed by the President in the District Court and the certified record had been docketed in the Court of Appeals. These actions all occurred on May 24, 1974.

UNITED STATES *v.* NIXON

in the administration of the criminal law justifies putting one who seeks to resist the production of desired information to a choice between compliance with a trial court's order to produce prior to any review of that order, and resistance to that order with the concomitant possibility of an adjudication of contempt if his claims are rejected on appeal." *United States* v. *Ryan*, 402 U. S. 530, 533 (1971).

The requirement of submitting to contempt, however, is not without exception and in some instances the purposes underlying the finality rule require a different result. For example, in *Perlman* v. *United States*, 247 U. S. 7 (1918), a subpoena had been directed to a third party requesting certain exhibits; the appellant, who owned the exhibits, sought to raise a claim of privilege. The Court held an order compelling production was appealable because it was unlikely that the third party would risk a contempt citation in order to allow immediate review of the appellant's claim of privilege. *Id.*, at 12–13. That case fell within the "limited class of cases where denial of immediate review would render impossible any review whatsoever of an individual's claims." *United States* v. *Ryan, supra,* at 533.

Here too the traditional contempt avenue to immediate appeal is peculiarly inappropriate due to the unique setting in which the question arises. To require a president to place himself in the posture of disobeying an order of a court merely to trigger the procedural mechanism for review of the ruling would be unseemly, and present an unnecessary occasion for constitutional confrontation between two branches of the Government. Similarly, a federal judge should not be placed in the posture of issuing a citation to a president simply in order to invoke review. The issue whether a president can be cited for contempt could itself engender protracted litigation, and

UNITED STATES *v.* NIXON

would further delay both review on the merits of his
claim of privilege and the ultimate termination of the
underlying criminal action for which his evidence is
sought. These considerations lead us to conclude that
the order of the District Court was an appealable order.
The appeal from that order was therefore properly "in"
the Court of Appeals, and the case is now properly before
this Court on the writ of certiorari before judgment. 28
U. S. C. § 1254; 28 U. S. C. § 2101 (e). *Gay* v. *Ruff*, 292
U. S. 25, 30 (1934).

II

JUSTICIABILITY

In the District Court, the President's counsel argued
that the court lacked jurisdiction to issue the subpoena
because the matter was an intra-branch dispute between
a subordinate and superior officer of the Executive
Branch and hence not subject to judicial resolution.
That argument has been renewed in this Court with
emphasis on the contention that the dispute does not
present a "case" or "controversy" which can be adjudicated in the federal courts. The President's counsel
argues that the federal courts should not intrude into
areas committed to the other branches of government.
He views the present dispute as essentially a "jurisdictional" dispute within the Executive Branch which he
analogizes to a dispute between two congressional committees. Since the Executive Branch has exclusive
authority and absolute discretion to decide whether to
prosecute a case, *Confiscation Cases*, 7 Wall. (74 U. S.)
454 (1869), *United States* v. *Cox*, 342 F. 2d 167, 171
(CA5), cert. denied, 381 U. S. 935 (1965), it is contended
that an executive decision is final in determining what
evidence is to be used in a given criminal case. Although
his counsel concedes the President has delegated certain
specific powers to the Special Prosecutor, he has not

UNITED STATES *v.* NIXON

"waived or delegated to the Special Prosecutor the President's duty to claim privilege as to all materials . . . which fall within the President's inherent authority to refuse to disclose to any executive officer." Brief of President 42. The Special Prosecutor's demand for the items therefore presents, in the view of the President's counsel, a political question under *Baker v. Carr,* 369 U. S. 186 (1962), since it involves a "textually demonstrable" grant of power under Art. II.

The mere assertion of a claim of an "intra-branch dispute," without more, has never operated to defeat federal jurisdiction; justiciability does not depend on such a surface inquiry. In *United States v. Interstate Commerce Commission,* 337 U. S. 426 (1949), the Court observed, "courts must look behind the names that symbolize the parties to determine whether a justiciable case or controversy is presented." 337 U. S., at 430. See also: *Powell v. McCormack,* 395 U. S. 486 (1969); *ICC v. Jersey City,* 322 U. S. 503 (1944); *United States ex rel. Chapman v. FPC,* 345 U. S. 153 (1953); *Secretary of Agriculture v. United States,* 347 U. S. 645 (1954); *Federal Maritime Board v. Isbrandtsen Co.,* 356 U. S. 481, 482 n. 2 (1958); *United States v. Marine Bank,* — U. S. — (1974), and *United States v. Connecticut National Bank,* — U. S. — (1974).

An essential starting point is the nature of the proceeding for which the evidence is sought—here a pending criminal prosecution. It is a judicial proceeding in a federal court alleging violation of federal laws and is brought in the name of the United States as sovereign. *Berger v. United States,* 295 U. S. 78 (1935). Under the authority of Art. II, § 2, Congress has vested in the Attorney General the power to conduct the criminal litigation of the United States Government. 28 U. S. C. § 516. It has also vested in him the power to appoint subordinate officers to assist him in the discharge of his

UNITED STATES *v* NIXON

duties. 28 U. S. C. §§ 509, 510, 515, 533. Acting pursuant to those statutes, the Attorney General has delegated the authority to represent the United States in these particular matters to a special prosecutor with unique authority and tenure.[8] The regulations give the Special Prosecutor explicit power to contest the invocation of executive privilege in the process of seeking evidence deemed relevant to the performance of these specially delegated duties." 38 Fed. Reg., at 30739.

---

[8] Regulations issued by the Attorney General pursuant to his statutory authority, vest in the Special Prosecutor plenary authority to control the course of investigations and litigation related to "all offenses arising out of the 1972 Presidential Election for which the Special Prosecutor deems it necessary and appropriate to assume responsibility, allegations involving the President, members of the White House staff, or Presidential appointees, and any other matters which he consents to have assigned to him by the Attorney General." 38 Fed. Reg., at 30739. In particular, the Special Prosecutor was given full authority, *inter alia*. "to contest the assertion of 'Executive Privilege' . . . and handl[e] all aspects of any cases within his jurisdiction." *Ibid.* The regulations then go on to provide:

"In exercising this authority, the Special Prosecutor will have the greatest degree of independence that is consistent with the Attorney-General's statutory accountability for all matters falling within the jurisdiction of the Department of Justice. The Attorney General will not countermand or interfere with the Special Prosecutor's decisions or actions. The Special Prosecutor will determine whether and to what extent he will inform or consult with the Attorney General about the conduct of his duties and responsibilities. In accordance with assurances given by the President to the Attorney General that the President will not exercise his Constitutional powers to effect the discharge of the Special Prosecutor or to limit the independence he is hereby given, the Special Prosecutor will not be removed from his duties except for extraordinary improprieties on his part and without the President's first consulting the Majority and Minority Leaders and Chairman and ranking Minority Members of the Judiciary Committees of the Senate and House of Representatives and ascertaining that their consensus is in accord with his proposed action."

[9] That this was the understanding of Acting Attorney General

UNITED STATES *v.* NIXON

It is argued that so long as these regulations are extant
they have the force of law. In *Accardi* v. *Shaughnessy,*
347 U. S. 260 (1953), regulations of the Attorney General
delegated certain of his discretionary powers to the Board
of Immigration Appeals and required that Board to exercise its own discretion on appeals in deportation cases.
The Court held that so long as the Attorney General's
regulation remained operative, he denied himself the
authority to exercise the discretion delegated to the
Board even though the original authority was his and
he could reassert it by amending the regulations. *Service*
v. *Dulles,* 354 U. S. 363, 388 (1957), and *Vitarelli v.
Seaton,* 359 U. S. 535 (1959), reaffirmed the basic holding
of *Accardi.*

Here, as in *Accardi,* it is possible for the Attorney
General to amend or revoke the regulations defining the
Special Prosecutor's authority. But he has not done

Robert Bork, the author of the regulations establishing the independence of the Special Prosecutor, is shown by his testimony before the
Senate Judiciary Committee:

"Although it is anticipated that Mr. Jaworski will receive cooperation
from the White House in getting any evidence he feels he needs to
conduct investigations and prosecutions, it is clear and understood
on all sides that he has the power to use judicial processes to pursue
evidence if disagreement should develop."

Hearings before the Senate Judiciary Committee on the Special
Prosecutor, 93d Cong., 1st Sess., pt. 2, at 470 (1973). Acting Attorney General Bork gave similar assurances to the House Subcommittee on Criminal Justice. Hearings before the House Judiciary
Subcommittee on Criminal Justice on H. J. Res. 784 and H. R. 10937,
93d Cong., 1st Sess. 266 (1973). At his confirmation hearings, Attorney General William Saxbe testified that he shared Acting
Attorney General Bork's views concerning the Special Prosecutor's
authority to test any claim of executive privilege in the courts,
Hearings before the Senate Judiciary Committee on the nomination
of William B. Saxbe to be Attorney General, 93d Cong., 1st Sess. 9
(1973).

UNITED STATES *v.* NIXON

so.[10] So long as these regulations remain in force the
Executive Branch is bound by them, and indeed the
United States as the sovereign composed of the three
branches is bound to respect and to enforce them.   Moreover, the delegation of authority to the Special Prosecutor
in this case is not an ordinary delegation by the Attorney
General to a subordinate officer; with the authorization
of the President, the Acting Attorney General provided
in the regulations that the Special Prosecutor was not to
be removed without the "consensus" of eight designated
leaders of Congress. Note 8, *supra.*

The demands of and the resistance to the subpoena
present an obvious controversy in the ordinary, colloquial
sense but that alone is not sufficient to meet constitutional standards.   In the constitutional sense, controversy means more than disagreement and conflict;
rather it means the kind of controversy courts traditionally resolve.   Here at issue is the production or
nonproduction of specified evidence preliminarily determined to be relevant and admissible in a pending criminal case.   It is sought by one official of the Government within the scope of his express authority; it is
resisted by the Chief Executive on the ground of his duty
to preserve the confidentiality of the communications of
the office of president.   Whatever is the correct answer on
the merits, these issues are "of the type which are traditionally justiciable." *United States v. ICC,* 337 U. S.,
at 430 (1949). The independent Special Prosecutor with
his asserted need for the subpoenaed material in the
underlying criminal prosecution is opposed by the Presi-

---

[10] At his confirmation hearings Attorney General William Saxbe
testified that he agreed with the regulations adopted by Acting Attorney General Bork and would not remove the Special Prosecutor
except for "extraordinary improprieties."   There is no contention
here that the Special Prosecutor is guilty of any "extraordinary"
improprieties."

UNITED STATES *v.* NIXON

dent with his steadfast assertion of privilege against disclosure of the material. This setting assures there is
"that concrete adverseness which sharpens the presentation of issues upon which the Court so largely depends
for illumination of difficult constitutional questions."
Baker v. *Carr,* 369 U. S. 186, 204 (1962). Moreover,
since the matter is one arising in the regular course of a
federal criminal prosecution, it is within the traditional
scope of Art. III power. *Id.,* at 217. In light of the
uniqueness of the setting in which the conflict arises, the
fact that both parties are officers of the Executive Branch
cannot be viewed as a barrier to justiciability. It would
be inconsistent with the applicable law and regulations
and the unique facts of this case to conclude other than
that the Special Prosecutor has standing to bring this
action and that a justiciable controversy is presented for
decision.

III

RULE 17 (c)

The subpoena duces tecum is challenged on the ground
that the Special Prosecutor failed to satisfy the requirements of Fed. Rule Crim. Proc. 17 (c), which governs
the issuance of subpoenas duces tecum in criminal proceedings. If we sustained this challenge, there would be
no occasion to reach the claim of privilege asserted with
respect to the subpoenaed material. Thus we will deal
first with the question whether the requirements of Rule
17 (c) have been satisfied. See *Arkansas-Louisiana Gas
Co.* v. *Dept. of Public Utilities,* 304 U. S. 61, 64 (1938);
Ashwander v. *Tennessee Valley Authority,* 297 U. S. 288,
346–347 (1936). (Brandeis, J., concurring.)

Rule 17 (c) provides:

> "A subpoena may also command the person to
> whom it is directed to produce the books, papers,
> documents or other objects designated therein,

UNITED STATES *v.* NIXON

The court on motion made promptly may quash or
modify the supoena if compliance would be unreasonable or oppressive. The court may direct that
books, papers, documents or objects designated in
the subpoena be produced before the court at a
time prior to the trial or prior to the time when they
are to be offered in evidence and may upon their
production permit the books, papers, documents or
objects or portions thereof to be inspected by the
parties and their attorneys."

A subpoena for documents may be quashed if their production would be "unreasonable or oppressive," but not
otherwise. The leading case in this Court interpreting
this standard is *Bowman Dairy Co. v. United States*, 341
U. S. 214 (1950). This case recognized certain fundamental characteristics of the subpoena duces tecum in
criminal cases: (1) it was not intended to provide a
means of discovery for criminal cases. 341 U. S., at 220;
(2) its chief innovation was to expedite the trial by providing a time and place *before* trial for the inspection of
subpoenaed materials.[11] *Ibid.* As both parties agree,
cases decided in the wake of *Bowman* have generally
followed Judge Weinfeld's formulation in *United States
v. Iozia*, 13 F. R. D. 335, 338 (D. C. N. Y. 1952), as to
the required showing. Under this test, in order to

---

[11] The Court quoted a statement of a member of the advisory
committee that the purpose of the Rule was to bring documents into
court "in advance of that time that they are offered in evidence, so
that they may then be inspected in advance, for the purpose . . . of
enabling the party to see whether he can use it or whether he
wants to use it." 341 U. S., at 220 n. 5. The Manual for Complex
and Multi-district Litigation published by the Administrative Office
of the United States Courts recommends that Rule 17 (c) be encouraged in complex criminal cases in order that each party may be
compelled to produce its documentary evidence well in advance of
trial in advance of the time it is to be offered. P. 142, CCH Ed.

UNITED STATES *v.* NIXON

require production prior to trial, the moving party must show: (1) that the documents are evidentiary [12] and relevant; (2) that they are not otherwise procurable reasonably in advance of trial by exercise of due diligence; (3) that the party cannot properly prepare for trial without such production and inspection in advance of trial and that the failure to obtain such inspection may tend unreasonably to delay the trial; (4) that the application is made in good faith and is not intended as a general "fishing expedition."

Against this background, the Special Prosecutor, in order to carry his burden, must clear three hurdles: (1) relevancy; (2) admissibility; (3) specificity. Our own review of the record necessarily affords a less comprehensive view of the total situation than was available to the trial judge and we are unwilling to conclude that the District Court erred in the evaluation of the Special Prosecutor's showing under Rule 17 (c). Our conclusion is based on the record before us, much of which is under seal. Of course, the contents of the subpoenaed tapes could not at that stage be described fully by the Special Prosecutor, but there was a sufficient likelihood that each of the tapes contains conversations relevant to the offenses charged in the indictment. *United States v.*

---

[12] The District Court found here that it was faced with "the more unusual situation . . . where the subpoena, rather than being directed to the government by the defendants, issues to what, as a practical matter, is a third party." *United States v. Mitchell*, —— F. Supp. —— (DC 1974). The Special Prosecutor suggests that the evidentiary requirement of *Bowman Dairy Co.* and *Iozia* does not apply in its full vigor when the subpoena duces tecum is issued to third parties rather than to government prosecutors. Brief for the United States, at 128–129. We need not decide whether a lower standard exists because we are satisfied that the relevance and the evidentiary nature of the subpoenaed tapes were sufficiently shown as a preliminary matter to warrant the District Court's refusal to quash the subpoena.

UNITED STATES *v.* NIXON

Gross, 24 F. R. D. 138 (SDNY 1959). With respect
to many of the tapes, the Special Prosecutor offered the
sworn testimony or statements of one or more of the
participants in the conversations as to what was said at
the time. As for the remainder of the tapes, the identity
of the participants and the time and place of the conversations, taken in their total context, permit a rational
inference that at least part of the conversations relate
to the offenses charged in the indictment.

We also conclude there was a sufficient preliminary
showing that each of the subpoenaed tapes contains evidence admissible with respect to the offenses charged in
the indictment. The most cogent objection to the admissibility of the taped conversations here at issue is that
they are a collection of out-of-court statements by declarants who will not be subject to cross-examination and
that the statements are therefore inadmissible hearsay.
Here, however, most of the tapes apparently contain conversations to which one or more of the defendants named
in the indictment were party. However, the hearsay rule
does not automatically bar all out-of-court statements by
a defendant in a criminal case. *On Lee v. United States,*
343 U. S. 747, 757 (1953). Declarations by one defendant may also be admissible against other defendants upon
a sufficient showing, by independent evidence,[13] of a con-

---

[13] As a preliminary matter, there must be substantial, independent
evidence of the conspiracy, at least enough to take the question to
the jury. *United States v. Vaught,* 385 F. 2d 320, 323 (CA4 1973);
United States v. Hoffa, 349 F. 2d 20, 41–42 (CA6 1965), *aff'd on
other grounds,* 385 U. S. 293 (1966); *United States v. Santos,* 385 F.
2d 43, 45 (CA7 1967), cert. denied, 390 U. S. 954 (1968); *United
States v. Morton,* 483 F. 2d 573, 576 (CA8 1973); *United States v.
Spanos,* 462 F. 2d 1012, 1014 (CA9 1972); *Carbo v. United States,*
314 F. 2d 718, 737 (CA9 1963), cert. denied, 377 U. S. 953 (1964).
Whether the standard has been satisfied is a question of admissibility
of evidence to be decided by the trial judge.

UNITED STATES *v.* NIXON

spiracy among one or more other defendants and the declarant and if the declarations at issue were in furtherance of that conspiracy. The same is true of declarations of co-conspirators who are not defendants in the case on trial. *Dutton v. Evans*, 400 U. S. 74, 81 (1970). Recorded conversations may also be admissible for the limited purpose of impeaching the credibility of any defendant who testifies or any other co-conspirator who testifies. Generally, the need for evidence to impeach witnesses is insufficient to require the production of evidence in advance of trial. See, *e. g., United States v. Carter*, 15 F. R. D. 367, 371 (D. C. D. C. 1954); *United States v. Hiss*, 9 F. R. D. 515, 516–517 (SDNY 1949). Here, however, there are other valid potential evidentiary uses for the same material and the analysis and possible transcription of the tapes may take a significant period of time.[14] Accordingly, we cannot say that the District Court erred in authorizing the issuance of the subpoena duces tecum.

Enforcement of a pretrial subpoena duces tecum must necessarily be committed to the sound discretion of the trial court since the necessity for the subpoena most often turns upon a determination of factual issues. Without a determination of arbitrariness or that the trial court finding was without record support an appellate court will not ordinarily disturb a finding that the applicant for a subpoena complied with Rule 17 (c). See, *e. g., Sue v. Chicago Transit Authority*, 279 F. 2d 416, 419 (CA7 1960); *Shotkin v. Nelson*, 146 F. 2d 402 (CA10 1944). In a case such as this, however, where a subpoena is directed to a President of the United States, appellate review, in deference to a coordinate branch of government, should be particularly meticulous to ensure that the

---

[14] The Special Prosecutor estimates two months time will be required. (Brief of Special Prosecutor, p. 139.)

UNITED STATES *v.* NIXON

standards of Rule 17 (c) have been correctly applied.
United States v. *Burr*, 25 Fed. Cas. 187, 191, No. 14694
(1807). From our close scrutiny of the materials submitted by the Special Prosecutor to the District Court in
support of his motion for the subpoena, we are persuaded
that the District Court's denial of the President's motion
to quash the subpoena was consistent with Rule 17 (c).
We also conclude that the Special Prosecutor has made a
sufficient showing to justify a subpoena for production
before trial. The subpoenaed materials are not available
from any other source, and their examination and processing should not await trial in the circumstances shown.
Bowman Dairy Co., supra; United States v. *Iozia, supra.*

IV

THE CLAIM OF PRIVILEGE

A

Having determined that the requirements of Rule
17 (c) were satisfied in this case, we turn to the claim
that the subpoena should be quashed because of a president's privilege covering confidential conversations with
aides and advisers, presidential correspondence and
records. The first contention is a broad claim that the
separation of powers doctrine precludes judicial review
of the claim of privilege by a president. The second
contention is that if he does not prevail on the claim of
absolute privilege, the court should hold as a matter of
constitutional law that the privilege prevails over the
subpoena duces tecum.

In the performance of assigned constitutional duties
each branch of the Government must initially interpret
the Constitution, and the interpretation of its powers by
any branch is due great respect from the others. The
President's counsel, as we have noted, reads the Constitu-

UNITED STATES *v.* NIXON

tion as providing an absolute privilege of confidentiality
for all presidential communications. Recent decisions
of this Court, however, have unequivocally reaffirmed the
holding of *Marbury* v. *Madison,* 1 Cranch (5 U. S.) 137
(1803), that "it is emphatically the province and duty
of the judicial department to say what the law is." *Id.,*
at 177.

No holding of the Court has defined the scope of judicial power specifically relating to the enforcement of a
subpoena for confidential presidential communications for
use in a criminal prosecution, but other exercises of powers
by the Executive Branch and the Legislative Branch have
been found invalid as in conflict with the Constitution.
Powell v. *McCormack, supra; Youngstown, supra.* In a
series of cases, the Court interpreted the explicit immunity conferred by express provisions of the Constitution
on Members of the House and Senate by the Speech or
Debate Clause, U. S. Const. Art. I, § 6. *Doe* v. *McMillan,* 412 U. S. 306 (1973); *Gravel* v. *United States,* 408
U. S. 606 (1973); *United States* v. *Brewster,* 408 U. S.
501 (1972); *United States* v. *Johnson,* 383 U. S. 169
(1966). Since this Court has consistently exercised the
power to construe and delineate claims arising under
express powers, it must follow that the Court has authority to interpret claims with respect to powers alleged to
derive from enumerated powers.

Our system of government "requires that federal courts
on occasion interpret the Constitution in a manner at
variance with the construction given the document by
another branch." *Powell* v. *McCormack, supra,* 549.
And in *Baker* v. *Carr,* 369 U. S. 186, 211 (1972), the
Court stated:

> "[d]eciding whether a matter has in any measure
> been committed by the Constitution to another

UNITED STATES *v.* NIXON

branch of government or whether the action of that
branch exceeds whatever authority has been committed, is itself a delicate exercise in constitutional
interpretation and is a responsibility of this Court
as ultimate interpreter of the Constitution. *Id.,* 211.

Notwithstanding the deference each branch must accord
the others, the "judicial power of the United States"
vested in the federal courts by Art. III, § 1 of the Constitution can no more be shared with the Executive
Branch than the Chief Executive, for example, can share
with the Judiciary the veto power, or the Congress share
with the Judiciary the power to override a presidential
veto. Any other conclusion would be contrary to the
basic concept of separation of powers and the checks and
balances that flow from the scheme of a tripartite government. The Federalist, No. 47, p. 313 (C. F. Mittel ed.
1938). We therefore reaffirm that it is "emphatically
the province and the duty" of this Court to pass on the
claim of privilege presented in this case.

B

In support of his claim of absolute privilege, the President's counsel urges two grounds one of which is common
to all governments and one of which is peculiar to our
system of separation of powers. The first ground is the
valid need for protection of communications between
high government officials and those who advise and assist
them in the performance of their manifold duties; the
importance of this confidentiality is too plain to require
further discussion. Human, experience teaches that
those who expect public dissemination of their remarks
may well temper candor with a concern for appearances
and for their own interests to the detriment of the decisionmaking process. Whatever the nature of the privilege of confidentiality of presidential communications in

UNITED STATES *v.* NIXON

the exercise of Art. II powers the privilege can be said to derive from the supremacy of each branch within its own assigned area of constitutional duties. Certain powers and privileges flow from the nature of enumerated powers; [15] the protection of the confidentiality of presidential communications has similar constitutional underpinnings.

The second ground asserted by the President's counsel in support of the claim of absolute privilege rests on the doctrine of separation of powers. Here it is argued that the independence of the Executive Branch within its own sphere, *Humphrey's Executor* v. *United States*, 295 U. S. 602, 629–630; *Kilbourn* v. *Thompson*, 103 U. S. 168, 190–191 (1880), insulates a president from a judicial subpoena in an ongoing criminal prosecution, and thereby protects confidential presidential communications.

However, neither the doctrine of separation of powers, nor the need for confidentiality of high level communications, without more, can sustain an absolute, unqualified presidential privilege of immunity from judicial process

---

[15] The Special Prosecutor argues that there is no provision in the Constitution for a presidential privilege as to his communications corresponding to the privilege of Members of Congress under the Speech or Debate Clause. But the silence of the Constitution on this score is not dispositive. "The rule of constitutional interpretation announced in *McCulloch* v. *Maryland*, 4 Wheat. 316, that that which was reasonably appropriate and relevant to the exercise of a granted power was considered as accompanying the grant, has been so universally applied that it suffices merely to state it." *Marshall* v. *Gordon, et al.*, 243 U. S. 521, 537. There is similarly nothing said in the Constitution authorizing the very subpoena at issue in this case. The only express provision in the Constitution for compulsory process is found in the Sixth Amendment guarantee that an accused shall have such process to secure evidence in his favor. But there can be no doubt whatever as to the power of the Courts to compel the attendance of witnesses and the production of evidence: without such power, the courts could not function.

UNITED STATES *v.* NIXON

under all circumstances.   The President's need for com=
plete candor and objectivity from advisers calls for great
deference from the courts.   However, when the privilege
depends solely on the broad, undifferentiated claim of
public interest in the confidentiality of such conversations, a confrontation with other values arises.   Absent
a claim of need to protect military, diplomatic or sensitive
national security secrets, we find it difficult to accept the
argument that even the very important interest in con=
fidentiality of presidential communications is significantly
diminished by production of such material for *in camera*
inspection with all the protection that a district court
will be obliged to provide.

The impediment that an absolute, unqualified privilege
would place in the way of the primary constitutional duty
of the Judicial Branch to do justice in criminal prosecutions would plainly conflict with the function of the
courts under Art. III.   In designing the structure of our
government and dividing and allocating the sovereign
power among three coequal branches, the Framers of the
Constitution sought to provide a comprehensive system,
but the separate powers were not intended to operate
with absolute independence.

> "While the Constitution diffuses power the better to
> secure liberty, it also contemplates that practice will
> integrate the dispersed powers into a workable gov-
> ernment.   It enjoins upon its branches separateness
> but interdependence, autonomy but reciprocity."
> *Youngstown Sheet & Tube Co.* v. *Sawyer,* 343 U. S.
> 579, 635 (1952) (concurring opinion of Jackson, J.).

To read the Art. II powers of the President as providing
an absolute privilege as against a subpoena essential to
enforcement of criminal statutes on no more than a generalized claim of the public interest in confidentiality of

UNITED STATES *v.* NIXON

nonmilitary and nondiplomatic discussions would upset the constitutional balance of "a workable government" and gravely impair the role of the courts under Art. III.

C

Since we conclude that the legitimate needs of the judicial process may outweigh presidential privilege, it is necessary in a given case to resolve these competing interests in a manner that preserves the essential functions of each branch. The right and indeed the duty to resolve that question does not free the judiciary from according high respect to the representations made on behalf of the President. *United States* v. *Burr*, 25 Fed. Cas. 187, 190, 191–192 (No. 14,694) (1807).

The right of a president to the confidentiality of his conversations and correspondence, like the claim of confidentiality of judicial deliberations, for example, has all the values to which we accord deference for the private citizen and added to that the necessity for protection of the public interest in candid, objective and even blunt or harsh opinions in presidential decisionmaking. A president and those who assist him must be free to explore alternatives in the process of shaping policies and making decisions and to do so in a way many would be unwilling to express except privately. These are the considerations justifying a presumptive privilege for presidential communications. The privilege is fundamental to the operation of government and inextricably rooted in the separation of powers under the Constitution. In *Nixon* v. *Sirica*, —— U. S. App. D. C. ——, 487 F. 2d 700 (1973), the Court of Appeals held that such presidential communications are "presumptively privileged," *id.*, at 717 (D. C. Cir. 1974) and this position is accepted by both parties in the present litigation. We agree with Chief Justice Marshall's observation, therefore, that "in

UNITED STATES *v.* NIXON

no case of this kind would a court be required to proceed
against the President as against an ordinary individual."
United States v. *Burr*, 25 Fed. Cas. 187, 191 (No. 14,694)
(CCD Va. 1807). Rather, the courts must follow stand=
ards and implement procedures that will adequately protect the undoubted need to preserve the legitimate confidentiality of that office.

The competing demands—the generalized privilege of
confidentiality on the one hand, and the function of Art.
III courts on the other—must be examined to ascertain
the relative importance of the presumptive privilege in
the whole scheme of Art. II, as compared with the importance which the need for relevant evidence occupies
in the fulfillment of Art. III duties of the Judicial Branch.
Under Art. II a president, for example, exercising certain
of his enumerated war powers, as in repelling a hostile
attack, or the veto power, or conducting foreign relations,
is performing duties at the very core of his constitutional role. The courts have shown the utmost deference
to presidential acts in the performance of Art. II core
functions. In *C. & S. Air Lines* v. *Waterman Steamship
Corp.,* 333 U. S. 103, 111 (1948), dealing with presidential
authority involving foreign policy considerations, the
Court said:

> "The President, both as Commander-in-Chief and as
> the Nation's organ for foreign affairs, has available
> intelligence services whose reports are not and ought
> not to be published to the world. It would be in-
> tolerable that courts, without the relevant informa-
> tion, should review and perhaps nullify actions of
> the Executive taken on information properly held
> secret." *Id.,* at 111.

In *United States* v. *Reynolds*, 345 U. S. 1 (1952) dealing

UNITED STATES *v.* NIXON

with a claimant's demand for evidence in a damage case
the Court said

"... Judicial control over the evidence in a case cannot be abdicated to the caprice of executive officers.
Yet we will not go so far as to say that the court may
automatically require a complete disclosure to the
judge before the claim of privilege will be accepted
in any case. It may be possible to satisfy the court,
from all the circumstances of the case, that there is a
reasonable danger that compulsion of the evidence
will expose military matters which, in the interest of
national security, should not be divulged. When
this is the case, the occasion for the privilege is appropriate, and the court should not jeopardize the
security which the privilege is meant to protect by
insisting upon an examination of the evidence, even
by the judge alone, in chambers."

○   •   •   •   •

"Where there is a strong showing of necessity, the
claim of privilege should not be lightly accepted, but
even the most compelling necessity cannot overcome the claim of privilege if the court is ultimately
satisfied that military secrets are at stake. A *fortiori*, where necessity is dubious, a formal claim of
privilege, made under the circumstances of this case,
will have to prevail." 345 U. S., at 10–11.

We see, therefore, that *Waterman Steamship, supra*, and
Reynolds, supra, each dealt with a presidential function
at the very core of Art. II authority. In the present
case, however, the reason for the claim is somewhat
removed from the central or core function of the Chief
Executive.

In contrast, the need for relevant evidence in the conduct of a criminal trial is central to the Art. III function
of a federal court. Although the administration of crim-

UNITED STATES *v.* NIXON

inal justice is shared by the Executive and Judicial Branches in the sense that the former investigates and initiates prosecutions under standards prescribed by Congress, the adjudicatory function is vested exclusively in the courts.[16] Under our adversary system of criminal justice not only do both sides have an interest in securing all relevant evidence that is probative on the issue of guilt, but the very integrity of the judicial system and public confidence in the system depends upon full disclosure of the facts within the framework of the rules of evidence. Without the power to compel the production of evidence the basic function of the courts could not be performed.

The effective functioning of the judicial system requires that courts obtain evidence in order to decide cases. Only recently the Court restated this ancient proposition of the law, albeit in the context of a grand jury inquiry rather than a trial,

> " 'that the public . . . has a right to every man's evidence' except for those persons protected by a constitutional, common law, or statutory privilege, *United States* v. *Bryan*, 339 U. S., at 331 (1949); *Blackmer* v. *United States*, 284 U. S. 421, 438

---

[16] Congress defines crimes, fixes penalties and prescribes procedures for the administration of criminal justice to be applied by the courts thus integrating "the dispersed powers into a workable government." 343 U. S., at 635. The discharge of Art. III functions requires the federal courts to enforce certain constitutional guaranties enumerated in the Bill of Rights, notably the right to a fair trial under the Due Process Clause of the Fifth Amendment and the rights of confrontation and compulsory process under the Sixth Amendment. Thus, the judiciary's need for all relevant evidence in a criminal trial derives not only from the general framework of Art. III but also from the specific requirements of the Bill of Rights.

UNITED STATES *v.* NIXON

(1932) . . . ." *Branzburg v. United States,* 408 U. S. 665. 688 (1973).[17]

Here, the core function of Art. III is pitted against a generalized need for presidential confidentiality without a showing that such confidentiality is necessary to protect a core function of Art. II. Under these circumstances the generalized assertion of privilege must yield to the demonstrated, specific need for evidence in a pending criminal trial.[18]

D

We have earlier determined that the District Court did not err in authorizing the issuance of the subpoena. If a president concludes that compliance with a subpoena would be injurious to the public interest he may properly, as was done here, invoke a claim of privilege on the return of the subpoena. Upon receiving a claim of privilege from the Chief Executive, it became the further duty of the District Court to treat the subpoenaed material as presumptively privileged and to require the Special Prosecutor to demonstrate, by extrinsic evidence, that the presidential material was "essential to the justice of the [pending criminal] case." *United States* v. *Burr, supra,* at 192. Here the District Court treated the material as presumptively privileged, proceeded to find that

---

[17] Because of the key role of the testimony of witnesses in the judicial process, courts have historically been cautious about privileges. Justice Frankfurter, dissenting in *Elkins* v. *United States,* 364 U. S. 206, 234 (1960), said of this:

"Limitations are properly placed upon the operation of this general principle only to the very limited extent that permitting a refusal to testify or excluding relevant evidence has a public good transcending the nominally predomnant principle of utilizing all rational means for ascertaining truth."

[18] We are not called on to decide what a district court should do when confronted by a categorical claim of privilege for military, foreign policy or national security secrets.

UNITED STATES *v.* NIXON

the Special Prosecutor had made a sufficient showing to
rebut the presumption and ordered an *in camera* examination of the subpoenaed material. On the basis of our
examination of the material submitted we are unable to
conclude that the District Court erred in ordering the
inspection. Accordingly the subpoenaed materials shall
be transmitted forthwith to the District Court. We now
turn to the important question of the District Court's
responsibilities in conducting the *in camera* examination
of presidential materials or communications delivered
under the compulsion of the subpoena duces tecum.

E

Enforcement the subpoena duces tecum was stayed
pending this Court's resolution of the issues raised by the
petitions for certiorari. Those issues now having been
resolved. the matter of implementation will rest with the
District Court. "[T]he guard, furnished to [the Presi-
dent] to protect him from being harassed by vexatious
and unnecessary subpoenas, is to be looked for in the
conduct of the [district] court after the subpoenas have
issued; not in any circumstances which is to precede their
being issued." *United States* v. *Burr, supra,* at 34. Statements that meet the test of admissibility and relevance
must be isolated; all other material must be excised. At
this stage the District Court is not limited to representations of the Special Prosecutor as to the evidence sought
by the subpoena; the recordings will be available to the
District Court. It is elementary that *in camera* inspection of evidence is always a procedure calling for scrupulous protection against any release or publication of
material not found by the court, at that stage to be both
admissible in evidence and relevant to the issues of the
trial for which it is sought. That being true of an ordinary situation, it is obvious that the District Court has

UNITED STATES *v.* NIXON

a very heavy responsibility to see to it that presidential conversations, which are either not admissible or not relevant, are accorded that high degree of respect due the President of the United States. Chief Justice Marshall sitting as a trial judge in the *Burr* case, *supra,* was extraordinarily careful to point out that:

> "[I]n no case of this kind would a Court be required to proceed against the President as against an ordinary individual." *United States* v. *Burr,* 25 Fed. Cases 187, 191 (No. 14,694).

Marshall's statement cannot be read to mean in any sense that a president is above the law, but relates to the singularly unique role under Art. II of a president's communications and activities. Moreover, a president's communications and activities encompass a vastly wider range of sensitive material than would be true of any "ordinary individual." It is therefore necessary [19] in the public interest to afford presidential confidentiality the greatest protection consistent with the fair administration of justice. The need for confidentiality even as to idle conversations with associates in which casual reference might be made concerning political leaders within the country or foreign statesmen is too obvious to call for further treatment. At all times the District Court has a heavy responsibility to see to it that until released to

---

[19] When the subpoenaed material is delivered to the District Judge *in camera* questions may arise as to the excising of parts and it lies within the discretion of that court to seek the aid of the Special Prosecutor and the President's counsel for *in camera* consideration on the validity of particular excisions, whether the basis of excision is relevancy or admissibility or under such cases as *Reynolds, supra,* or *Waterman Steamship, supra.* Any order releasing material to the Special Prosecutor over objections of the President's counsel shall, of course, be stayed for a reasonable time to provide opportunity for appellate review; the record should be sealed for any review that may be sought.

UNITED STATES *v.* NIXON

the Special Prosecutor no *in camera* material is revealed
to anyone.   This burden applies with even greater force
to excised material: once the decision is made to excise,
the material is restored to its privileged status and should
be returned under seal to its lawful custodian.

Since this matter came before the Court during the
pendency of a criminal prosecution, and on representations that time is of the essence, the mandate shall issue
forthwith.

Affirmed.

JUSTICE STEWART'S REDRAFT†

C

Since we conclude that the legitimate needs of the judicial process may outweigh presidential privilege, it is necessary to resolve those competing interests in a manner that preserves the essential functions of each branch. The right and indeed the duty to resolve that question does not free the judiciary from according high respect to the representations made on behalf of the President. *United States* v. *Burr*, 25 Fed. Cas. 187, 190, 191–192 (No. 14,694) (1807).

The right of a president to the confidentiality of his conversations and correspondence, like the claim of confidentiality of judicial deliberations, for example, has all the values to which we accord deference for the private citizen and added to that the necessity for protection of the public interest in candid, objective and even blunt or harsh opinions in presidential decisionmaking. A president and those who assist him must be free to explore alternatives in the process of shaping policies and making decisions and to do so in a way many would be unwilling to express except privately. These are the considerations justifying a presumptive privilege for presidential communications. The privilege is fundamental to the operation of government and inextricably rooted in the separation of powers under the Constitution.* In *Nixon* v. *Sirica*, —— U. S. App. D. C. ——, 487, F. 2d 700 (1973), the Court of Appeals held that such presidential

---

† Original in typescript.

* "Freedom of communication vital to fulfillment of wholesome relationships is obtained only by removing the specter of compelled disclosure. . . . [G]overnment . . . needs open but protected channels for the kind of plain talk that is essential to the quality of its functioning." *Carl Zeiss Stiftung* v. *V. E. B. Carl Zeiss, Jena,* 40 FRD 318, 325 (DDC 1966). See *Nixon* v. *Sirica*, —— U. S. App. D. C. ——, ——, 487 F. 2d 700, 713 (1973); *Kaiser Aluminum & Chem. Corp.* v. *United States,* 157 F. Supp. 939 (Ct. Cl. 1958) (*per* Reed, J.); *The Federalist* No. 64 (S. F. Mittel ed. 1938).

communications are "presumptively privileged," *id.*, at 717, and this position is accepted by both parties in the present litigation. We agree with Chief Justice Marshall's observation, therefore, that "in no case of this kind would a court be required to proceed against the President as against an ordinary individual." *United States* v. *Burr,* 25 Fed. Cas. 187, 191 (No. 14,694) (CCD Va. 1807).

But we are a nation governed by the rule of law. Nowhere is our commitment to this principle more profound than in the enforcement of the criminal law, "the twofold aim of which is that guilt shall not escape or innocence suffer." *Berger* v. *United States,* 295 U. S. 78, 88 (1935). Conviction of the guilty and exoneration of the innocent are matters of the greatest consequence for a people devoted to equal justice under law. Individuals are subject to criminal penalties for conduct proscribed by society. The imposition of such penalties turns on what was done and by whom and with what intent. Enforcement of the criminal law requires ascertainment of these facts. It is, in short, a search for truth.

We have committed that pursuit to an adversary system in which the parties contest issues before a court of law. To develop their opposing contentions of fact, the parties are entitled to invoke the court's authority to compel production of relevant evidence. Because the adversary nature of our system is tempered by an overriding concern for fairness to the individual, the prosecutor has an obligation to reveal evidence that may be favorable to the defense. See *Brady* v. *Maryland,* 373 U. S. 83 (1963). In addition, the accused has the right to a fair trial by making the best possible defense on the basis of all material evidence. And the court itself has the paramount duty to ensure that justice is done, by making compulsory process available for the production of evidence needed by either the prosecution or the defense. Accordingly, the need to develop all relevant facts is both elemental and comprehensive, for the ends of the criminal law would be defeated if judgments were founded on a fragmentary or speculative presentation of the facts. To the extent that the search for truth is restrained, the integrity of the process of criminal justice is impaired. As a general proposition, therefore, the law is entitled to every man's evidence. See *Branzburg* v. *Hayes*, 408 U. S. 665, 688 (1972).

This rule, however, is not absolute. It admits of exceptions designed to protect weighty and legitimate competing interests. Thus, the Fifth Amendment to the Constitution provides that no man "shall be compelled in any criminal case to be a witness against himself." And generally an attorney may not be required to reveal what his cilent has told him in confidence. These and other interests are recognized at law by privileges against forced disclosure. Such privileges may be established in the Constitution, by statute, or at common law. Whatever their origins, these exceptions to the demand for every man's evidence are not lightly created nor expansively construed, for they are in derogation of the search for truth.*

In this case the President challenges a subpoena requiring the production of materials for use in certain criminal prosecutions. He claims that he has a privilege against compliance with that subpoena. He does not claim that disclosure of the subpoenaed material would comprise state secrets. There is no claim that the conversations at issue involved the President's functions under Article II as Commander in Chief, or the conduct of international relations. Compare *United States* v. *Reynolds*, 345 U. S. 1 (1952) ; *C & S Air Lines* v. *Waterman*

---

* Because of the key role of the testimony of witnesses in the judicial process, courts have historically been cautious about privileges. Justice Frankfurter, dissenting in *Elkins* v. *United States*, 364 U. S. 206, 234 (1960), said of this:

Limitations are properly placed upon the operation of this general principle only to the very limited extent that permitting a refusal to testify or excluding relevant evidence has a public good transcending the normally predominant principle of utilizing all rational means for ascertainig truth.

Steamship Corp., 333 U. S. 103, 111 (1948). Rather, the President grounds his assertion of privilege in the generalized interest in preserving the confidentiality of his discussions with his advisers. Because maintaining confidentiality for such discussions is essential to his high office, he claims a privilege against forced disclosure.

The Constitution does not explicitly mention the President's interest in confidentiality. Yet to the extent that the interest in confidentiality pertains to the President's effective exercise of his executive powers, it is nevertheless constitutionally based. The Constitution does explicitly confer the right upon every defendant in a criminal trial "to be confronted with the witnesses against him" and "to have compulsory process for obtaining witnesses in his favor." (Am. VI) And, of course, the Constitution also guarantees that no person shall be deprived of liberty without due process of law. (Am. V) Because the production of all material evidence in a criminal trial effectuates those guarantees, it too is a matter of constitutional import.

We must balance the importance of the privilege to the President's performance of the responsibilities vested in him against the inroads of such a privilege on the fair administration of criminal justice. The interest in confidentiality, as distinct from the preservation of state secrets, is a generalized concern. The goal is to promote candor by maintaining an expectation of confidentiality rather than to preserve secrecy for the substance of any particular communication. The asserted need to refuse to comply with a subpoena presumes that rare and isolated instances of disclosure would negate the general expectation of confidentiality and thus defeat the ability of the President to obtain candid advice. We think that this assumption is unfounded. The willingness to speak plainly is not so fragile that it would be undermined by some remote prospect of disclosure in narrowly defined and isolated circumstances. At least this is true where the prospect of disclosure is limited to demands for evidence demonstrably material to a criminal prosecution.

It requires no clairvoyance to foresee that such demands will arise with the greatest infrequency nor any special insight to recognize that few advisers will be moved to temper the candor of their remarks by such an unlikely possibility. Thus, while the general interest in confidentiality is weighty [it] is general in nature, [and] the constitutional need for protection of material evidence in a criminal proceeding is not. The enforcement of the criminal laws does not depend on an assessment of the broad sweep of events but on a limited number of specific historical facts concerning the conduct of identified individuals at given times. The President's broad interest in confidentiality would not be vitiated by disclosure of a limited number of confidential conversations, but nondisclosure of those same conversations could gravely impair the pursuit of truth in a criminal prosecution.

Thus, where the President's ground for withholding subpoenaed materials from use in a criminal trial is only the generalized interest in confidentiality, it cannot prevail over the needs of due process of law in the fair administration of criminal justice. Under these circumstances the generalized assertion of privilege must yield to the demonstrated, specific need for evidence in a pending criminal trial.

In discussing the final *Nixon* opinion with me, a Justice who took part in the case characterized it as "opinion by committee." His characterization is supported by a paper in his file on the case. Typed on one page and without any identification, it reads simply:

Opinion Outline

I.   Facts [HAB]
II.   Appealability [WOD]
III. Intra-branch dispute [WJB or beefed-up WEB version]
IV.   Rule 17(c) [BRW]
V.   [Merits of executive privilege: WEB: LFP as revised by PS]
VI.   Standards to be met before in camera inspection is ordered [LFP as revised by WJB]
VII. The Court's judgment and order [WJB]

This means that the different sections of the opinion identified in the paper were to be drafted primarily by the Justices whose initials are stated next to the sections concerned. How this happened will be discussed in the remainder of this chapter. Why it happened can be seen from the unsatisfactory nature of the Chief Justice's draft opinion reprinted on p. 202. It is fair to say that none of the sections circulated (sent around, as we saw, in installments) satisfied the other Justices—with the exception of the section headed "Jurisdiction," which was based on the Douglas draft reprinted on p. 163. When the Justices saw how weak the Burger draft was, they concluded that substantial revisions were necessary. Rather than wait for new drafts by the Chief Justice, they decided to send him their own drafts of the different sections for him to use in later redrafts circulated by him.

The attitude of the others was indicated in a July 10 "Dear Chief" letter sent by Justice Brennan with a draft on the standing issue—that is, the section headed "Justiciability" in the Burger draft. "Needless to say," Brennan wrote of his draft, "insofar as its incorporation, or any part of it, furthers your preparation of the opinion I freely deed it to you in fee simple absolute. I don't think I presume in saying that that is also the thought of the brethren who have sent you memos on this and other issues."

It is said that the Chief Justice was offended by the tone of this letter. The Justice was telling Burger that he was free to use the Brennan draft as he saw fit; but, if he did not use it, the others would not support the Burger draft. This was also the implication in the other drafts sent to the Chief Justice as substitutes for the sections prepared by him.

An important consequence of the *Nixon* drafting process was the absence of a vital ingredient of almost all the memorable Supreme Court opinions since John Marshall substituted the one opinion of the Court for the seriatim opinions by each Justice that had been delivered before Marshall's day—the sense of one strong hand that has molded the outstanding opinions in our legal history.

Equally significant, the "committee" had to use as its foundation the unsatisfactory Burger draft sections. To avoid making the rebuff to the Chief Justice even harsher than it was, the other Justices used the Burger draft language as much as possible. The result was that much of the final opinion reads as though the work of at least two authors laid side by side. The final opinion was weaker than it would have been had it been authored solely by one of the other Justices or even had the sections been the work only of those who redrafted them, without their having to incorporate as much as possible of the original Burger sections.

In actuality, the best characterization of the end product in *Nixon* was the Burger characterization of another opinion in a 1969 case. The final draft in that case, wrote the Chief Justice in a *Memorandum for the Conference,* "resembles the proverbial 'horse put together by a committee' with a camel as the end result. But then even the camel has proven to be useful."[18] That was also true of the final *Nixon* opinion. With all its faults, it did reject the extreme claim of absolute executive privilege and was the catalyst that led to the forced Nixon departure from the White House.

The *Nixon* redrafting process began with a July 12 "Dear Chief" letter from Justice White that stated, "With respect to your draft on the Rule 17(c) question, it seems to me something more should be said with respect to the relevance and admissibility of the tapes. The attached is the bare bones of an alternative treatment which I am now embellishing to some extent."

The White redraft of the Rule 17(c) section (as recirculated by White on July 13) is reprinted on p. 229 because it formed the basis of the final opinion's section on the subject. The White redraft stressed the point made by the Justice at the July 9 conference—that the ordinary standard under Rule 17(c) applied here and not the higher standard urged by Justice Powell. The key question, wrote White, was "whether the requirements of [the rule] have been satisfied." White shows that they were, emphasizing that the tapes were both relevant and admissible. But all that was necessary was "to ensure that the standards of Rule 17(c) have been correctly applied." This was as true in this case involving the President, as in other pretrial subpoena enforcement cases.

The ending of the White redraft was taken from a Brennan redraft of Justice Powell's draft on Rule 17(c), reprinted on p. 199, which Justice Brennan had circulated July 8. Brennan's "particularly meticulous" language was inserted in Justice White's recirculated version as a compromise between his view and the Powell approach. But it did not really detract from the White position, since it stressed that the court should only be meticulous to ensure that the normal Rule 17(c) standard had been properly applied.

On July 12, the day that the Chief Justice received the White redraft, he also received a redraft of his first section by Justice Blackmun. The latter's covering letter informed the Chief Justice: "With your letter of July 10, you recommended and invited suggestions. Accordingly, I take the liberty of suggesting herewith a revised statement of facts and submit it to you for your consideration."

The Blackmun redraft of the statement of facts was substantially similar to the version contained in the final *Nixon* opinion. The one important difference was the paragraph—omitted from the final opinion— that ended the Blackmun redraft:

> In the interim, the fact that the President had been named by the grand jury as an unindicted co-conspirator was discovered by the news media and made public. This Court denied the joint motion of the Special Prosecutor and Counsel for the President to unseal those portions of the record that had been ordered sealed by the District Court, except an extract therefrom relating to the co-conspirator identification. —— U.S. —— (1974).

As already seen, Chief Justice Burger circulated his draft of the executive privilege section on July 17. Before that time, he received notes from several of the others approving the Blackmun and White redrafts. Particularly striking was a July 12 letter from Justice Douglas refusing to join the Burger Rule 17(c) section on the ground that it "seems to reintroduce a phase of 'compelling need.' My difficulty is that when the President is discussing crimes to be committed and/or crimes already committed with and/or by him or by his orders, he stands no higher than the mafia with respect to those confidences."

Soon after he had sent around his July 17 draft of the section on executive privilege (supra p. 216) Chief Justice Burger began to receive comments on it. After he had read the draft, Justice Stewart wrote a July 17 "Dear Chief" letter criticizing the beginning of "B" of the draft, which read, "Although the President's counsel asserts that the privilege of confidentiality of presidential communications is absolute he does not challenge the authority of this Court to interpret the law."

According to Stewart, this sentence "is misleading. Unless I have completely misunderstood Mr. St. Clair's brief and oral argument, his primary contention on the merits is that the President alone has the power to decide the question of privilege, and that the Judicial Branch has no role to play."

Because of this, Stewart asserted, "I strongly believe . . . that the Court opinion must contain an unambiguous response to this argument. It seems to me that this response should probably come at the beginning of the discussion of the claim of executive privilege."

On July 18, Justices Brennan, White, and Marshall wrote to the Chief Justice supporting Stewart. Their view was expressed in Marshall's statement, "I also agree with Potter's suggested addition rejecting the President's argument that it is he who finally decides whether the public interest would be served by release of the subpoenaed material; I, too, think that it is important to reject this argument firmly and unequivo-cally."

The Marshall letter also objected to the Burger footnote, discussed on p. 161, that had cast doubt on the subpoena served on the President. Marshall urged that the note "should be eliminated. . . . I see no sig-nificance for this case in the lack of mention in the Constitution of sub-poenas, and see no reason to raise any doubt on this score or to discuss the question at all."

In addition, Marshall suggested deletion of the reference to "highly sensitive domestic policies" as coming within the Burger notion of execu-tive privilege, "The issue raised there is too speculative to explore in the context of the narrow issue involved in this case. Your discussion also clearly indicates a view on the merits of that question, with which I disagree."

Justice White's letter again stressed that all that had to be met here was the normal Rule 17(c) standard. In the Burger draft, White wrote, "You . . . imply that there must be a compelling need for the material to overcome presumptively privileged executive documents. I take it that you are suggesting that there is a dimension to overcoming the privilege beyond the showing of relevance and admissibility." White disagreed with such a view. "As I have already indicated, my view is that relevance and admissibility themselves provide whatever compelling need must be shown. I would also doubt that the Prosecutor has made any showing of necessity beyond that of relevance and admissibility."

White also objected to the Burger draft's implication that *Marbury* v. *Madison*[19] had created judicial review. "Because I am one of those who thinks that the Constitution on its face provides for judicial review, especially if construed in the light of what those who drafted it said at the time or later, I always wince when it is inferred that the Court cre-ated the power or even when it is said that the 'power of judicial review [was] first announced in *Marbury* v. *Madison.*' See page 4 of your draft. But perhaps this is only personal idiosyncrasy."

The Brennan and Marshall letters took a conciliatory approach to the Burger draft on executive privilege. Brennan wrote "that your 'work-ing draft' circulated July 17, of 'The Claim of Executive Privilege' re-flects for me a generally satisfactory approach to the decision of that important question," and Marshall "that it provides a good starting point with which we can work."

But the Justices were more dissatisfied with the privilege draft than these comments indicated. The White letter gave voice to the general reluctance to accept the Burger draft. Toward the end of his letter, Jus-tice White told the Chief Justice flatly, "it is likely that I shall write separately if your draft becomes the opinion of the Court."

At this point, the other Justices were unwilling to accept the Burger draft on executive privilege with its doctrine of "core functions," which they felt tilted the balance unduly in favor of the presidential claim. Even before the Chief Justice had sent around his draft, three of the Justices had prepared their own proposed version of the privilege section. My copy of this draft has at its head, in the writing of a Justice, "Draft agreed to by BRW, PS, & WJB, but not circulated pending Chief's merits section."

This draft was prepared by Justice Stewart and gone over by Justices White and Brennan. It was based on Stewart's redrafting of Justice Powell's draft on executive privilege (supra p. 190) and is reprinted on p. 233.

The Stewart draft is much more direct than the Powell version in asserting the judicial power to decide the privilege issue, "We unreservedly reject the claim that the President alone, by simple assertion of privilege, had the unreviewable power to decide not to deliver the subpoenaed materials to the District Court." Instead, it is the constitutional responsibility of the courts to decide the issue. "The existence and scope of Presidential privilege is thus a judicial question for the Judicial Branch alone to decide."

In this case, Stewart went on, there is a need for confidentiality in government. But, though "constitutionally based," it must give way to the need for "the production of all material evidence in a criminal trial" which is itself "a matter of constitutional import." Such a narrow exception to the general expectation of confidentiality will not defeat the Presidential ability to obtain candid advice. "The President's broad interest in confidentiality would not be vitiated by disclosure of a limited number of confidential conversations, but nondisclosure of those same conversations could gravely impair the pursuit of truth in a criminal prosecution." In this case, "the President's . . . generalized interest in confidentiality . . . cannot prevail over the needs of due process of law in a federal criminal trial."

As already noted, this Stewart draft on privilege was not circulated, but it was apparently shown to Justices Powell and Marshall, who indicated their approval. On Saturday afternoon, July 20, the Chief Justice circulated the first printed draft of his *Nixon* opinion. It was the first time the proposed opinion was presented as a whole; headed "1st DRAFT," it contained 29 printed pages. It is reprinted on p. 242.

The printed draft was substantially improved over the original version, sent out in sections, which is reprinted on p. 202. The statement of facts was taken largely from Justice Blackmun's July 12 draft; the section on appealability was based even more directly on the Douglas July 15 memorandum (supra p. 163); that on standing made use of a Brennan draft; and the Rule 17(c) section was based on Justice White's July 13 draft (supra p. 229).

Even the executive privilege section was improved by the use of language from Justice Powell's draft (supra p. 190) as well as the stronger rejection urged by Justice Stewart in his July 17 letter of the President's claim that the courts might not review his privilege claim. The new Burger draft asserted categorically, "We therefore reaffirm that it is 'emphatically the province and the duty' of this Court to pass on the claim of privilege presented in this case."

But the printed draft still contained the Burger "core function" concept, with its statement that the courts must observe "the utmost deference to presidential acts in the performance of Art. II core functions." There was still the plain implication that there would be no review in cases that "dealt with a presidential function at the very core of Art. II authority."

The continued use of the "core function" approach was unacceptable to Justice Stewart and the Justices who had approved his privilege draft (supra p. 233). What happened next in the drafting process may be seen from the following memorandum sent around by Justice Stewart on July 22.

July 22, 1974
Re: *Nixon Cases*
MEMORANDUM TO: Mr. Justice Douglas
Mr. Justice Brennan
Mr. Justice Blackmun
Mr. Justice Powell

Byron, Thurgood, and I were here in the building on Saturday afternoon when the printed draft of the tentative proposed opinion was circulated. After individually going over the circulation, we collected our joint and several specific suggestions and met with the Chief Justice in order to convey these suggestions to him.

With respect to IV(C), beginning on page 22 of the proposed opinion, our joint suggestions were too extensive to be drafted on Saturday afternoon, and I was accordingly delegated to try my hand at a draft over the week-end. The enclosed draft embodies the views of Byron, Thurgood, and me, and we have submitted it to the Chief Justice this morning.

As of now, Byron, Thurgood, and I are prepared to join the proposed opinion, if the recasting of IV(C) is acceptable to the Chief Justice, and on the assumption that problems re the specificity *vel non* of IV(C), beginning on page 27, are resolved.

At this late stage it seems essential to me that there be full intramural communication in the interest of a cooperative effort, and it is for this reason that I send you this memorandum bringing you up to date so far as I am concerned.

P.S.

P.S. As you will observe, the enclosed draft borrows generously from the draft of the Chief Justice as well as Lewis Powell's earlier memorandum.
Copies to: The Chief Justice
Mr. Justice White
Mr. Justice Marshall

Justices Stewart, White, and Marshall had met after they had received the Burger printed draft. The three of them were dissatisfied with the "core function" analysis in Section IV(C) and agreed that the Stewart version was far preferable. Because (as seen) Justices Brennan and Powell had previously approved the Stewart draft, that meant that a five-man majority now backed it. Stewart, White, and Marshall discussed the matter with the Chief Justice. The three Justices then agreed that Stewart would redraft section IV(C) and he did so during the remainder of the weekend. The other two went over the redraft and the three submitted it to the Chief Justice. Stewart then sent the redraft to the other four Justices in the case, together with the July 22 memo apprising them of these developments.

The Stewart redraft of section IV(C), consisting of seven double-spaced typed pages, is reprinted on p. 271. It is essentially a combination of the Burger and Stewart versions of Section IV(C). So far as possible, Justice Stewart used the Chief Justice's language. But he eliminated the "core function" analysis that the Justices had found objectionable. In its place was inserted the approach followed in the Stewart draft (supra p. 233). This was essentially the approach also taken in the final *Nixon* opinion.

After he had received the Stewart July 22 memo and section IV(C) redraft, the Chief Justice sent the following July 22 *MEMORANDUM TO THE CONFERENCE,* headed *PERSONAL:*

> Potter's memo of July 22, 1974 enclosing a revision of Part "C" prompts me to assure you that I will work on it promptly with the hope to accommodate those who wish to get away this week.
>
> The two versions can be accommodated and harmonized and, indeed, I do not assume it was intended that I cast aside several weeks work and take this circulation as a total substitute.
>
> I will have a new draft of Part "C" along as soon as possible. I take it for granted voting will be deferred until the revised opinion is recirculated. There are miscellaneous changes throughout but none of great moment.

By this point, however, it had been made clear to Chief Justice Burger that he could not secure a majority (indeed, he would remain virtually alone in his opinion) if he did not abandon his "core function" analysis for the Stewart approach. Rather than lose the opinion, the Chief Justice gave way. On July 23, he circulated a new draft of section IV(C). It was a modified version of the Stewart IV(C) redraft. The "core function" concept was now completely eliminated from the draft.

The Burger redraft and the opinion as a whole was approved at a conference that met at 1:30 P.M. on July 23. The final printed draft was sent around later that day and met no objection. The next day the decision was announced and the opinion summarized by the Chief Justice in a packed courtroom. Seventeen days later the President resigned.

Notes

1. Mason, *Harlan Fiske Stone: Pillar of the Law* 406 (1956).
2. *United States* v. *Nixon*, 418 U.S. 683 (1974).
3. *New York Times*, July 10, 1974, p. 1; May 26, 1974, p. 1.
4. Dissenting, in *Northern Securities Co.* v. *United States*, 193 U.S. 197, 400 (1904).
5. Id. at 400–401.
6. 5 Burke, *Works* 67 (Rev. ed. 1865).
7. 418 U.S. 683 (1974).
8. McLellan, *Karl Marx: His Life and Thought* 72 (1973).
9. See Berger, *Executive Privilege: A Constitutional Myth* 254 (1974).
10. Id. at 254–55.
11. *Submission of the Recorded Presidential Conversations to the Committee on the Judiciary of the House of Representatives by President Richard M. Nixon* 111 (1974).
12. *Nixon* v. *Administrator of General Services*, 433 U.S. 425, 447 (1977).
13. Quoted in Schwartz, *Super Chief: Earl Warren and His Supreme Court— A Judicial Biography* 637 (1983).
14. 417 U.S. 960 (1974).
15. I.e., *Marbury* v. *Madison*, 1 Cranch 137 (U.S. 1803).
16. Counsel for the President.
17. Concurring, in *Rochin* v. *California*, 342 U.S. 165, 177 (1952).
18. Quoted in Schwartz, *Swann's Way: The School Busing Case and the Supreme Court* 85 (1986).
19. Supra note 15.

6

O'Connor v. Donaldson (1975)
Mental Commitment and the Right
to Treatment

In August 1956, Kenneth Donaldson, a forty-eight-year-old carpenter from Camden, New Jersey, went to Florida for an extended visit with his eighty-year-old parents. A few months later, while still in Florida, he began to feel unusually tired and told his father that someone might have put a sedative in his food. He had a basis for such a fear. A few years earlier, he had become drowsy after eating lunch at a diner he frequented, and laboratory tests of his urine disclosed the presence of a large amount of codeine; Donaldson, a Christian Scientist, had not been taking medication that contained codeine. In this latest incident, Donaldson's father filed a petition requesting that his son be committed to a mental hospital. Donaldson was taken to the county jail where he was examined for less than two minutes by two physicians, who were not psychiatrists, and a layman. On the basis of this examination, the doctors concluded that Donaldson was a paranoid schizophrenic.

Shortly thereafter, a commitment hearing before a county judge was held. The hearing was completed in a matter of minutes. The judge agreed with the doctors' diagnosis and committed Donaldson to Florida State Hospital. This action was contrary to a Florida law that limited involuntary commitment to persons resident in Florida for at least one year, whereas Donaldson had been in Florida for only four months. The examining physicians had erroneously reported that Donaldson had been in Florida for four years.

Donaldson was confined in Florida State Hospital for over fourteen years. For religious reasons, he refused both medication and electroshock therapy, and his wishes were honored. He was given little other treatment. He was allowed to speak to a psychiatrist for only three hours in fourteen years; he was denied grounds privileges and occupational therapy. Yet, the hospital continued to confine him, reasoning that he was mentally ill because he insisted (1) that he had been in Florida for only four months prior to commitment, (2) that someone had once put codeine in his food, and (3) that he was not mentally ill.[1]

In 1971, Donaldson sued his attending physicians for denying him treatment in violation of his constitutional rights. A jury awarded him $38,500 damages, and the court of appeals upheld the verdict, reasoning that if "the 'purpose' of commitment is treatment, and treatment is not provided, then the 'nature' of the commitment bears no 'reasonable relation' to its 'purpose,' and the Constitutional rule [requiring due process] is violated." The court declared that "a person involuntarily civilly committed to a state mental hospital has a constitutional right to receive such individual treatment as will give him a reasonable opportunity to be cured or to improve his mental condition."[2]

The court of appeals had relied on "the landmark case of Rouse v. Cameron,"[3] where the Court of Appeals for the District of Columbia had first held that committed mental patients had a right to treatment.[4] This holding was reaffirmed by the D.C. Court on numerous occasions,[5] but it had been vigorously contested by Judge Warren E. Burger (then a member of that court).[6] Now that he was Chief Justice, Burger saw the *Donaldson* case as an opportunity to repudiate the right-to-treatment holding that he had opposed on the U.S. Court of Appeals.

At the conference after the January 15, 1975, oral argument,[7] the Chief Justice stated his view on what he saw as the main issue. He began by categorically summarizing the holding below on the matter, "Treatment was held to be the quid pro quo for confinement as a constitutional matter." Burger rejected this holding in strong language, declaring, "The instruction that he is entitled to treatment giving him a realistic opportunity to be cured or improved is nonsense." The Chief Justice was referring to the district court's instruction to the jury on the matter, which (as summarized in a Burger June 9, 1975, *MEMORANDUM TO THE CONFERENCE*) "could not be more unequivocal in stating that there is a constitutional right to psychiatric treatment for any involuntary confined mental patient." The Chief Justice concluded his conference presentation, "I can't see how we can sustain the judgment on this instruction.

Justices Powell and Rehnquist agreed that there was no constitutional right to treatment. But only Powell followed Burger's view that the decision should turn on that issue: "I'd have the opinion say no constitutional right to treatment." Rehnquist said that they could "get round[8] the mistake that there's a constitutional right to treatment and say that the case is like a jailer keeping a man after his term runs out."

The other Justices kept away from the right to treatment issue. Justices Brennan and Marshall stressed that Donaldson had clearly been injured and was entitled to damages. Justice Stewart, who was to play a crucial role in the case, said that the constitutional right involved here was the "right to release from unconstitutional state custody." As Stewart put the key question, "Is the fellow not dangerous to anyone and not getting treated?" If so, said the Justice, he is "constitutionally entitled not to be confined. I'd go further and say he can get out whether or not he's getting treatment if he's not a danger to himself or others."

Justice Powell (as seen) agreed with the Chief Justice on the right to treatment, saying, "I don't think there is a constitutional right to medical treatment." But he also expressed agreement on the issue stated by Stewart, "The constitutional right here is against incarceration; can't detain against a patient's will without justifiable grounds for doing so—along the lines of Potter's statement." Justice Blackmun also expressed the same view. As he saw it, "Evidence supports the jury finding that maliciously O'Connor refused to release him. He was unconstitutionally confined when not dangerous to himself or anyone else."

The one Justice who stated that the verdict for Donaldson should be reversed was White. "Up to now," he asserted, "the state has been entitled to warehouse people who are ill. I don't think there was a glimmer of that constitutional duty [i.e., to release Donaldson] that this doctor knew of. The jury was not entitled to [inquire] in the [doctor's] good faith and that's a plain error in the instructions." White did, however, also express support for the Stewart position, "Rather than get into treatment, I'd say you can't hold just for treatment; they must prove that you're dangerous or not able to take care of yourself."

The tally sheet of the Justice whose conference notes I have used summarized the vote on the case as follows (with Justice Douglas, then undergoing treatment at the Rusk Institute in New York, not participating):

REVERSE:	White
AFFIRM:	Brennan, Marshall, Blackmun, Powell, Rehnquist
PASS:	Chief Justice, Stewart

Despite this vote and the fact that only Justice Powell had supported his view that the opinion should reject the holding that there was a right to treatment (and Powell [as seen] also stated agreement with Justice Stewart's position), Chief Justice Burger assigned the *Donaldson* opinion to himself. Once again, as in *Roe* v. *Wade* (supra Chapter 4), the Chief Justice assigned a case although he had not voted with the majority. Once again, the majority did not challenge the Burger action, inconsistent though it was with long-settled Court practice.[9] Justice Douglas, who had protested the Chief Justice's making the assignment in *Roe* v. *Wade* (even though he ultimately gave way on the assignment to Justice Blackmun), was seriously ill at the time and the others let the matter pass without objection.

On May 15, the Chief Justice circulated his draft opinion of the Court reprinted on p. 288. It contained a complete rejection of the right to treatment approach which Burger had opposed on the D.C. Court of Appeals and which had been the basis of the lower court holding in *Donaldson* itself. The Burger draft minced no words on the subject. It began by making the point stressed by the Chief Justice at the conference—that this case was before the Court for it "to decide whether there is a constitutional right to treatment for persons involuntarily committed to state institutions by reason of mental abnormality."

The Burger draft gave short shrift to the notion that there was any such constitutional right to treatment. There was, it stated, no historical or logical basis for such a right, "In short, the idea that States may not confine the mentally ill except for the purpose of providing them with treatment is of very recent origin, and there is no historical basis for imposing such a limitation on state power. Analysis of the sources of the civil commitment power likewise affords no basis for the conclusion that its only legitimate purpose is treatment."

Though there are due process limitations on governmental authority in this area, Burger denies that it follows from them "that a State is without power under all conditions to confine a nondangerous mentally ill person except for treatment." On the contrary, there was no legal justification for the lower court's right to treatment holding. The Burger conclusion on this was categorical, "In sum, we reject the reasoning of the Court of Appeals and can discern no other basis for equating the federal constitutional right not to be confined without due process of law with an absolute constitutional right for involuntarily committed mental patients to either receive adequate psychiatric treatment or be released." Indeed, the draft asserted, "few things would be more fraught with peril than to irrevocably condition the power to protect the mentally ill upon the providing of 'such treatment as will give [them] a realistic opportunity to be cured.' Nothing in the Constitution mandates such a rule."

But the Burger draft did not stop with the effort to inter what the Chief Justice's conference presentation had termed the right-to-treatment "nonsense." There was also language in the draft that might have even greater potential for the rights of those in involuntary confinement. "There can be little doubt," declares the draft, "that in the exercise of its police power a State may confine individuals solely to protect society from the dangers of significant antisocial acts or communicable disease." By indicating that people could be confined for "significant antisocial acts," the Chief Justice was opening the door to a drastic expansion of the substantive power of confinement itself.

1st DRAFT

SUPREME COURT OF THE UNITED STATES

No. 74–8

J. B. O'Connor,
Petitioner,
v.
Kenneth Donaldson.

On Writ of Certiorari to the
United States Court of Appeals
for the Fifth Circuit.

[May —, 1975]

MR. CHIEF JUSTICE BURGER delivered the opinion of the Court.

We granted certiorari in this case to decide whether there is a constitutional right to treatment for persons involuntarily committed to state institutions by reason of mental abnormality. The issue arises in the context of an action for damages under 42 U. S. C. § 1983 brought by a former patient against individual physicians employed by the State of Florida.

I

On December 10, 1956, respondent's father instituted civil proceedings in the County Judge's Court of Pinellas County, Florida, to commit him as an incompetent. The petition alleged that respondent was incompetent by virtue of a longstanding "persecution complex" and "increasing signs of paranoid delusions . . . ," and expressed his father's belief that he was potentially dangerous. Accordingly, the County Judge appointed a committee of two physicians and a layman to examine respondent as required by Fla. Stat. § 394.22.[1]

---

[1] That statute governed judicial proceedings regarding a person believed to be "incompetent by reason of mental illness, sickness, drunkenness, excessive use of drugs, insanity, or other mental or

O'CONNOR *v.* DONALDSON

The committee reported that respondent was incompetent and suffering from paranoid schizophrenia, that his condition was "acute and chronic," that he was destitute, and that he required "mechanical restraint to prevent him from self-injury or violence to others." On January 3, 1957, respondent was adjudged incompetent and eight days later was committed to the Florida State Hospital at Chattahoochee, Florida. The orders entered at the conclusion of these proceedings stated that a hearing had been held, that respondent had appeared personally with an attorney, and that evidence had been taken. The County Judge adopted the committee's findings and the commitment order concluded that respondent required "confinement or restraint to prevent self-injury or violence to others, or to insure proper treatment, and the court having taken other evidence . . . and the said Kenneth Donaldson has been . . . adjudged mentally incompetent within the meaning of the statute in such cases . . . ."

Respondent remained at Florida State Hospital for slightly less than 15 years. During that time he filed numerous petitions for release by habeas corpus in the

physical condition, so that he is incapable of caring for himself or managing his property or is likely to dissipate or lose his property or become the victim of designing persons, or inflict harm on himself or others . . . ." 14A Fla. Stat. § 394.22 (1) (West 1960). Commitment of a person adjudicated incompetent was permitted if the judge found that he "requires confinement or restraint to prevent self-injury or violence to others," but an incompetent person could be adjudicated "harmless" and released to a guardian upon a finding that he did "not require confinement or restraint to prevent self-injury or violence to others and that treatment in the Florida state hospital is unnecessary or would be without benefit to such person . . . ." *Id.,* §§ 394.22 (11)(a), (b). Entry of an order of commitment required that the patient be remanded to the custody of the sheriff for eventual delivery to "the proper officer for the purpose of care, custody and treatment." *Id.,* § 394.09. This procedure was repealed by 1971 Fla. Laws, c. 71, §§ 16, 17.

O'CONNOR *v.* DONALDSON

Florida and federal courts, alleging that he was not mentally ill and had not been when he was committed, that
he had not received proper treatment, that he had been
denied procedural due process in the commitment proceedings, and that his commitment papers were "fraudu-
lent." None of these claims was ever resolved on its
merits; respondent's federal petitions were rejected for
failure to exhaust state remedies, and the Florida courts
referred him to the Pinellas County Court for a judicial
determination of his present competence. No evidentiary hearings were ever held. On four occasions this
Court denied petitions for certiorari filed by respondent.
In re Donaldson, 364 U. S. 808 (1960); *Donaldson v.
Florida*, 371 U. S. 806 (1962); *Donaldson v. O'Connor*,
390 U. S. 971 (1968); *Donaldson v. O'Connor*, 400 U. S.
869 (1970). The latter order stated that it was "without prejudice to petitioner's right to apply to appropriate United States District Court for relief." [2] *Ibid.*

On February 26, 1971, five months prior to his release
from Florida State Hospital,[3] respondent instituted the
present action in the United States District Court for
the Northern District of Florida. His amended complaint charged petitioner J. B. O'Connor, who had been
one of respondent's attending physicians and superintendent of the state hospital, and two other staff members with violating his constitutional rights and sought
damages under 42 U. S. C. § 1983.[4] The essence of the

---

[2] Petitioner has never contended that the actions of these courts
each constituted an independent intervening cause justifying continued confinement, and no instructions on this score were requested.

[3] On July 31, 1971, respondent received a competency discharge
pursuant to Fla. Stat. § 394.22 and his rights were subsequently
restored by the Pinellas County Court.

[4] In addition, the complaint sought an injunction against Florida's
civil commitment statutes, prayed that a three-judge court be convened, and alleged causes of action against the judge and committee
who had ordered respondent's commitment and certain other mental

O'CONNOR *v.* DONALDSON

charge was that petitioner and his codefendants had confined respondent "against his will, knowing that [he] was not receiving adequate treatment, and knowing that absent such treatment the period of his hospitalization would be prolonged," and intentionally limited his " 'treatment' program to 'custodial care' for the greater part of his hospitalization." Respondent alleged that the defendants had denied him specific types of treatment such as occupational training, grounds privileges, and group therapy, had refused to let him consult with a psychiatrist, had kept him in a locked ward with convicted criminals, and had frustrated the attempts of interested persons to obtain his release. He prayed for both compensatory and punitive damages.

At trial, respondent's evidence showed that Florida State Hospital was overcrowded and understaffed while he was there and that he received little, if any, professionally recognized psychiatric treatment. There was no testimony that while in the hospital respondent had ever been violent or otherwise shown signs of being physically dangerous, and it was conceded that an organization to which respondent had written and a family friend had made repeated unsuccessful attempts to have him released in their custody.

Petitioner and his codefendants contended, however, that respondent was mentally ill and in need of care during the entire time that he was confined, and that they had not denied him treatment. Their position was that respondent had been unwilling to acknowledge his illness or otherwise cooperate, that he refused various types of therapy which had been offered, and that, in the face of these impediments to providing effective

---

health officials. However, the request for injunctive relief was abandoned and the other defendants were either not served or dismissed prior to trial.

O'CONNOR *v.* DONALDSON

treatment, they had done the best they could with the
limited resources available to them. They maintained
that all of their actions with respect to respondent had
been professionally motivated and in good faith.

The District Court instructed the jury that, in order
for respondent to recover, he was required to prove that
the defendants had "confined him against his will, knowing that he was not mentally ill or dangerous or knowing that if mentally ill he was not receiving treatment,"
that they had acted under color of state law, and that these
actions violated respondent's constitutional right not to
be deprived of his liberty without due process of law.
The court defined that right as follows:

> "[A] person who is involuntarily civilly com-
> mitted to a mental hospital does have a constitu-
> tional right to receive such treatment as will give
> him a realistic opportunity to be cured or to im-
> prove his mental condition.
>
> "Now, the purpose of involuntary hospitalization
> is treatment and not mere custodial care or punish-
> ment if a patient is not a danger to himself or
> others. Without such treatment there is no justi-
> fication from a constitutional standpoint for con-
> tinued confinement unless you should also find that
> the Plaintiff was dangerous to either himself or
> others."

The District Court also charged that respondent could
not recover damages for failure to receive any treatment
that he had refused, and that the defendants were entitled to a verdict if they established by a preponderance
of the evidence that they "reasonably believed in good
faith that detention of [respondent] was proper for the
length of time he was so confined . . . ."

The defendants did not object to these instructions,
and the jury returned an aggregate verdict of $38,500

O'CONNOR *v.* DONALDSON

against petitioner and one of his codefendants, including $10,000 in punitive damages. The third defendant was absolved of liability. The Court of Appeals affirmed, holding that the evidence supported the jury's verdict and the trial court's instructions correctly stated the law. Specifically, the Court of Appeals agreed that the Due Process Clause of the Fourteenth Amendment guarantees a "right to treatment" to persons who are involuntarily civilly committed to state mental hospitals. It reasoned that recognition of such a right was necessary to insure that the nature of commitment bear a reasonable relationship to its purpose, and to compensate for the lack of certain safeguards in commitment proceedings. 493 F. 2d 507, 520–522.

We granted certiorari and we affirm the jury verdict, but reject the reasoning of the Court of Appeals.

II

At the outset it is important to emphasize that although this case began as a comprehensive attack upon Florida's scheme for civilly committing the mentally ill, see n. 4, *supra,* it comes to us in the far more modest form of a jury verdict for damages against a specific individual. Our review is accordingly narrowly limited to considering petitioner's specifications of error in the trial and, if errors occurred, whether challenges to them were properly preserved or are otherwise open for our consideration.

The limited and specific nature of our review also precludes consideration of various issues which we have touched upon in other contexts, and it will help to isolate the present area of concern to describe them briefly. First, this is not a case of a person seeking release because he has been confined "without ever obtaining a judicial determination that such confinement is war-

ranted." *McNeil* v. *Director, Patuxent Institution,* 407
U. S. 245, 249 (1972). Although respondent's amended
complaint alleged that his 1956 hearing before the
Pinellas County Court was procedurally defective and
ignored various factors relating to the necessity for commitment, the persons to whom those allegations applied
were either not served with process or dismissed by the
District Court prior to trial. Respondent has not sought
review of the latter rulings, and we are therefore not
here dealing with the rights of a person in an initial
competency or commitment proceeding. Cf. *Jackson* v.
Indiana, 406 U. S. 715, 738 (1972); *Specht* v. *Patterson,* 386 U. S. 605 (1967); *Minnesota ex rel. Pearson* v.
Probate Court, 309 U. S. 270 (1940).

Further, it was not alleged that respondent was singled
out for discriminatory treatment by the staff of Florida
State Hospital or that patients at that institution were
denied privileges generally available to other persons
under commitment in Florida. Thus, the question
whether different bases for commitment justify differences in conditions of confinement is not involved in this
litigation. Cf. *Jackson* v. *Indiana,* 406 U. S. 723–730;
Baxstrom v. *Herold,* 383 U. S. 107 (1966).

Finally, there was no evidence whatever that respondent was abused or mistreated at Florida State Hospital
or that the failure to provide him with treatment aggra-
vated his condition. There was testimony regarding the
general quality of life at the hospital, but the jury was
not asked to consider whether respondent's confinement
was in effect "punishment" for being mentally ill. The
record provides no basis for concluding, therefore, that
respondent was denied rights secured by the Eighth and
Fourteenth Amendments. Cf. *Robinson* v. *California,*
370 U. S. 660 (1962).

In sum, the narrow question here is whether, on the

O'CONNOR *v.* DONALDSON

evidence presented and under the instructions given, the jury could properly conclude that petitioner's actions toward respondent subjected him to personal liability for damages under 42 U. S. C. § 1983. We need not and do not decide whether respondent's confinement comported with the Constitution in every respect.

III

Petitioner's primary contention, and the only one meriting extended discussion,[5] is that the District Court erred in instructing the jury that persons involuntarily committed to state mental hospitals have a constitutional right either to receive treatment which will give them a realistic opportunity to improve or be released. This is so, he says, because the "alleged right to treatment is incapable of definition, implementation, or enforcement . . . ." Brief for Petitioner 15. We agree that the instructions were erroneous, but for different reasons.

A

There can be no doubt that involuntary commitment to a mental hospital, like involuntary confinement of an individual for any reason, is a deprivation of liberty which the State cannot accomplish without due process

---

[5] Petitioner's only other contention of even arguable merit is that he acted in the good-faith belief that his treatment of respondent was lawful, that this belief was reasonable, and that an award of damages against him was therefore improper. These assertions obviously involve questions of fact for resolution by the jury. See *Scheuer* v. *Rhodes*, 416 U. S. 232, 249–250 (1974). Moreover, regardless of whether the District Court's instructions properly defined the scope of the good-faith defense available to a state official such as petitioner, the jury's award of punitive damages required it to conclude that he had acted "maliciously or wantonly or oppressively . . . ." This award forecloses petitioner's good-faith defense. See *Wood* v. *Strickland*, —— U S —— (1975).

O'CONNOR *v.* DONALDSON

of law. *Specht* v. *Patterson,* 386 U. S. 608. Cf. *In re
Gault,* 387 U. S. 1, 12–13 (1967). Commitment must
be justified on the basis of a legitimate state interest, and
the reasons for committing a particular individual must
be established in an appropriate proceeding. Equally
important, confinement must cease when those reasons
no longer exist. See *McNeil* v. *Director, Patuxent Institution,* 407 U. S. 249–250; *Jackson* v. *Indiana,* 406
U. S. 738.

The Court of Appeals purported to be applying these
principles in developing the first of its theories supporting a constitutional right to treatment. It stated:

> "[W]here, as in Donaldson's case, the rationale
> for confinement is the *'parens patriae'* rationale that
> the patient is in need of treatment, the due process
> clause requires that minimally adequate treatment
> be in fact provided . . . . 'To deprive any citizen
> of his or her liberty upon the altruistic theory that
> the confinement is for humane therapeutic reasons
> and then fail to provide adequate treatment violates
> the very fundamentals of due process." 493 F. 2d
> 521.

The Court of Appeals did not explain its conclusion
that the rationale for respondent's commitment was that
he needed treatment. The Florida statutes in effect
during the period of his confinement did not require that
nondangerous persons who had been adjudicated incompetent either be provided with psychiatric treatment
or released; and there was no such condition in respondent's order of commitment, which was at least par-
tially based upon the findings of court-appointed physicians that he was paranoid and potentially dangerous.
Cf. *Rouse* v. *Cameron,* —— U. S. App. D. C. ——, 373
F. 2d 451 (1966). More important, the District Court's
instructions did not require the jury to focus upon the

O'CONNOR *v.* DONALDSON

reasons for respondent's confinement nor to make any findings regarding his rights under state law." Thus, the premise of the Court of Appeals' holding must have been that a State has no power to confine nondangerous mentally ill persons other than for the purpose of treatment. We find nothing in the Constitution to support such a conclusion.

In the first place, that proposition is certainly not descriptive of the power traditionally exercised by the States in this area. For a considerable period of time, subsidized custodial care in private foster homes or boarding houses was the most benign form of care provided incompetent or mentally ill persons for whom the States assumed responsibility. Until well into the 19th century the vast majority of such persons were simply restrained in poorhouses, almshouses, or jails. See A. Deutsch, The Mentally Ill in America 38–54, 114–131 (2d ed. 1949). The few States that established institutions for the mentally ill during this early period were concerned primarily with providing a more humane place of confinement and only secondarily with "curing" the persons sent there. See *id.*, at 98–113.

As the trend toward state care of the mentally ill expanded, eventually leading to the present statutory schemes for protecting such persons,[7] the dual functions of institutionalization continued to be recognized. While one of the goals of this movement was to provide medical treatment to those who could benefit from it, it was ac-

---

[6] Florida has recently enacted a complete revision of its civil commitment law which includes a statutory right to receive individual medical treatment. 144 Fla. Stat. Ann. § 394.459 (1972). See generally Note, Involuntary Hospitalization of the Mentally Ill Under the Baker Act: Procedural Due Process and the Role of the Attorney, 26 U. Fla. L. Rev. 508 (1974).

[7] See generally American Bar Foundation, The Mentally Disabled and the Law (S. Brakel & R. Rock ed. 1971).

O'CONNOR *v.* DONALDSON

knowledged that this could not be done in all cases and that there was a large number of mental illnesses for which no known "cure" existed. In time, providing places for the custodial confinement of the so-called "dependent insane" again emerged as the major goal of the State's programs in this area and continued to be so well into this century. See *id.*, at 228–271; D. Rothman, The Discovery of the Asylum 264–295 (1971).

In short, the idea that States may not confine the mentally ill except for the purpose of providing them with treatment is of very recent origin,[*] and there is no historical basis for imposing such a limitation on state power. Analysis of the sources of the civil commitment power likewise affords no basis for the conclusion that its only legitimate purpose is treatment. There can be little doubt that in the exercise of its police power a State may confine individuals solely to protect society from the dangers of significant antisocial acts or communicable disease. Cf. *Minnesota ex rel. Pearson v. Probate Court*, 309 U. S. 270; *Jacobson v. Massachusetts*, 197 U. S. 1, 25–29 (1905). Additionally, the States are vested with the historic *parens patriae* power, including the duty to protect "persons under legal disabilities to act for themselves." *Hawaii v. Standard Oil Co.*, 405 U. S. 251, 257 (1972). See also *Mormon Church v. United States*, 136 U. S. 1, 56–58 (1890). The classic example of this role is when a State undertakes to act as " 'the general guardian of all infants, idiots, and lunatics.' " *Hawaii v. Standard Oil Co., supra*, quoting 3 W. Blackstone, Commentaries *47.

Of course, an inevitable consequence of exercising the *parens patriae* power is that the ward's personal freedom will be substantially restrained, whether a guardian is appointed to control his property, he is placed in the cus-

---

[*] See Editorial, A New Right, 46 A. B. A. J. 516 (1960)

O'CONNOR *v.* DONALDSON

today of a private third party, or committed to an institution. Thus, however the power is implemented, due process requires that it not be invoked indiscriminately. At a minimum, a particular scheme for protection of the mentally ill must rest upon a legislative determination that it is compatible with the best interests of the affected class because they are unable to act for themselves. Cf. *Mormon Church* v. *United States, supra.* Moreover, the use of alternative forms of protection may be motivated by different considerations, and the justifications for one may not be invoked to rationalize another. Cf. *Jackson* v. *Indiana,* 406 U. S. 737–738. See also American Bar Foundation, The Mentally Disabled and the Law, 254–255 (S. Brakel & R. Rock ed. 1971).

Notwithstanding these due process limitations, it does not follow that a State is without power under all conditions to confine a nondangerous mentally ill person except for treatment. Despite many recent advances in medical knowledge, it remains a stubborn fact that there are still forms of mental illness which are not understood, some which are untreatable in the sense that no effective therapy has yet been discovered for them, and that rates of "cure" are generally low. See Schwitzgebel, The Right to Effective Mental Treatment, 62 Calif. L. Rev. 936, 941–948 (1974). There can be little responsible debate regarding "the uncertainty of diagnosis in this field and the tentativeness of professional judgment." *Greenwood* v. *United States,* 350 U. S. 366, 375 (1957). See also Ennis and Litwack, Psychiatry and the Presumption of Expertise: Flipping Coins in the Courtroom, 62 Calif. L. Rev. 693, 697–719 (1974).[9] Similarly, it is universally recognized as fundamental to effective therapy that the patient acknowledge his

---

[9] Indeed, there is considerable debate regarding what constitutes "mental disease" and "treatment." See Szasz, The Right to Health 57 Geo. L. J. 734 (1969).

O'CONNOR v. DONALDSON

illness and cooperate with those attempting to give
treatment; yet the failure of a large proportion of mentally ill persons to do so is a common phenomenon. See
Katz, The Right to Treatment—An Enchanting Legal
Fiction?, 36 U. Chi. L. Rev. 755, 768–769 (1969). It
may be that some persons in either of these categories,[10]
and there may be others, are unable to function in society and will suffer real harm to themselves unless provided with care in a sheltered environment. See, e. g.,
Lake v. *Cameron*, —— U. S. App. D. C. ——, 364 F. 2d
657, 663–664 (1966) (dissenting op.). At the very least,
we cannot say that a state legislature is powerless to
make that kind of judgment. See *Greenwood* v. *United
States, supra.*

B

Alternatively, it is argued that a Fourteenth Amendment right to treatment for involuntarily confined
mental patients derives from the fact that many of the
safeguards of the criminal process are not present in
civil commitment. The Court of Appeals described this
theory as follows:

> "[A] due process right to treatment is based on
> the principle that when the three central limitations
> on the government's power to detain—that deten-
> tion be in retribution for a specific offense; that it
> be limited to a fixed term; and that it be permitted
> after a proceeding where the fundamental proce-
> dural safeguards are observed—are absent, there

---

[10] Indeed, respondent may have shared both of these characteristics. His illness, paranoid schizophrenia, is notoriously unsusceptible
to treatment, see Livermore, Malmquist, and Meehl, On the Justifications for Civil Commitment, 117 U. Pa. L. Rev. 75, 93 & n. 52
(1968), and the reports of the Florida State Hospital Staff which
were introduced into evidence expressed the view that he was unwilling to acknowledge his illness and generally uncooperative

O'CONNOR *v* DONALDSON

> must be a *quid pro quo* extended by the governments to justify confinement. And the *quid pro quo* most commonly recognized is the provision of rehabilitative treatment." [11] 493 F. 2d 522.

To the extent that this theory may be read to permit a State to confine an individual simply because it is willing to provide treatment, regardless of the subject's ability to function in society, it raises the gravest of constitutional problems, and we have no doubt the Court of Appeals would agree on this score. As a justification for a constitutional right to such treatment, the *quid pro quo* theory suffers from equally serious defects.

It is too well established to require extended discussion that due process is not an inflexible concept. Rather, its requirements are determined in particular instances by identifying and accommodating the interests of the individual and society. See, *e. g., Morrissey* v. *Brewer,* 408 U. S. 471, 480–484 (1972); *McNeil* v. *Director, Patuxent Institution,* 407 U. S. 249–250; *McKeiver* v. *Pennsylvania,* 403 U. S. 528, 545–555 (1971). Where claims that the State is acting in the best interests of the individual are said to justify reduced procedural and substantive safeguards, our decisions require that they be "candidly appraised." *In re Gault,* 387 U. S. 1, 21, 27–19. However, in so doing we are not free to read our private notions of public policy or public health into the Constitution. *Olsen* v. *Nebraska,* 313 U. S. 236, 246-247 (1941).

The *quid pro quo* theory is a sharp departure from, and cannot coexist with, these due process principles. As an initial matter, the theory presupposes that essen-

---

[11] The Court of Appeals was of the view that this theory justified a constitutional right to treatment or release even for persons confined on the ground that they are dangerous to society. 493 F. 2d 522.

O'CONNOR *v.* DONALDSON

tially the same interests are involved in every situation
where a State seeks to confine an individual; as these
illustrations suggest, that assumption is incorrect.   It is
elementary that the justification for the criminal process
and the unique deprivation of liberty which it can impose
requires that it be invoked only for commission of a
specific offense prohibited by legislative enactments.   See
Powell v. *Texas*, 392 U. S. 514, 541–544 (1968) (opinion of Black, J.).[12]   But it would be incongruous to apply
the same limitation when quarantine is imposed by the
State to protect the public from a highly communicable
disease.   See *Jacobson* v. *Massachusetts*, 197 U. S. 29–30.

A more troublesome feature of the *quid pro quo* theory
is that it elevates a concern for essentially procedural
safeguards into a new substantive constitutional right.[13]
Rather than inquiring whether strict standards of proof
or periodic redetermination of a patient's condition are
required in civil confinement, the theory accepts the
absence of such safeguards but insists that the State provide benefits which, in the view of a court, are adequate
"compensation" for confinement.   In light of the wide
divergence of medical opinion regarding the diagnosis of
and proper therapy for mental abnormalities, that prospect is especially troubling in this area and cannot be
squared with the principle that "courts may not substitute for the judgments of legislators their own under-

---

[12] This is not to imply that we accept all of the Court of Appeals'
conclusions regarding the limitations upon the States' power to
detain persons who commit crimes.   For example, the notion that
confinement must be "for a fixed term" is difficult to square with
the widespread practice of indeterminate sentencing, at least where
the upper limit is life.

[13] Even advocates of a right to treatment have criticized the *quid
pro quo* theory on this ground.   *E. g.,* Note, Developments in the
Law—Civil Commitment of the Mentally Ill, 87 Harv. L. Rev.
1190, 1325, n. 39 (1974).

O'CONNOR v DONALDSON

standing of the public welfare, but must instead concern themselves with the validity of the methods which the legislature has selected." *In re Gault*, 387 U. S. 71 (opinion of Harlan, J.). Of course, questions regarding the adequacy of procedure and the power of a State to continue particular confinements are ultimately for the courts, aided by expert opinion to the extent that is found helpful. But we are not prepared to abandon the traditional limitations on the scope of judicial review.

C

In sum, we reject the reasoning of the Court of Appeals and can discern no other basis for equating the federal constitutional right not to be confined without due process of law with an absolute constitutional right for involuntarily committed mental patients to either receive adequate psychiatric treatment or be released. In the context of this case, a jury finding that respondent's treatment program was limited to custodial care, standing alone, would not establish liability under 42 U. S. C. § 1983. Because the District Court's instructions were such as to permit a verdict for respondent based solely upon such a finding, the instructions were, in that respect, erroneous.

IV

The conclusion that the jury was incorrectly instructed does not automatically entitle petitioner to reversal of the verdict. It remains to be determined whether his present attack on those instructions was properly preserved and, if not, whether any failure to do so may be excused.

Rule 51, Federal Rules of Civil Procedure, provides in pertinent part:

"No party may assign as error the giving or failure to give an instruction unless he objects thereto.

O'CONNOR *v.* DONALDSON

> before the jury retires to consider its verdict, stating
> distinctly the matter to which he objects and the
> grounds of his objection."

This Rule reflects the historic federal practice and "is
founded upon considerations of fairness to the court and
to the parties and of the public interest in bringing litigation to an end after fair opportunity has been afforded
to present all issues of law and fact." *United States* v.
Atkinson, 297 U. S. 157, 159 (1936). See also *Palmer*
v. *Hoffman,* 318 U. S. 109, 119 (1943); *Pennslyvania R.
Co.* v. *Minds,* 250 U. S. 368, 374–375 (1919); *Allis* v.
United States, 155 U. S. 117, 122–123 (1894).

As observed, neither petitioner nor his codefendants
objected to the District Court's instructions regarding
respondent's alleged constitutional right to be treated or
else promptly released, and his challenge would therefore
seem to be foreclosed by a literal application of Rule 51.
It is argued, however, that formal objection was not required to preserve the claim for review because petitioner
had made his position clear and further argument
or specific objection would have been fruitless. See 9 C.
Wright and A. Miller, Federal Practice and Procedure,
§ 2553, at 639–640 (1971). Whatever the validity of
such an argument in some contexts, it is not supported
by this record.

Despite its central importance to the litigation, respondent's claim that he had a constitutional right to
treatment received little attention prior to the beginning
of trial. In a "Pre-Trial Stipulation" submitted pursuant to an order of the District Court the parties identified six "[i]ssues of law that remain to be determined,"
none of which was remotely related to a "constitutional
right" of a mental patient to receive treatment, and their
trial briefs argued only the issues set out in the stipulation. Similarly, in response to respondent's proposed

O'CONNOR *v.* DONALDSON

instructions No. 37 and 38, from which the District Court's instructions on this point were taken, petitioner stated only that they

> "should be corrected to read . . . that a person who is committed to a mental hospital has a right to be released through judicial process when through no fault of his own treatment is not afforded and he is not dangerous to society or himself."

Even accepting that this "correction" is inconsistent with the instructions eventually given by the District Court, this Court has consistently held that a request for a different or contradictory instruction is not a substitute for the specific objection required to preserve appellate review. See *Palmer* v. *Hoffman,* 318 U. S. 116–120; *Beaver* v. *Taylor,* 93 U. S. 46, 55 (1876). That rule obtains even where the request is for a more nearly correct statement of the law, and the reasons for it are obvious:

> "It is not the duty of a judge at the [district] court, or of an appellate court, to analyze and compare the requests and the charge, to discover what are the portions thus excepted to. One of the objects of an exception is to call the attention of the [district] judge *to the precise point as to which it is supposed he has erred, that he may then and there consider it,* and give new and different instructions to the jury, if in his judgment it should be proper to do so. An exception in the form we are considering entirely defeats that object." *Ibid.* (citation omitted; emphasis added).

On no other occasion did petitioner even express disagreement with the proposition that involuntarily confined mental patients have a constitutional right to receive treatment or be released, despite the fact that he

O'CONNOR v. DONALDSON

was offered the opportunity to do so both before and after the jury was charged. In such circumstances, the District Court would have been justified in believing that the parties were in essential agreement regarding the elements of respondent's case, and to hold that the requirements of Rule 51 had been met here would be to negate their clear intent.

Nor do we think that petitioner's failure to comply with the Rule can be disregarded. The doctrine of plain error in federal cases [14] is confined to situations in which "errors are obvious, or . . . otherwise seriously affect the fairness, integrity or public reputation of judicial proceedings." *United States* v. *Atkinson*, 297 U. S. 160. In light of the unsettled state of the law regarding the State's power to confine mentally ill persons, see *Jackson* v. *Indiana*, 406 U. S. 736–737, the fact that some courts had recognized the supposed constitutional right to treatment at the time this case was tried, *e. g., Wyatt* v. *Stickney*, 325 F. Supp. 781 (ND Ala. 1971), and the award of punitive damages, implying a jury finding that petitioner acted maliciously, this is not a case in which an appellate court should rescue a litigant from his tactical errors at trial.

V

Government does not have plenary power to deprive mentally ill persons of their liberty. The requirements of due process must be adhered to not only in initial competency or commitment proceedings, but throughout the period of an individual's confinement as well. However, given the present state of medical knowledge regarding

---

[14] Rule 52 (b), Federal Rule of Criminal Procedure, states that, "Plain errors or defects affecting substantial rights may be noticed although they were not brought to the attention of the court." There is no similar provision in the civil rules.

O'CONNOR *v.* DONALDSON

abnormal human behavior and its treatment, few things would be more fraught with peril than to irrevocably condition the power to protect the mentally ill upon the providing of "such treatment as will give [them] a realistic opportunity to be cured." Nothing in the Constitution mandates such a rule.

In this case, however, the issues were resolved by a jury under instructions which, although erroneous in some respects, were given without objection from petitioner. In such circumstances it is not the function of appellate courts, and particularly of this Court, to reach out to correct specific trial error for the benefit of a private litigant.

Affirmed.

1st **DRAFT**   Recirculated:_____

SUPREME COURT OF THE UNITED STATES

No. 74–8

J. B. O'Connor,
Petitioner,
v.
Kenneth Donaldson.

On Writ of Certiorari to the
United States Court of Appeals
for the Fifth Circuit.

[June —, 1975]

MR. JUSTICE STEWART, dissenting.

The respondent, Kenneth Donaldson, was civilly committed to the Florida State Hospital at Chattahoochee in January 1957 and was confined there against his will for nearly 15 years.[1] During most of that period, the

---

[1] The judicial commitment proceedings were initiated by Donaldson's father, pursuant to a state statute, now repealed, which provided:

"Whenever any person who has been adjudged mentally incompetent requires confinement or restraint to prevent self-injury or violence to others, the said judge shall direct that such person be forthwith delivered to the superintendent of the Florida state hospital, for care, maintenance, and treatment, as provided in §§ 394.09, 394.24, 394.25, 394.26 and 394.27, or make such other disposition of him as he may be permitted by law."

14 A Fla. Stat. § 394.22 (11) (a) (West 1960)

Donaldson had been adjudged "incompetent" several days earlier under § 394.22 (1), which provided for such a finding as to any person who was

"incompetent by reason of mental illness, sickness, drunkenness, excessive use of drugs, insanity, or other mental or physical condition, so that he is incapable of caring for himself or managing his property, or is likely to dissipate or lose his property or become the victim of designing persons, or inflict harm on himself or others . . ."

It would appear that § 394.22 (11) (a) contemplated that involuntary commitment would be imposed only on those "incompetent" persons who "require[d] confinement or restraint to prevent self-

O'CONNOR *v.* DONALDSON

petitioner, Dr. J. B. O'Connor, was superintendent of the hospital. The evidence at the trial showed that the hospital staff could release a patient who was not dangerous to himself or to others, even if committed under a valid judicial order and still mentally ill.[2] Donaldson

injury or violence to others." But this is not certain, for the statute further provided that the judge could adjudicate the person a "harmless incompetent" and release him to a guardian upon a finding that he did "not require confinement or restraint to prevent self-injury or violence to others *and* that treatment in the Florida state hospital is unnecessary or would be without benefit to such person. . . ." § 394.22 (11)(b) (emphasis added). In this regard, it is noteworthy that Donaldson's "Order for Delivery" to the Florida State Hospital provided that he required "confinement or restraint to prevent self-injury or violence to others, *or* to insure proper treatment." (Emphasis added.) At any rate, the Florida commitment statute provided no judicial procedure whereby one still incompent could secure his release on the ground that he was no longer dangerous to himself or others. It might be thought that state habeas corpus procedures would serve this purpose. But Donaldson instituted numerous habeas corpus actions and never succeeded in securing an adjudication on the merits.

Whether the Florida statute provided a "right to treatment" for involuntarily committed patients is also open to dispute. Under § 394.22 (11)(a), commitment "to prevent self-injury or violence to others" was "for care, maintenance, and treatment." Recently Florida has totally revamped its civil commitment law and now provides a statutory right to receive individual medical treatment. 144 Fla. Stat. Ann. § 394.459 (1972)

[2] The sole *statutory* procedure for release required a judicial reinstatement of a patient's "mental competency." 14 A Fla. Stat. § 394.22 (15) & (16) (West 1960). But this procedure could be initiated by the hospital staff. Indeed, it was at the staff's initiative that Donaldson was finally restored to competency, and liberty, almost immediately after O'Connor retired from the superintendency.

In addition, witnesses testified that the hospital had always had its own procedure for releasing patients—for "trial visits," "home visits," "furloughs," or "out of state discharges"—even though the patients had not been judicially restored to competency. Those conditional releases often became permanent, and the hospital merely

O'CONNOR *v.* DONALDSON

repeatedly asked O'Connor to exercise that power in his case, and, on numerous occasions, responsible private parties offered to give Donaldson whatever care he might need on release. O'Connor nonetheless refused to allow Donaldson to leave the hospital.[3] O'Connor testified that he had believed that Donaldson would not make a "successful adjustment outside the institution," but he could not recall the basis for his conclusion. As soon as O'Connor retired as superintendent, the hospital staff secured Donaldson's release and a judicial restoration of his competency.

The record is scanty as to Donaldson's condition when he was first committed. But evidence at the trial showed that, at least from an early point in his confine-

---

closed its books on the patient. O'Connor did not deny at trial that he had the power to release patients; he conceded that it was his "duty" as superintendent cf the hospital "to determine whether that patient having once reached the hospital was in such a condition as to request that he be considered for release from the hospital."

[3] In June 1963, a representative of Helping Hands, Inc., a half-way house for mental patients, wrote O'Connor asking him to release Donaldson to its care. The request was accompanied by a supporting letter from the Minneapolis Clinic of Psychiatry and Neurology, which a defense witness conceded was a "good clinic." O'Connor rejected the offer, replying that Donaldson could be released only to his parents. This rule was apparently of O'Connor's own making. At the time, Donaldson was 55 years old. As O'Connor knew, Donaldson's parents were too elderly and infirm to take responsibility for him. Though he had a continuing correspondence with the parents, O'Connor never informed them of the Helping Hands offer.

On four separate occasions, between 1964 and 1968, John Lembcke, a college classmate of Donaldson, and a long-time family friend, asked O'Connor to release Donaldson to his care. On each occasion O'Connor refused. The record shows that Lembcke is a serious and responsible person, who had been willing and able to assume responsibility for Donaldson's welfare

O'CONNOR *v.* DONALDSON

ment, he was not dangerous to himself or others [4] and could have lived safely in the private community.[5] The record is equally persuasive that his confinement was a simple regime of enforced custodial care, not a program designed to cure his illness.[6]

At the trial O'Connor did not seriously deny this. He claimed, however, that he had acted in good faith and was therefore, immune from any award of damages. His position, in short, was that state law, which he had believed valid, had authorized indefinite custodial confinement of the "sick," even when their release could harm no one.[7]

---

[4] O'Connor conceded that he had neither personal nor second hand knowledge of any instance of Donaldson committing or threatening to commit an act dangerous to himself or others. The other witnesses agreed that Donaldson's release would have posed no threat.

[5] See n. 3, *supra*. O'Connor's codefendant admitted that Donaldson could have earned his own living outside the hospital, as he had for many years prior to his involuntary commitment. Donaldson had never been on welfare. Immediately after his release, Donaldson secured a responsible job in hotel administration.

[6] Numerous witnesses, including one of O'Connor's codefendants, testified that Donaldson had received nothing but custodial care. O'Connor described Donaldson's treatment as "milieu therapy." Witnesses from the hospital staff conceded that, in the context of this case, this was euphemism for confinement in the "milieu" of a mental hospital. For much of his stay at the hospital, Donaldson was kept in a large room that housed 60 patients, many of whom were under criminal commitment.

There was some evidence that Donaldson, who is a Christian Scientist, on occasion refused to take medication. The trial judge instructed the jury not to award damages for any period of confinement during which Donaldson had declined treatment.

[7] At the close of Donaldson's case-in-chief, O'Connor moved for a directed verdict on the ground that state law at the time of Donaldson's confinement authorized institutionalization of the mentally ill even if they posed no danger to themselves or others. This motion was denied. At the close of all the evidence, O'Connor

O'CONNOR v. DONALDSON

The trial judge instructed the members of the jury, in essence, that they should find that O'Connor had violated Donaldson's constitution right to liberty if they found that he had subjected Donaldson to simple custodial confinement, with the knowledge that Donaldson's release would threaten neither his own safety nor that of others.[8] The trial judge further instructed the jury that O'Connor was immune from damages if he

"reasonably believed in good faith that detention of

---

asked that the jury be instructed that "if the defendants acted pursuant to a statute which was not declared unconstitutional at the time, they cannot be held accountable for such action." The District Court declined to give this requested instruction.

[8] The pertinent instructions, to which O'Connor's counsel did not object, were as follows:

"The Plaintiff claims in brief that throughout the period of his hospitalization he was not mentally ill or dangerous to himself, and claims further that if he was mentally ill, or if Defendants believed he was mentally ill, Defendants withheld from him the treatment necessary to improve his mental condition.

"The Defendants claim, in brief, that Plaintiff's detention was legal and proper, or if his detention was not legal and proper, it was the result of mistake, without malicious intent.

"In order to prove his claim under the Civil Rights Act, the burden is upon the Plaintiff in this case to establish by a preponderance of the evidence in this case the following facts:

'That the Defendants confined Plaintiff against his will, knowing that he was not mentally ill or dangerous, or knowing that if mentally ill he was not receiving treatment for his mental illness . . . .'

"That the Defendants' acts and conduct deprived Plaintiff of his Federal Constitutional right not to be denied or deprived of his liberty without due process of law as that phrase is defined and explained in these instructions . . . .

"You are instructed that a person who is involuntarily civilly committed to a mental hospital does have a constitutional right to recieve such treatment as will give him a realistic opportunity to be cured or to improve his mental condition.

"Now the purpose of involuntary hospitalization is treatment and not mere custodial care or punishment if a patient is not a danger

O'CONNOR *v.* DONALDSON

Plaintiff was proper for the length of time he was so confined . . .

    o   •   o   o   o

"[M]ere good intentions which do not give rise to a reasonable belief that detention is lawfully required cannot justify Plaintiff's confinement in the Florida State Hospital."

The jury returned a verdict for Donaldson against O'Connor and a codefendant, and awarded damages of $38,500, including $10,000 in punitive damages.[9] The Court of Appeals affirmed the judgment. 493 F. 2d 507.[10]

---

to himself or others. Without such treatment there is no justification from a constitutional standpoint for continued confinement unless you should also find that the Plaintiff was dangerous either to himself or others."

Given those instructions, it is possible that the jury went so far as to find that O'Connor knew that Donaldson was not only harmless to himself and others but also that he was not mentally ill at all. If it so found, the jury was permitted by the instructions to rule against O'Connor regardless of the nature of the involuntary confinement imposed. If we were to construe the jury's verdict in that fashion, there would remain no substantial issue in this case: That a wholly sane and innocent person has a constitutional right not to be physically confined by the State when his freedom will pose a danger neither to himself nor to others cannot be seriously doubted.

   [9] The trial judge had instructed that punitive damages should be awarded only if "the act or omission of the Defendant or Defendants which proximately caused injury to the Plaintiff was maliciously or wantonly or oppressively done."

   [10] Athough O'Connor did not object to the jury instructions that Donaldson had a right to release if he was not receiving treatment and was not dangerous to himself or others, this basic constitutional question was preserved for appeal by O'Connor's answer in the District Court, which alleged that Donaldson had failed to state a claim upon which relief could be granted. See Fed. Rule Civ. Proc. 12 (h) (2).

O'CONNOR *v.* DONALDSON

I

The jury's verdict makes the issue in this case a narrow one. We need not decide whether, when, or by what procedures, a mentally ill person may be confined by the State on any of the grounds traditionally asserted to justify the involuntary confinement of such a person—that is, to prevent injury to the public, to ensure his own survival or safety,[11] or to alleviate or cure his illness. See *Jackson* v. *Indiana,* 406 U. S. 715, 736–737; *Humphrey* v. *Cady,* 405 U. S. 504, 509. Because involuntary civil commitment represents a "massive curtailment of liberty," *Humphrey* v. *Cady, supra,* at 509, even those grounds are subject to "substantive constitutional limitations." *Jackson* v *Indiana, supra,* at 737. But the nature and scope of those limitations need not detain us, for the jury found that none of the traditionally asserted grounds for continued confinement was presented in Donaldson's case.[12]

---

[11] The judge's instructions used the phrase "danger to himself." Of course, even if there is no foreseeable risk of self-injury or suicide, a person is literally a "danger to himsef" if he cannot economically survive safey in freedom, either through his own efforts or with the aid of willing family members or friends. While it might be argued that the judge's instructions could have been more detailed on this point, O'Connor raised no objection to them, presumably because the evidence clearly showed that Donaldson was not a "danger to himself" however broadly that phrase might be defined.

[12] O'Connor argues that, despite the jury's verdict, the Court must assume that Donaldson was receiving treatment sufficient to justify his confinement, because the adequacy of treatment is a "nonjusticiable" question that must be left to the discretion of the psychiatric profession. That argument is unpersuasive. Where "treatment" is the sole asserted ground for depriving a person of liberty, it is plainly unacceptable to suggest that the courts are powerless to determine whether the asserted ground is present. See *Jackson* v. *Indiana, supra.* Neither party objected to the jury instruction concerning the type and quantum of treatment sufficient

O'CONNOR *v.* DONALDSON

Given the jury's findings, what was left as justification for keeping Donaldson in continued confinement? The fact that state law may have authorized confinement of the harmless mentally ill does not itself establish a constitutionally adequate purpose for the confinement. See *Jackson* v. *Indiana, supra,* at 720–721; *McNeil* v. *Director, Patuxent Institution,* 407 U. S. 245, 248–250. Nor is it enough that Donaldson's original confinement was founded upon a constitutionally adequate basis, if in fact it was, because even if his involuntary confinement was initially permissible, it could not constitutionally continue after that basis no longer existed. *Jackson* v. *Indiana, supra,* at 738; *McNeil* v. *Director, Patuxent Institution, supra.*

In my opinion, a finding of "mental illness" cannot in itself justify the extinguishment of personal liberty. The term "mental illness" is notoriously vague and variable.[13] To permit incarceration upon a criterion with such uncertain dimensions invites evils too obvious to require cataloguing. See *Papachristou* v. *City of Jacksonville,* 405 U. S. 156. But even assuming that the term could be given a reasonably precise content and that the "mentally ill" could be identified with reasonable accuracy, I can perceive no constitutional basis

---

to justify confinement. There is, accordingly, no occasion in this case to decide whether the provision of treatment, standing alone, can ever constitutionally justify involuntary confinement or, if it can, how much or what kind of treatment would suffice for that purpose. In its present posture this case involves not involuntary treatment but involuntary custodial confinement. See n. 6, *supra.*

[13] See, *e. g.*, Sarbin, The Scientific Status of the Mental Illness Metaphor, in Changing Perspectives in Mental Illness 1 (S. Plog & R. Edgerton eds.); Livermore, Malmquist & Meehl, On the Justifications for Civil Commitment, 117 U. Pa. L. Rev. 75, 80. See also, Developments in the Law—Civil Commitment of the Mentally Ill, 87 Harv. L. Rev. 1190, 1254–1256.

O'CONNOR *v.* DONALDSON

for confining such pesrsons against their will if they are
dangerous to no one and can live safely in freedom.

May the State confine the mentally ill merely to
ensure them a living standard superior to that they
enjoy in the private community? At best, this ground
could justify the enforced confinement only of those incapable of surviving safely on their own or with the help
of family or friends, for involuntary confinement is
hardly a necessary condition for providing financial aid to a
person who can live in liberty to the detriment of no
one. See *Shelton* v. *Tucker,* 364 U. S. 479, 488–490.
May the State fence in the harmless mentally ill solely
to save its citizens from exposure to those whose ways
are different? One might as well ask if the State, to
avoid public unease, could incarcerate all who are physically handicapped or socially eccentric. Mere public
intolerance or animosity cannot constitutionally justify
the deprivation of a person's physical liberty. See, *e. g.,*
Coates v. *City of Cincinnati,* 402 U. S. 611, 615; *Street*
v. *New York,* 394 U. S. 576, 592.

In my view a State cannot constitutionally confine
without more a nondangerous individual who is capable
of caring for himself or who has responsible family members or friends willing and able to care for him. Since
the jury found, upon ample evidence, that O'Connor,
as an agent of the State, knowingly did so confine
Donaldson, it properly concluded that O'Connor violated
Donaldson's constitutional right to freedom.

II

O'Connor contends that in any event he should not
be held personally liable for monetary damages because
his decisions were made in "good faith." Specifically,
O'Connor argues that he was acting pursuant to state
law which, he believed, authorized confinement of the
mentally ill even when their release would not compro-

O'CONNOR *v.* DONALDSON

mise their safety or constitute a danger to others, and that he could not reasonably have been expected to know that the state law as he understood it was constitutionally invalid. A proposed instruction to this effect was rejected by the District Court.[14]

The District Court did instruct the jury, without objection, that monetary damages could not be assessed against O'Connor if he had believed reasonably and in good faith that Donaldson's continued confinement was "proper," and that punitive damages could be awarded only if O'Connor had acted "maliciously or wantonly or oppressively." The Court of Appeals approved those instructions.

But both the District Court and the Court of Appeals acted without the benefit of this Court's most recent decision on the scope of the qualified immunity available to state officials under 42 U. S. C. § 1983, *Wood* v. *Strickland,* —— U. S. ——. Under that decision, the relevant question is whether O'Connor "knew or reasonably should have known that the action he took within his sphere of official responsibility would violate the constitutional rights of [Donaldson], or if he took the action with the malicious intention to cause a deprivation of constitutional rights or other injury to [Donaldson]." *Id.,* ——. For the purposes of this question, an official has a duty to know of constitutional rights that are "clearly established," but no duty to forecast unforeseeable constitutional developments. *Id.,* ——. I would vacate the judgment of the Court of Appeals and remand the case to enable that court to consider, in light of *Wood* v. *Strickland,* whether the District Court's failure to instruct on the effect of O'Connor's claimed reliance on state law rendered inadequate the instructions given on the issue of his immunity from liability for monetary damages.

---

[14] See n. 7, *supra.*

The Chief Justice's *Donaldson* draft opinion of the Court went far beyond the conference consensus on the case. It is true that the draft concluded by affirming the verdict in Donaldson's favor. But it did so on a theory none of the others had approved—that the erroneous instructions of the district court had not been specifically objected to and that "an appellate court should [not] rescue a litigant from his tactical errors at trial." The affirmance could not mask the fact that the Burger draft focused almost entirely on the right-to-treatment issue and that the Chief Justice's effort to render that right stillborn had not been approved by the conference majority.

On June 2, Justice Stewart gave voice to the majority view in the matter by circulating the draft dissent reprinted on p. 308. The approach taken in this Stewart draft was explained by the Justice in a June 6 *MEMORANDUM TO THE CONFERENCE*. Explaining his reluctance to deal with the broad issue on which the Burger draft had focused, Stewart noted, "The constitutional problems raised by civil commitment of the mentally ill are many and difficult. I remain persuaded that the Court should proceed cautiously and deliberately in this area. The present case can be decided on a narrow, though hardly trivial, ground—i.e. that a person cannot be incarcerated, without more, merely because he is mentally ill."

Stewart wrote, "I am opposed to plunging into these extraneous issues" such as the right to treatment. The court of appeals may have held that Donaldson's "detention is constitutionally permissible, but only if treatment is provided along with confinement. The constitutional arguments on all sides are novel and complicated. They were not joined in this case; nor was there any need to join them, for Donaldson was found to be non-dangerous." Then, emphasizing his disagreement with the Burger approach, Stewart concluded, "I would therefore dispose of the present case on its facts. The Court of Appeals used the case as a vehicle for an expansive essay on the constitutional law of civil commitment. This was unnecessary, and perhaps we should say so. But surely we should not make the same mistake."

In line with the memo's approach, the Stewart draft dissent (supra p. 308) ignores the right-to-treatment issue. Its first section (after the statement of facts) begins by stressing that "the issue in this case [is] a narrow one." The treatment issue, to which the Burger draft had been devoted, was relegated to a footnote. There was no occasion here, the note said, to decide that issue. "In its present posture this case involves not involuntary treatment but involuntary custodial confinement."

The key question in the case, according to the Stewart draft was, "Given the jury's findings, what was left as justification for keeping Donaldson in continued confinement?" That an individual was "mentally ill" was not a sufficient justification. "In my opinion, a finding of 'mental illness' cannot in itself justify the extinguishment of personal liberty." On the contrary, even as far as the "mentally ill" are concerned, "I can perceive no constitutional basis for confining such persons against their will if they are dangerous to no one and can live safely in freedom."

This approach leads to a simple resolution of this case. Stewart concludes:

> a State cannot constitutionally confine without more a nondangerous individual who is capable of caring for himself or who has responsible family members or friends willing and able to care for him. Since the jury found, upon ample evidence, that O'Connor, as an agent of the State, knowingly did so confine Donaldson, it properly concluded that O'Connor violated Donaldson's constitutional right to freedom.

The Stewart draft took particular aim at the Burger indication that people could be confined for "significant antisocial acts." "May the State," Stewart asks, "fence in the harmless mentally ill solely to save its citizens from exposure to those whose ways are different?" The answer is self-evident. "One might as well ask if the State, to avoid public unease, could incarcerate all who are physically handicapped or socially eccentric. Mere public intolerance or animosity cannot constitutionally justify the deprivation of a person's physical liberty."

The Stewart draft did not, however, affirm the judgment for Donaldson. Like the final opinion, it remanded because the lower courts had acted without the benefit of the high Court's most recent decision on the scope of the immunity available to state officials.[10] The court of appeals was to consider whether, in light of that decision, the district court's instructions on immunity were adequate.

After the Stewart draft was circulated, the Chief Justice attempted to persuade the others that his approach was the correct one and that the right to treatment issue should not be avoided, as had been done in the Stewart draft. In a June 4 *MEMORANDUM TO THE CONFERENCE,* Burger wrote:

> Potter's proposed dissent furnishes a possible avenue for disposing of this case but it does not deal with a crucial aspect should the Court of Appeals remand for a new trial. In that situation we should deal with the instruction that Donaldson had a "constitutional right" to treatment. I believe a majority were of the view that no such right existed. It would hardly be wise if a new trial were held and this instruction given anew if five here think it wrong.

The Burger memo proposed a new footnote to his draft showing that the lower court decisions turned squarely on the right to treatment. In conclusion, the memo stated, "I surely favor almost any disposition that clarifies the constitutional right as a right not to be confined as opposed to a 'right to treatment.'"

Thus far, no one had agreed to join the Burger draft opinion of the Court and, soon after receiving the Chief Justice's memo, Justice Powell sent him a brief June 4 note about "this troublesome case." Powell wrote, "as of now, I lean toward Potter's basic approach."

The lack of response, other than the negative Powell letter, led the Chief Justice to circulate a stronger *MEMORANDUM TO THE CONFERENCE* on the next day, June 5. This memo read:

> In my view, even to give tacit approval to the instruction that there is a "constitutional right" to "realistically" effective treatment will (a) leave the instruction binding on all district judges in the largest circuit and (b) lead other courts to consider such an instruction as required. That will bring us quite a volume of business as "jackleg" lawyers begin to look for new fields to conquer.

The memo concluded by reiterating the main Burger theme on the matter: "The constitutional issue is fairly presented and ought to be met."

Justice Stewart replied to this Burger memo with his own June 6 *MEMORANDUM TO THE CONFERENCE*, which has already been quoted. The Chief Justice came back with a three-page June 9 *MEMORANDUM TO THE CONFERENCE*. Most of this memo was devoted to an effort to show that the court of appeals had definitely decided on the right to treatment issue and not, "as Potter suggests [only] adopted a strained reading of the District Court's instructions in order to write an essay regarding the supposed constitutional right-to-treatment."

Burger wrote that he was convinced that his approach was correct. "Thus, while I am open to some other disposition which would not only vacate that court's judgment but leave no doubt that the *opinion* is 'washed out,' I continue to believe that we risk disservice to courts faced with claims such as respondent's if we do not decide the right-to-treatment question."

The right-to-treatment issue, Burger asserted, had to be confronted. "In short, the question whether there is a constitutional right-to-treatment is fairly presented by this case and that we relieve ourselves of no difficult problems, and indeed will create serious problems, by brushing it under the rug, unless, as suggested above, we make clear that the opinion approving such instruction is no longer a valid holding of the Court of Appeals."

The memo concluded with a statement that the Chief Justice was not necessarily insisting on his as the only possible approach. "I am perfectly willing to consider alternatives so long as they make clear that the Court of Appeals' opinion is not to be considered precedent or the law of this case."

By now, however, it was too late for the Chief Justice to control the disposition of the case. No one had joined his draft; instead a Court was forming behind Justice Stewart's draft dissent. This was made clear when Justice White circulated a two-page June 10 *MEMORANDUM TO THE CONFERENCE*. White started with a diplomatic bow to the Chief Justice, stating, "There is . . . much to be said for deciding the right to treatment issue." In this case, however, we "may rationally avoid it." This can be done by following the Stewart approach. "Potter says that whether or not respondent had a right to be treated, no treatment was given and respondent therefore should have been released since the State may not confine a person against his will solely because he is mentally ill. . . . I agree with him."

Yet, even here, the White memo sought to assuage the Chief Justice by suggesting that the Chief Justice might be correct in his fears that Stewart had really also dealt with the right-to-treatment issue, "[I]t should be understood that his opinion decides that nondangerous, mentally ill persons who are not being treated must be released and that in this sense Potter deals with the right to treatment issue—at least he is not disagreeing with the Court of Appeals' pronouncement insofar as persons in respondent's situation are concerned."

The White memo then further broadened the debate by asking "whether a State may confine a nondangerous, mentally ill person solely for treatment purposes." White wrote that he would prefer to decide that issue, noting, "My vote at the conference was that the State may not do so."

Still, the key part of the White memo was his statement that he agreed with Justice Stewart. Justice White had been the strongest conference opponent of Donaldson's damage award. If Chief Justice Burger could not hold him, he knew that he had little chance of securing a majority for his draft opinion.

At this point, the Chief Justice decided to yield to Stewart. On June 11, he sent around the following *MEMORANDUM TO THE CONFERENCE:*

> Potter seems to have four and a fraction votes (with Bill Douglas not voting), and I am happy to have him try his hand at an opinion. As I stated, I can go along with a remand, but the opinion must explain how a new trial can be confined to the immunity issue. Also can we avoid passing on the correctness of the right-to-treatment issue in view of the CA5 opinion with its categorical approval of the District Court instruction?
>
> Bon voyage!

Burger's continued insistence on the need to decide the right-to-treatment issue did not change the fact of his abandonment of his effort to obtain a Court for his repudiation of the right to treatment. Now the Stewart draft would speak for the entire Court (though the Chief Justice also issued an abbreviated version of his draft as a concurring opinion, first circulated June 19).

Stewart's new status as spokesman for the Court was underlined by a June 11 "Dear Potter" letter from Justice Douglas (the senior Justice in the majority now supporting the Stewart draft): "Please join me. Since Bill Brennan, Byron, Thurgood, and Lewis have already joined you, isn't your dissent the basis for the Court opinion? If so, to avoid any delay at this late hour, and if, as I assume, it is my task formally to assign the opinion for the Court, I assign, of course, to you."

Interestingly, this letter was signed only with Douglas's typed initials. The Justice was still at the Rusk Institute and presumably had dictated the letter to his chambers.

In pursuance of the dual reassignment to him, Justice Stewart circulated a typed draft opinion of the Court on June 13, essentially similar to his final *Donaldson* opinion. The Stewart opinion went through five drafts (the last circulated June 23) before being announced as the opinion of the Court on June 26.

The Justices' refusal to join the Chief Justice's draft *Donaldson* opinion has made a substantial difference so far as the rights of those confined for mental illness are concerned. Even apart from the broader implications in the Burger extension of commitment power to protection against "significant antisocial acts," his draft would have left the right to treatment developed by the lower federal courts stillborn as a constitutional right.

Justice Stewart's final *Donaldson* opinion of the Court (as seen) did not deal with the right to treatment. This left it open to the lower federal courts to continue their development and enforcement of that right. Thus, the lower court in *Donaldson* recently affirmed that a person involuntarily confined in a mental hospital "has a constitutional right to such individual treatment as will help him to be cured or to improve his mental condition." Furthermore, there is the right to have the treatment accomplished "in the least restrictive setting" and both rights "could be implemented through judicially manageable standards."[11]

This means that there is a judicially enforceable right to treatment whenever an individual is involuntarily committed. The courts will require that treatment be provided to those committed, " '[W]here treatment is the sole asserted ground for depriving a person of liberty, . . .' . . . it is the court's duty to insist on appropriate treatment or that the plaintiff be released."[12]

Thus, the lower *Donaldson* court approach to the right to treatment issue is now established federal constitutional doctrine.[13] The Supreme Court's *Donaldson* opinion has not affected this at all and the post-*Donaldson* cases have been able to refine and enforce the right. This would, of course, have been impossible had the Burger draft come down as the opinion of the Court. *Donaldson* is a prime example of a case where the "might have been" would have made all the difference to the law on the subject.

Notes

1. This statement of facts is taken from Brian M. Schwartz, "In the Name of Treatment: Autonomy, Civil Commitment, and Right to Refuse Treatment," 50 *Notre Dame Lawyer* 808 (1975).
2. *Donaldson v. O'Connor*, 493 F.2d 507, 521 (5th Cir. 1974).

3. Id. at 526.
4. *Rouse* v. *Cameron*, 373 F.2d 451 (D.C. Cir. 1966).
5. *Donaldson* v. *O'Connor*, 493 F.2d 507, 523 (5th Cir. 1974).
6. See *Dobson* v. *Cameron*, 383 F.2d 519, 523 (D.C. Cir. 1967); *Lake* v. *Cameron*, 364 F.2d 657, 663 (D.C. Cir. 1966).
7. My reconstruction of the conference and vote, which is based on the conference notes and tally sheet of a Justice who was present, differs substantially from the version in Woodward and Armstrong, *The Brethren: Inside the Supreme Court* 372–73 (1979).
8. The word *round* is not clear in the conference notes used by me.
9. For a similar situation, see Schwartz, *Swann's Way: The School Busing Case and the Supreme Court* 111–13 (1986).
10. *Wood* v. *Strickland*, 420 U.S. 308 (1975).
11. *Doe* v. *Public Health Trust*, 696 F.2d 901, 902 (11th Cir. 1983).
12. *Romeo* v. *Youngberg*, 644 F.2d 147, 165 (3d Cir. 1980).
13. Id. at 176.

7

Michelin Tire Corp. v. *Wages* (1976): "Time Low Was Laid Low"

From John Marshall's day until the 1976 decision in *Michelin Tire Corp.* v. *Wages*,[1] interpretation of the Constitution's Import Clause had been governed by the original-package doctrine laid down in *Brown* v. *Maryland*.[2] The opinion there has been called the seminal opinion on forbidden state taxes on imports.[3] In *Brown*, a state law required all importers to obtain a license, for which they had to pay fifty dollars, before they could sell their goods. The state argued that its tax was an occupational tax, not a forbidden tax on imports, but the Court rejected that contention. The tax on the importer was treated like a tax on the imports themselves. It thus contravened the Constitution, which the Court interpreted as absolutely prohibiting states from levying a tax on imports.

Brown precludes the states from subjecting imports to even a general nondiscriminatory tax. This raises the further question of how long imported goods retain their immunity from state taxation. This question, too, was discussed by Marshall. As he put it, "[T]here must be a point of time when the prohibition ceases, and the power of the state to tax commences."[4] This point of time occurs when the goods no longer retain their status as imports. In words grown familiar with judicial repetition, the *Brown* opinion stated the guide for determining when imported goods cease to be imports:

> It is sufficient for the present to say, generally, that when the importer has so acted upon the thing imported, that it has become incorporated and mixed up with the mass of property in the country, it has, perhaps, lost its distinctive character as an import, and has become subject to the taxing power of the State; but while remaining the property of the importer, in his warehouse, in the original form or package in which it was imported, a tax upon it is too plainly a duty on imports to escape the prohibition in the constitution.[5]

Under this original-package doctrine, imports remain immune as long as they keep their status as imports. When they have become part of the general "mass of property" within the state, then state taxes are no longer barred. But while in the hands of the importer in its "original package," the import remains free from state levies.

The most controversial application of *Brown* occurred in the 1871 case of *Low* v. *Austin*.[6] The Court there held that the states were prohibited by the Import Clause from imposing a nondiscriminatory *ad valorem* property tax on imports until they lost their character as imports and became incorporated into the mass of property in the state. *Low* rejected the argument that the Import Clause prohibited only taxes on the goods as imports and not nondiscriminatory taxes on goods as property.

Not only did *Michelin* overrule *Low*, it all but did away with the doctrine laid down by Marshall in *Brown* v. *Maryland*. The *Michelin* decision did not, however, start out as such a far-reaching one. Under the original draft opinion of the Court, *Michelin* did not reconsider *Low* v. *Austin* or raise any doubts about the original-package doctrine.

In *Michelin*, a Georgia county assessed *ad valorem* property taxes against tires imported by Michelin that were included, on assessment dates, in an inventory maintained at its wholesale distribution warehouse in the county. The Georgia court held that the tires stacked in the warehouse had lost their status as imports and had thus become subject to ad valorem taxation. The Supreme Court ruled that the tires were subject to the tax regardless of whether the Georgia court was correct in holding that they had lost their status as imports because the "assessment of a nondiscriminatory ad valorem property tax against the imported tires [was] not within the constitutional prohibition against laying 'any Imposts or Duties on Imports.' Insofar as *Low* v. *Austin* [was] to the contrary, that decision [was] overruled."[7]

At the conference following the *Michelin* argument, however, the Justices did not decide to overrule *Low* v. *Austin*. Instead the conference vote—as explained by Justice Brennan in his November 21, 1975, *MEMORANDUM TO THE CONFERENCE*—was "to affirm the holding of the Georgia Supreme Court that the tires had lost their status as imports by reason of the sorting, segregating by size and style and co-mingling of the tires with other shipments." This enabled the Georgia decision to be affirmed without any need to reconsider *Low* or the original-package doctrine.

The original draft opinion of the Court (infra p. 326), which Justice Brennan circulated on November 21, was intended—in the words of the Brennan memo—"to reflect what I understand was the conference vote." As such, it affirmed the Georgia court because "the situation revealed by the facts of this case establishes that the tires had lost their status as imports on the assessment dates." That was true because "the tires were sorted, segregated by size and style, and commingled with other shipments . . . 'for use or trade and . . . exposed or offered for sale.' "

Under this holding, "we have no occasion in this case to reconsider *Low* v. *Austin* and its progeny." Instead, the Brennan draft applied the original-package doctrine and did not question *Low*'s continuing validity.

2nd DRAFT

SUPREME COURT OF THE UNITED STATES

No. 74–1396

Michelin Tire Corporation, | On Writ of Certiorari to the
Petitioner, | Supreme Court of Georgia.
v. |
W. L. Wages, Tax Com- |
missioner, et al. |

[December —, 1975]

MR. JUSTICE BRENNAN delivered the opinion of the Court.

Respondents, the Tax Commissioner and Tax Assessors of Gwinnett County, Ga., assessed ad valorem taxes against tires and tubes imported by petitioner from France and Nova Scotia and added to the inventory at one of its wholesale distribution warehouses which was located in the County. The business conducted at the warehouse was that of filling orders for tires and tubes from petitioner's 250–300 franchised dealers selling the tires and tubes at retail in six southeastern States. Petitioner brought this action for declaratory and injunctive relief in the Superior Court of Gwinnett County, alleging that with the exception of certain passenger tubes that had been removed from the original shipping cartons,[1] the ad valorem taxes assessed against its merchandise inventory of imported tires and tubes were

---

[1] Petitioner's complaint conceded the taxability of certain passenger tubes that had been removed from the original shipping cartons. These had a value of $633.92 on the assessment date January 1, 1972, and of $664.22 on the assessment date January 1, 1973. The tax for 1972 on the tubes was $8.03 and for 1973 was $8.72.

MICHELIN TIRE CORP *v.* WAGES

prohibited by the Import Clause, Art. I, § 10, cl. 2,
of the Constitution, which provides in pertinent part,
"No State shall, without the consent of Congress, lay
any Imposts or Duties on Imports or Exports, except
what may be absolutely necessary for executing its Inspection Laws . . ." After trial, the Superior Court
sustained petitioner's contention as to both tires and
tubes and granted the requested declaratory and injunctive relief. On Appeal, the Supreme Court of Georgia
affirmed in part and reversed in part, agreeing with the
holding of the Superior Court that the tubes in the corrugated shipping cartons were immune from ad valorem
taxation under the "original package" doctrine, but disagreeing with the holding of the Superior Court that the
bulk imports of the tires that had been mingled with
other bulk imports, sorted and arranged for sale, were
not subject to such taxation. *Wages* v. *Michelin Tire
Corp.*, 233 Ga. 712, 214 S. E. 349 (1975). We granted
petitioner's petition for certiorari, 422 U. S. 1040 (1975).
The only question presented is whether the Georgia Supreme Court was correct in holding that the tires were
subject to the ad valorem tax. On that question we
affirm. The respondents did not cross-petition from the
affirmance of the holding of the Superior Court that the
tubes in the corrugated shipping cartons were immune
from the tax, and that holding is therefore not before
us for review.

I

Petitioner, a New York corporation qualified to do
business in Georgia, operates as an importer and wholesale distributor in the United States of automobile and
truck tires and tubes manufactured in France and Nova
Scotia by Michelin Tires, Ltd. The business is operated
from its distribution warehouses in various parts of the
country. Distribution and sale of tires and tubes from

MICHELIN TIRE CORP *v.* WAGES

the Gwinnett County warehouse is confined to the 250–300 franchised dealers with whom petitioner does all of its business in six southeastern States. Some 25% of the tires and tubes are manufactured in and imported from Nova Scotia, and are brought to the United States in tractor-driven over-the-road trailers packed and sealed at the Nova Scotia factory. The remaining 75% of the imported tires and tubes are brought to the United States by sea from France and Nova Scotia in sea vans. Sea vans are over-the-road trailers from which the wheels are removed before being loaded aboard ship. The sea vans, like the over-the-road trailers, are owned by the shipper and not by petitioner. The sea vans are also packed and sealed at the foreign factories, and are hauled by tractor to ship-side where the wheels are removed before loading aboard ship. Upon arrival of the ship at the United States port of entry, the vans are unloaded, the wheels are replaced, and the vans are tractor-hauled to petitioner's distribution warehouse after clearing customs upon payment of a 4% import duty. The Gwinnett County distribution warehouse is located inland and not at seaboard

The imported tires and tubes are packaged for shipment differently. The tires, each of which has its own serial number, are packed in bulk into the trailers and vans, without otherwise being packaged or bundled. They lose their identity as a unit, however, when unloaded from the trailers and vans at the distribution warehouse. When unloaded they are sorted by size and style, without segregation of French from Nova Scotia manufacture, stacked on wooden pallets each bearing four stacks of five tires of the same size and style, and stored in pallet stacks of three pallets each. This is the only processing required or performed to ready the tires for sale and delivery to the franchised dealers.

MICHELIN TIRE CORP *v.* WAGES

The imported tubes, however, are packaged individually in small boxes a number of which are put in large corrugated shipping cartons at the manufacturing plant and shipped by trailer or sea van to the United States. Upon arrival at the distribution warehouse, the large corrugated shipping cartons are sorted by size and style, much like the tires, without regard to place of manufacture. After sorting, the corrugated cartons are stored in a "full case" area of the distribution warehouse. When a sale requires opening of a carton, the carton is removed from the "full case" area to a "shelf area" where, after opening of the carton, the individual packages are removed and placed on shelves pending sales in less-than-carton quantities.

Sales of tires and tubes from the Gwinnett County distribution warehouse average 4,000–5,000 pounds per sale. Orders are filled without regard to the shipments in which the tires and tubes arrived in the United States or the place of their manufacture. Delivery of orders to the franchised dealers is by common carrier or customer pickup.

II

The Superior Court of Georgia held, citing *Low* v. *Austin*, 13 Wall. 29 (1872), and *Hooven & Allison Co.* v. *Evatt*, 324 U. S. 652 (1945), that the Import Clause immunized imported goods from local nondiscriminatory ad valorem taxes until the goods lose their character as imports and have become intermingled with the common mass of property in the State, and that they retain their character as imports as long as they remain the property of the importer in the original form or package in which imported. The Superior Court concluded that "The automobile and truck tires here involved while perhaps not in an original package are without doubt in the original form in which they were imported into this

MICHELIN TIRE CORP *v* WAGES

Country , , . Insofar as the tubes in [petitioner's]
inventory are concerned, those which remain intact in
their original shipping cartons are likewise exempt from
ad valorem tax and those which may be removed from
the original shipping cartons and placed in [petitioner's]
general inventory would be subject to an *ad valorem*
tax. , , Petition for Writ of Cert., at A4–A5.

The Supreme Court of Florida agreed that *Low* v.
Austin and *Hooven & Allison Co v Evatt* required
the holding that a nondiscriminatory ad valorem tax is
a "tax on imports within the meaning of the federal
constitutional provision." 233 Ga. ——, 214 S. E. 2d,
at 355 The State Supreme Court also rejected respondent tax officials' argument that the "original package"
is the sea van so that the imports lose their character
as such when removed from the van, stating, *ibid :*

> "Sea vans are a normal means of transportation
> available through common carriers. To make the
> act of unloading the imports from the carrier a
> breaking of the original package' is to make it
> impossible for importers who use that means of
> transportation to maintain the character of the
> goods as imports after the goods are in this country."

The Georgia Supreme Court held, however, that the
Superior Court erred in holding that the tires had not
lost their status as imports, stating. 233 Ga ——, 214
S. E. 2d. at 355

> 'As we read *Brown* v *Maryland, supra,* it estab-
> lishes a 'two-hat' approach to importers for resale
> Such importers are free to deal with their goods as
> imports after the goods are in this country, and.
> if they do so. the goods remain immune from state
> taxation When, however, the importer deals with
> his goods as a seller, he becomes Chief Justice Mar-
> shall's 'itinerant peddler', and the goods become

MICHELIN TIRE CORP *v* WAGES

subject to state taxation. The original package
doctrine is not a mechanical, universally applicable
test, it is, instead, a useful means in many cases of
determining which hat the importer-seller is wear-
ing, because frequently the act of breaking the
original package is preliminary to converting the
imports to salable units.

In the case at bar the entire Michelin tire inventory was unpackaged, and all shipments in the
inventory were commingled and stored by size and
type to make the individual units immediately
available for resale. We therefore hold that the
tires, imported in bulk without packaging, which
have been sorted, segregated by size and style, and
commingled with other shipments have lost their
status as 'imports' and are subject to taxation. ... .
Bulk imports that have been mingled with other
bulk imports, sorted, and arranged for sale do not
retain their status as imports . . . ."

III

The seminal opinion construing the Import Clause is
Brown v *Maryland*, 12 Wheat. 419 (1827), written a
century and a half ago by Chief Justice Marshall.
Brown held that the prohibition of the Import Clause
invalidated a Maryland statute that required all importers of foreign goods by the bale or package, and other
persons selling the same wholesale, by bale or package,
to take out a license, for which the fee was $50, and that
specified that neglect or refusal to take out such license
would subject them to certain forfeitures and penalties.
That holding was clearly mandated by the wording of the
Clause, but Marshall's sensitivity to the impact of the
Clause as a restriction on the taxing power of the States
prompted him to articulate limitations upon its reach,

MICHELIN TIRE CORP *v.* WAGES

". . the words of the prohibition ought not to be pressed
to their utmost extent;   . in our complex system, the
object of the powers conferred on the government of the
Union, and the nature of the often conflicting powers
which remain in the States, must always be taken into
view . . . ." *Id.,* at 441. ". . there must be a point of
time when the prohibition ceases, and the power of the
State to tax commences . . . ." *Ibid.* But insofar as the
prohibition applied, it forbade "imposts, or duties on
imports" after as well as before they were landed in this
country, this because the prohibition is against such levies
"on the thing imported." *Id.,* at 437–438.

The Chief Justice believed that this construction would
be consistent with the objects of the prohibition. The
primary design of the prohibition, he said, was to prevent
"[t]he great importing States [from laying] a tax on the
nonimporting States" to which the imported property is
or might ultimately be destined, which would not only
discriminate against them but also "would necessarily
produce countervailing measures on the part of those
States whose situation was less favorable to importation."
Id., at 440. Other objects were "to maintain unimpaired
our commercial connexions with foreign nations [and]
to confer this source of revenue on the government of
the Union." *Id*, at 439

The Chief Justice raised questions, however, not fully
answered, as to what state levies fall within the prohibited "imposts, or duties on imports," and as to when
the imported goods lose their status as imports so as to
be subject to any otherwise applicable taxes. In answering the first question, Chief Justice Marshall was of the
view that the obvious referrent was the express exception of the Clause authorizing "imposts or duties"
that "may be absolutely necessary for executing [the
State's] Inspection Laws"; he said, ". . this exception

MICHELIN TIRE CORP *v.* WAGES

in favour of duties for the support of inspection laws,
goes far in proving that the framers of the constitution
classed taxes of a similar character with those imposed
for the purposes of inspection, with duties on imports
and exports, and supposed them to be prohibited." *Id.,*
at 438. Thus, "imposts and duties' are restricted to
state exactions that "intercept the import, as an import,
in its way to become incorporated with the general mass
of property, and denies it the privilege of becoming so
incorporated . It denies to the importer the right of
using the privilege which he has purchased from the
United States, until he shall have also purchased it from
the State." *Id.,* at 443.

In answering the second question—when did the goods
lose their status as imports—the Chief Justice devised
an evidentiary tool to make that determination—the
'original package" test—for, he said, "the constitutional
prohibition . . may certainly come in conflict with [the
States'] acknowledged power to tax persons and property within their territory . . . . [T]he distinction exists,
and must be marked as the cases arise." *Id.,* at 441.
"It is a matter of hornbook knowledge that the original
package statement of Justice Marshall was an illustration, rather than a formula, and that its application
is evidentiary, and not substantive . . . ." *Galveston* v.
Mexican Petroleum Corp., 15 F. 2d 208 (SD Tex. 1926).
The evidentiary inquiry to be made "as the cases arise,"
Marshall suggested, was in general terms: "It is sufficient
for the present to say, generally, that when the importer
has so acted upon the thing imported, that it has become
incorporated and mixed up with the mass of property in the country, it has, perhaps, lost its distinctive character as an import, and has become
subject to the taxing power of the State; but while
remaining the property of the importer, in his ware-

MICHELIN TIRE CORP *v.* WAGES

house, in the original form or package in which it was
imported, a tax upon it is too plainly a duty on imports to escape the prohibition of the constitution." *Id.,*
at 441–442. Later in the opinion, the Chief Justice illustrated the situations in which the evidence might prove
that the status as imports of the goods has ceased: where
the evidence is that the importer "sells them, or otherwise mixes them with the general property of the State,
by breaking up his packages, and travelling with them
as an itinerant pedlar." In such cases, "the [state]
tax finds the article already incorporated with the mass
of property by the act of the importer. He has used
the privilege he had purchased, and has himself mixed
them up with the common mass, and the law may treat
them as it finds them." *Id.,* at 443.

IV

Some decisions of this Court since *Brown* v. *Maryland*
have seemed to convert the "original package" concept
from an evidentiary tool into a mechanical, universally
applicable substantive doctrine, and also to condemn
any state tax affecting an "original package" without
inquiry whether the state exaction constitutes an "impost or duty" within the meaning of the Import Clause.
Low v. *Austin,* 13 Wall. 29 (1871); *Cook* v. *Pennsylvania,* 7 Otto 566 (1878); *Anglo-Chilean Nitrate Sales
Corp* v. *Alabama,* 288 U. S. 218 (1933); *Department of
Revenue* v. *James B. Beam Distilling Co.,* 377 U. S. 341
(1964).[2] State taxing authorities have prevailed, how-

---

[2] For comments see Powell, State Taxation of Imports—When
Does an Import Cease to Be an Import?, 58 Harv. L. Rev. 858
(1945). The Supreme Court, 1958 Term, 73 Harv L. Rev. 126,
176 (1959) See also, *e g.,* Early & Weitzman, A Century of
Dissent. The Immunity of Goods Imported for Resale From Nondiscriminatory State Personal Property Taxes, 7 S. W. U. L Rev.
247 (1975), Dakin, The Protective Cloak of the Export-Import

MICHELIN TIRE CORP *v.* WAGES

ever, in several cases where the decision turned on whether given imported goods had lost their state tax immunity because, through intermingling with the mass of property, the goods had lost their distinctive character as imports. *Waring* v. *The Mayor*, 8 Wall. 110 (1868); *Gulf Fisheries Co.* v. *MacInerney*, 276 U. S. 124 (1928); *May* v. *New Orleans*, 178 U. S. 496 (1900); *Burke* v. *Wells*, 208 U. S. 14 (1908). Moreover, the expansion of the "original package" concept to goods imported for use rather than sale, *Hooven & Allison Co.* v. *Evatt*, 324 U. S. 652 (1954), was sharply abridged, if not overruled, in *Youngstown Sheet & Tube Co.* v. *Bowers*, 358 U. S. 534 (1959).

In this case, the Georgia Superior Court (in this respect affirmed by the Georgia Supreme Court) cited *Low* v. *Austin, supra,* and *Hooven & Allison Co.* v. *Evatt* as reading *Brown* v. *Maryland* to hold that "Imposts or Duties on Imports" in the Import Clause include "local *ad valorem* property taxes." Petition for Writ of Cert., at A–3. It is true that the Court in *Low* v. *Austin*, in reversing the holding of the Supreme Court of California that sustained a nondiscriminatory ad valorem property tax against imported goods—on the ground that the tax prohibited must be a tax upon the character of the goods

---

Clause. Immunity for the Goods or Immunity for the Process?, 19 La. L. Rev. 747 (1958)

State court decisions attempting to apply the "original package" concept include *Florida Greenheart Corp.* v. *Gautier*, 172 So. 2d 589 (Fla. 1965); *Citroen Cars Corp.* v. *City of New York*, 30 N. Y. 2d 300, 283 N. E. 2d 758 (1972); *Wilson* v. *County of Wake*, 19 N. C. App. 536, 199 S. E. 2d 665 (1973); *Volkswagen Pacific, Inc.* v. *City of Los Angeles*, 7 Cal. 2d 48, 101 Cal. Rpts. 869, 496 P. 2d 1237 (1972); *E. J. Stanton & Sons* v. *Los Angeles County*, 78 Cal. App. 2d 181, 177 P. 2d 804 (1945); *American Manner Corp.* v. *Cronvich*, 251 La. 1014, 207 So. 2d 778 (1968), and *Columbus Steel Supply Co.* v. *Kosydar*, 38 Ohio St. 2d 258, 313 N. E. 2d 389 (1974).

MICHELIN TIRE CORP *v.* WAGES

as importations, rather than upon the goods themselves as property—said, 13 Wall., at 34

"The Supreme Court of California appears, from its opinion, to have considered the present case as excepted from the rule laid down in *Brown v. The State of Maryland*, because the tax levied is not directly upon imports as such, and consequently the goods imported are not subjected to any burden as a class, but only are included as port of the whole property of its citizens which is subjected equally to an *ad valorem* tax. But the obvious answer to this position is found in the fact, which is, in substance, expressed in the citations made from the opinions of Marshall and Taney, that the goods imported do not lose their character as imports, and become incorporated into the mass of property of the State, until they have passed from the control of the importer or been broken up by him from their original cases. Whilst retaining their character as imports, a tax upon them, in any shape, is within the constitutional prohibition. The question is not as to the extent of the tax, or its equality with respect to taxes on other property, but as to the power of the State to levy any tax. If, at any point of time between the arrival of the goods in port and their breakage from the original cases, or sale by the importer, they become subject to State taxation, the extent and the character of the tax are mere matters of legislative discretion."

There is a substantial question whether a nondiscriminatory ad valorem property tax is the type of exaction which the Constitution or Chief Justice Marshall had in mind as being an "impost" or "duty." See Powell, State Taxation of Imports—When Does an Import Cease to Be an Import?, 58 Harv. L. Rev. 858 (1945); T Cooley,

MICHELIN TIRE CORP *v* WAGES

The General Principles of Constitutional Law in the United States, c. V, § 3, c. VII, § 14 (Bruce ed. 1931); 1 W. Crosskey, Politics and the Constitution in the History of the United States 295–296 (1953); 2 J. Story, Commentaries on the Constitution § 946–950, 1013–1014 (1933). See also, *e. g.*, Hamilton, The Federalist Nos. 12, 30, 32. Is a nondiscriminatory ad valorem tax a tax (as Marshall suggested was the limit of the reach of "imposts or duties") "of a similar character with those required for the purposes of inspection," that is, one "that intercepts the import, as an import, in its way to become incorporated with the general mass of property?" See *License Cases*, 5 How. 504, 576 (1847) (Taney, C. J.)

But we have no occasion in this case to reconsider *Low v. Austin* and its progeny. And we may assume, without deciding, that the Georgia Supreme Court was correct in its holding that the tires did not lose their status as imports the instant of unloading from the trailers and sea vans, and by reason of that fact alone. It suffices to support our affirmance of the Georgia Supreme Court's judgment to state our reasons for our agreement with its holding that "the tires, imported in bulk without packaging, which have been sorted, segregated by size and style, and commingled with other shipments have lost their status as 'imports' and are subject to taxation." 233 Ga., at ——, 214 S. E. 2d, at 355.

Inasmuch as "'the reconciliation of the competing demands of the constitutional immunity and of the state's power to tax, is an extremely practical matter' . . . we must approach the question whether these [tires] had been 'put to the use for which they [were] imported' . . . with full awareness of realities and treat with them in a practical way." *Youngstown Sheet & Tube Co v. Bowers*, 358 U. S. 534, 545 (1959). Since,

MICHELIN TIRE CORP *v.* WAGES

as we have seen, the "original package" concept invented by Chief Justice Marshall was not a substantive doctrine but only an evidentiary tool, our task is to determine whether the situation revealed by the facts of this case establishes that the tires had lost their status as imports on the assessment dates.

Petitioner's distribution warehouse was not a mere waystop for the tires on their way to an inland destination. The center was the headquarters of the ongoing domestic business of maintaining an inventory of tires and tubes adequate to fill any order by size and quantity that might be received from any of the 250–300 franchised retail dealers selling Michelin products in the southeast area of the country. The operations of sorting, segregating by size and style, and commingling with other tires were essential to the efficient handling and filling of orders. As the Georgia Supreme Court said, "all shipments in the inventory were commingled and stored by size and type to make the individual [tires] immediately available for resale." 233 Ga. ——, 214 S. E. 2d, at 355. These operations are identical to those performed by any wholesaler preparing his goods for immediate sale to retailers.

Conclusions reached in our decisions addressing the question whether the importer has so acted as to incorporate and mix up the imported goods with the mass of property in the country are not always reconcilable. We think, however, that *May* v. *New Orleans, supra,* and *Gulf Fisheries Co.* v. *MacInerney, supra,* are persuasive authorities that the holding of the Georgia Supreme Court in this case should be affirmed.

May v *New Orleans* sustained an assessment by Orleans Parish on "merchandise and stock in trade." The stock in trade consisted of imported goods brought here in shipping cases. Packed in each case were many

MICHELIN TIRE CORP *v* WAGES

packages separately marked and wrapped, each of which
was separately sold by the importer. For that purpose
the importer opened each shipping case and sold the
goods therein, wrapped in separate parcels, in his store
from shelves or counters upon which the parcels had been
placed for examination and sale. In those circumstances,
the Court concluded, 178 U. S., at 509–510:

> "Without further reference to authorities we state
> our conclusion to be that within the decision in
> *Brown* v *Maryland* the boxes, cases or bales in
> which plaintiffs' goods were shipped were the orig-
> inal packages, and the goods imported by them lost
> their distinctive character as imports and became a
> part of the general mass of the property of Louisi-
> ana, and subject to local taxation as other property
> in that State, the moment the boxes, cases or bales
> in which they were shipped reached their destina-
> tion for use or trade and were opened and the sep-
> arate packages therein exposed or offered for sale;
> consequently, the assessment in question was not in
> violation of the Constitution of the United States."

If the goods in *May* lost their status as imports "the moment the boxes, cases or bales in which they were shipped
reached their destination for use or trade and were
opened and the separate packages therein exposed or
offered for sale," we think it follows that the tires too
lost their status as imports when sorted, segregated by
size and style, and commingled with other shipments "for
use or trade and   . exposed or offered for sale."

Gulf Fisheries Co. v. *MacInerney* sustained application to an importer of fish of a Texas criminal statute
making it an offense to engage in the business of wholesale dealer of fish without a license. The appellant's
fish were caught in the Gulf of Mexico and were landed,
in bulk, by the fishing boats on a wharf where appellant

MICHELIN TIRE CORP. v. WAGES

carried on its business. After unloading, all of the fish were weighed, washed and iced, 75% were beheaded and gutted, 7 to 10% were gutted and gilled with heads on, and the remaining 15 to 18% were weighed, washed, and iced but left for sale without beheading or removing gills and entrails. On these facts the Court held that all of the fish had lost their alleged distinctive character as imports and had become, through processing, handling, and preparation for sale, a part of the mass of property subject to taxation by the State. The Court said, 276 U. S., at 127

> All the fish sold have, after landing and before laying the tax, been so acted upon as to become part of the common property of the state. They have lost their distinctive character as imports and have become taxable by the state.

Plainly the processing, limited to washing and icing, of the 15 to 18% of the fish not beheaded or gutted is the precise counterpart of the processing, by sorting and segregation by size and style, of the tires in this case. Since the Court held that the fish "lost their distinctive character as imports," it follows that the tires did also.

Moreover, in *Youngstown Sheet & Tube Co.* v. *Bowers, supra,* we considered whether certain veneers received "in bundles" and kept in that form in piles for use as needed in that form in day-to-day operations of a manufacturing plant had lost their character as imports. In holding that they had lost that character, the Court said, 358 U. S. 548-549

> Breaking the original package is only one of the ways by which packaged goods that have been imported for use in manufacturing may lose their distinctive character as imports. Another way is by putting them 'to the use for' which they [were] imported. *Id.* That the package has not been

MICHELIN TIRE CORP *v* WAGES

broken is, therefore, only one of the several factors
to be considered in factually determining whether
the goods are being 'used for the purpose for which
they [were] imported. *Hooven & Allison Co.* v.
Evatt, supra, at 665. Here the fact that the bundles
are not opened until the veneers are put into the
day-to-day manufacturing operations of the plant
was fully considered by the Wisconsin courts before
they made the finding that the veneers that were
taxed were 'necessarily required to be kept on hand
to meet [petitioner's] current operational needs,'
and were actually being 'used' to supply those
needs

Of course, the tires here involved were imported for
sale and not for use in manufacture, and *Youngstown*
left open "[w]hatever may be the significance of retaining in the 'original package' goods that have been . . .
imported for sale." *Id.,* at 548. But no substantial
basis for confining *Youngstown* to goods imported for
use in manufacturing occurs to us. In any event we
see no distinction in this case of importation for sale
where the goods lost their character as imports when the
tires were sorted, segregated by size and style, and commingled with other shipments, as said in *May,* "for use
or trade and   exposed or offered for sale "

Affirmed.

The Brennan draft *Michelin* opinion assumed that the prohibited "Imposts or Duties on Imports" in the Import Clause included local *ad valorem* property taxes such as those imposed by Georgia on the Michelin tires. The draft did, however, also raise the question of whether such an assumption was correct. This was pointed out by Justice Brennan in his November 21 covering memorandum. It begins with the quoted passage (supra p. 325) summarizing the draft. "You will note, however," the memo goes on, "that the opinion at pages 10–12 [supra pp. 335–37] discusses the question whether a nondiscriminatory *ad valorem* property tax is a[n] 'impost or duty' prohibited by the Import and Export Clause."

The Brennan memo then briefly reviews the prior law on the question, "Marshall never said it was in *Brown* v. *Maryland*,[8] and Taney in the *License Cases*[9] said it was not. Research by some distinguished scholars has lead [*sic*] them unanimously to conclude that Taney was right and that the *ad valorem* tax is not an 'impost or duty.' But one decision of this Court a century ago, *Low* v. *Austin*, written by Mr. Justice Field, held squarely without any analysis or discussion, that it was an 'impost or duty.' "

The Brennan draft stated expressly that it was not questioning the authority of *Low* v. *Austin*. In his covering memo, however, Justice Brennan took a different approach. "For myself," the memo declared, "I'd be willing to grapple with the question in this case and overrule *Low* v. *Austin*." He was willing to do so even though the issue had not been raised by the parties. Brennan asserted, "I don't see any reason for a reargument asking the parties to address that specific question since there is a very voluminous amicus brief from California that fully canvasses all the authorities."

Brennan was also willing to overrule *Low* v. *Austin* without further argument, even though he recognized the impact of such a decision. "I agree," he wrote, "that overruling *Low* will have far-reaching consequences particularly in this day when such an enormous quantity of goods marketed in this country is imported from Japan and West Germany. In its amicus brief Los Angeles County said it would make a difference of $15,000,000 annually to that county alone."

The Brennan memo was, in this respect, a bid for support for the more far-reaching decision that its author preferred. Without such support, of course, the Justice could not expect to have the Court go beyond his draft. As his memo concluded, "Unless there are four or more of the Brethren who feel as I do, I'll say no more about it."

Soon after they received Brennan's draft and covering memo, the Justices sent replies indicating their views. Only Justice White objected to the proposal to go beyond the draft and discard *Low* v. *Austin*. On December 2, White sent a "Dear Bill" letter: "I join your opinion and would prefer not to overrule *Low* v. *Austin* without briefing and argument and a better feel for the ramification of departing from that precedent."

All the others, however, stated support for the Brennan preference to overrule *Low*. On November 24, Justice Thurgood Marshall wrote to Brennan, "I will give a vote to overrule *Low* v. *Austin* and straighten this mess out." On the same day, Justice Rehnquist sent a letter agreeing "that this might be a logical case in which to overrule *Low* v. *Austin*."

Justice Powell also wrote on November 24, stating, "I think there is a good deal to be said, certainly in theory, for the view that a nondiscriminatory ad valorem property tax is not an 'impost or duty' prohibited by the Import and Export Clause." In view of this, Powell wrote, "I would therefore be interested—sympathetically—in an attempt to clarify the law by adopting that view, even though this required overruling *Low* v. *Austin*. Of course, I would like to see how this 'writes'."

The next day, Justice Stewart wrote to Brennan that he had "voted to [affirm][10] in this case upon the assumption that *Low* v. *Austin* would not be re-examined." Nevertheless, his mind remained open to Brennan's suggestion.

On December 3, Justice Blackmun went even further, writing to Brennan that he could not join his draft opinion as "I am not yet fully persuaded that what was done here served to have these shipments lose their status as imports." On the other hand, "If *Low* were overruled, my difficulties would disappear."

Thus, Blackmun went on, "I would be willing to join an opinion that overrules *Low*." If, on the contrary, the Brennan draft "remains as it is, the alternatives left to me, therefore, are (1) either to concur separately, contending that, despite the Court's disavowal, the facts of this case and the Court's ruling making it clear that *Low* is overruled *sub silentio*, or (2) to dissent on the theory that so long as the Court refuses to overrule *Low*, that case controls this one."

The developing consensus for overruling *Low* v. *Austin* also received the support of Chief Justice Burger. In a December 3 letter the Chief Justice informed Brennan, "[Y]our suggestion intrigues me. If you get any (more) encouragement I would like to see your full dress treatment of *Low*. Maybe it's time *Low* was laid low! Things have changed since John Marshall's time."

"In short," Burger told Brennan, "you have one potential vote to go the whole route." By then, of course, Brennan had a solid majority for his suggestion "to go the whole route." As already seen, except for Justice White, all the others had proved receptive to the suggested Brennan approach.

This led Justice Brennan to circulate a completely revised *Michelin* draft on December 19. This was basically the opinion that was issued as the final *Michelin* opinion of the Court on January 14, 1976. Another draft containing further minor changes was circulated by Brennan on January 5.

The Brennan redraft was quickly agreed to by the others, except for Justice White, who issued a short concurrence stating that there was no need to overrule *Low* v. *Austin*. Justice Blackman wrote in his December 22, 1975, letter joining the revised Brennan opinion, "I think this will clean away some of the cobwebs in this area." The *Michelin* opinion not only did that; it also completely changed the Court's approach to the Import Clause. On its face, Brennan's *Michelin* opinion merely overruled the *Low* v. *Austin* holding that a nondiscriminatory *ad valorem* property tax came within the Import Clause's prohibited "Imposts or Duties." But the *Michelin* opinion is actually far more sweeping. In effect, it repudiates the jurisprudence on the matter that had prevailed since the Marshall Court and all but eliminates one of the oldest constitutional doctrines—the original-package doctrine—from our constitutional law.

Michelin's ultimate importance is that it initiated a new approach to the Import Clause. Before *Michelin*, the primary consideration was whether the tax at issue reached imports or exports. The *Brown* "original package" doctrine was used to determine when the goods remained imports immune from state taxation. *Michelin* ignored the simple question whether the tires were imports. "Instead," a more recent case explains, "it analyzed the tax to determine whether it was an 'Impost or Duty.' "[11] More specifically, the *Michelin* analysis examined whether the challenged tax offended any of the policies underlying the Import Clause: (1) that the states not usurp the federal government's authority to regulate foreign relations; (2) that the states not deprive the federal government of revenues to which it is entitled; and (3) that harmony among the inland states and the seaboard states not be disturbed. Because the Georgia *ad valorem* property tax offended none of these policies, the *Michelin* Court concluded that it was not an "Impost or Duty" within the meaning of the Import Clause.

Under *Michelin*, the "original package" doctrine no longer exempts imported goods, even though still in their original packages, from nondiscriminatory *ad valorem* property taxes imposed by the state in which they are located. The prohibition of the Import Clause does not apply to a state tax that treats imported goods in their original packages no differently from domestically produced property in the state. Only imposts and duties now come within the bar of the Import Clause. Nondiscriminatory property taxation of goods not in import transit is permitted.

The revised *Michelin* approach abandons the mechanical original-package doctrine as the determining criterion for taxes involving imports. Property in an importer's warehouse is no longer exempt from *ad valorem* taxes to which all other property is subject merely because it still remains in the original package in which it was imported. Under the three-policy test enunciated in *Michelin*, it is probable that no nondiscriminatory state tax would offend any of the three *Michelin* policy considerations. If that is true, the Court's approach reduces the Import Clause to a mere ban on state tariffs. All other forms of taxation may no longer be considered "Imposts or Duties" within the meaning of the Clause.

Notes

1. *Michelin Tire Corp.* v. *Wages,* 423 U.S. 276 (1976).
2. 12 Wheat. 419 (U.S. 1827).
3. Supra note 1 at 282.
4. Supra note 2 at 441.
5. Id. at 441–442.
6. 13 Wall. 29 (U.S. 1871).
7. Supra note 1 at 279.
8. Supra note 2.
9. 5 How. 504 (U.S. 1847).
10. The original reads "reverse," but this appears to be an error.
11. *Department of Revenue* v. *Association of Washington Stevedoring Cos.,* 435 U.S. 734, 752 (1978).

8

Houchins v. *KQED* (*1978*): Right of Access to News

The First Amendment prohibits restrictions on freedom of the press. This, of course, gives the news media the right to publish free from governmental restraints. Any system of censorship or other prior restraints on publication is patently invalid. The First Amendment erects an absolute barrier between government and the media so far as government tampering with news and editorial content is concerned.[1]

The right to publish may, however, be an empty one if the press does not have access to information in the control of governmental officials. Does the Constitution confer on the press a judicially enforceable right of access to the news? This is the question at issue in *Houchins* v. *KQED*[2] as well as the *Gannett* and *Richmond Newspapers* cases discussed in Chapter 10.

The right of access to news was first dealt with by the Warren Court in the 1965 case of *Estes* v. *Texas*,[3] the first case involving the issue of television in the courtroom. The original draft opinions in *Estes* rejected the notion of a press right of access.[4] Both the draft opinion of the Court by Justice Stewart and the draft dissent of Justice Clark expressly denied, in the words of the Clark draft, that "the First Amendment grants any of the news media such a privilege." Had these statements remained in the final *Estes* opinions, they might have foreclosed their fresh consideration by the Burger Court in *Houchins*, *Gannett*, and *Richmond Newspapers*. Instead, the final Clark opinion of the Court in *Estes* stated only that the press was "entitled to the same rights as the general public,"[5] whereas the Stewart dissent contained an intimation that the First Amendment did support a press right of access.[6]

The statements in the final *Estes* opinions were the only ones by the Court on the issue when *Houchins* v. *KQED* came before the Justices in the 1977 Term. Houchins was the Sheriff of Alameda County, just across the Bay from San Francisco (where Chief Justice Warren had served as district attorney for many years). The sheriff controlled access to the county jail. KQED operated television and radio stations that reported the suicide of a prisoner in the Greystone portion of the jail as well as a psychiatrist's statement that conditions there were responsible. KQED requested permission to inspect and take pictures within the Greystone facility. After permission was refused, KQED filed suit. They alleged that Houchins had violated the First Amendment by refusing to provide any effective means by which the public could be informed of conditions prevailing in the Greystone facility or learn of the prisoners' grievances.

Houchins then announced a program of regular monthly tours open to the public (limited to 25 persons) of parts of the jail—not including Greystone. Cameras and tape recorders were not allowed on the tours— nor were interviews with inmates. The lower court preliminarily enjoined petitioner from denying KQED news personnel and responsible news-media representatives reasonable access to the jail, including Greystone; from preventing their use of photographic or sound equipment; or from their carrying out inmate interviews.

The conference after the November 29, 1977, argument was closely divided on *Houchins*. The case for reversal was stated bluntly by Justice White, "I don't see any right of access for anyone or why, if [they] let the public in, [they] must let the press in with their cameras." On the other side, Justice Stevens asked, "Can a policy denying all access be constitutional? I think not." Stevens emphasized the public interest "as to how prisons are run."

Of particular interest, in view of his position as the "swing vote," was the ambivalent statement of Justice Stewart. "The First Amendment," he declared, "does not give [the press] access superior to that of the general public. Moreover, there is no such thing as a constitutional right to know." Nevertheless, the Justice concluded, "Basically, I think the injunction here does not exceed [the permitted] bounds." Stewart also noted, "If the sheriff had not allowed public tours, he did not have to allow the press in."

The conference, with Justices Marshall and Blackmun not participating, divided four (Justices Brennan, Stewart, Powell, and Stevens) to three (the Chief Justice and Justices White and Rehnquist) in favor of affirmance. The opinion was assigned to Justice Stevens who circulated the draft opinion of the Court reprinted on p. 349 on March 15, 1978. This draft is essentially similar to the *Houchins* dissent ultimately issued by Justice Stevens. It contains a broad recognition of a constitutional right of access to information on the part of the press—a right that "is not for the private benefit of those who might qualify as representatives of the 'press' but to insure that the citizens are fully informed regarding matters of public interest and importance."

The Stevens starting point is the First Amendment itself. "The preservation of a full and free flow of information to the general public has long been recognized as a core objective of the First Amendment to the Constitution." The amendment's reach is not limited to the protection of news dissemination. "Without some protection for the acquisition of information about the operation of public institutions such as prisons by the public at large, the process of self-governance contemplated by the Framers would be stripped of its substance."

It follows that "information-gathering is entitled to some measure of constitutional protection." Here, the restrictions on access "concealed from the general public the conditions of confinement within the facility [and] abridged the public's right to be informed about those conditions."

In these circumstances, there was a clear constitutional violation. "An official prison policy of concealing such knowledge from the public by arbitrarily cutting off the flow of information at its source abridges the freedom of speech and of the press protected by the First and Fourteenth Amendments to the Constitution." It follows that the injunction against Houchins was properly issued. Consequently, the Stevens draft concludes, "The judgment of the Court of Appeals is

Affirmed."

1st DRAFT

SUPREME COURT OF THE UNITED STATES

No. 76–1310

Thomas L. Houchins, Sheriff of the County of Alameda, California, Petitioner,

v.

KQED, Inc., et al.

On Writ of Certiorari to the United States Court of Appeals for the Ninth Circuit.

[March —, 1978]

MR. JUSTICE STEVENS, delivered the opinion of the Court.

The question presented is whether a preliminary injunction requiring the Sheriff of Alameda County, Cal., to allow representatives of the news media access to the county jail is consistent with the holding in *Pell* v. *Procunier,* 417 U. S. 817, 834, that "newsmen have no constitutional right of access to prisons or their inmates beyond that afforded the general public."

Respondent KQED, Inc., operates a public service television station in Oakland, Cal. It has televised a number of programs about prison conditions and prison inmates. KQED reporters have been granted access to various correctional facilities in the San Francisco Bay area, including San Quentin State Prison, Soledad Prison and the San Francisco County Jails at San Bruno and San Francisco, to prepare program material. They have taken their cameras and recording equipment inside the walls of those institutions and interviewed inmates. No disturbances or other problems have occurred on those occasions.

KQED has also reported newsworthy events involving the Alameda County Jail in Santa Rita, including a 1972 newscast reporting a decision of the United States District Court finding

HOUCHINS *v.* KQED, INC.

that the "shocking and debasing conditions which prevailed [at Santa Rita] constituted cruel and unusual punishment for man or beast as a matter of law." [1]   Petitioner is the Sheriff of Alameda County and has general supervision and control of the Santa Rita facility.[2]

On March 31, 1975, KQED reported the suicide of a prisoner in the Greystone portion of the Santa Rita jail. That program also carried a statement by a psychiatrist assigned to Santa Rita to the effect that conditions in the Greystone facility were responsible for illnesses of inmates.[3]   Petitioner's disagreement with that conclusion was reported on the same newscast.

KQED requested permission to visit and photograph the area of the jail where the suicide occurred.   Petitioner refused, advising KQED that it was his policy not to permit any access to the jail by the news media.   This policy was also invoked by petitioner to deny subsequent requests for access to the jail in order to cover news stories about conditions and alleged incidents within the facility.[4]   Except for a carefully supervised tour in 1972, the news media were completely excluded from the inner portions of the Santa Rita jail until after this action was commenced.[5]

Respondents KQED, and the Alameda and Oakland branches of the National Association for the Advancement of Colored

---

[1] See *Brenneman* v. *Madison*, 343 F. Supp. 128, 132–133 (ND Cal. 1972). Based on a personal visit to the facility, Judge Zirpoli reached the "inescapable conclusion that Greystone should be razed to the ground."

[2] Petitioner has been employed by the Sheriff's Department for 30 years, including five as commanding officer of the jail at Santa Rita. He was elected to his present office in 1974.

[3] The psychiatrist was discharged after the telecast.

[4] Access was denied, for example, to cover stories of alleged gang rapes and poor physical conditions within the jail, Tr. 208, and of recent escapes from the jail, Tr. 135–136.

[5] A previous sheriff had conducted one "press tour" in 1972, attended by reporters and cameramen.   But the facility had been "freshly scrubbed" for the tour and the reporters were forbidden to ask any questions of the inmates they encountered (App. 16–17).

HOUCHINS *v.* KQED, INC.

People,[6] filed their complaint for equitable relief on June 17, 1975. The complaint alleged that petitioner had provided no "means by which the public may be informed of conditions prevailing in Greystone or by which prisoners' grievances may reach the public." It further alleged that petitioner's policy of "denying KQED and the public" access to the jail facility violated the First and Fourteenth Amendments to the Constitution and requested the court to enjoin petitioner "from excluding KQED news personnel from the Greystone cells and Santa Rita facilities and generally preventing full and accurate news coverage of the conditions prevailing therein." App. 6–7.

With the complaint, respondents filed a motion for a preliminary injunction, supported by affidavits of representatives of the news media, the Sheriff of San Francisco County, and the attorney for respondents. The affidavits of the news media representatives and the sheriff described the news coverage in other penal institutions and uniformly expressed the opinion that such coverage had no harmful consequences and in fact served a significant public purpose.[7]

---

[6] The NAACP alleged a "special concern with conditions at Santa Rita because the prisoner population at the jail is disproportionately black, and the members of the NAACP depend on the news media for information about conditions in the jail so that they can meaningfully participate in the current public debate on jail conditions in Alameda County." Complaint Paragraph 3.

Since no special relief was requested by or granted to the NAACP, the parties have focused on the claim of KQED.

[7] The sheriff has a master's degree in criminology from the University of California at Berkeley and 10 years experience in law enforcement with the San Francisco Police Department. As sheriff he has general supervision and control over the jail facilities in San Francisco. He expressed the "opinion, based on my education and experience in law enforcement and jail administration, that such programs made an important contribution to public understanding of jails and jail conditions. In my opinion jails are public institutions and the public has a right to know what is being done with their tax dollars being spent on jail facilities and programs." App. 15.

HOUCHINS *v.* KQED, INC.

The affidavit of the attorney for KQED described a series of telephone conversations with counsel for the County between May 12, 1975 and June 17, when this suit was filed. In the first conversation, respondents' counsel explained KQED's problem regarding access to the Santa Rita facility. In the second, County Counsel stated that a rule or regulation regarding press access would be forthcoming within a week. In the third conversation, more than two weeks later, County Counsel stated that no access rule had yet been developed, and agreed to forward a copy of the prison rules which were then in effect for maximum security inmates.[8] In the last communication, on June 10, 1975, County Counsel stated that petitioner was contemplating monthly public tours for 25 persons, with the first tour tentatively scheduled for July 14. The tours, however, would not include the cell portions of Greystone and would not allow any use of cameras or communication with inmates. Respondents filed suit on June 17, 1975.

In a letter to the County Board of Supervisors dated June 19, 1975, petitioner outlined a pilot public tour program along the lines of that described to respondents' counsel. The Board approved six tours. Petitioner then filed his answer and supporting affidavit explaining why he had refused KQED access to the jail and identifying the recent changes in policy regarding access to the jail and communication between inmates and persons on the outside. Petitioner stated that if KQED's request had been granted, he would have felt obligated to honor similar requests from other representatives of the press and this could have disrupted mealtimes, exercise times, visiting times, and court appearances of inmates.[9] He pointed out

---

[8] The inmates at Santa Rita include pretail detainees as well as prisoners who have been convicted and sentenced. The rules in effect on June 3, 1975, contained no rule on press access. Visiting was limited to three hours on Sunday. All outgoing mail, except letters to judges or lawyers, was inspected. The rule prohibited any mention of "the names or actions of any officers" of the jail.

[9] In contrast to the floodgate concerns expressed by petitioners, the

HOUCHINS *v.* KQED, INC.

that the mail regulations had recently been amended to delete a prohibition against mentioning the names or actions of any correctional officers. Petitioner also stated that KQED had been advised about the contemplated program of guided tours before the suit was filed and that the tours had since been approved and publicly announced. With respect to the scope of the proposed tours, petitioner explained that the use of cameras would be prohibited because it would not be possible to prevent 25 persons with cameras from photographing inmates and security operations. Moreover, communication with inmates would not be permitted because of excessive time consumption, "problems with control" of inmates and visitors, and a belief "that interviews would be excessively unwieldy." [10]

An evidentiary hearing on the motion for a preliminary injunction was held after the first four guided tours had taken place. The evidence revealed the inadequacy of the tours as a means of obtaining information about the inmates and their conditions of confinement for transmission to the public. The tours failed to enter certain areas of the jail.[11] They afforded no opportunity to photograph conditions within the facility, and the photographs which the County offered for sale to tour visitors omitted certain jail characteristics, such as catwalks above the cells from which guards can observe the inmates.[12] The tours provided no opportunity to question randomly encountered inmates about jail conditions. Indeed, to the

Information Officer at San Quentin testified that after the liberalization of access rules at that institution media requests to enter the facility actually declined. Tr. 152. This testimony may suggest that the mere existence of inflexible access barriers generates a concern that conditions within the closed institution require especially close scrutiny.

[10] App., at 24.

[11] The tour did not include Little Greystone, which was the subject of reports of beatings, rapes and poor conditions, or the disciplinary cells.

[12] There were also no photos of the women's cells, of the "safety cell," of the "disciplinary cells," or of the interior of Little Greystone. In addition, the photograph of the dayroom omits the television monitor that maintains continuous observation of the inmates and the open urinals.

HOUCHINS *v.* KQED, INC.

extent possible inmates were kept out of sight during the tour, preventing the tour visitors from obtaining a realistic picture of the conditions of confinement within the jail. In addition, the fixed scheduling of the tours prevented coverage of newsworthy events at the jail.

Of most importance, all of the remaining tours were completely booked and there was no assurance that any tour would be conducted after December of 1975. The District Court found that KQED had no access to the jail and that the broad restraints on access were not required by legitimate penological interests.[13]

---

[13] "Sheriff Houchins admitted that because Santa Rita has never experimented with a more liberal press policy than that presently in existence, there is no record of press disturbances. Furthermore, the Sheriff has no recollection of hearing of any disruption caused by the media at other penal institutions. Nevertheless Sheriff Houchins stated that he feared that invasion of inmates' privacy, creation of jail 'celebrities,' and threats of jail security would result from a more liberal press policy. While such fears are not groundless, convincing testimony was offered that such fears can be substantially allayed.

"As to the inmates' privacy, the media representatives commonly obtain written consent from those inmates who are interviewed and/or photographed, and coverage of inmates is never provided without their full agreement. As to pre-trial detainees who could be harmed by pre-trial publicity, consent can be obtained not only from such inmates but also from their counsel. Jail 'celebrities' are not likely to emerge as a result of a random interview policy. Regarding jail security, any cameras and equipment brought into the jail can be searched. While Sheriff Houchins expressed concern that photographs of electronic locking devices could be enlarged and studied in order to facilitate escape plans, he admitted that the inmates themselves can study and sketch the locking devices. Most importantly, there was substantial testimony to the effect that ground rules laid down by jail administrators, such as a ban on photographs of security devices, are consistently respected by the media.

"Thus, upon reviewing the evidence concerning the present media policy at Santa Rita, the Court finds the plaintiffs have demonstrated irreparable injury, absence of an adequate remedy at law, probability of success on the merits, a favorable public interest, and a balance of hardships which must be struck in plaintiffs' favor." App., at 69.

HOUCHINS *v.* KQED, INC.

The District Court thereafter issued a preliminary injunction, enjoining petitioner "from denying to KQED news personnel and responsible representatives of the news media access to the Santa Rita facilities, including Greystone, at reasonable times and hours," or from preventing such representatives "from utilizing photographic and sound equipment or from utilizing inmate interviews in providing full and accurate coverage of the Santa Rita facilities." The court, however, recognized that petitioner should determine the specific means of implementing the order and, in any event, should retain the right to deny access when jail tensions or other special circumstances require exclusion.

Petitioner took an interlocutory appeal to the United States Court of Appeals for the Ninth Circuit.[14] The Court of Appeals affirmed, holding that the District Court did not abuse its discretion in framing the preliminary injunction under review.[15] MR. JUSTICE REHNQUIST, acting as Circuit Justice, stayed the mandate and in his opinion on the stay application fairly stated the legal issue we subsequently granted certiorari to decide:

"The legal issue to be raised by applicant's petition for certiorari seems quite clear. If the 'no greater access' doctrine of *Pell* and *Saxbe* applies to this case, the Court of Appeals and the District Court were wrong, and the injunction was an abuse of discretion. If, on the other hand, the holding in *Pell* is to be viewed as impliedly limited to the situation where there already existed substantial press and public access to the prison, then *Pell* and *Saxbe* are not necessarily dispositive, and review by this Court of the propriety of the injunction, in light of

---

[14] Two circuit judges granted a stay of the District Court's order pending disposition of petitioner's appeal.

[15] 546 F. 2d 284 (1976). A petition for rehearing, a suggestion for rehearing en banc, and a motion to stay the mandate were all denied by the Ninth Circuit.

HOUCHINS *v.* KQED, INC.

those cases, would be appropriate, although not necessary." 429 U. S. 1341, 1344.

For two reasons, which shall be discussed separately, the
decisions in *Pell* and *Saxbe* do not control the propriety of the
District Court's preliminary injunction. First, the unconstitutionality of petitioner's policies which gave rise to this
litigation does not rest on the premise that the press has a
greater right of access to information regarding prison conditions than do other members of the public. Second, relief
tailored to the needs of the press may properly be awarded to
a representative of the press which is successful in proving that
it has been harmed by a constitutional violation and need not
await the grant of relief to members of the general public who
may also have been injured by petitioner's unconstitutional
access policy but have not yet sought to vindicate their rights.

I

This litigation grew out of petitioner's refusal to allow
representatives of the press access to the inner portions of the
Santa Rita facility. Following those refusals and the institution of this suit, certain remedial action was taken by petitioner. The mail censorship was relaxed and an experimental
tour program was initiated. As a preliminary matter, therefore we must consider the relevance of the actions after
March 31, 1975, to the question whether a constitutional violation had occurred.

It is well settled that a defendant's corrective action in
anticipation of litigation or following commencement of suit
does not deprive the court of power to decide whether the
previous course of conduct was unlawful. See *United States*
v. *W. T. Grant Co.,* 345 U. S. 629 and cases cited, at 632–633.[16]

---

[16] Moreover, along with the power to decide the merits, the Court's
power to grant injunctive relief survives the discontinuance of illegal conduct. "It is the duty of the courts to beware of efforts to defeat injunctive relief by protestations of repentance and reform, especially when

HOUCHINS *v.* KQED, INC.

The propriety of the court's exercise of that power in this case is apparent. When this suit was filed, there were no public tours. Petitioner enforced a policy of virtually total exclusion of both the public and the press from those areas within the Santa Rita jail where the inmates were confined. At that time petitioner also enforced a policy of reading all inmate correspondence addressed to persons other than lawyers and judges and censoring those portions that related to the conduct of the guards who controlled their daily existence. Prison policy as well as prison walls significantly abridged the opportunities for communication of information about the conditions of confinement in the Santa Rita facility to the public.[17] Therefore,

abandonment seems timed to anticipate suit, and there is a probability of resumption." *United States* v. *Oregon Medical Society*, 343 U. S. 326, 333. When the District Court issued the preliminary injunction, there was no assurance that the experimental public tours would continue beyond the next month. Thus, it would certainly have been reasonable for the court to assume that, absent injunctive relief, the access to the inner portions of the Santa Rita facility would soon be reduced to its prelitigation level.

[17] Thus, when this suit was filed, there existed no opportunity for outsiders to observe the living conditions of the inmates at Santa Rita. And the mail regulations prohibited statements about the character of the treatment of prisoners by correctional officers.

We cannot agree with petitioner that the inmates' visitation and telephone privileges were reasonable alternative means of informing the public at large about conditions within Santa Rita. Neither offered an opportunity to observe those conditions. Even if a member of the general public or a representative of the press were fortunate enough to obtain the name of an inmate to visit, access to the facility would not have included the inmate's place of confinement. The jail regulations do not indicate that an inmate in the minimum security portion of the jail may enlist the aid of Social Service Officers to telephone the press or members of the general public to complain of the conditions of confinement. App. 38. Even if a maximum security inmate may make collect telephone calls, it is unlikely that a member of the general public or representative of the press would accept the charges, especially without prior knowledge of the call's communicative purpose.

Although sentenced prisoners may not be interviewed under any cir-

HOUCHINS *v.* KQED, INC.

even if there would not have been any constitutional violation
had the access policies adopted by petitioner following commencement of this litigation been in effect all along, it was
appropriate for the District Court to decide whether the
restrictive rules in effect when KQED first requested access
were constitutional.

In *Pell* v. *Procunier*, 417 U. S. 817, 834, the Court stated
that "newsmen have no constitutional right of access to prisons
or their inmates beyond that afforded the general public."
But the Court has never intimated that a nondiscriminatory
policy of excluding entirely both the public and the press from
access to information about prison conditions would avoid
constitutional scrutiny.[18]   Indeed, *Pell* itself strongly suggests
the contrary.

---

cumstances, pretrial detainees may, according to petitioner, be interviewed
with the consents of the inmates, defense counsel and prosecutor and with
an order from the court. Not only would such an interview take place
outside the confines of the jail, but the requirement of a court order makes
this a patently inadequate means of keeping the public informed about the
jail and its inmates.

Finally, petitioner suggests his willingness to provide the press with
information regarding the release of prisoners which, according to petitioner, would permit interviews of former prisoners regarding the conditions of their recent confinement. This informal offer was apparently only
made in response to respondents' lawsuit. Moreover, it too fails to afford
the public any opportunity to observe the conditions of confinement.

Hence, the means available at the time this suit was instituted for
informing the general public about conditions in the Santa Rita jail were,
as a practical matter, nonexistent.

[18] In *Zemel* v. *Rusk*, 381 U. S. 1, 17, the Court said:

"The right to speak and publish does not carry with it the *unrestrained*
right to gather information." (Emphasis added.)

And in *Branzburg* v. *Hayes*, 408 U. S. 665, 681:

"We do not question the significance of free speech, press, or assembly
to the country's welfare. Nor is it suggested that news gathering does not
qualify for First Amendment protection; without some protection for seeking out the news, freedom of the press could be eviscerated."

Both statements imply that there is a right to acquire knowledge that

HOUCHINS *v.* KQED, INC.

In that case, representatives of the press claimed the right to interview specifically designated inmates. In evaluating this claim, the Court did not simply inquire whether prison officials allowed members of the general public to conduct such interviews. Rather, it canvassed the opportunities already available for both the public and the press to acquire information regarding the prison and its inmates. And the Court found that the policy of prohibiting interviews with inmates specifically designated by the press was "not part of an attempt by the state to conceal the conditions in its prisons." The challenged restriction on access, which was imposed only after experience revealed that such interviews posed disciplinary problems, was an isolated limitation on the efforts of the press to gather information about those conditions. It was against the background of a record which demonstrated that both the press and the general public were "accorded full opportunities to observe prison conditions," [19] that the Court considered the constitutionality of the single restraint on access challenged in *Pell.*

The decision in *Pell*, therefore, does not imply that a state policy of concealing prison conditions from the press, or a policy denying the press any opportunity to observe those conditions, could have been justified simply by pointing to like

---

derives protection from the First Amendment. See *Branzburg, supra,* at 728 n. 4, STEWART, J., dissenting.

[19] "The Department of Corrections regularly conducts public tours through the prisons for the benefit of interested citizens. In addition, newsmen are permitted to visit both the maximum security and minimum security sections of the institutions and to stop and speak about any subject to any inmates whom they might encounter. If security considerations permit, corrections personnel will step aside to permit such interviews to be confidential. Apart from general access to all parts of the institutions, newsmen are also permitted to enter the prisons to interview inmates selected at random by the corrections officials. By the same token, if a newsman wishes to write a story on a particular prison program, he is permitted to sit in on group meetings and to interview the inmate participants." 417 U. S., at 830.

HOUCHINS *v.* KQED, INC.

concealment from, and denial to, the general public. If that
were not true, there would have been no need to emphasize
the substantial press and public access reflected in the record
of that case.[20] What *Pell* does indicate is that the question
whether respondents established a probability of prevailing on
their constitutional claim is inseparable from the question
whether petitioner's policies unduly restricted the opportunities of the general public to learn about the conditions of
confinement in Santa Rita jail. As in *Pell*, in assessing its
adequacy, the total access of the public and the press must
be considered.

Here, the broad restraints on access to information regarding
operation of the jail that prevailed on the date this suit was
instituted are plainly disclosed by the record. The public and
the press had consistently been denied any access to those

---

[20] Nor would it have been necessary to note, as the *Pell* opinion did, the
fact that the First Amendment protects the free flow of information to
the public:

"The constitutional guarantee of a free press 'assures the maintenance
of our political system and an open society,' *Time, Inc.* v. *Hill*, 385 U. S.
374, 389 (1967), and secures 'the paramount public interest in a free flow
of information to the people concerning public officials,' *Garrison* v. *Louisiana*, 379 U. S. 64, 77 (1964). See also *New York Times Co.* v. *Sullivan*,
376 U. S. 254 (1964). By the same token, '[a]ny system of prior restraints of expression comes to this Court bearing a heavy presumption
against its constitutional validity.' *New York Times Co.* v. *United States*,
403 U. S. 713, 714 (1971); *Organization for a Better Austin* v. *Keefe*, 402
U. S. 415 (1971); *Bantam Books, Inc.* v. *Sullivan*, 372 U. S. 58, 70 (1963);
Near v. *Minnesota ex rel. Olson*, 283 U. S. 697 (1931). Correlatively,
the First and Fourteenth Amendments also protect the right of the public
to receive such information and ideas as are published. *Kleindienst* v.
Mandel, 408 U. S., at 762–763; *Stanley* v. *Georgia*, 394 U. S. 557, 564
(1969).

"In *Branzburg* v. *Hayes*, 408 U. S. 665 (1972), the Court went further
and acknowledged that 'news gathering is not without its First Amendment protections,' *id.*, at 707, for 'without some protection for seeking out
the news, freedom of the press could be eviscerated,' *id.*, at 681." 417
U. S., at 832–833.

HOUCHINS *v.* KQED, INC.

portions of the Santa Rita facility where inmates were confined and there had been excessive censorship of inmate correspondence. Petitioner's no-access policy, modified only in the wake of respondents' resort to the courts, could survive constitutional scrutiny only if the Constitution affords no protection to the public's right to be informed about conditions within those public institutions where some of its members are confined because they have been charged with or found guilty of criminal offenses.

II

The preservation of a full and free flow of information to the general public has long been recognized as a core objective of the First Amendment to the Constitution.[21] It is for this reason that the First Amendment protects not only the dissemination but also the receipt of information and ideas. See, *e. g., Virginia Pharmacy Board* v. *Virginia Consumer Council,* 425 U. S. 748, 756; *Procunier* v. *Martinez,* 416 U. S. 396, 408–409; *Kleindienst* v. *Mandel,* 408 U. S. 753, 762–763.[22] Thus, in *Procunier* v. *Martinez, supra,* the Court invalidated prison regulations authorizing excessive censorship of outgoing inmate correspondence because such censorship abridged the rights of the intended recipients. See also *Morales* v. *Schmidt,* 489 F. 2d 1335, 1346, n. 8 (CA7 1973). So here, petitioner's prelitigation prohibition on mentioning the conduct of jail officers in outgoing correspondence must be considered an impingement

---

[21] See, *e. g., Virginia Pharmacy Board* v. *Virginia Consumer Council,* 425 U. S. 748, 764–765; *Garrison* v. *Louisiana,* 379 U. S. 64, 77; *New York Times Co.* v. *Sullivan,* 376 U. S. 254, 266–270; *Associated Press* v. *United States,* 326 U. S. 1, 20; *Grosjean* v. *American Press Co.,* 297 U. S. 233, 250. See also *Branzburg* v. *Hayes,* 408 U. S. 665, 726 n. 2 (STEWART, J., dissenting.)

[22] See also *Lamont* v. *Postmaster General,* 381 U. S. 301; *Red Lion Broadcasting Co.* v. *FCC,* 395 U. S. 367, 390; *Stanley* v. *Georgia,* 394 U. S. 557, 564; *Martin* v. *City of Struthers,* 319 U. S. 141; *Marsh* v. *Alabama,* 326 U. S. 501.

HOUCHINS *v.* KQED, INC.

on the noninmate correspondent's interest in receiving the intended communication.

In addition to safeguarding the right of one individual to receive what another elects to communicate, the First Amendment serves an essential societal function.[23] Our system of self-government assumes the existence of an informed citizenry.[24] As Madison wrote:

> "A popular Government, without popular information or the means of acquiring it, is but a prologue to a farce or a tragedy; or perhaps both. Knowledge will forever govern ignorance. And a people who mean to be their own governors, must arm themselves with the power knowledge gives." Writings of James Madison 103 (G. Hurst ed. 1910).

It is not sufficient, therefore, that the channels of communication be free of governmental restraints. Without some pro-

---

[23] "What is at stake here is the societal function of the First Amendment in preserving free public discussion of governmental affairs. No aspect of that constitutional guarantee is more treasured than its protection of the ability of our people through free and open debate to consider and resolve their own destiny. . . . It embodies our Nation's commitment to popular self-determination and our abiding faith that the surest course for developing sound national policy lies in a free exchange of views as public issues. And public debate must not only be unfettered; it must also be informed. For that reason this Court has repeatedly stated that First Amendment concerns encompass the receipt of information and ideas as well as the right of free expression." *Saxbe* v. *Washington Post Co.*, 417 U. S. 843, 862–863 (POWELL, J., dissenting).

[24] See A. Meiklejohn, Free Speech and its Relation to Self-Government 26 (1948):

"Just as far as . . . the citizens who are to decide an issue are denied acquaintance with information or opinion or doubt or disbelief or criticism which is relevant to that issue, just so far the result must be ill-considered, ill-balanced planning, for the general good. It is that mutilation of the thinking process of the community against which the First Amendment to the Constitution is directed.

HOUCHINS *v.* KQED, INC.

tection for the acquisition of information about the operation of public institutions such as prisons by the public at large, the process of self-governance contemplated by the Framers would be stripped of its substance.[25]

For that reason information-gathering is entitled to some measure of constitutional protection. See, *e. g., Branzburg* v. *Hayes,* 408 U. S. 665, 681; *Pell* v. *Procunier,* 417 U. S., at 833; "a right to gather news, of some dimensions, must exist." [26] As this Court's decisions clearly indicate, however, this protection is not for the private benefit of those who might qualify as representatives of the "press" but to insure that the citizens are fully informed regarding matters of public interest and importance.

In *Grosjean* v. *American Press Co.,* 297 U. S. 233, representatives of the "press" challenged a state tax on the advertising revenues of newspapers. In the Court's words, the issue raised by the tax went "to the heart of the natural right of the members of an organized society, united for their common good, to impart and acquire information about their common interests." *Id.,* at 243. The opinion described the long struggle

---

[25] Admittedly, the right to receive or acquire information is not specifically mentioned in the Constitution. But "the protection of the Bill of Rights goes beyond the specific guarantees to protect from . . . abridgement those equally fundamental personal rights necessary to make the express guarantees fully meaningful. . . . The dissemination of ideas can accomplish nothing if otherwise willing adherents are not free to receive and consider them. It would be a barren marketplace of ideas that had only sellers and no buyers." *Lamont* v. *Postmaster General,* 381 U. S., at 380 (BRENNAN, J., concurring). It would be an even more barren marketplace that had willing buyers and sellers and no meaningful information to exchange.

[26] See *Branzburg* v. *Hayes, supra,* at 727 (STEWART, J., dissenting):
"No less important to the news dissemination process is the gathering of information. News must not be unnecessarily cut off at its source, for without freedom to acquire information the right to publish would be impermissibly compromised. Accordingly, a right to gather news, of some dimensions, must exist."

HOUCHINS *v.* KQED, INC.

in England against the stamp tax and tax on advertisements—
the so-called "taxes on knowledge":

> "[I]n the adoption of the . . . [taxes] the dominant and
> controlling aim was to prevent, or curtail the opportunity
> for, the acquisition of knowledge by the people in respect
> of their governmental affairs. . . .   The aim of the strug-
> gle [against those taxes] was . . . to establish and pre-
> serve the right of the English people to full information in
> respect of the doings or misdoings of their government.
> Upon the correctness of this conclusion, the very charac-
> terizations of the exactions as 'taxes on knowledge' sheds
> a flood of corroborative light.   In the ultimate, an in-
> formed and enlightened public opinion was the thing at
> stake." *Id.*, at 247.

Noting the familiarity of the Framers with this struggle,
the Court held:

> "[S]ince informed public opinion is the most potent of
> all restraints upon misgovernment, the suppression or
> abridgement of the publicity afforded by a free press
> cannot be regarded otherwise than with grave concern.
> The tax involved here is bad . . . because, in light of its
> history and its present setting, it is seen to be a deliberate
> and calculated device . . . to limit the circulation of
> information to which the public is entitled in virtue of the
> constitutional guaranties." *Id.*, at 250.

A recognition that the "underlying right is the right of the
public generally" [27] is also implicit in the doctrine that "newsmen have no constitutional right of access to prisons or their
inmates beyond that afforded the general public." *Pell* v.
Procunier, 417 U. S., at 834.   In *Pell* it was unnecessary to
consider the extent of the public's right of access to information regarding the prison and its inmates in order to adjudicate

---

[27] *Saxbe* v. *Washington Post Co.*, 417 U. S., at 864.   (POWELL, J.,
dissenting.)

HOUCHINS *v.* KQED, INC.

the press claim to a particular form of access, since the record demonstrated that the flow of information to the public, both directly and through the press, was adequate to survive constitutional challenge; institutional considerations justified denying the single, additional mode of access sought by the press in that case.

Here, in contrast, the restrictions on access to the inner portions of the Santa Rita jail that existed on the date this litigation commenced concealed from the general public the conditions of confinement within the facility. The question is whether petitioner's policies, which cut off the flow of information at its source, abridged the public's right to be informed about those conditions.

The answer to that question does not depend upon the degree of public disclosure which should attend the operation of most governmental activity. Such matters involve questions of policy which generally must be resolved by the political branches of government. Moreover, there are unquestionably occasions when governmental activity may properly be carried on in complete secrecy. For example, the public and the press are commonly excluded from "grand jury proceedings, our own conferences, [and] the meetings of other official bodies gathering in executive session . . . ." *Branzburg* v. *Hayes*, 408 U. S., at 684; *Pell* v. *Procunier*, 417 U. S., at 834. In such situations the reasons for withholding information from the public are both apparent and legitimate.[28]

---

[28] In the case of grand jury proceedings, for example, the secrecy rule has been justified on several grounds:

"(1) to prevent the escape of those whose indictment may be contemplated; (2) to insure the utmost freedom to the grand jury in its deliberations, and to prevent persons subject to indictment or their friends from importuning the grand jurors; (3) to prevent subornation of perjury or tampering with the witnesses who may testify before grand jury and later appear at the trial of those indicted by it; (4) to encourage free and untrammeled disclosures by persons who have information with respect to the commission of crimes; (5) to protect innocent accused who is exoner-

HOUCHINS *v.* KQED, INC.

In this case, however, "[r]espondents do not assert a right
to force disclosure of confidential information or to invade in
any way the decisionmaking processes of governmental officials." [29] They simply seek an end to petitioner's policy of
concealing prison conditions from the public. Those conditions are wholly without claim to confidentiality. While prison
officials have an interest in the time and manner of public
acquisition of information about the institutions they administer, no one even suggests that there is any legitimate,
penological justification for concealing from citizens the conditions in which their fellow citizens are being confined.[30]

The reasons which militate the favor of providing special
protection to the flow of information to the public about
prisons relate to the unique function they perform in a democratic society. Not only are they public institutions, financed
with public funds and administered by public servants; [31]
they are an integral component of the criminal justice system.
The citizens confined therein are temporarily, and sometimes
permanently, deprived of their liberty as a result of a trial
which must conform to the dictates of the Constitution. By

---

ated from disclosure of the fact that he has been under investigation, and
from the expense of standing trial where there was no probability of
guilt." *United States* v. *Procter & Gamble,* 356 U. S. 677, 681 n. 6.

[29] *Saxbe* v. *Washington Post Co.,* 417 U. S., at 861 (POWELL, J.,
dissenting).

[30] The Court in *Saxbe* noted that " 'prisons are institutions where public access is generally limited.' " 417 U. S., at 849 (citation omitted).
This truism reflects the fact that there are legitimate penological interests served by regulating access, *e. g.,* security and confinement. But concealing prison conditions from the public is not one of those legitimate
objectives.

[31] "The administration of these institutions, the effectiveness of their
rehabilitative programs, the conditions of confinement that they maintain,
and the experiences of the individuals incarcerated therein are all matters
of legitimate societal interest and concern." *Saxbe* v. *Washington Post Co.,*
417 U. S., at 861 (POWELL, J., dissenting).

HOUCHINS *v.* KQED, INC.

express command of the Sixth Amendment the proceeding must be a "public trial." [32] It is important not only that the trial itself be fair, but also that the community at large have confidence in the integrity of the proceeding.[33] That public interest survives the judgment of conviction and appropriately carries over to an interest in how the convicted person is treated during his period of punishment and hoped-for rehabilitation. While a ward of the State and subject to its stern discipline, he retains constitutional protections against cruel and unusual punishment, see. *e. g., Estelle* v. *Gamble*, 429 U. S. 97, a protection which may derive more practical support from access to information about prisons by the public than by occasional litigation in a busy court.[34]

Some inmates—in Santa Rita, a substantial number—are pretrial detainees. Though confined pending trial, they have not been convicted of an offense against society and are entitled to the presumption of innocence. Certain penological objectives, *i. e.,* punishment, deterrence and rehabilitation, which are legitimate in regard to convicted prisoners, are inap-

---

[32] In all criminal prosecutions, the accused shall enjoy the right to a speedy and public trial, by an impartial jury of the State and district wherein the crime shall have been committed, which district shall have been previously ascertained by law, and to be informed of the nature and cause of the accusations; . . ." U. S. Const., Amend. VI.

[33] "The right to a public trial is not only to protect the accused but to protect as much the public's right to know what goes on when men's lives and liberty are at stake . . . ." *Lewis* v. *Peyton*, 352 F. 2d 791, 792 (CA4 1965). See also *In re Oliver*, 333 U. S. 257, 270: "The knowledge that every criminal trial is subject to contemporaneous review in the forum of public opinion is an effective restraint on possible abuse of judicial power."

[34] In fact, conditions within the Greystone portion of the Santa Rita facility had been found to constitute cruel and unusual punishment. *Brenneman* v. *Madigan*, 343 F. Supp. 128, 132–133 (ND Cal. 1972). The public's interest in ensuring that these conditions have been remedied is apparent. For, in final analysis, it is the citizens who bear responsibility for the treatment accorded those confined within penal institutions.

HOUCHINS *v.* KQED, INC.

plicable to pretrial detainees.[35]   Society has a special interest
in ensuring that unconvicted citizens are treated in accord with
their status.

In this case, the record demonstrates that both the public
and the press had been consistently denied any access to the
inner portions of the Santa Rita jail, that there had been
excessive censorship of inmate correspondence, and that there
was no valid justification for these broad restraints on the flow
of information.   An affirmative answer to the question whether
respondent established a likelihood of prevailing on the merits
did not depend, in final analysis, on any right of the press to
special treatment beyond that accorded the public at large.
Rather, the probable existence of a constitutional violation
rested upon the special importance of allowing a democratic
community access to knowledge about how its servants were
treating some of its members who have been committed to
their custody.   An official prison policy of concealing such
knowledge from the public by arbitrarily cutting off the flow of
information at its source abridges the freedom of speech and
of the press protected by the First and Fourteenth Amendments to the Constitution.[36]

---

[35] "Incarceration after conviction is imposed to punish, to deter, and to
rehabilitate the convict. . . .   Some freedom to accomplish these ends must
of necessity be afforded prison personnel.   Conversely, where incarceration
is imposed prior to conviction, deterrence, punishment, and retribution
are not legitimate functions of the incarcerating officials.   Their role is
but a temporary holding operation, and their necessary freedom of action
is concomitantly diminished. . . .   Punitive measures in such a context are
out of harmony with the presumption of innocence."   *Anderson* v. *Nosser,*
438 F. 2d 183, 190 (CA5 1971).

[36] When fundamental freedoms of citizens have been at stake, the Court
has recognized that an abridgement of those freedoms may follow from a
wide variety of governmental policies.   See, *e. g., American Communications Assn.* v. *Douds,* 339 U. S. 382; *NAACP* v. *Alabama,* 357 U. S. 449;
Boyd v. *United States,* 116 U. S. 616; *Grosjean* v. *American Press Co.,* 297
U. S. 233.

HOUCHINS *v.* KQED, INC.

III

The preliminary injunction entered by the District Court granted relief to KQED without providing any specific remedy for other members of the public. Moreover, it imposed duties on petitioner that may not be required by the Constitution itself. The injunction was not an abuse of discretion for either of these reasons.

If a litigant can prove that he has suffered specific harm from the application of an unconstitutional policy, it is entirely proper for a court to grant relief tailored to his needs without attempting to redress all the mischief that the policy may have worked on others. Though the public and the press have an equal right to receive information and ideas, different methods of remedying a violation of that right may sometimes be needed to accommodate the special concerns of the one or the other. Preliminary relief could therefore appropriately be awarded to KQED on the basis of its proof of how it was affected by the challenged policy without also granting specific relief to the general public. Indeed, since our adversary system contemplates the adjudication of specific controversies between specific litigants, it would have been improper for the District Court to attempt to provide a remedy to persons who have not requested separate relief. Accordingly, even though the Constitution provides the press with no greater right of access to information than that possessed by the public at large, a preliminary injunction is not invalid simply because it awards special relief to a successful litigant which is a representative of the press.[37]

---

[37] Moreover, the relief granted to KQED will redound to the benefit of members of the public interested in obtaining information about conditions in the Santa Rita jail. The press may have no greater constitutional right to information about prisons than that possessed by the general public. But when the press does acquire information and disseminate it to the public, it performs an important societal function.

"In seeking out the news the press therefore acts as an agent of the public at large. It is the means by which the people receive that free flow of

HOUCHINS *v.* KQED, INC.

Nor is there anything novel about injunctive relief which goes beyond a mere prohibition against repetition of previous unlawful conduct. In situations which are both numerous and varied the chancellor has required a wrongdoer to take affirmative steps to eliminate the effects of a violation of law even though the law itself imposes no duty to take the remedial action decreed by the court.[38] It follows that if prison regulations and policies have unconstitutionally suppressed information and interfered with communication in violation of the First Amendment, the District Court has the power to require, at least temporarily, that the channels of communication be opened more widely than the law would otherwise require in order to let relevant facts, which may have been concealed, come to light. Whether or not final relief along the lines of that preliminarily awarded in this case would be "aptly tailored to remedy the consequences of the constitutional violation," *Milliken* v. *Bradley,* 433 U. S. 267, 287, it is perfectly clear that the Court had power to enter an injunction which was broader than a mere prohibition against illegal conduct.

The Court of Appeals found no reason to question the specific preliminary relief ordered by the District Court. Nor would it be appropriate for us to review the scope of the

---

information and ideas essential to intelligent self-government. By enabling the public to assert meaningful control over the political process, the press performs a critical function in effecting the societal purpose of the First Amendment." *Saxbe* v. *Washington Post Co.,* 417 U. S., at 863–864 (POWELL, J., dissenting).

See also *Branzburg* v. *Hayes,* 408 U. S., at 726–727 (STEWART, J., dissenting).

In the context of fashioning a remedy for a violation of rights protected by the First Amendment, consideration of the role of the press in our society is appropriate.

[38] For an extensive discussion of this practice in the context of desegregation decrees, see the Court's opinion last Term in *Milliken* v. *Bradley,* 433 U. S. 267.

HOUCHINS *v.* KQED, INC.

order.[39] The order was preliminary in character, and is subject to revision in the light of experience and such evidence and argument as may be presented before the litigation is finally concluded.

The judgment of the Court of Appeals is

Affirmed.

MR. JUSTICE MARSHALL and MR. JUSTICE BLACKMUN took no part in the consideration or decision of this case.

---

[39] We note, however, that the District Court was presented with substantial evidence indicating that the use of cameras and interviews with randomly selected inmates neither jeopardized security nor threatened legitimate penological interests in other prisons where such access was permitted. See *Procunier* v. *Martinez*, 416 U. S., at 414 n. 14.

Had the Stevens draft (supra p. 349) come down as the *Houchins* opinion of the Court, it would have established a First Amendment right of access to news on the part of the press. But it soon became apparent that the Stevens draft would not be able to retain its majority. On April 24, Justice Stewart, whose vote had helped to make up the bare majority for affirmance at the conference, informed Justice Stevens that he could not join his opinion. "Try as I may," Stewart wrote, "I cannot bring myself to agree that a county sheriff is constitutionally required to open up a jail that he runs to the press and the public. Accordingly, I shall not be able to subscribe to the opinion you have circulated, affirming the judgment of the Court of Appeals."

The Stewart letter summarized its author's own "tentative view, which may not stand up." Under his view, "[I]t would be permissible in this case to issue an injunction assuring press access equivalent to existing public access, but not the much broader injunction actually issued by the District Court."

Justice Stewart ended his letter, "I shall in due course circulate an expression of these views." On May 22, Stewart circulated the opinion to whch he referred. It became his concurring opinion in the *Houchins* case.

On April 25, apparently before he had been informed of the changed Stewart position, Chief Justice Burger sent around a *MEMORANDUM TO THE CONFERENCE* informing the others, "I have devoted a substantial amount of time on a dissent in this case with some emphasis on systems of citizen oversight procedures which exist in many states." According to Burger, "This approach, rather than pushy TV people interested directly in the sensational, is the way to a solution." The Chief Justice also noted, "I agree with Potter's view that media have a right of access but not beyond that of the public generally."

On May 19, the Chief Justice circulated his opinion. But it was no longer in the form of a dissent. "Since John's opinion has been 'in limbo' for some time," read the Burger covering memo, "I have put my hand to an alternative, proposing reversal." Justice Stewart's refusal to join the Stevens opinion of the Court affirming the judgment below meant that the Burger draft could be circulated as "an alternative, proposing reversal."

The decision for reversal received a majority when Justice Stewart circulated his May 22 opinion. Though it refused to join the Burger opinion, it did concur in the judgment of reversal on the ground that the injunction against the sheriff was overbroad.

After he had received Justice Stewart's concurrence, the Chief Justice sent a May 23 "Dear Potter" letter that pointed out that any press right of access could hardly be limited to the news media: "[T]here are literally dozens of people—law teachers, judges, penologists, writers, lawyers—who tour prisons (as I did for 25 years in Europe and U.S.A.). Many of them write books, articles, or give lectures or a combination. I'm sure you will agree they have the same rights as a TV reporter doing a 'documentary.' Can they have greater First Amendment rights than these others whose form and certainty of communications is not so fixed?" "I do not believe," the Burger letter declared, "First Amendment rights can be circumscribed by the scope of the audience. If so, the early pamphleteers who could afford only 100 sheets were 'suspect.' " On the contrary, the Chief Justice noted, "a team of TV cameramen (camera-persons!) will tend to produce far more disruption than the serious student or judge, lawyer, or penologist who wants to exercise First Amendment rights with a somewhat different objective."

Then, on June 9, Chief Justice Burger sent around a second draft of his *Houchins* opinion. His covering memo succinctly summarized his approach in the case: "As a legislator I would vote for a reasonably orderly access to prisons, etc., by media, because it would be useful. But that is not the issue. The question is whether special access rights are *constitutionally compelled.*" The Burger *Houchins* opinion, unlike the original Stevens draft opinion of the Court (supra p. 349) answered this question in the negative.

Ultimately, the Burger opinion was joined by only Justices White and Rehnquist. This made it the plurality opinion of a seven-Justice Court, as Justice Stewart's concurrence enabled the decision for reversal to come down as the majority decision. The Stevens affirmation of a First Amendment right of access was relegated to the dissenting view.

In a June 12 "Dear Chief" letter joining the Burger opinion, Justice White explained the basis of the *Houchins* decision in the broad implications of the result reached by the Stevens draft. "If the First Amendment," White wrote, "requires a government to turn over information about its prisons on the demand of the press or to open its files and properties not only to routine inspections but for filming and public display, it would be difficult to contain such an unprecedented principle. I would suppose there are many government operations that are as important for the public to know about as prisons, or more so; yet I cannot believe that the press has a constitutional right to be at every administrator's elbow and to read all of his mail."

It is not for the courts, the White letter urged, to impose a duty on "governments to submit themselves to daily or periodic auditing by the press." What the *Houchins* majority did, as White saw it, was to "resist taking over what is essentially a legislative task and by reinterpreting the First Amendment assigning to ourselves and other courts the duty of determining whether the state and Federal Governments are making adequate disclosures to the press."

Notes

1. *Miami Herald Pub. Co.* v. *Tornillo,* 418 U.S. 241, 259 (1974).
2. 438 U.S. 1 (1978).
3. 381 U.S. 532 (1965).
4. Schwartz, *The Unpublished Opinions of the Warren Court* 193, 222 (1985).
5. Supra note 3 at 540.
6. Id. at 614–15.

9

Barry v. *Barchi* (*1979*): *Expanding and Contracting Due Process Concepts—From Goldberg* v. *Kelly to a More Restrictive Approach*

One of the most important accomplishments of the Burger Court was its expansion of procedural due process in administrative proceedings. Before 1970, it was settled law that the right to notice and hearing guaranteed by due process applied only in cases in which personal or property rights were adversely affected by administrative action. "Due process of law is not applicable unless one is being deprived of something to which he has a right."[1] If the individual was being given something by government to which he had no preexisting "right," he was being given a mere "privilege." Such a privilege "may be withdrawn at will and is not entitled to protection under the due process clause."[2]

This privilege concept was applied to licenses to sell liquor, operate billiard parlors, and to engage in other occupations deemed of little social value.[3] But its broadest application was in the burgeoning field of social welfare. During this century, government has been assuming welfare functions in a geometric progression, becoming a gigantic fount that pours out largess on which an ever-increasing number of people depend. Under the traditional approach, all of this public largess involves mere privileges.[4] In consequence, an ever-larger area of administrative power was being insulated from the safeguards of due process. There was danger that the joyless reaches of the welfare state would be littered with dependents outside the pale of procedural protection.

Goldberg v. Kelly

All this was changed by the landmark case of *Goldberg* v. *Kelly*[5] decided during Chief Justice Burger's first term. At issue was whether welfare payments could be terminated without a pretermination hearing where there was a right to a hearing after the decision to terminate. The lower court held that only a pretermination hearing could satisfy the demands of due process. There was a similar companion case from California in which the lower court had reached the opposite result.[6]

At the conference after the *Goldberg* v. *Kelly* argument on October 13, 1969, Chief Justice Burger and Justices Black and Stewart favored upholding the state procedures. The question posed by the cases, said the Chief Justice, was, "Is due process satisfied by a procedure which allows an appearance before termination, but also a full hearing afterward?" He stated that the states should be allowed to experiment, "[P]erhaps we should let it alone for now." Justice Black agreed, saying, "I think the procedures are okay so long as later there is a full hearing." Black did not explain why he adopted this view. His later discussion during the decision process indicated that he felt that welfare payments are a "gratuity," and not the kind of "property" protected by the "words" of the Due Process Clause. No other Justice expressed that view—including the Chief Justice, who, when he was on the D.C. Court of Appeals,[7] had authored the most important pre-*Goldberg* v. *Kelly* opinion rejecting the privilege-right dichotomy. Justice Stewart, who voted with Burger and Black, went out of his way to indicate his disagreement with the privilege concept. "I don't think," he declared, "the distinction between vested right and gratuity is significant to what requirements of due process obtain." On the other hand, Stewart said, "the totality of procedures here for me satisfies due process."

The other five at the conference voted to affirm. Justice Douglas strongly rejected the Black notion of welfare as a privilege not protected by due process. "Can a state," he asked, "create these things and withdraw them without the kind of due process we required in *Willner* [v. *Committee on Character and Fitness*[8]—a decision preventing disbarment of an attorney without notice and hearing]? Aren't they a species of property?" Justice Brennan spoke even more strongly along similar lines, summarizing the view he was to take in his opinion of the Court.

Justice Harlan also declared categorically, "This is not a gratuity. It's an entitlement or right . . . a vested right so long as the state chooses to give it." Harlan adopted a flexible approach to the type of hearing that might be required: "[the] full panoply of a trial type hearing is not required." As he saw it, "Confrontation, cross-examination, etc., [are needed] where termination turns on questions of fact. Where other things are involved maybe more flexibility is required."

Justice White said that he was "more with John than with the two Bills." Though, in other cases the government may cut off benefits before a full hearing, "the impact here is so severe that the balance should be cast for a full hearing before termination." White was not sure, however, whether the hearing would have to be held before "an independent judge."

The conference vote was five (Douglas, Brennan, Harlan, White, and Marshall) to three (Burger, Black, and Stewart) to affirm in *Goldberg* v. *Kelly*. Justice Douglas, senior in the majority, assigned the opinion to Justice Brennan. Brennan's main problem was to keep the votes of Justices Harlan and White. Though they had voted with the majority, they did not go as far as the others who had urged a more sweeping application of due process. Thus, the Brennan opinion went out of its way to indicate reliance on the opinion of the lower court. Justice Harlan had suggested that he would have been content to affirm on the basis of that opinion had Court practice permitted that and Harlan was, of course, crucial to a majority. Not too long before, the Court did at times affirm on the opinion below. However, Justice Frankfurter succeeded in ending the practice on the ground that it hurt the egos of those other lower court judges whose decisions were affirmed but not on the basis of their opinions.

The Brennan opinion-writing process in *Goldberg* v. *Kelly* well illustrates the need to compromise in order to hold votes. In Part I of his opinion, Brennan enunciated a rationale rejecting the privilege concept that had previously barred welfare recipients from procedural protection. Brennan stated that the constitutional claim could not be answered by the argument that "public assistance benefits are 'a privilege' and not a 'right.' " The opinion then characterized welfare benefits as a "matter of statutory entitlement" and added in a note that it "may be realistic today to regard welfare entitlements as more like 'property' than a 'gratuity.' "

I have been told that the Justice himself would have preferred to go further and hold that welfare payments in today's economic and social setting constitute "property"—in the same sense that land ownership constitutes property. Brennan did not, however, go that far in his opinion; instead he felt that he had to write narrowly for fear of losing Justices Harlan and White. The latter was particularly concerned that the opinion not reach the interest in governmental employment. The result was that the *Goldberg* v. *Kelly* opinion replaced the privilege concept with that of "entitlement"—"more like 'property' than a 'gratuity',"but not "property" itself.

The original Brennan draft, circulated November 24, contained a different approach to the role of welfare than that stated in the final opinion. The key draft passage on this reads:

Whatever may have been true in the past, today we cannot confidently saddle the poor with the blame for their poverty. It has become increasingly clear that indigency is now largely a product of impersonal forces— among others, technological change, economic policy, racial prejudice. In a complex, highly industrial nation such as ours "[I]t is closer to the truth to say that the poor are affirmative contributors to . . . society, for we are so organized as virtually to compel this sacrifice by a segment of the population." In other words, welfare is not charity but a means for treating a disorder in our society. Government, accordingly, has an overriding interest in providing uninterrupted assistance to the eligible, both to help maintain the dignity and well-being of a large segment of the population and to protect against the societal malaise that may flow from a widespread sense of unjustified frustration and insecurity.

Justice White, however, refused to accept this passage. He conferred with Justice Brennan the day after receiving the draft and said that he thought our society had always been committed to spreading as widely as possible the opportunities to participate fully in economic, social, and political life—witness universal free public schools, universal suffrage, and so on. He thought it wrong to suggest that people in this country had once blamed the poor for their poverty and wrong to say that today welfare is given because society is responsible for poverty. Rather, as he saw it, welfare is given to enable people to maintain their dignity, and to participate in, and contribute to society, economically and otherwise. Welfare functions to enable people to stand on their own feet and thus get off the dole and go out on their own to compete and otherwise participate in society.

Justice Brennan said he thought Justice White's views failed to recognize the conditions of endemic poverty in large cities and depressed areas. But White refused to accept the Brennan approach and Brennan saw that to hold White's essential vote he would have to revise the statement on poverty. A revised statement on poverty was drafted incorporating certain ideas of each Justice in a combination acceptable to White, who joined the Brennan opinion on December 2.

This provided the fourth vote. Justice Douglas had joined the first draft on November 24. Justice Marshall had joined the next day. On that same day, the Chief Justice and Justice Black had announced that they would dissent. Justices Harlan and Stewart were still to be heard from.

On December 11, Justice Harlan sent Justice Brennan a letter indicating general agreement with the opinion, but requesting several changes. None was of great significance. The most important was the suggestion that the term "trial-type hearing," which Brennan had used to describe the type of proceeding to be provided, be replaced by "evidentiary hearing." The use of the latter term in the final Brennan opinion has led to its employment during recent years as the generic administrative law term for what used to be called trial-type hearings.

Justice Brennan accepted all the Harlan suggestions but one. Justice Harlan wanted Brennan to add a clear statement that there was no right to an evidentiary hearing when the only issues were legal, that is, when questions of fact were not at issue. The Brennan draft had intimated that a hearing was required in that circumstance. Here, however, Brennan refused to yield. If he was not to decide that a hearing was necessary when only legal issues were presented, he was not going to decide that question the other way. The result was the addition of a footnote[9] that reserved the issue.

On December 15, Justice Brennan told Justice Harlan of his general agreement with the Harlan suggestions. The latter then said that he would join the opinion. There was now a majority and the opinion could come down as soon as the dissents were ready. Justice Black circulated his dissent on January 29, 1970, and Chief Justice Burger on February 12. The Chief Justice suggested in his first draft that the cases should be dismissed as improvidently granted—overlooking the facts that each was an appeal and that the two lower courts had reached contrary conclusions. Burger himself came to realize that the cases could not be avoided as improvident grants and the suggestion does not appear in his final dissent. However, at Justice Harlan's suggestion, the Brennan opinion pointed out that a decision by the Supreme Court was necessary because the courts below were in direct conflict.

Justice Stewart also circulated a brief dissent on February 17. He had indicated that he was favorably disposed toward the Brennan opinion, but in the end, he adhered to his initial statement at the conference—that under the circumstances, due process was satisfied by the state procedures.

The dissents did not, however, detract from the force of the *Goldberg* v. *Kelly* opinion. Compromise or not, it repudiated the notion that welfare payments were a mere "privilege" or "gratuity" that might be taken away without compliance with procedural due process. From this point of view *Goldberg* v. *Kelly* was a seminal decision: it worked what a federal judge terms a "due process" explosion under which "we have witnessed a greater expansion of due process . . . than in the entire period since ratification of the Constitution."[10] The post-*Goldberg* v. *Kelly* cases extended its hearing requirement to virtually all the cases that used to be treated as involving only privileges not protected by procedural due process.[11] In many respects, the culmination of this development came in *Goss* v. *Lopez*,[12] where the Court ruled in 1975 that public school pupils might not be suspended for even short periods (ten days or less), without a hearing.

The next year, however, the due process development suffered a serious setback. If the *Goldberg* v. *Kelly* revolution reached its apogee in *Goss* v. *Lopez*, it may have met its Thermidor in *Mathews* v. *Eldridge*.[13] The majority there upheld the termination of disability benefits, even though there was no provision for a hearing until after the administrative decision to end the payments. *Eldridge* held that due process did not require a pretermination hearing; instead, due process was satisfied by the posttermination procedures provided in the agency.

Brennan's *Barchi* Draft

The Burger Court adhered to the *Eldridge* holding, contrary though it may be to the *Goldberg* v. *Kelly* requirement of a hearing before the welfare payments were ended. In *Barry* v. *Barchi*,[14] however, the Court almost returned to the *Goldberg* v. *Kelly* due process demand of a pre-termination hearing—that is, one given before the adverse administrative decision is made. That would have happened had Justice Brennan's draft opinion of the Court come down as the final opinion. Ultimately, as we shall see, it did not, and the *Barry* decision remains as another confirmation of the *Mathews* v. *Eldridge* retreat from the categorical *Goldberg* v. *Kelly* holding.

Barchi was licensed as a harness racing trainer by the New York Racing Board. Two days after a horse trained by him finished second in a race, he was informed by the board steward that a test had revealed that the horse had been drugged. Barchi denied that he had drugged the horse and took two lie detector tests, which indicated that his denials were truthful. Despite this, the steward summarily suspended Barchi for fifteen days without giving him any opportunity to rebut the charge. The notice of suspension relied on the board's "trainer responsibility rule," which creates a presumption that when a horse has been drugged, the drug was administered by the trainer or resulted from his negligence. The lower court held that Barchi had been denied procedural due process.

The Chief Justice spoke strongly at the postargument conference, in early November 1978, in favor of reversal. He summarized his position in a February 12, 1979, *MEMORANDUM TO THE CONFERENCE:* "[M]y view on the merits is that the New York statute should not be held unconstitutional either on its face or as applied to Barchi in the circumstances of this case." Justices Blackmun and Powell were also for reversal, but they did so on the ground that the federal courts should abstain from deciding what was initially a question of New York law. Justice Rehnquist voted the same way, as he put it in a letter of April 10, 1979 to Justice White, "both on substantive grounds and on abstention grounds."

The other five Justices were for affirmance, and the opinion was assigned by Justice Douglas (the senior Justice in the bare majority) to Justice Brennan. Early in February 1979, the latter circulated the draft opinion of the Court reprinted on p. 382. The Brennan draft contains a categorical holding that "summary suspension without prior hearing of trainers of harness race horses for violation of the trainer's responsibility rule, fail to satisfy the requirements of procedural due process."

Justice Brennan starts by applying the *Goldberg* v. *Kelly* holding that Barchi had an interest protected by due process. "There is no doubt that appellee's trainer's license clothes him with a constitutionally protected interest of which he cannot be deprived without procedural due process." The draft notes the contention by appellants that Barchi's license was a mere "privilege" and states flatly, "This contention is without merit." The Court "has fully and finally rejected the wooden distinction between 'rights' and 'privileges' that once seemed to govern the applicability of due process rights." Barchi's interest is thus plainly protected by the Due Process Clause.

To determine what process is due, a "balancing process weighing the competing interests involved" is required. The balance in this case clearly tilts in favor of the presuspension hearing requirement. The key element here is the harm caused by the suspension:

> [E]ven a temporary suspension can irreparably damage a trainer's liveli-hood. Not only does a trainer lose the income from races during the sus-pension, but, even more harmful, he is likely to lose the clients he has collected over the span of his career. Thus, the harm to Barchi from a summary suspension can be devastating. . . . [T]he procedures appellee requests would significantly decrease the chances of erroneous suspensions without imposing any significant additional administrative burden.

On the other side, there is only "the State's interests in protecting horses from harm and in protecting the repute of racing and the State's income derived from racing." This is hardly significant enough "to jus-tify summary procedures in light of appellants' concession that Barchi is likely to suffer substantial and irreparable harm." The Brennan conclusion is that the lower court was right in ruling that "on balance . . . the ab-sence of a pre-suspension hearing . . . denies [Barchi] the meaningful review due process requires."

1st DRAFT

SUPREME COURT OF THE UNITED STATES

No. 77–803

William G. Barry, Etc., et al., Appellants, *v.* John Barchi.	On Appeal from the United States District Court for the Southern District of New York.

[January —, 1979]

MR. JUSTICE BRENNAN delivered the opinion of the Court.

Appellee John Barchi is duly licensed as a harness racing trainer by appellant New York State Racing and Wagering Board (Board).[1] The Board suspended his license without first affording him a prior hearing after a post-race test indicated traces of a drug in the urine of one of Barchi's horses. Barchi brought this suit in the District Court for the Southern District of New York challenging the constitutionality of the statutory provision and administrative rules that authorized the summary suspension. A three-judge court sustained his challenge, declared the statutory provision unconstitutional, and nullified Barchi's suspension. *Barchi v. Sarafan*, 436 F. Supp. 775 (SDNY 1977). We noted probable jurisdiction. 435 U. S. 921 (1978). We affirm.

I

On June 22, 1976, one of the horses trained by Barchi, "Be

---

[1] Section 8010 of New York's Unconsolidated Laws authorizes the "state harness racing commission," whose powers are now exercised by the Board, see N. Y. Uncon. Laws §§ 7951-a, 8162 (McKinney Supp. 1978), to "license drivers and such other persons participating in harness horse race meets, as the commission may by rule prescribe . . . ." The administrative regulation authorizing the licensing of trainers of harness race horses is 9 N. Y. C. R. R. § 4101.24 (1974).

BARRY *v.* BARCHI

Alert," finished second in the third race at Monticello Raceway. Two days later John Fay, the Board Steward and Presiding Judge at Monticello, informed Barchi that a post-race urine test on "Be Alert" had revealed that the horse had been treated with the drug "Lasix" within 48 hours of the race, a violation of Board Rule 4120.4.[2] Barchi denied to both Fay and Daniel Goldberg, the Board's Chief Investigator, that he had given the drug to "Be Alert." On June 28 Barchi took a lie-detector test on his own initiative, and on June 29 took a second lie-detector test administered at the request of the Board. Both tests indicated that his claims to have no knowledge of the violation were truthful.[3]

Nonetheless, on July 8, Steward Fay, without giving Barchi a prior hearing or access to any information concerning the urine test, summarily suspended him for 15 days beginning July 10.[4] The notice of suspension relied on several Board

[2] This rule provides in relevant part:

"*Prohibition.* No person shall, or attempt to, or shall conspire with another or others to:

"(a) Stimulate or depress a horse through the administration of any drug, medication, stimulant, depressant, hypnotic or narcotic.

·   ·   ·   ·   ·

"(d) Administer any drug, medicant, stimulant, depressant, narcotic or hypnotic to a horse within 48 hours of its race."

[3] Among the questions asked in the lie-detector test were the following:
"Did you ever give Be Alert Lasix? No.
"Do you know of anyone ever giving Be Alert Lasix? No.
"Did you ever direct anyone to give Be Alert Lasix? No.
"Did you ever authorize anyone to give Be Alert Lasix? No."

Appendix, at 18a.

[4] See N. Y. Unconsol. Laws § 8009 (McKinney Supp. 1978); 9 N. Y. C. R. R. § 4105.8 (f) (authorizing presiding judges "[w]here a violation of any rule is suspected to conduct an inquiry promptly and to take such action as may be appropriate . . . ."). Section 8010 of the Unconsolidated Laws provides the grounds for suspension:

". . . The commission may suspend or revoke a license issued pursuant to this section if it shall determine that (a) the applicant or licensee (1) has

BARRY *v.* BARCHI

rules which, taken together, create the "trainer's responsibility rule," [5] a rebuttable evidentiary presumption that "when a
harness racing horse has been drugged, [the durg] was either

been convicted of a crime involving moral turpitude; (2) has engaged in
bookmaking or other form of illegal gambling; (3) has been found guilty
of any fraud in connection with racing or breeding; (4) has been guilty
of any violation or attempt to violate any law, rule or regulation of any
racing jurisdiction for which suspension from racing might be imposed in
such jurisdiction; (5) or who has violated any rule, regulation or order
of the commission, or (b) that the experience, character or general fitness
of any applicant or licensee is such [that] the participation of such person in harness racing or related activities would be inconsistent with the
public interest, convenience or necessity or with the best interests of
racing generally."

[5] The relevant rules provide as follows:

"4116.11. *Trainer's responsibility.* A trainer is responsible for the condition, fitness, equipment, and soundness of each horse at the time it is
declared to race and thereafter when it starts in a race.

"4120.5 *Presumptions.* Whenever [certain tests required to be made on
horses that place first, second, or third in a race] disclose the presence in
any horse of any drug, stimulant, depressant or sedative, in any amount
whatsoever, it shall be presumed:

"(a) that the same was administered by a person or persons having the
control and/or care and/or custody of such horse with the intent thereby
to affect the speed or condition of such horse and the result of the race
in which it participated;

"(b) that it was administered within the period prohibited [by
§ 4120.4 (d), see note 2, supra]; and

"(c) that a sufficient quantity was administered to affect the speed or
condition of such animal.

"4120.6. *Trainer's responsibility.* A trainer shall be responsible at all
times for the condition of all horses trained by him. No trainer shall
a horse or permit a horse in his custody to be started if he knows, or if
by the exercise of reasonable care he might have known or have cause
to believe, that the horse has received any drug, stimulant, sedative,
depressant, medicine, or other substance that could result in a positive
test. Every trainer must guard or cause to be guarded each horse
trained by him in such manner and for such period of time prior to racing
the horse so as to prevent any person not employed by or connected with

BARRY *v.* BARCHI

administered by the trainer or resulted from his negligence in failing to adequately protect against such occurrence." [6]

Barchi brought this action in the District Court under 42 U. S. C. § 1983 and 28 U. S. C. § 1343 (3) without first seeking administrative review under § 8022 of New York Unconsolidated Laws, which provides for a post-suspension hearing. Although declaring that "[p]ending such hearing and final determination thereon, the action of the commission in . . . suspending a license . . . shall remain in full force and effect." the section specifies no time within which the hearing must be held.[7] Barchi's complaint challenged the constitutionality of the trainer's responsibility rule and of the procedures under § 8022 and sought declaratory and injunctive relief. The District Court stayed Barchi's suspension and convened a three-judge District Court pursuant to 28 U. S. C. § 2281

---

the owner or trainer from administering any drug, stimulant, sedative, depressant, or other substance resulting in a positive test."

[6] *Barchi* v. *Sarafan*, No. 76 Civ. 3070 (SDNY, Dec. 23, 1976), reprinted in Appendix, at 24a; See *Barchi* v. *Sarafan*, 436 F. Supp. 775, 784 (SDNY 1977). The Assistant Attorney General of New York interpreted the presumption in this way both before the three-judge court and in oral argument before this Court:

"QUESTION: What this is is a presumption to get the matter started and that can be rebutted by other evidence.

"MR. HAMMER: Absolutely, Your Honor. This is a permissive presumption. It is a rule of evidence, nothing more."

Tr. of Oral Arg., at 7. See *id.*, at 5; *Barchi* v. *Sarafan*, No. 76 Civ. 3070 (SDNY, Tr .of Oral Arg., May 4, 1977), at 33–34 (trainer not held absolutely responsible for drugging of horse "if it is shown that the trainer was not culpable, that he, himself, could not administer the drug and he was not found to be negligent in supervising the people under him").

[7] Section 8022 provides that a licensee whose license has been suspended may within 10 days demand a hearing before the Board. However, the statute specifies no time for the hearing but only that the Board must give "prompt notice" of the time and place. Moreover, once the hearing commences, the Board "may continue such hearing from time to time for the convenience of the parties." After the conclusion of the hearing, the Board has up to 30 days to issue its final order.

BARRY *v.* BARCHI

(1970). *Barchi* v. *Sarafan*, No. 76 Civ. 3070 (SDNY, Dec. 23, 1976). Rejecting appellants' contentions that it should abstain from determining Barchi's claims until after the New York State courts had been given the opportunity authorita‑ tively to interpret § 8022, the District Court upheld the rebut‑ table trainer's responsibility presumption,[8] but held the proce‑ dural structure established under § 8022 unconstitutional on grounds of both procedural due process and denial of equal protection.[9]

II

We first address appellants' argument that the District Court should have abstained from determining appellee's con‑ stitutional claims because state court resolution of allegedly uncertain issues of state law might have avoided or materially altered the Federal Constitution questions. See, *e. g., Railroad Commission* v. *Pullman Co.*, 312 U. S. 496 (1941); *Carey* v. *Sugar*, 425 U. S. 73 (1976); *Harman* v. *Forssenius*, 380 U. S. 528, 534 (1965); *Lake Carriers' Assn.* v. *MacMullan*, 406 U. S. 498 (1972). Appellants contend that the New York courts

---

[8] Lower court decisions conflict on the question whether an irrebuttable presumption of trainer responsibility is constitutional. Compare *Brennan* v. *Illinois Racing Board*, 42 Ill. 2d 352, — N. E. 2d — (1969) (irrebut‑ table presumption unconstitutional), with *Hubel* v. *West Va. Racing Comm.*, 513 F. 2d 240 (CA4 1975) (irrebuttable presumption constitu‑ tional). See generally Note, Brennan v. Ilinois Racing Board: The Validity of Statutes Making a Horse Trainer the Absolute Insurer for the Condition of his Horse, 74 Dick. L. Rev. 303 (1970). We need not address the District Court's holding in this case that the rebuttable presumption is constitutional; appellee did not cross-appeal, and he is not to be heard upon the challenge to that holding made in his brief, since agreement with that challenge would result in greater relief than was awarded him by the District Court. See *Federal Energy Administration* v. *Algonquin SNG, Inc.*, 426 U. S. 548, 560 n. 11 (1976); *United States* v. *Raines*, 362 U. S. 17, 27 n. 7 (1960).

[9] Appellee's equal protection claim was based on the differences between § 8022, applicable to harness racing, and § 7915, applicable to thoroughbred racing. In light of our decision, we need not address this claim.

BARRY *v.* BARCHI

might have construed the New York racing laws to give the Board discretion to stay suspensions pending the decision of the post-suspension hearing provided by § 8022.

The District Court properly refused to abstain in this case. Abstention is appropriately denied when the state law is clear. See *California New Motor Vehicle Board* v. *Orrin W. Fox Co.*, — U. S. — (1978); *Wisconsin* v. *Constantineau*, 400 U. S. 433, 437–439 (1971). We agree with the District Court that there is no ambiguity in the challenged statute; it is "not fairly susceptible of a reading that would avoid the necessity of constitutional adjudication." *Kusper* v. *Pontikes*, 414 U. S. 51, 55 (1973). The clear import of the statute's wording that "[p]ending such hearing and final determination thereon, the action of the commission in . . . suspending a license shall remain in full force and effect," is that summary suspension without prior hearing is authorized.[10] Moreover, even the construction of state law urged by appellants at most gives the Board "discretion" to grant stays, and appellants have failed to identify any standards for the exercise of that discretion.[11] The existence of such unfettered discretion, without even the requirement of a hearing in which its exercise may be urged, would not avoid or substantially

---

[10] Appellants suggest that the clear statutory language notwithstanding, the Board's practice is to exercise discretion to stay suspensions pending the outcome of hearings. Given the clarity of the statute, even a conclusively established administrative practice contrary to the express legislative mandate might not justify abstention. In any event, the alleged administrative practice is by no means conclusively established. Appellants rely on an affidavit of the Board's Supervising Steward, but the affidavit fails to cite a single instance in which a stay has been granted. Affidavit of John M. Dailey, Aug. 26, 1976, Appendix, at 32a. Affidavits by counsel for appellee vigorously contest the availability of such stays. Supplemental Affidavit of Joseph Feraldo, July 19, 1976, Appendix, at 30a, Affidavit of Joseph Feraldo, September 3, 1976, Appendix, at 36a.

[11] See Tr. of Oral Arg., at 20–21.

BARRY *v.* BARCHI

modify the question whether the state scheme satisfies procedural due process.[12]

Appellants further contend that Barchi should have exhausted the procedure outlined under § 8022. But there is no requirement that a plaintiff exhaust inadequate remedies, and thus no requirement of exhaustion where, as here, a plaintiff challenges the constitutionality of the procedures he has failed to exhaust. In such cases, "the question of the adequacy of the administrative remedy, an issue which under federal law the District Court [is] required to decide, [is] for all practical purposes identical to the merits of appellees' lawsuit." *Gibson* v. *Berryhill,* 411 U. S. 564, 575 (1973).

III

Turning to the merits, we agree with the District Court that the procedures established by § 8022, as applied to permit

---

[12] After the District Court rendered its decision, the Appellate Division of the New York Supreme Court annulled a Board order summarily suspending a veterinarian's license to practice medicine at racetracks because the Board had not made "any finding that the public health, safety, or welfare imperatively required such emergency action as a suspension prior to a hearing." *Gerard* v. *Barry,* 59 App. Div. 2d 901 (1977). The court relied on § 401 (3) of the State Administrative Procedure Act, which provides as follows:

"If the agency finds that public health, safety, or welfare imperatively requires emergency action, and incorporates a finding to that effect in its order, summary suspension of a license may be ordered, effective on the date specified in such order or upon service of a certified copy of such order on the licensee, whichever shall be later, pending proceedings for revocation or other action. These proceedings shall be promptly instituted and determined."

Since § 401 (3) did not become effective until September 1, 1976—two months after appellee was suspended—that section can have no bearing on our decision of this case. We therefore have no occasion to consider whether the constitutional issue presented would be avoided or substantially modified if the New York Courts were to interpret § 401 (3) as altering the procedures governing the suspension after September 1, 1976, of harness racing trainers' licenses.

BARRY v. BARCHI

summary suspension without prior hearing of trainers of harness race horses for violation of the trainer's responsibility rule, fail to satisfy the requirements of procedural due process.

There is no doubt that appellee's trainer's license clothes him with a constitutionally protected interest of which he cannot be deprived without procedural due process. What was said of automobile drivers' licenses in *Bell* v. *Burson*, 402 U. S. 535, 539 (1971), is even more true of occupational licenses such as Barchi's:

> "Once licenses are issued. . . . their continued possession may become essential in the pursuit of a livelihood. Suspension of issued licenses . . . involves state action that adjudicates important interests of the licensees. In such cases the licenses are not to be taken away without that procedural due process required by the Fourteenth Amendment."

See *Dixon* v. *Love*, 431 U. S. 105, 112 (1977); *Gibson* v. *Berryhill*, 411 U. S. 565 (1973); cf. *New Motor Vehicle Bd.* v. *Orrin W. Fox Co., supra*, 43– U. S., at ——.

Appellants seek to avoid these cases by characterizing appellee's license as a "privilege" and arguing that one who has accepted the benefits of a license is precluded from challenging the conditions attached to it, including the procedures for suspension and revocation. This contention is without merit. *Board of Regents* v. *Roth*, 408 U. S. 564, 571 (1972), emphasized that "[t]he Court has fully and finally rejected the wooden distinction between 'rights' and 'privileges' that once seemed to govern the applicability of due process rights." Having once determined that the interest at stake is protected by the Due Process Clause, we have occasion only to inquire what process is due. See *Dixon* v. *Love, supra*, 431 U. S., at 112; *Matthews* v. *Eldridge*, 424 U. S. 319, 332–333 (1976).

We turn then to the question whether the process due Barchi required a hearing prior to his suspension. Although

BARRY *v.* BARCHI

the Constitution does not require that a hearing must always
be a prior hearing. *Armstrong* v. *Manzo*, 380 U. S. 545. 552
is 'the opportunity to be heard'. . . at a meaningful time and in
a meaningful manner," quoting *Grannis* v. *Ordean*, 234 U. S.
385. 394 (1914). See *Mullane* v. *Central Hanover Trust Co.*,
339 U. S. 306. 313–314 (1950). The Court has thus found it
necessary. despite statutory authorization of a summary procedure. to inquire into the asserted justifications for such a
procedure in each case—a balancing process weighing the
competing interests involved. *Goldberg* v. *Kelly*, 397 U. S.
254. 263–266 (1970); see *Cafeteria Workers* v. *McElroy*, 367
U. S. 886. 895 (1961). See generally J. Freedman. Crisis and
Legitimacy 211–232 (1978). *Bell* v. *Burson, supra*, 402 U. S..
at 542. our prior case most analogous to this one. asserted as
"fundamental" that "except in emergency situations . . . due
process requires that when a State seeks to terminate an interest such as that here involved. it must afford 'notice and
opportunity for hearing appropriate to the nature of the case'
before the termination becomes effective." Subsequent cases
have elaborated on the factors to be evaluated in this balancing
process. see. *e. g., Matthews* v. *Eldridge, supra*, 424 U. S.. at
335. and have emphasized the flexibility of the notion of a
"hearing appropriate to the nature of the case." see. *e. g., Goss*
v. *Lopez*, 419 U. S. 565 (1975). These refinements did not
purport to change the basic interest-balancing analysis. however. and lead us in this case to the same result we reached in
Bell.

Matthews v. *Eldridge, supra*, 424 U. S.. at 335. articulated
the factors to be evaluated and balanced against one another
in determining whether a summary procedure can be justified:

> "First. the private interest that will be affected by the
> official action; second. the risk of an erroneous depriva-
> tion of such interest through the procedures used. and
> the probable value, if any, of additional or substitute pro-
> cedural safeguards; and finally, the Government's inter-

BARRY *v*. BARCHI

est, including the function involved and the fiscal and administrative burdens that the additional or substitute procedural requirement would entail."

First, then, we consider the nature of Barchi's interest.

The District Court found that, in harness racing, even a temporary suspension can irreparably damage a trainer's livelihood. Not only does a trainer lose the income from races during the suspension, but, even more harmful, he is likely to lose the clients he has collected over the span of his career.[13] Thus, the harm to Barchi from a summary suspension can be devastating.

Evaluation of the second factor—the risk of erroneous suspensions under present procedures and the tendency of a presuspension hearing to reduce those risks—must be made in terms of the grounds for suspension. Under the Board's rules applied in this case, the threshold issue is whether a urine test has revealed traces of a drug in the trainer's horse

---

[13] "Race horse trainers may be entrusted with the care of a number of trotters at any given time. A trainer's income is derived in large measure from the proceeds of horse races (as opposed to a salary), and, since, harness race meetings are sporadic, trainers cannot recapture the racing opportunities lost by missed meetings. Once a trainer is suspended, even for a brief period, an owner will immediately seek the services of another trainer so that the horse is not barred from racing. This change is often permanent in order to avoid further disruption in the care of the animal. Significantly, plaintiff has proffered the affidavit of a third-party trainer/driver who experienced just such a loss during a suspension for a similar drug infraction. He had also suffered irreparable damage for a subsequent *ex parte* suspension that was later reversed. Racing opportunities lost because of a suspension cannot be recovered by a later reversal in an review hearing for obvious reasons. Furthermore, defendants do not dispute the fact that a loss of horses in a trainer's stable occasioned during his suspension can often be an irremediable injury, even though such suspension is erroneous and without justification." *Barchi* v. *Sarafan, supra,* 436 F. Supp., at 778.

See Affidavit of John Barchi, July 12, 1976, Appendix, at 23a; Affidavit of Lucien Fontaine, August 17, 1976, Appendix, at 39a.

BARRY *v.* BARCHI

within the prohibited time. Barchi contends that urine tests are often "drawn from a number of horses and the possibility of a mixup in labeling is present." He complains that in this case he was "never confronted with the urine specimen, nor the circumstances under which it was taken." [14] At least one case supports Barchi's claim of laxity in the Board's approach to evidence of this critical finding. *Strain* v. *Sarafan*, 57 App. Div. 2d 525 (1977). Thus the risks of an erroneous deprivation are substantial under the Board's procedures that give the trainer no opportunity to challenge the finding of drugs, or in any event to assert his innocence of knowledge of the drugging and his exercise of due care to prevent drugging. [15]

Appellants do not deny that even temporary suspensions of a trainer's license are likely to cause the trainer irreparable harm. Nor do they question that the procedures appellee requests would significantly decrease the chances of erroneous suspensions without imposing any significant additional administrative burden. Appellants' only asserted justifications are the State's interests in protecting horses from harm and in protecting the repute of racing and the State's income

---

[14] Affidavit of John Barchi, *supra*, n. 15, at 24a.

[15] A trainer without knowledge of the drugging and not negligent in guarding the horse to prevent drugging is not subject to suspension when drugs are found. See n. 6, *supra*. This case is not like *Dixon* v. *Love*, 431 U. S. 105 (1977), which involved the application of a valid rule mandating the revocation of a driver's license if the license had been suspended three times within a 10-year period. As the Court pointed out:

"Under the Secretary's regulations, suspension and revocation decisions are largely automatic. Of course, there is the possibility of clerical error, but written objection will bring a matter of that kind to the Secretary's attention. In this case appellee had the opportunity for a full judicial hearing in connection with each of the traffic convictions on which the Secretary's decision was based. Appellee has not challenged the validity of those convictions or the adequacy of his procedural rights at the time they were determined. . . . We conclude that requiring additional procedures would be unlikely to have significant value in reducing the number of erroneous deprivations." *Id.*, at 113–114.

BARRY *v.* BARCHI

derived from racing.[16]   The asserted importance of these
interests is plainly depreciated, however, by the Board's practice of not suspending trainers innocent of detected druggings
and by the claimed practice of staying suspensions where
appropriate.[17]   Moreover, in this case 16 days elapsed
between the positive urine test and the suspension order.
These practices are hardly consistent with appellants' claim
that summary suspensions are necessary to serve important
state interests whenever a drug test is positive.   In any event,
the State's interest would have to be extremely significant to
justify summary procedures in light of appellants' concession
that Barchi is likely to suffer substantial and irreparable
harm.[18]

---

[16] Cf. *Hubel* v. *West Virginia Racing Comm..* 513 F. 2d 240 (1975),
which described West Virginia's interests as follows:

"The state has at least two substantial interests to be served.   It has
a humanitarian interest in protecting the health of the horse, and it has
a broader and more weighty interest in protecting the purity of the sport,
both from the standpoint of protecting its own substantial revenues
derived from taxes on legalized pari-mutuel betting and protecting patrons
of the sport from being defrauded. . . .   If a horse is fleeter or slower than
his normal speed because of having been drugged, the integrity of the
race is irretrievably lost.   Of course, if stimulated, his artificial position at
the finish may be corrected and he may be deprived of any purse that he
apparently won.   But the interests of bettors cannot be protected.   Win-
ning tickets must be paid promptly at the end of the race before the dis-
qualification of the horse, except for the most obvious reasons, can be
accomplished."

[17] See Tr. of Oral Arg., at 10–12; Tr. of May 4 Hearing, *supra*, n. 3, at
27–30; Affidavit of John M. Dailey, Aug. 26, 1976, Appendix, at 34a.

[18] Our decision in *Bell* v. *Burson*, 408 U. S. 535 (1971), see *supra*,
at 9, indicates that when the private interest is as strong as the appellants concede it is in this case, summary procedures can be justified only
by state interests that rise to the level of an "emergency situation."
Examples of "emergency situations" in which the government's interest
has been held to justify summary procedures include regulations in time
of war, *Stoehr* v. *Wallace*, 255 U. S. 239 (1921); *Bowles* v. *Willingham*,
321 U. S. 503 (1944); regulations affecting the collection of taxes, *Phillips*

BARRY *v.* BARCHI

The evaluation of the three factors required by *Matthews* v. *Eldridge* therefore leads us to agree with the District Court that "on balance . . . the absence of a pre-suspension hearing . . . denies [Barchi] the meaningful review due process requires." 436 F. Supp., at 782. In light of the State's interest in "taking a . . . licensee who has probable misconducted himself . . . off the track," Tr. of Oral Arg., at 18, and since "the [full post-suspension hearing available under the statute] will provide [a licensee] with a full administrative review," *Goldberg* v. *Kelly,* 397 U. S. 254, 266–267 (1970), procedural due prouess would be satisfied at a presuspension hearing by a finding of probable cause to believe that the Board's rules were violated by the trainer. See *Bell* v. *Burson,* *supra,* 402 U. S., at 540,

Affirmed.

---

v. *Commissioner,* 283 U. S. 589 (1931), and regulations to protect the public health against foods and drugs unwholesome and unfit for use, *North American Cold Storage* v. *Chicago,* 211 U. S. 306 (1908); *Ewing* v. *Mytinger & Casselberry,* 339 U. S. 594 (1950). The state interests in this case clearly fall short of the significant interests necessary to justify summary deprivation of the substantial private interests involved here.

BARRY *v.* BARCHI, No. 77–803

MEMORANDUM TO THE CONFERENCE:*

The core issue on this appeal is whether the New York statute violates due process guarantees by authorizing summary suspension of a racehorse trainer when tests showed a horse in his care had been drugged. The three-judge District Court declared the state statute authorizing summary suspension unconstitutional on its face and permanently enjoined the Board from enforcing it.

The Court affirms that judgment today. With all deference it seems to me the Court misreads the relevant state law and misapplies the governing federal law. That holding will have drastic consequences on the ability of state and local governments to deal with a wide range of immediate dangers which they can cope with only by summary procedures.

1

Paradoxically, the Court holds the statute unconstitutional on its face but deals with it in traditional terms of unconstitutionality *as applied.* See *ante,* at 10–13. Moreover, the Court's opinion ignores relevant state law bearing on the facial constitutionality of § 8022 on the ground that statutory provisions enacted after Barchi's suspension have no bearing in this case. *Ante,* at 7, n. 12. The Court plainly frames its holding in "as applied" language. See *ante,* at 7–8, 13.

But the District Court did not hold § 8022 unconstitutional only as applied to Barchi. He attacked the constitutionality of that statute on its face, claiming it failed to protect his "right to opportunity for hearing prior to the imposition of administrative punishment."—[Amended Complaint ¶ 15.] In holding that § 8022 violated the Due Process Clause because that statute "permits the State" to suspend a racing trainer's license "without a pre-suspension or prompt, post-suspension hearing," the

---

* Original in typescript. Notes at end in original.

District Court necessarily held the statute unconstitutional on its face. It inescapably rested on the absence of a pre-suspension hearing *requirement* in the statute, since there is nothing on the face of § 8022 to preclude the State Racing Board from giving a licensee a prompt, post-suspension hearing if requested and habitually does so. Moreover, only a ruling that the statute was unconstitutional on its face would support the sweeping order issued by the District Court, permanently enjoining the Board members from enforcing the summary-suspension procedures authorized by § 8022 against any licensee under any circumstances.[1]

Given the sweep of the District Court's judgment, the Court's emphasis on the particular facts of this case is puzzling at least. The facial constitutionality of § 8022, *i. e.*, what process is due, must be discerned by focus on interests affected by the procedures used; hence, it is the *generality* of cases, not the rare or exceptional cases, that control. See *Matthews* v. *Eldridge*, 424 U.S. 319, 344 (1976). To the extent the Court's opinion in this case is intended to do no more than declare § 8022 unconstitutional *as applied to Barchi* in the circumstances of this case, its opinion is at war with its judgment. For, in affirming the District Court's judgment and injunction without modification, this Court's judgment strips the New York State Racing Board of its power to summarily suspend any racing trainer's license no matter what circumstances prompted the suspension. In so doing the Court leaves no room for resort to the summary-suspension procedures of § 8022 in even the most acute "emergency" situations.

2

We are told by the Court that the constitutional question presented here must be decided solely by reference

---

[1] The District Court order adjudges § 8022 unconstitutional on its face and unconditionally decrees that the "defendants be and they are hereby enjoined from enforcing such statute." [App. to Juris. Statement 2a.]

to the provisions of § 8022 under which Barchi was suspended. The Court acknowledges the exisence of Section 401 (3) of the New York State Administrative Procedure Act, which would substantially alter the constitutional question presented. Yet it cavalierly dismisses that provision as without "bearing" on this case because it was enacted after the suspension. *Ante,* at 7, n. 12. But, like the Court's emphasis on the particular facts of this case, its focus solely on the state law applicable at the time of Barchi's suspension is error.

When confronted with a constitutional holding of the facial invalidity of a state statute, as we are here, we are bound under *Fusari* v. *Steinberg*, 419 U. S. 379, 389 (1975), to review the District Court's judgment in light of the state law as it stands *at the time of our decision,* not the law as it was at the time of the District Court's judgment. Accord, *Thorpe* v. *Housing Authority*, 393 U. S. 268, 281–82 (1969).

The question then arises whether the provisions of N.Y. State Administrative Procedure Act § 401 (3) have modified or limited the impact of the unconditional summary-suspension power granted the State Racing Board in § 8022. The Court suggests the question is an open one as a matter of state law. See *ante,* at 7, n. 12. *It is not open.* The Appellate Division of the Supreme Court of New York has already resolved that question in *Gerard* v. *Barry*, 59 App. Div. 2d 901 (2d Dept. 1977), *appeal dismissed,* 44 N.Y. 2d 729 (1978). There, the State Racing Board had summarily suspended the license of a veterinarian who attended thoroughbred racehorses at various tracks within the State. The Board's suspension of the veterinarian without a prior hearing pursuant to N.Y. Unconsolidated Laws § 7915, however, was annulled by a state trial court. On appeal, the Appellate Division affirmed because the Board had not complied with the provisions of Section 401 (3) of the State Administrative Procedure Act. There being "no indication in the record that the [Board had] made any finding that the public health, safety or welfare imperatively required such emergency action as a suspension prior to a hearing," the court held that the petition annulling the Board's suspension order had properly issued. 50 App. Div. 2d at 901–02.

Although *Gerard* involved the applicability of Section 401 (3) of the State Administrative Procedure Act to summary suspension of thoroughbred racing licensees pursuant to § 7915, there can be little question that *Gerard* controls as to § 8022. Indeed, that is what Barchi argued in this Court. [Tr. of Oral Arg. 33–34, 39–40.] And, as the District Court itself observed, the procedure for suspension of thoroughbred racing licensees embodied in § 7915 is "substantially identical" to the suspension procedure set out in § 8022. *Barchi* v. *Sarafan*, 436 F. Supp. 775, 782 (S.D.N.Y. 1977). Necessarily, then, *Gerard* means the State Racing Board may not resort to the summary-suspension procedures authorized by §§ 7915 and 8022 without complying with the mandate of Section 401 (3) of the State Administrative Procedure Act.

Only one state appellate court has passed on this question; hence, this declaration of state law is binding on this Court unless persuasive evidence appears that New York's highest court would hold otherwise.[2] *Commissioner* v. *Estate of Basch*, 387 U. S. 456, 465 (1967); *Fidelity Trust Co.* v. *Field*, 311 U. S. 169, 177–78 (1940).

Section 401 (3) (which was enacted *after* Barchi's suspension but *before* the District Court judgment) provides:

> "If the agency finds that public health, safety, or welfare imperatively requires emergency action, and incorporates a finding to that effect in its order, summary suspension of a license may be ordered, . . .

---

[2] There is no evidence that the highest court of the State would decide otherwise. Indeed, Barchi's counsel argues that the New York Court of Appeals' dismissal of the Board's appeal from the Appellate Division's judgment in *Gerard* amounts to placing an "official imprimatur" on the decision below. [Tr. of Oral Arg. 34.]

pending proceedings for revocation or other action. These proceedings shall be promptly instituted and determined."

As is apparent from the face of this statute, and by extrapolation from the holding in *Gerard,* § 401 (3) effectively precludes any summary suspension of a harness racing licensee under § 8022 except in "emergency" situations. But summary suspension is authorized when such action is expressly found to be "imperatively require[d]" to maintain the public health, safety, or welfare. Moreover, § 401 (3) mandates that the post-suspension hearing proceedings made available in § 8022 be "promptly instituted and determined." On this record it is beyond doubt Barchi could have had his claims "promptly . . . determined" had he but asked.

Accordingly, if we determine the facial constitutionality of § 8022, as limited and modified by the mandate of Section 401 (3) of the State Administrative Procedure Act, as we must, there can be no doubt that the New York statutory scheme is constitutional; even Barchi's counsel seemed to agree to that. [See Tr. of Oral Arg. 40–41.]

3

Even if we were to ignore the bearing § 401 (3) has on this case, as the Court chooses to do, affirmance of the District Court's judgment holding § 8022 unconstitutional on its face still would be unwarranted. In affirming that judgment, the Court today starts from the premise that, except in emergency situations, the Due Process Clause *invariably* requires that an opportunity for hearing precede any adverse administrative action. *Ante,* at 9–10, quoting *Bell* v. *Burson,* 402 U. S. 535, 542 (1971). The Court then purports to apply evenhandedly the balancing test announced in *Matthews* v. *Eldridge,* 424 U. S. 319, 335 (1976) Relying on the particular facts of this case, it concludes that Barchi was entitled to an adversary evidentiary hearing prior to any suspension; it is unconvinced of the need for any "emergency" action in the circumstances of this case. *Ante,* at 10–13, & n. 19. Of course if we accept the Court's dubious predicate as to absence of any need for summary suspension, it is not surprising the Court affirms the District Court's judgment without modification.

We need to examine carefully the erroneous premise from which the Court proceeds and the uniqueness of its "balancing" of the relative interests of the licensee and the State. But we must first to ask whether the Court may appropriately reach the merits on the record before us.

a

Although I concur in the Court's conclusion that under our holdings Barchi was not bound to exhaust his state administrative remedy *as a jurisdictional prerequisite* to bringing this action in federal court,[3] I do so only because he has alleged in his complaint that the post-suspension administrative remedy open to him was untimely and inadequate as a matter of law. [Amended Complaint ¶ 15.] Accordingly, the question of the timeliness and adequacy of the state administrative remedy open to Barchi was "for all practical purposes identical to the merits of [his] lawsuit," *Gibson* v. *Berryhill,* 411 U. S. 564, 575 (1973), for the timeliness and adequacy of the post-suspension review procedures available is an integral factor in assessing the constitutionality of the entire process by which Barchi was suspended. *Fusari* v. *Steinberg,* 419 U. S. 379, 387–89 (1975).

Under our holdings Barchi's bare, conclusory allega-

_____

[3] Because § 8022 unequivocally mandates that a suspension remain "in full force and effect" pending the outcome of any post-suspension hearing, I agree that *Pullman* abstention was unwarranted in the circumstances of this case. See *ante,* at 6–7. The Courts errs, however, in suggesting that abstention would have been unwarranted if the statute were "fairly susceptible" to a construction authorizing the Board to stay any suspension order pending the outcome of a post-suspension hearing. Such a construction would have entirely mooted the equal protection claim advanced by Barchi.

tion of the inadequacy of the available administrative remedy allowed him to go directly into federal court without troubling himself to seek a post-suspension hearing. But, he should not prevail on the merits of his due process claim without first *proving* the inadequacy and untimeliness of the state remedy he deliberately by-passed. He has not done so.

The problem, perhaps, lies with both Barchi and the District Court, which precipitously ruled that the post-suspension remedy afforded by § 8022 was inadequate and untimely on its face without entertaining any evidence regarding the Racing Board's post-suspension practices. This was clearly erroneous. Although the statute does not on its face mandate that the Board hold an immediate post-suspension hearing, there was nothing to prevent Barchi from asking for such a hearing and nothing to preclude the Board from granting him one and reaching a prompt decision, and we have the State's affirmative representation that a prompt hearing was available. Until it is shown that prompt, post-suspension review *is unavailable,* the statute cannot be deemed unconstitutional on its *face.* Surely the Court cannot be of the view that the availability of post-suspension review—no matter how timely—is wholly irrelevant to the due process claim urged here.

If I am correct in the view that the District Court clearly erred in holding the post-suspension remedy available under § 8022 untimely and inadequate on its face as a matter of law, the record support for such a finding assumes critical importance. I see no such record supports.

To be sure, Barchi *alleged* the untimeliness of the Board's post-suspension review process and supported his claim with two affidavits, which simply parrot the conclusory allegations of his complaint regarding the untimeliness of the Board's post-suspension review process. Those conclusory affidavits provide no evidentiary support for the District Court's cryptic reference to the "time the state is currently taking in such matters." *Barchi* v. *Sarafan,* 436 F. Supp. 775, 781 (S.D.N.Y.

1977). If the court intended this as a finding of fact upon which it premised its conclusion of law that the Board's post-suspension review process was inadequate and untimely, it falls far short of what is demanded. Review of the record suggests that the District Court's failure to specify the undue time the Board is taking in "such matters" is not merely the product of an oversight, but rather reflects the lack of any record *evidence* as to the timeliness of the Board's post-suspension decisionmaking processes.

The record does show, however, that the Board controverted Barchi's allegations concerning the untimeliness the § 8022's post-suspension remedy in its pleadings. [Answer to Amended Complaint ¶ 1.] The Board submitted an affidavit of its counsel asserting that "a prompt hearing is always offered" a licensee when no stay of the suspension order is granted. [App. at 34a.] Moreover, at oral argument before the District Court—and in this Court—the Board's counsel represented that Board policy was to offer licensees subject to brief suspension orders a hearing *and* determination within *24 to 48 hours* of any request. And, the Board offered to prove its representation with evidence if necessary. [Hearing Tr. of May 4, 1977 at 29–30, 36.]

The District Court's failure to hear evidence on the timeliness of the Board's post-suspension practices, standing alone, is reversible error. On this record it could not be *assumed* that Barchi would have been denied a prompt, post-suspension hearing had he asked for one. Barchi's conclusory allegations regarding the untimeliness of the Board's post-suspension administrative remedy fall far short of proof. Here those allegations were specifically controverted, and the District Court had a duty to resolve the factual dispute once it was raised by the pleadings. Its failure to do so in itself commands reversal. There is no way that we can properly assess the constitutionality of the process by which Barchi was suspended without a clear picture of the consequences that would flow from requiring him to await a post-suspension hearing.

As we observed recently in *Fusari* v. *Steinberg, supra,* at 387–89, the requirements of due process can vary with the nature of the private interests affected by the timeliness of post-deprivation proceedings. The possible length of any potentially wrongful deprivation of private property interests is an important factor in assessing the constitutionality of the entire process. Indeed, this was thought so important in *Fusari* that we vacated the District Court's judgment and remanded the case for reconsideration in light of intervening changes in the applicable state law bearing on the adequacy and timeliness of the post-deprivation review process. If I had any doubt about the applicability of Section 401 (3) of the State Administrative Procedure Act in the circumstances of this case, which I do not, a remand would make sense— even though not necessary.

b

The District Court's failure to resolve the issues raised by the pleadings relates not only to the question of the adequacy and timeliness of the Board's post-suspension administrative remedy, but also on other questions of fact relevant to the constitutionality of § 8022, either on it face or as applied to Barchi in the circumstances of this case. For example, in affirming the District Court's judgment, the Court makes much of the "irreparable" and "substantial" injury Barchi would have suffered because of the unavailability of prompt, post-suspension review. But neither this Court nor the District Court can tell to what degree he would have been injured by being required to seek and await the outcome of a post-suspension hearing. It does not even allude to the risk of Barchi's drugging a few more horses in the interim.

We recognize, as the Board's counsel has conceded, that any injury Barchi would have suffered, had his suspension been permitted to take effect, would have been "irreparable" in the sense that the State could not restore the races held while Barchi awaited the outcome of a hearing. But, the mere fact that Barchi or any other suspended licensee might suffer "irreparable injury" by missing out on some races in no sense compels the conclusion that he is *constitutionally* entitled to a pre-suspension hearing. *See, e. g., Dixon* v. *Love,* 431 U. S. 105, 113 (1977); *Bob Jones University* v. *Simon,* 416 U. S. 725, 746–48 (1974). And, however "irreparable" Barchi's potential injury, we can only speculate as to its degree. On this record this Court simply cannot know— anymore than the District Court knew—that Barchi would have suffered "substantial" injury. *Ante,* at 13. The Board correctly argues there is no way of telling the degree to which Barchi would have been injured. [Tr. of Oral Arg. 21–22.] And, that is, of course, the case.

Indeed, both this Court and the District Court can do no more than guess as to how much Barchi would have been injured had no post-suspension review been available. There is, for example, no evidence as to how many horses under Barchi's care—if any—were scheduled to compete during the 15 days for which he was suspended; nor any evidence of record that *any,* let alone many, of the owners whose horses were entrusted to Barchi's care had threatened to switch trainers on even a *temporary,* let alone permanent, basis as a consequence of his suspension. There is, thus, no warrant in the record for the District Court's sweeping conclusion that Barchi's "right to a livelihood" was at stake in this proceeding; nor any basis for the District Court's supositions on which this Court bases its assertion that a trainer suspended for as brief a period as 15 days "is *likely* to lose the clients he has collected over the span of his career." *Ante,* at 10 & n. 14 (emphasis added).[4]

---

[4] The only matter of record providing any support whatsoever for the District Court's suppositions on which this Court bases its assertion is the affidavit of another trainer, one Lucien Fontaine. That affidavit provides no real support at all, for Fontaine was suspended for 90 days, not 15; in Pennsylvania, not New York; and

The Court's holding, thus, rests on suppositions about what *might* have happened, not on any evidence as to what injury Barchi *actually* faced. Given the state of the record before us, there was no justification for reaching the merits of this case. Any decision reached here that is not based solely on the language of § 8022 itself amounts to constitutional adjudication on the basis of sheer speculation.

c

Apart from the problems generated by the want of evidence in the record before us, it seems to me the Court also errs in its analysis of the merits. It arrives at an erroneous conclusion with regard to the constitutionality of § 8022 because it starts from the erroneous premise that an opportunity for a pre-suspension hearing is a constitutional predicate for the suspension of a state licensee absent an emergency situation.

The Court's reliance on *Bell* v. *Burson,* 402 U. S. 535, 542 (1971), is curious. Since *Bell,* this Court has unequivocally declared that "the ordinary principle established by our decisions [is] that *something less* than an evidentiary hearing is sufficient prior to adverse administrative action." *Dixon* v. *Love,* 431 U. S. 105, 133 (1977) (emphasis added). Indeed, that general rule was set forth in *Matthews* v. *Eldridge,* 424 U. S. 319 (1976), which supplies the balancing test the Court purports to apply in this case. In *Matthews,* we canvassed prior holdings, including *Bell,* and observed that the requirement of a full evidentiary hearing prior to adverse administrative action is the exception, not the rule. *Id.,* at 333–34, 343. Today the Court turns prior decisions on their respective heads by following as the *rule,* what is properly only an *exception.*

---

there is nothing to indicate whether Fontaine had the same opportunity for prompt, post-suspension review that Barchi may well have been given if he had but asked for it. In sum, the consequences of Fontaine's summary suspension are not remotely relevant here.

The general rule that a prior hearing is not a constitutional predicate to any adverse administrative action is not of recent origin. Long ago, in *Phillips* v. *Commissioner*, 283 U. S. 589 (1931), the Court declared:

> "Where *only property rights* are involved, mere postponement of the judicial inquiry *is not a denial* of due process, if the opportunity given for ultimate judicial determination of the liability is adequate. . . . Delay in the adjudication of property rights is not uncommon where it is essential that governmental needs be immediately satisfied." *Id.*, at 596–97 (emphasis added).

The *Phillips* rule authorizing summary deprivation of a property interest prior to any determination of liability did not rest on any "emergency" conditions, at least not in the time/essence sense. The national government, after all, would not have ground to a standstill had it been required to await a judicial determination of Phillips' tax liability prior to seizure of his assets. Yet, long before *Phillips*, this Court had recognized that "prompt payment of taxes is always important to the public welfare." *Springer* v. *United States*, 102 U. S. 586, 594 (1880). Surely a temporary blocking of Barchi's license on a showing that a horse in his charge was drugged is as much a matter of public interest as prompt payment of taxes.

In *Ewing* v. *Mytinger & Casselberry*, 339 U. S. 594 (1950), for another example, the Court upheld the Food and Drug Administration's authority to seize misbranded drugs by summary administrative action against a due process attack. No hearing prior to such action was deemed necessary for, to protect an important public interest, "[i]t is sufficient, *where only property rights* are concerned, that there is at some stage an opportunity for hearing and a judicial determination." *Id.*, at 599 (emphasis added). Interestingly, *Ewing* involved no claim that immediate seizure of the mislabelled drugs was essential to protect the public health and safety as such; the Government conceded that the drugs contained no ingredients that were dangerous or harmful to health. *Id.,* at 596. The sole basis for the summary action was the need to protect the public from misleading claims made in marketing the drugs while a determination of the alleged violations of the Food and Drug Act was being made. So it must be with a closely regulated activity.

More recently, in *Mitchell* v. *W. T. Grant,* 416 U. S. 600, 611–20 (1974), we reaffirmed the holding of *Phillips* that postponement of an evidentiary hearing to determine liability is not a denial of due process when only property rights have been adversely affected by preliminary governmental action. This, we said, was the "usual" rule that had served to decide recent, as well as older, cases. *Id.,* at 611.

To be sure, *Phillips* and *Ewing* are cited by the Court as involving unusual situations in which an "emergency" justified postponement of notice or hearing. *Ante,* at 13 n.19. But these cases were not decided upon any such ground and cannot be so cavalierly distinguished. Rather, they embody the general rule, acknowledged in such post-*Bell* decisions as *Love* and *Eldridge,* that an evidentiary hearing on questions of liability is not ordinarily a constitutional predicate for adverse administrative action affecting an individual's property rights. That general rule should be the starting point for the Court's analysis.

d

But, whatever the premise from which the court should proceed, *Matthews* v. *Eldridge, supra,* makes clear that, in the final analysis, the constitutionality of the procedures employed by the State Racing Board must depend upon a weighing of the competing interests of the State and the citizen affected by the procedures to be employed. More precisely,

"identification of the specific dictates of due process
generally requires consideration of three distinct
factors: first, the private interest that will be affected by the official action; second, the risk of an
erroneous deprivation of such interest through the
procedures used, and the probable value, if any, of
additional or substitute procedural safeguards; and
finally, the function involved and the fiscal and administrative burdens that the additional substitute
procedural requirements would entail." *Id.*, at 335.

Although the Court correctly recognizes this as the applicable law, the Court gravely misapplies it by focusing
solely on the importance of the alleged private interests
of the racing trainer responsible for keeping his animals
drug-free—and presumptively liable if they are not—and
ignoring the legitimate governmental interests affected.
Even a brief suspension of any occupational licensee is a
serious matter, of course, and there is a risk that an
erroneously suspended licensee will, indeed, suffer harm.
But I find it puzzling that the Court ignores the "irreparable" and "substantial" harm that would be suffered
by *the public* if the State is constitutionally prohibited
from acting summarily for the protection of its legitimate interest in trying to keep a notoriously corrupt
business "reasonably honest."

We are not dealing with one of the "common occupations" of life, but with licensees engaged in activities historically subject to the State's police power. We have
long held that licensees necessarily subject to close governmental regulation because they are engaged in activities affecting the public health, safety, or welfare are
likewise subject to warrantless inspection and summary
procedures. *E. g., United States* v. *Biswell*, 419 U. S.
311 (1972) (warrantless inspection of gun dealers);
Colonnade Catering Corp. v. *United States*, 397 U. S. 72
1970) (warrantless inspection of liquor dealers); *North
American Cold Storage* v. *Chicago*, 211 U. S. 306 (1908)
(summary seizure of unwholesome food). We cannot

blind ourselves to the reality that racing presents significant potential for corrupt exploitation not unlike securities, for example. That is why such activities must be subject to strict regulation under the State's police power. Just as the need to protect the public from fraud justifies summary suspension of securities trading, *e. g.,* *SEC* v. *Sloan,* 436 U. S. 103 (1978), or summary seizure of harmless but mislabelled drugs, *e. g., Ewing* v. *Mytinger & Casselberry,* 339 U. S. 594 (1950), so also it justifies summary suspension of a racing licensee pending the outcome of a prompt, post-suspension hearing.

The essence of the matter is this: either the licensee's *claimed* interests or the State's interest in protecting the integrity of races—and the attendant betting—will be impaired no matter how the Court resolves this case. Either Barchi or the public will suffer injury if the vindication of the interests of either must await the outcome of an evidentiary hearing, for the racing will go on while the parties litigate the validity of any suspension order. The two interests, therefore, are in square conflict, and one must give way to the other; historically the public interest has been regarded as paramount.

For me, it is clear that Barchi's "[p]roperty rights must yield to governmental need." *Phillips* v. *Commissioner,* 283 U. S. 589, 595 (1931). The State's legitimate interest in protecting the integrity of horse racing meets and the public from fraud outweighs the licensee's interest in the prospect of deriving personal gain from those meets. Surely summary suspension of a licensee *prima facie* shown to be responsible for drugging a race horse entrusted to his care, followed by a prompt, post-suspension hearing as mandated by current New York law, strikes a fair procedural balance.

For these reasons, I will dissent from the Court's judgment along these lines, but, with more time, I will do so more briefly.

Regards
[signed]
WEB

As already indicated, had the Brennan draft (supra p. 382) come down as the opinion of the Court in *Barry* v. *Barchi*, it would have been a substantial step away from *Mathews* v. *Eldridge*,[15] and a return to the categorical pretermination hearing requirement laid down in *Goldberg* v. *Kelly*.[16] But that eventuality was avoided when the Brennan draft could not hold the majority that had voted for affirmance at the conference.

Soon after the conference itself, well before the Brennan draft opinion of the Court had been circulated, Chief Justice Burger sent around a note, "I will be noting a dissent in this case." When he received the Brennan draft, the Chief Justice circulated an undated *MEMORANDUM TO THE CONFERENCE*, which contains the substance of a dissenting opinion and is, as such, reprinted on p. 395.

A major part of the Burger draft dissent is devoted to technical points not dealt with in the Brennan draft—particularly, the effect of section 401(3) of the New York Administrative Procedure Act, which precludes summary suspensions except in "emergency" situations. With the statute authorizing Barchi's suspension limited by this provision, the Burger draft asserts "there can be no doubt that the New York statutory scheme is constitutional."

On the right to a presuspension hearing (i.e., the subject to which the Brennan draft was devoted), the Chief Justice disagreed with what he said was the "erroneous" Brennan "premise that, except in emergency situations, the Due Process Clause *invariably* requires that an opportunity for hearing precede any adverse administrative action." The Burger draft stressed that the availability of postsuspension review was directly relevant to the due process claim. The Chief Justice states that there was no record support for the holding below that there was no timely and adequate postsuspension remedy. Nor was there such support for the finding on the extent of Barchi's injury, "[N]either this Court nor the District Court can tell to what degree he would have been injured by being required to seek and await the outcome of a post-suspension hearing. It does not even allude to the risk of Barchi's drugging a few more horses in the interim."

On the merits, the Burger draft asserts that there is a "general rule that a prior hearing is not a constitutional predicate to any adverse administrative action." On the contrary, "the requirement of a full evidentiary hearing prior to adverse administrative action is the exception, not the rule. . . . Today the Court turns prior decisions on their respective heads by following as the *rule*, what is properly only an *exception*."

According to the Chief Justice, the "rule authorizing summary deprivation of a property interest prior to any determination of liability did not rest on any 'emergency' conditions." Hence, the "general rule" should also be the basis of decision here. This is especially true under the balancing test, which the Brennan opinion "gravely misapplies." Barchi may, indeed, suffer harm from the suspension, "But I find it puzzling that the Court ignores the 'irreparable' and 'substantial' harm that would be suffered by *the public* if the State is constitutionally prohibited from acting summarily for the protection of its legitimate interest in trying to keep a notoriously corrupt business 'reasonably honest.'" In this case, the public interest should be "regarded as paramount." The summary suspension, followed by a prompt postsuspension hearing "strikes a fair procedural balance."

"For these reasons," the Chief Justice concluded his memo, "I will dissent from the Court's judgment along these lines, but, with more time, I will do so more briefly."

The refined dissent thus promised did not materialize. Of "the Chief's earlier dissenting opinion," writes Justice Rehnquist to Justice White in a letter of April 10, 1979, ". . . he has now abandoned it." It is fortunate that this happened. The Burger draft dissent (supra p. 395) takes a rigid approach to due process that would have had baneful effects on the law of administrative procedure. The Chief Justice's approach would turn around the general requirement of a hearing before adverse administrative action except in emergency cases.[17] Despite the Burger disclaimer, a careful survey of the cases he uses to support *his* "general rule" reveals that they are emergency cases, where summary action was justified by the need to deal expeditiously with an emergency situation. To treat these emergency cases as the general rule is drastically to restrict procedural rights.

No other Justice was willing to join the Burger draft dissent. Justice Powell wrote to the Chief Justice on February 7, agreeing with the Burger view on section 401(3) of the New York Administrative Procedure Act. However, Powell also wrote, "I would hesitate to concur in the remainder of your memorandum, as some of the issues discussed are difficult ones for me, and I do not believe it necessary to reach them."

Correspondence between Justices Powell and Brennan eliminated the state Administrative Procedure Act from the case. The state APA became effective after Barchi's suspension was imposed. A February 8 note from Brennan pointed out to Powell that, by its express provision, the state APA's provisions were not retroactive. Powell replied the next day, "you are quite right that the non-retroactivity . . . disposes of the view that heretofore I have taken of this case."

The crucial role in the case was now played by Justice White who wrote to Justice Brennan on March 1. White noted that he was troubled by the Brennan approach. "Your judgment is, I take it, that at least absent opportunity for an immediate full hearing after summary suspension, the State must extend more pre-suspension procedures than it did here even if probable cause is the appropriate standard. But would you be satisfied if Barchi had had available an immediate post-suspension hearing which the District Court found he did not have? I would be satisfied. Is there no way of our getting together?"

At this point, the Brennan draft opinion of the Court (supra p. 382) had been joined by Justices Stewart, Marshall, and Stevens. But as a Brennan March 14 letter to them pointed out, "[T]here is not, and is apparently no possibility of, a fifth vote." Brennan noted, however, that, "Byron, supported by Lewis, might join an opinion that held that the due process defect lay in the absence of either a pre-suspension or a *prompt* post-suspension hearing."

A new Brennan draft was sent to Justice White to attract the latter's vote. As explained in a Brennan March 15 "Dear Byron" letter, "It abandons the holding that the absence of a pre-suspension hearing in New York's statute and rules governing suspension of harness race horse trainers denied Barchi the meaningful review due process requires (leaving that question open, p. 12 n.15) and replaces it with a holding that the due process defect lay in the absence of *either* a pre-suspension or a *prompt* post-suspension hearing and determination." After stating that Justices Stewart, Marshall, and Stevens would go along with the new draft if it received a fifth vote, the Brennan letter asked, "How does it look?"

Justice White replied on March 17 that he could not join the new draft, "I can do no more than concur in the judgment and will file the enclosed concurrence." White enclosed a concurrence that was a much shorter version of his final *Barry* v. *Barchi* opinion of the Court.

The White concurrence soon received the support of the Chief Justice (who wrote on April 9, "I am prepared to 'abdicate' and yield to you") and Justices Blackmun, Rehnquist, and Powell. On June 18, Justice White sent around a *"MEMO TO THE CONFERENCE,"* "In view of the way the votes have fallen in this case, Bill Brennan suggested to me that I circulate a draft opinion. This will at least pose the question of what we should do with this pipsqueak of a case." Justice White then circulated the draft that became his opinion of the Court.

As it turned out, *Barry* v. *Barchi* may have been Justice White's "pipsqueak of a case," for it only confirmed the trend away from *Goldberg* v. *Kelly*'s pretermination hearing requirement. The situation would have been different had Justice Brennan's draft (supra p. 382) come down as the final opinion of the Court. Had that happened, *Barry* v. *Barchi* might now be considered the leading case that reversed the post-*Goldberg* v. *Kelly* trend and restored the right to a hearing before decision as a categorical imperative of our administrative law.

Notes

1. *Bailey* v. *Richardson*, 182 F.2d 46, 58 (D.C. Cir. 1950), affirmed by equally divided Court, 341 U.S. 918 (1951).
2. *Gilchrist* v. *Bierring*, 14 N.W.2d 724, 730 (Iowa 1944).
3. The cases are summarized in Schwartz *Administrative Law* § 5.12 (2 ed. 1984).
4. Ibid.

5. 397 U.S. 254 (1970).

6. *Montgomery* v. *Wheeler*, 397 U.S. 280 (1970).

7. *Gonzalez* v. *Freeman*, 334 F.2d 570 (D.C. Cir. 1964).

8. 373 U.S. 96 (1963).

9. Note 15 of the *Goldberg* v. *Kelly* opinion.

10. Friendly, "Some Kind of Hearing," 123 *University of Pennsylvania Law Review*. 1267, 1268, 1271 (1975).

11. The one exception is alien entry, which is still treated as a privilege. *Landon* v. *Plasencia*, 459 U.S. 21 (1982).

12. 419 U.S. 565 (1975).

13. 424 U.S. 319 (1976).

14. 443 U.S. 55 (1979).

15. Supra note 13.

16. Supra note 5.

17. See Schwartz, *Administrative Law* § 5.10.

10

Gannett Co. v. DePasquale (1979): Right of Access to Criminal Proceedings

"This case would have been unnecessary," asserted Justice White in *Richmond Newspapers* v. *Virginia*,[1] now the leading case on public and press access to criminal trials, "had *Gannett Co.* v. *DePasquale*, 443 U.S. 368 (1979), construed the Sixth Amendment to forbid excluding the public from criminal proceedings except in narrowly defined circumstances. But the Court there rejected the submission of four of us to this effect, thus requiring that the First Amendment issue involved here be addressed."[2] There was more than a bit of I-told-you-so in Justice White's tone, for the first draft opinion of the Court in the *Gannett* case had done just what Justice White said that the Court failed to do in its final decision. Had that draft come down as the final *Gannett* opinion, it would have established a public and press right of access to criminal proceedings broader than that recognized in *Richmond Newspapers* itself and would, indeed, have made the decision in the second case unnecessary.

The difficult constitutional cases are not those in which the courts are asked to protect a given right against arbitrary assault, but those in which conflicting rights—each by itself deserving of judicial protection—are at issue. The courts must then balance the rights in light of the social and other values involved and define the precise course and texture of the interface between the competing rights. Just such a bumping together of conflicting rights was presented in the *Gannett* case.[3] On the one hand, criminal defendants asserted their right to a fair trial, which could require exclusion of the public and press from a pretrial hearing at which would be aired evidence and issues not permitted at the trial itself. On the other hand, a reporter claimed that the press and the public had a right of access to judicial proceedings even where the accused, the prosecutor, and the trial judge all had agreed to closure.

Gannett arose out of a murder prosecution in New York. Defendants moved to suppress certain evidence. At the pretrial hearing on the motion, defendants requested that the public and the press be excluded from the hearing, arguing that the unabated buildup of adverse publicity had jeopardized their ability to receive a fair trial. The district attorney did not oppose the motion, and it was granted by the trial judge. A newspaper challenged the closure order, but it was upheld by the highest New York court.

The claims of the press in *Gannett* rested on both the Sixth Amendment guaranty of a public trial and the First Amendment guaranty of freedom of the press. At the postargument conference on the case in early November 1979, the Chief Justice indicated that neither amendment supported a reversal. In his view, the Sixth Amendment public-trial right did not apply "because the motion to suppress [is] not part of the trial." And, as for the "First Amendment argument, there isn't any for me."

Justice Stewart, who ultimately wrote the *Gannett* opinion, also spoke for affirmance. He agreed with the Chief Justice on the First Amendment, "I don't think the First Amendment claim is valid, since the press has no greater rights than the public." On the Sixth Amendment issue, the Justice reached the same result as the Chief Justice, but he refused to follow the Burger approach, saying, "I can't agree it's not part of the trial."

Justice Stewart, nevertheless, reached the same result "because the right to a public trial is explicitly given to the accused; but there is a public interest and who but the accused can trigger that?" Stewart answered this query, "I'm inclined to hold that only the prosecutor can speak for the public where a motion for closure is made by the defendant."

Justices Rehnquist and Stevens also were in favor of affirmance. "The Sixth Amendment," said Rehnquist, "means for me only protection for the rights of the accused. . . . [T]he Framers didn't give the public a right to access." Stevens relied on what he called "a critical difference between seeing a live hearing and reading a transcript of it. If the public has a right of access to the live performance, we'll be holding that the electronic media must be allowed."

The other five Justices spoke in favor of reversal. They were led by Justice Brennan, who was for establishing a constitutional right of access for the press and the public. Justices White and Marshall took the same approach. Both agreed that the suppression hearing was part of the trial. "The public," Marshall declared, "has a right because, if the accused is done dirt, the public interest is hurt. The public is entitled to know what happens when it happens."

Of particular interest were the statements of Justice Blackmun, who wrote the first *Gannett* draft, and Justice Powell, who was ultimately the swing vote in the case. Blackmun said that he agreed that the Sixth Amendment provided for the "public character of trial. . . . I think the public directly and the press indirectly have an interest in preventing the abuse of public business. I'd take the Sixth Amendment approach." Powell, who was to change his mind on this point, agreed. As he put it, "This is Sixth [Amendment] and not First." Powell also agreed that this "suppression hearing is part of a criminal trial." In his view, "the trial judge didn't do enough when he heard the accused and the prosecutor, [who] agreed to closure." The judge should also have allowed the press to be heard.

In a May 9, 1979, letter to Justice Blackmun, Justice Powell wrote, "I do not think a majority of the Court agreed [at the *Gannett* conference] as to exactly how the competing interests in this case should be resolved." On the other hand, the tally sheet of a Justice present at the conference, which I have used, indicates that a bare majority (Justices Brennan, White, Marshall, Blackmun, and Powell) favored reversal.

The opinion was assigned to Justice Blackmun, who circulated the draft opinion of the Court reprinted on p. 418. The draft contains a broadside rejection of the decision below. In his final *Gannett* dissent, Blackmun began by stating that he could not "join" the Court's phrasing of the 'question presented.' "[4] How he saw that question was indicated by the first sentence of the Blackmun draft opinion of the Court. "This case presents the issue whether, and to what extent, the First, Sixth, and Fourteenth Amendments of the Constitution restrict a State, in a criminal prosecution, from excluding the public and the press from a pretrial suppression-of-evidence hearing, when the request to exclude is made by the defendant himself."

Justice Blackmun's draft is virtually the same as his *Gannett* dissent, with the omission of the statement of facts (which was used by Justice Stewart in the opinion of the Court ultimately issued) and those changes made to convert the draft from a majority opinion to a dissent (e.g., changing "we" in the draft opinion of the Court to "I"). The Blackmun draft reads a broad right of public and press access to all criminal proceedings into the Sixth Amendment's public trial guaranty, "The public trial guarantee . . . insures that not only judges but all participants in the criminal justice system are subjected to public scrutiny as they conduct the public's business of prosecuting crime."

Much of the draft is devoted to a lengthy summary of the historical practice in both England and this country. The Blackmun conclusion is stated at the beginning of this summary, "The importance we as a Nation attach to the public trial is reflected both in its deep roots in the English common law and in its seemingly universal recognition in this country since the earliest times."

Blackmun's crucial emphasis is on the role of open courts in protecting the public "from the abuses to which secret tribunals would be prone." The draft declares, "Open trials . . . enable the public to scrutinize the performance of police and prosecutors in the conduct of public judicial business." Where the prosecution's interest "in hiding police or prosecutorial misconduct or ineptitude may coincide with the defendant's desire to keep the proceedings private, . . . the result [is] that the public interest is sacrificed from both sides."

The conclusion logically follows of a Sixth Amendment right of access not limited to the accused's right to a public trial:

We therefore conclude that the Due Process Clause of the Fourteenth Amendment, insofar as it incorporates the public trial provision of the Sixth Amendment, prohibits the States from excluding the public from a proceeding within the ambit of the Sixth Amendment's guarantee without affording full and fair consideration to the public's interests in maintaining an open proceeding. And we believe that the Sixth and Fourteenth Amendments require this conclusion notwithstanding the fact it is the accused who seeks to close the trial.

This conclusion is as applicable to this pretrial proceeding as it is to the criminal trial itself:

> Accordingly, we hold that the Sixth and Fourteenth Amendments prohibit a State from conducting a preliminary hearing in private, even at the request of the accused, unless full and fair consideration is first given to the public's interest, protected by the Amendments, in open trials.

This does not, however, mean "that the Sixth Amendment imposes an absolute requirement that the court be open at all times." The Sixth Amendment may establish a strong presumption in favor of open proceedings, but "it does not require that all proceedings be held in open court when to do so would deprive a defendant of a fair trial." For closure to be ordered, it must be established (with specific findings to support this conclusion) "that it is strictly and inescapably necessary in order to protect the fair trial guarantee."

The Blackmun draft concludes its legal discussion by stressing that the Sixth Amendment gives the press the same general right of access to a criminal trial and a pretrial proceeding as the general public has. Blackmun refuses to accept the broader claim that the press has a First Amendment right of access. To the First Amendment argument, the Blackmun draft replies, "We do not agree." The case does not involve restraint on publication or comment, "It involves an issue of access to a judicial proceeding. To the extent the Constitution protects a right of public access to the proceeding, the standards enunciated under the Sixth Amendment suffice to protect that right. We therefore need not reach the issue of First Amendment access."

1st DRAFT   Recirculated: _____

SUPREME COURT OF THE UNITED STATES

No 77-1301

Gannett Co., Inc., Petitioner. | On Writ of Certiorari to the
v, | Court of Appeals of New
Daniel A. DePasquale. Etc., et al. | York.

[April — 1979]

Mr. Justice Blackmun delivered the opinion of the Court.

This case presents the issue whether, and to what extent, the First. Sixth. and Fourteenth Amendments [1] of the Con-

---

[1] The Court long ago held that the First Amendment's guaranty of the freedom of the press "is within the liberty safeguarded by the due process clause of the Fourteenth Amendment from invasion by state action." *Near* v. *Minnesota*, 283 U. S. 697, 707 (1931).

The Sixth Amendment reads:

In all criminal prosecutions, the accused shall enjoy the right to a speedy and public trial, by an impartial jury of the State and district wherein the crime shall have been committed, which district shall have been previously ascertained by law, and to be informed of the nature and cause of the accusation; to be confronted with the witnesses against him; to have compulsory process for obtaining witnesses in his favor, and to have the Assistance of Counsel for his defence."

Many of the elements of the Sixth Amendment have been recognized as subsumed in the Fourteenth Amendment's guaranty of due process of law and, thus, as applicable to the States, *Powell* v. *Alabama*. 287 U. S. 45 (1932). Specifically, the Court has held that the States must adhere to the Sixth Amendment's requirements with respect to trial by jury and an impartial jury in a criminal prosecution, *Duncan* v. *Louisiana*, 391 U. S. 145 (1968); *Irvin* v. *Dowd*, 366 U. S. 717 (1961), a speedy trial, *Klopfer* v. *North Carolina*, 386 U. S. 213 (1967). confrontation of witnesses, *Pointer* v. *Texas*, 380 U. S. 400 (1965); assistance of counsel, *Gideon* v. *Wainwright*, 372 U. S. 335 (1963); compulsory process, *Washington* v. *Texas*, 388 U. S. 14 (1967); and notice of the charge, *In re Oliver*, 333 U. S. 257 (1948). The last cited case also demands of the State certain minimal aspects of a "public trial.

GANNETT CO. *v.* DePASQUALE

stitution restrict a State, in a criminal prosecution, from excluding the public and the press from a pretrial suppression-of-evidence hearing, when the request to exclude is made by the defendant himself

The court order here at issue, excluding the public and the press, was entered by respondent, the Honorable Daniel A. DePasquale, judge of the County Court of Seneca County, N. Y., in connection with the prosecution of respondents Kyle Edwin Greathouse and David Ray Jones for second-degree murder and other offenses. Greathouse and Jones requested Judge DePasquale to exclude the press and public from a pretrial hearing on their motion to suppress certain evidence. The judge granted their motion and conducted the suppression hearing *in camera*

The facts leading to the issuance of the order and its ultimate affirmance on appeal are not in any real dispute. They are of importance for the resolution of the legal issues, however, and we therefore set those facts out in some detail

I

Wayne Clapp, aged 42 and residing at Henrietta, a Rochester, N. Y., suburb, disappeared in July 1976. He was last seen on July 16 when, with two male companions, he went out on his boat to fish in Lake Seneca, about 40 miles from Rochester. The two companions returned in the boat the same day and drove away in Clapp's pickup truck. Clapp was not with them. When he failed to return home by July 19, his family reported his absence to the police. An examination of the boat, laced with bulletholes, seemed to indicate that Clapp had met a violent death aboard it. Police then began an intensive search for the two men. They also began lake dragging operations in an attempt to locate Clapp's body

Petitioner Gannett Co., Inc., publishes two Rochester newspapers, the morning Democrat & Chronicle and the evening

GANNETT CO. *v.* DePASQUALE

Times-Union.[2]   On July 20, each paper carried its first story
about Clapp's disappearance. App. 32, 33. Each reported
the few details that were then known and stated that the
police were theorizing that Clapp had been shot on his boat
and his body dumped overboard. Each stated that the body
was missing. The Times-Union mentioned the names of
respondents Greathouse and Jones and said that Greathouse
"was identified as one of the two companions who accompanied Clapp Friday" on the boat; said that the two were
aged 16 and 21, respectively; and noted that the police were
seeking the two men and Greathouse's wife, also aged 16.
Accompanying the evening story was a 1959 photograph of
Clapp. The report also contained an appeal from the state
police for assistance.

Michigan police apprehended Greathouse, Jones, and the
woman on July 21. This came about when an interstate
bulletin describing Clapp's truck led to their discovery in
Jackson County, Mich., by police who observed the truck

[2] The Democrat & Chronicle and the Times-Union are published in
Rochester, N. Y. Rochester, in Monroe County, is approximately 40 miles
from the Seneca County line. The circulation of the newspapers is
primarily in Monroe County. There are some subscribers, however, in
Seneca County. In 1976, when this case arose, the Democrat & Chronicle
had a Seneca County daily circulation of 1,022, giving it a 9.6% share of
the market in that county, and a Sunday circulation of 1,532, for a 14.3%
share of the market. The Times-Union publishes only a daily edition and
had but 1 subscriber in Seneca County. American Newspaper Markets,
Inc., Circulation 77/78, pp. 522, 541. The Bureau of the Census estimated Seneca County's 1976 population at 34,000. U. S. Department of
Commerce, Bureau of the Census, Current Population Reports, Series
P-26, No 76-32, Population Estimates 3 (Aug. 1977)

Petitioner in 1976 also owned a Rochester, N. Y., television station.
And there were other newspapers in Seneca County at that time. See
Circulation 77/78, at 522. The record in this case, however, contains no
evidence concerning newspaper coverage of Clapp's disappearance and the
subsequent prosecution of respondents Greathouse and Jones other than
that which appeared in the Democrat & Chronicle and the Times-Union.

GANNETT CO. *v.* DePASQUALE

parked at a local motel. Petitioner's two Rochester papers on July 22 reported the details of the capture. App. 34–35, 36. The stories recounted how the Michigan police, after having arrested Jones in a park, used a helicopter and dogs and tracked down Greathouse and the woman in some woods. They recited that Clapp's truck was located near the park.

The stories also stated that Seneca County police theorized that Clapp was shot with his own pistol, robbed, and his body thrown into Lake Seneca. The articles provided background on Clapp's life, sketched the events surrounding his disappearance, and said that New York had issued warrants for the arrest of the three persons. One of the articles reported that the Seneca County District Attorney would seek to extradite the suspects and would attempt to carry through with a homicide prosecution even if Clapp's body were not found. The paper also quoted the prosecutor as stating, however, that the evidence was still developing and "the case could change." The other story noted that Greathouse and Jones were from Texas and South Carolina, respectively.

Both papers carried stories on July 23. App. 37–38, 40. These revealed that Jones, the adult, had waived extradition and that New York police had traveled to Michigan and were questioning the suspects. The articles referred to police speculation that extradition of Greathouse and the woman might involve "legalities" because they were only 16 and considered juveniles in Michigan. The morning story provided details of an interview with the landlady from whom the suspects had rented a room while staying in Seneca County at the time Clapp disappeared. It also noted that Greathouse, according to state police, was on probation in San Antonio, Tex., but that the police did not know the details of his criminal record

The Democrat & Chronicle carried another story on the morning of July 24. App. 39. It stated that Greathouse had led the Michigan police to the spot where he had buried a

GANNETT CO. *v.* DePASQUALE

,357 magnum revolver belonging to Clapp and that the gun was being returned to New York with the three suspects. It also stated that the police had found ammunition at the hotel where Greathouse and the woman were believed to have stayed before they were arrested. The story repeated the basic facts known about the disappearance of Clapp and the capture of the three suspects in Michigan. It stated that New York police continued to search Lake Seneca for Clapp's body.

On July 25, the Democrat & Chronicle reported that Greathouse and Jones had been arraigned before a Seneca County magistrate on second-degree murder charges shortly after their arrival from Michigan; that they and the woman also had been arraigned on charges of second-degree grand larceny; that the three had been committed to the Seneca County jail; that all three had "appeared calm" during the court session; and that the magistrate had read depositions signed by three witnesses, one of whom testified to having heard "five or six shots" from the lake on the day of the disappearance, just before seeing Clapp's boat "veer sharply" in the water. App. 41.

Greathouse, Jones, and the woman were indicted by a Seneca County grand jury on August 2. The two men were charged, in several counts, with second-degree murder, robbery, and grand larceny. The woman was indicted on one count of grand larceny. Both the Democrat & Chronicle and the Times-Union on August 3 reported the filing of the indictments. This was the first time either paper had carried any comment about the case since July 25. Each story stated that the murder charges specified that the two men had shot Clapp with his own gun, had weighted his body with anchors and tossed it into the lake, and then had made off with Clapp's credit card, gun, and truck. Each reported that the defendants were held without bail, and each again provided background material with details of Clapp's disappearance. The

GANNETT CO. *v.* DePASQUALE

fact that Clapp's body still had not been recovered was mentioned. App. 42, 43. One report noted that, according to the
prosecutor, if the body were not recovered prior to trial, "it
will be the first such trial in New York State history." *Id.,*
at 43. Each paper on that day also carried a brief notice
that a memorial service for Clapp would be held that evening
in Henrietta. *Id.,* at 44. These notices repeated that Greathouse and Jones had been charged with Clapp's murder and
that his body had not been recovered.

On August 6, each paper carried a story reporting the details
of the arraignments of Greathouse and Jones the day before. The papers stated that both men had pleaded not guilty
to all charges. Once again, each story repeated the basic facts
of the accusations against the men and noted that the woman
was arraigned on a larceny charge. The stories noted that
defense attorneys had been given 90 days in which to file
pretrial motions. *Id.,* at 45, 46.

No further story about the Clapp case appeared in petitioner's Rochester papers until after the pretrial suppression
hearing on November 4. Thus, for the 90 days preceding that
hearing, there was no publicity. From July 20, when the first
story appeared, until August 6 (when coverage ceased until
after the pretrial hearing), a period of 18 days, 14 different
articles appeared in the two papers. Because the evening
paper usually reprinted or substantially duplicated the morning story, articles appeared on only seven different days during this 18-day period, with the evening story containing little
that differed from the morning story on the five days that
accounts appeared in both papers.

There is no dispute, moreover, that the stories consisted
almost entirely of straightforward reporting of the facts surrounding the investigation of Clapp's disappearance, and of
the arrests and indictments. The stories contained no editorializing and nothing that a fair-minded person could char-
acterize as sensational journalism. Only one photograph
appeared; it was the one of Clapp that accompanied the first

GANNETT CO. *v.* DePASQUALE

story printed by the Times-Union. There is nothing in the
record to indicate that the stories were placed on the page
or within the paper so as to play up the murder investigation.
The headline accompanying each story was factual. The
stories were relatively brief. They appeared only in connection with some development in the investigation, and they
gave no indication of having been published simply to sustain
popular interest in the case.

During the 90-day period fixed by the County Court for the
filing of any pretrial motions, Greathouse and Jones moved to
suppress statements made to the police. The ground they
asserted was that those statements had been given involuntarily. They also sought to suppress physical evidence seized
as fruits of the allegedly involuntary confessions; the primary
physical evidence they sought to suppress was the gun to
which, as petitioner's newspaper had reported, Greathouse led
the Michigan police.

The motions to suppress came on before Judge DePasquale
on November 4. Despite the absence of any publicity in
petitioner's newspapers for three months, both defendants, at
the commencement of the hearing, and without previously
having indicated their intent so to do, asked for the exclusion
of all members of the public and press present in the court-

Under N. Y. Crim. Proc. Law, §§ 710.40 and 255.10 (Supp. 1974–1975)
(McKinney), a defendant was required to file in advance of trial any
motion to suppress evidence. The statutes permitted a defendant to make
such a motion for the first time during trial only when he did not have a
reasonable opportunity to do so prior to trial, or when the State failed to
provide notice before trial that it would seek to introduce a confession of
the defendant. §§ 710.30 and 710.40.2.

The hearing on the motion of defendants Greathouse and Jones to
suppress their confessions as involuntary was held before trial in accordance with the decision in *People* v. *Huntley*, 15 N. Y. 2d 72, 204 N. E. 2d
179 (1965). In *Huntley*, the New York Court of Appeals ruled that the
separate inquiry into the voluntariness of a confession, required by this
Court's decision in *Jackson* v. *Denno*, 378 U. S. 368 (1964), was to be
made in a preliminary hearing. 15 N. Y. 2d, at 78, 204 N. E. 2d, at 183.

GANNETT CO. *v.* DePASQUALE

room. They urged as ground for their motions that "we are going to take evidentiary matters into consideration here that may or may not be brought forth subsequently at a trial." App. 4. After being reminded by the court that the defendants had a constitutional right to a public trial and that such exclusion might abridge that right, Greathouse's attorney, joined by Jones' lawyer, stated: "I fully understand that, your Honor, but this is not a trial, it is a hearing, and I think the dilatorious [*sic*] effects far outweigh the constitutional rights." *Id.*, at 5. When the District Attorney stated that he would not oppose the motion, the court, without further inquiry, granted it. He noted that "it is not the trial" and that "matters may come up in the testimony of the People's witnesses that may be prejudicial to the defendant[s]." *Id.*, at 6.

Among those excluded from the courtroom was Carol Ritter, a reporter employed by petitioner to cover Seneca County. Ritter, in fact, had written some of the published accounts of the Clapp case and was in court to continue her coverage. She did not immediately object to her exclusion. On November 5, however, she wrote to Judge DePasquale and stated that, on the advice of petitioner's counsel, she believed she had a right to attend the hearing. She asked that the hearing, if it was still underway, be postponed so that petitioner's attorneys could argue the point or, if the hearing had been completed, that "we . . . be given access to the transcript." *Id.*, at 7. The judge responded by letter the same day. He stated that the hearing had been concluded and that he was reserving decision. "Under no circumstances, therefore, will a transcript be made available to you before I have rendered my decision, at which time you may renew your request for a transcript through your attorney in the form of a Motion." *Id.*, at 8.

On November 16, however, while the motions to suppress were still pending, the judge acceded to the request and heard

GANNETT CO. *v.* DePASQUALE

argument on the propriety of the closure order. He adhered, nonetheless, to his previous conclusion. He stated that he had granted the original motion to exclude the public and the press "on the theory that under the special and unusual circumstances—one of these two defendants being 16 years of age—that there was a reasonable probability of . . . prejudice to the defendants." *Id.*, at 14. He rejected petitioner's contention that no adequate factual basis for exclusion had been established, and held that it was not incumbent upon the defendants "to present a factual basis for the exclusion of the public and press," *ibid.*, and that any such requirement would be "unreasonable." *Id.*, at 17. "With the age of the defendants and everything being taken into consideration and the fact that the People were joining in, or not objecting to the motion, the Court [was justified in ruling] that there was a reasonable probability of prejudice to the defendants." *Ibid.*

The following day, petitioner instituted an original proceeding in the Supreme Court, Appellate Division, pursuant to Art. 78 of the N. Y. Civil Practice Law & Rules, § 7801 *et seq.* (McKinney), in the nature of a petition for a writ of mandamus directing Judge DePasquale to vacate his order of exclusion and to grant petitioner immediate access to the pretrial hearing.

The Appellate Division ruled, first, that the order entered by the County Court violated the Sixth Amendment's public trial guarantee. It held that that provision afforded protection to the public's independent interest in observing judicial proceedings and that the exclusion order lacked the requisite factual basis to support a finding that the defendants' rights to a fair trial were so endangered that infringement of the

---

Respondents in the original proceeding were Judge DePasquale, defendants Greathouse and Jones, and the Seneca County district attorney. All four remain respondents in this Court, although the current district attorney has been substituted for the respondent who occupied that position in 1976.

GANNETT CO. *v.* DePASQUALE

public's interest was justified. The trial court's "only factual reason," that is, "that one of the defendants is sixteen years of age," was insufficient to justify a finding of reasonable probability of prejudice. Second, and more importantly for the Appellate Division, the exclusion order offended the First Amendment's prohibition on prior restraints against publication. The denial of access to information usually available to the public was a gag order of the type condemned in *Nebraska Press Assn. v. Stuart,* 427 U. S. 539 (1976). Since the record did not reveal facts sufficient to overcome the heavy burden that is required to justify a prior restraint, the order was invalid. The Court also found that petitioner was entitled to notice and a hearing prior to the entry of any such order. Accordingly, it vacated the order of the County Court and granted petitioner immediate access to the transcript of the suppression hearing. 55 A. D. 2d 107, 389 N. Y. S. 2d 719 (1976).

The New York Court of Appeals, by a 4–2 vote, took a different view. 43 N. Y. 2d 370, 372 N. E. 2d 544 (1977). The court noted that shortly prior to the entry of judgment by the Appellate Division, Greathouse and Jones had pleaded guilty to lesser included offenses in satisfaction of the charges against them,[6] and that shortly thereafter petitioner had been granted access to the transcript. The court said: "We would ordinarily . . . dismiss the appeal . . . for mootness. But this is far from an ordinary appeal." *Id.,* at 376, 372 N. E. 2d, at 547. Because the issue was a recurring one "of concrete significance both to the courts and the news media," which presented a challenge to the power of the courts "to control their own process," and because such a dispute typically evaded review, the court "retained jurisdiction to entertain the

---

[6] Respondent Greathouse pleaded guilty to one count of manslaughter and received a 20-year indeterminate sentence. Respondent Jones pleaded guilty to one count of second-degree grand larceny and received a 5-year indeterminate sentence.

GANNETT CO. *v.* DePASQUALE

appeal" and proceeded to the merits. *Ibid.,* 372 N. E. 2d,
at 547

The court recognized that all criminal trials were presumptively open to the public and the press, but that the right to
a public trial was a right " 'the accused shall enjoy,' " and
that the attenuated interest of the public, in context of a pretrial suppression hearing, was subordinate to the trial court's
obligation to ensure "that tainted evidence never see the light
of day . . . and certainly not before trial through publication
of illegally obtained evidence by the media." *Id.,* at 376,
379, 372 N. E. 2d, at 547, 549. "At the point where press
commentary [about a pretrial hearing] would threaten the
impaneling of a constitutionally impartial jury in the county
of venue, pretrial evidentiary hearings in this State are presumptively to be closed to the public." *Id.,* at 380, 372 N. E.
2d. at 550.

The court then ruled that the presumption of closure was
raised in this case because the public knew that respondents
Greathouse and Jones "had been caught 'red-handed' by
Michigan police with fruits of the crime," and because it was
"widely known" that they "had made incriminating statements before being returned to" New York. *Id.,* at 381, 372
N. E. 2d, at 550. And the court found the level of "legitimate
public interest" necessary to overcome the presumption of
closure had not been demonstrated:

> "Widespread public awareness kindled by media satura-
> tion does not legitimize mere curiosity. Here the pub-
> lic's concern was not focused on prosecutorial or judicial
> accountability; irregularities, if any, had occurred out
> of State. The interest of the public was chiefly one of
> active curiosity with respect to a notorious local happen-
> ing. While the defendants were still in jeopardy, any
> true public interest could be fully satisfied, consonant
> with constitutional free press guarantees, by affording the
> media access to transcripts redacted to exclude matters

GANNETT CO. *v.* DePASQUALE

ruled inadmissible during the closed suppression hearing."
Ibid., 372 N. E. 2d, at 550–551.

Although it noted that this conclusion "would ordinarily
lead to a reversal," the court held that in light of the mootness
of the underlying dispute it would simply modify the judgment of the Appellate Division to the extent of dismissing the
proceeding as moot." *Ibid.* 372 N. E. 2d, at 551.

We granted certiorari to consider the important and fundamental issues involved. 435 U. S. 1006 (1978).

II

We consider, first, the suggestion of mootness, noted and
rejected by the New York Court of Appeals. 43 N. Y. 2d,
at 376, 372 N. E. 2d, at 547. We readily conclude that this
aspect of the case is governed by *Nebraska Press Assn.* v.
Stuart, 427 U. S., at 546–547, and that the controversy is not
moot. Petitioner, of course, has obtained access to the transcript of the suppression hearing. But this Court's jurisdiction is not defeated, *id.*, at 546, "simply because the order
attacked has expired, if the underlying dispute between the
parties is one 'capable of repetition, yet evading review.'
Southern Pacific Terminal Co. v. ICC, 219 U. S. 498, 515
(1911)." To meet that test, two conditions must be satisfied:
"(1) the challenged action was in its duration too short to be
fully litigated prior to its cessation or expiration, and (2) there
was a reasonable expectation that the same complaining
party would be subjected to the same action again." *Wein-
stein* v. *Bradford*, 423 U. S. 147, 149 (1975).

Those conditions have been met. The order closing a pretrial hearing is too short in its duration to permit full review.

---

⁷ The dissenters would have found the order entered by the County
Court to be of the type of prior restraint prohibited by *Nebraska Press
Assn.* v. *Stuart*. 427 U. S. 539 (1976), and would have affirmed the
Appellate Division on the ground that the evidence did not support entry
of the order. 43 N. Y. 2d, at 382, 372 N. E. 2d, at 551.

GANNETT CO. *v.* DePASQUALE

And to the extent the order has effect of denying access to the transcript, termination of the underlying criminal proceeding by a guilty plea, as in this case, or by a jury verdict, nearly always will lead to a lifting of the order before appellate review is completed. The order is "by nature short-lived." *Nebraska Press*, 427 U. S., at 547. Further, it is reasonably to be expected that petitioner, as publisher of two New York newspapers, will be subjected to similar closure orders entered by New York courts in compliance with the judgment of that State's Court of Appeals. We therefore turn to the merits.

III

We confront in this case another aspect of the recurring conflict that arises whenever a defendant in a criminal case asserts that his right to a fair trial clashes with the right of the public in general, and of the press in particular, to an open proceeding. This Court has considered other aspects of the problem in deciding whether publicity was sufficiently prejudicial to have deprived the defendant of a fair trial. Cf. *Murphy* v. *Florida*, 421 U. S. 794 (1975), with *Sheppard* v. *Maxwell*, 384 U. S. 333 (1966). And recently we examined the extent to which the First and Fourteenth Amendments protect news organizations' rights to publish, free from prior restraint, information learned in open court during a pretrial suppression hearing. *Nebraska Press Assn.* v. *Stuart*, *supra*. But the Court has not yet addressed the precise issue raised by this case, whether and to what extent the Constitution prohibits the States from excluding, at the request of a defendant, members of the public from such a hearing. See *Nebraska Press*, 427 U. S., at 564 n. 8; *id.*, at 584 n. 11 (BRENNAN, J., concurring); *Times-Picayune Publishing Corp.* v. *Schulingkamp*, 419 U. S. 1301, 1308 n. 3 (1974) (POWELL, J., in chambers).

It is clear that this case does not involve the type of prior restraint that was in issue in cases like *Nebraska Press*,

GANNETT CO. *v.* DePASQUALE

Neither the County Court nor the Court of Appeals restrained publication of, or comment upon, information already known to the public or the press, or about the case in general. The issue here, then, is not one of prior restraint on the press but is, rather, one of access to a judicial proceeding.

This Court heretofore has not found any First Amendment right of access to judicial or other governmental proceeding. See, *e. g., Nixon v. Warner Communications, Inc.*, 435 U. S. 589, 608–610 (1978); *Pell v. Procunier*, 417 U. S., 817, 834 (1974). Before considering whether such a right is now to be recognized for the first time, we turn to that provision of the Constitution that speaks most directly to the question of access to judicial proceedings, namely, the public trial provision of the Sixth Amendment.

A

The familiar language of the Sixth Amendment reads: "In all criminal prosecutions, the accused shall enjoy the right to a speedy and public trial." This provision reflects the tradition of our system of criminal justice that a trial is a "public event" and that "[w]hat transpires in the court room is public property." *Craig v. Harney*, 331 U. S. 367, 374 (1947). And it reflects, as well, "the notion, deeply rooted in the common law, that 'justice must satisfy the appearance of justice.'" *Levine v. United States*, 362 U. S. 610, 616 (1960), quoting *Offutt v. United States*, 348 U. S. 11, 14 (1954).

More importantly, the requirement that a trial of a criminal case be public embodies our belief that secret judicial proceedings would be a menace to liberty. The public trial is rooted in the "principle that justice cannot survive behind walls of silence," *Sheppard v. Maxwell*, 384 U. S., at 349, and in the "traditional Anglo-American distrust for secret trials," *In re Oliver*, 333 U. S. 257, 268 (1948). This Nation's accepted practice of providing open trials in both federal and state courts "has always been recognized as a safeguard against any attempt to employ our courts as instruments of persecution.

GANNETT CO. *v.* DePASQUALE

'The knowledge that every criminal trial is subject to contemporaneous review in the forum of public opinion is an effective restraint on possible abuse of judicial power." *Id.,* at 270.

The public trial guarantee, moreover, insures that not only judges but all participants in the criminal justice system are subjected to public scrutiny as they conduct the public's business of prosecuting crime. This publicity "guards against the miscarriage of justice by subjecting the police, prosecutors, and judicial processes to extensive public scrutiny and criticism." *Sheppard* v. *Maxwell,* 384 U. S., at 350. Publicity "serves to guarantee the fairness of trials and to bring to bear the beneficial effects of public scrutiny upon the administration of justice." *Cox Broadcasting Corp. v. Cohn,* 420 U. S. 469, 492 (1975). "The commission of crime, prosecutions resulting from it, and judicial proceedings arising from the prosecutions . . . are without questions events of legitimate concern to the public." *Ibid.* Indeed, such information is 'of critical importance to our type of government in which the citizenry is the final judge of the proper conduct of public business." *Id.,* at 495.[8] Even in those few cases in which

---

[8] Although we are dealing here with access under the Sixth Amendment, it is worthy of note that this Court's decisions emphasizing the protection afforded reporting of judicial proceedings under the First Amendment also point up the grave concern that information relating to the administration of criminal justice be widely available. In *Landmark Communications, Inc.* v. *Virginia,* 435 U. S. 829 (1978), for example, the Court noted that 'the operation of the judicial system itself [ ] is a matter of public interest," *id.,* at 839, and that reporting judicial disciplinary proceedings "lies near the core of the First Amendment." *Id.,* at 838. And in *Nebraska Press,* 427 U. S., at 559, the Court recognized that "[t]ruthful reports of public judicial proceedings have been afforded special protection against subsequent punishment" because of the importance of free commentary about the conduct of the criminal justice system. Any question of access under the Sixth Amendment aside, the "extraordinary protections afforded by the First Amendment" with respect to the reporting of judicial proceedings, *id.,* at 560, indicate the importance attached to making the public·

GANNETT CO. *v.* DePASQUALE

the Court has permitted limits on courtroom publicity out
of concern for prejudicial coverage, it has taken care to emphasize that publicity of judicial proceedings "has always been
regarded as the handmaiden of effective judicial administration, especially in the criminal field." *Sheppard* v. *Maxwell,*
384 U. S., at 350. And in *Estes* v. *Texas,* 381 U. S. 532, 541
(1965), the Court found that it "is true that the public has
the right to be informed as to what occurs in its courts." See
also *id.,* at 614–615 (STEWART, J., dissenting).

The importance we as a Nation attach to the public trial
is reflected both in its deep roots in the English common law
and in its seemingly universal recognition in this country since
the earliest times. When *In re Oliver* was decided in 1948,
the Court was "unable to find a single instance of a criminal
trial conducted in camera in any federal, state, or municipal
court during the history of this country," 333 U. S., at 266
(footnote omitted), with the exception of cases in courts mar-
tial and the semiprivate conduct of juvenile court proceedings.
Id., at 266 n. 12. Nor could it uncover any record "of even
one such secret criminal trial in England since abolition of the
Court of Star Chamber in 1641." *Ibid.* This strong tradition
of publicity in criminal proceedings, and the States' recognition of the importance of a public trial, led the Court in *In re
Oliver* to conclude that the Sixth Amendment's guarantee of a
public trial, as applied to the States through the Fourteenth
Amendment, proscribed conviction through the type of secret
process at issue in that case.

The public trial concept embodied in the Sixth Amendment
remains a fundamental and essential feature of our system of
criminal justice in both the federal courts and in the state

---

aware of business of the courts. "The administration of the law is not the
problem of the judge or prosecuting attorney alone, but necessitates the
active cooperation of an enlightened public." *Wood* v. *Georgia,* 370 U. S.
375, 391 (1962). See *Bridges* v. *California,* 314 U. S. 252 (1941);
Pennekamp v. *Florida,* 328 U. S. 331 (1946).

GANNETT CO. *v.* DePASQUALE

courts." We reaffirm that the Due Process Clause of the Fourteenth Amendment requires that in criminal cases the States
act in conformity with the public trial provision of the Sixth
Amendment. *Duncan* v. *Louisiana,* 391 U. S. 145, 148
(1968); *Argersinger* v. *Hamlin,* 407 U. S. 25, 28 (1972).

B

By its literal terms the Sixth Amendment secures the right
to a public trial only to "the accused." And in this case, the

---

" 48 of the 50 States protect the right to a public trial in one way or
another. 45 have constitutional provisions specifically guaranteeing the
right: Ala. Const., Art. 1, § 6; Alaska Const., Art. 1, § 11; Ariz. Const.,
Art. 2, §§ 11, 24; Ark. Const., Art. 2, § 10; Calif. Const., Art. 1, § 15;
Colo. Const., Art. 2, § 16; Conn. Const., Art. 1, §§ 8, 19; Dela. Const.,
Art. 1, §§ 7, 9; Florida Const., Art. 1, § 16; Ga. Const., Art. 1, ¶ 11;
Haw. Const., Art. 1, § 11; Idaho Const., Art. 1, § 13; Ill. Const., Art. 1,
§ 8; Ind. Const., Art. 1, §§ 12, 13; Iowa Const., Art. 1, § 10; Kan. Const.,
Bill of Rights, § 10; Ky. Const., Bill of Rights, §§ 11, 14; La. Const.,
Art. 1, §§ 16, 22, Me. Const., Art. 1, § 6; Mich. Const., Art. 1, § 20;
Minn. Const., Art. 1, § 6; Miss. Const., Art. 3, §§ 24, 26; Mo. Const.,
Art. 1, § 18 (a); Mont. Const., Art. 2, § 24; Neb. Const., Art. 1, § 11;
N. J. Const., Art. 1, ¶ 10; N. M. Const., Art. 2, § 14; N. C. Const., Art 1,
§§ 18, 24; N. D. Const., Art. 1, §§ 13, 22; Ohio Const., Art. 1, §§ 10, 16;
Okla. Const., Art. 2, § 20; Ore. Const., Art. 1, § 11; Pa. Const., Art. 1,
§§ 9, 11; R. I. Const., Art. 1, § 10; S. C. Const., Art. 1, §§ 9, 14; S. D.
Const., Art. 6, §§ 7, 20; Tenn. Const., Art. 1, §§ 9, 17; Texas Const.,
Art. 1, § 10; Utah Const., Art. 1, §§ 11, 12; Vt. Const., Ch. 1, Art. 10th;
Va. Const., Art. 1, § 8; Wash. Const., Art. 1, § 22; W. Va. Const., Art. 3,
§§ 14, 17; Wis. Const., Art. 1, § 7; Wyo. Const., Art. 1, § 8.

In addition, New Hampshire has held that the Due Process Clause of its
Constitution, pt. 1, Art. 15, requires that criminal trials be held in public.
Martineau v. *Helgemoe,* — N. H. —, —, 379 A. 2d 1040, 1041 (1977).
Maryland by judicial decision has provided for open proceedings. *Dutton*
v. *State,* 123 Md. 373, 386–387, 91 A. 417, 422–423 (1914). New York by
statute provides for open trials. N. Y. Civil Rights Law, Art. 1, § 12
(McKinney)

Only Masschusetts and Nevada appear to have no state provision for
public trials. But see *Commonwealth* v. *Marshall,* 356 Mass. 432, 253
N. E. 2d 333 (1969).

GANNETT CO. *v.* DePASQUALE

accused were the ones who sought to waive that right, and to have the public removed from the pretrial hearing in order to guard against publicity that possibly would be prejudicial to them. We are urged, accordingly, to hold that the decision of respondents Greathouse and Jones to submit to a private hearing is controlling.

The Court, however, previously has recognized that the Sixth Amendment may implicate interests beyond those of the accused. In *Barker* v. *Wingo*, 407 U. S. 514 (1972), for example, the Court unanimously found this to be so with respect to the right to a speedy trial. "In addition to the general concern that all accused persons be treated according to decent and fair procedures," the Court wrote, "there is a societal interest in providing a speedy trial which exists separately from, and at times in opposition to, the interests of the accused." *Id.*, at 519. This separate public interest led the Court to reject a rule that would have made the defendant's assertion of his speedy trial right the critical factor in deciding whether the right had been denied, for a rule dependent entirely on the defendant's demand failed to take into account that "society has a particular interest in bringing swift prosecutions." *Id.*, at 527.

The same is true of other provisions of the Sixth Amendment. In *Singer* v. *United States*, 380 U. S. 24 (1965), the Court rejected a contention that, since the constitutional right to a jury trial was the right of the accused, he had an absolute right to be tried by a judge alone if he considered a bench trial to be to his advantage. Rejecting a mechanistic waiver approach, the Court reviewed the history of trial by jury at English common law and the practice under the Constitution. The common law did not indicate that the accused had a right to compel a bench trial. Although there were isolated instances where such a right had been recognized in the American colonies, the court could find no "general recognition of a defendant's right to be tried by the court instead of by a jury.

GANNETT CO. *v.* DePASQUALE

Indeed, if there had been recognition of such a right, it would
be difficult to understand why Art. III and the Sixth Amendment were not drafted in terms which recognized an option."
Id., at 31. Noting that practice under the Constitution simi-
larily established no independent right to a bench trial, the
Court held that neither the jury trial provision in Art. III,
§ 2,[°] nor the Sixth Amendment empowered an accused to
compel the opposite of what he was guaranteed specifically by
the Constitution

The Court in *Singer* recognized that in *Patton v. United
States,* 281 U. S. 276 (1930), it had held that a defendant
could waive his jury trial right, but it held that a proffered
waiver need not be given effect in all cases. Quoting *Patton,*
at 312, the Court observed: "Trial by jury has been established by the Constitution as the 'normal and . . . preferable
mode of disposing of issues of fact in criminal cases.'"
Singer v. United States, 380 U. S., at 35. The Court rejected
"the bald proposition that to compel a defendant in a criminal
case to undergo a jury trial against his will is contrary to his
right to a fair trial or to due process." *Id.,* at 36. Rather,
the Court said, a defendant's "only constitutional right concerning the method of trial is to an impartial trial by jury."
Ibid. Accordingly, the Court concluded that the Constitution was no impediment to conditioning the grant of a request
for a bench trial upon the consent of the court and the
Government.

In *Singer,* the Court also recognized that similar reasoning
is applicable to other provisions to the Sixth Amendment.
"The ability to waive a constitutional right does not ordinarily
carry with it the right to insist upon the opposite of that
right." *Id.,* at 34–35. For example, although the accused
"can waive his right to be tried in the State and district where
the crime was committed, he cannot in all cases compel trans-

---

[°] "The trial of all Crimes, except in cases of Impeachment, shall be by
Jury."

GANNETT CO. *v.* DEPASQUALE.

fer of the case to another district." *Id.,* at 35. While he "can waive his right to be confronted by the witnesses against him," he cannot thereby compel the prosecution "to try the case by stipulation." And, most relevant here, "although a defendant can, under some circumstances, waive his constitutional right to a public trial, he has no absolute right to compel a private trial." *Ibid.*

Indeed, in only one case, apparently, *Faretta* v. *California,* 422 U. S. 806 (1975), has this Court ever inferred from the Sixth Amendment a right that fairly may be termed the "opposite" of an explicit guarantee. In *Faretta,* the Court found that not only did the Amendment secure the assistance of counsel to the defendant in a criminal prosecution, but, by inference, it also granted him the right to self-representation. In so ruling, however, the Court was careful to stress that it followed *Singer's* holding that the ability to waive a Sixth Amendment right did not carry with it the automatic right to insist upon its opposite. "The inference of rights is not, of course, a mechanical exercise." 422 U. S., at 819 n. 15. By inferring the existence of a right to self-representation, the Court did not mean to "suggest that this right arises mechanically from a defendant's power to waive the right to the assistance of counsel . . . . On the contrary, the right must be independently found in the structure and history of the constitutional text." *Id.,* at 819–820, n. 15. Following the approach of *Singer,* then, the Court found that "the structure of the Sixth Amendment, as well as . . . the English and colonial jurisprudence from which the Amendment emerged," *id.,* at 818, established the existence of an independent right of self-representation.

C

It is thus clear from *Singer, Barker,* and *Faretta* that the fact the Sixth Amendment casts the right to a public trial in terms of the right of the accused is not sufficient to permit the inference that the accused may compel a private proceeding

GANNETT CO. *v.* DePASQUALE

simply by waiving that right. Any such right to compel a private proceeding must have some independent basis in the Sixth Amendment. In order to determine whether an independent basis exists, we examine, as did the Court in *Singer*, the common law and colonial antecedents of the public trial provision as well as the original understanding of the Sixth Amendment. If no such basis is found, we then must turn to the function of the public trial in our system so that we may decide under what circumstances, if any, a trial court may give effect to a defendant's attempt to waive his right.

1 The Court, in *In re Oliver*, 333 U. S. 257, 266 (1948), recognized that this Nation's "accepted practice of guaranteeing a public trial to an accused has its roots in our English common law heritage." Study of that heritage reveals that the tradition of conducting the proceedings in public came about as an inescapable concomitant of trial by jury, quite unrelated to the rights of the accused, and that the practice at common law was to conduct all criminal proceedings in public.

Early Anglo-Saxon criminal proceedings were "open-air meetings of the freemen who were bound to attend them." F. Pollock, The Expansion of the Common Law 140 (1904) (hereinafter Pollock). Criminal trials were by compurgation or by ordeal, and took place invariably before the assembled community, many of whom were required to attend. 1 W. Holdsworth, A History of English Law 7–24 (1927) (hereinafter Holdsworth). This Anglo-Saxon tradition of conducting a judicial proceeding "like an ill-managed public meeting." Pollock, at 30, persisted after the Conquest, when the Norman kings introduced in England the Frankish system of conducting inquests by means of a jury. Wherever royal justice was introduced, the jury system accompanied it, and both spread rapidly throughout England in the years after 1066. 1 Holdsworth, at 316. The rapid spread of royal courts led to the replacement of older methods of trial, which were always public, with trial by jury with little procedural change. The

GANNETT CO. *v.* DePASQUALE

jury trial "was simply substituted for [older methods], and was adapted with as little change as possible to its new position." *Id.*, at 317. This substitution of royal justice for traditional law served the Crown's interests by "enlarging the king's jurisdiction and bringing well-earned profit in fines and otherwise to the king's exchequer, and the best way of promoting those ends was to develop the institution, or let it develop itself, along the lines of least resistance." Pollock, at 40.

Thus, the common law from its inception was wedded to the Anglo-Saxon tradition of publicity, and the "ancient rul[e that] Courts of justice are public," *id.*, at 51, was in turn strengthened by the hegemony the royal courts soon established over the administration of justice. Bentham noted that by this accommodation of the common law to the Anglo-Saxon practice of holding open courts, "publicity . . . became a natural, and, as good fortune would have it, at length an inseparable, concomitant" of English justice. 1 J. Bentham, The Rationale of Judicial Evidence 584–585 (1827). See 2 F. Pollock and F. Maitland, The History of English Law 604 (1909).

Publicity thus became intrinsically associated with the sittings of the royal courts. Coke noted that the very words "In curia Domini Regis" ("In the King's Courts"), in the Statutum de Marleberg, ch. 1, enacted in 1267, 52 Hen. III, indicated public proceedings. 2 E. Coke, Institutes of the Laws of England 103 (6th ed. 1681).[11]

---

[11] "These words are of great importance, for all Causes ought to be heard, ordered, and determined before the Judges of the Kings Courts openly in the Kings Courts, whither all persons may resort; and in no chambers, or other private places: for the Judges are not Judges of chambers, but of Courts, and therefore in open Court, where the parties Councel and Attorneys attend, ought orders, rules, awards, and Judgments to be made and given, and not in chambers or other private places. . . . Nay, that Judge that ordereth or ruleth a Cause in his chamber, though his order or rule be just, yet offendeth he the Law, (as here it appeareth) because he doth it not in Court."

GANNETT CO. v. DePASQUALE

This and other commentary [12] indicate that by the 17th century the concept of a public trial was firmly established under the common law. Indeed, there is little record, if any, of secret proceedings, criminal or civil, having occurred at any time in known English history. Apparently, not even the Court of Star Chamber, the name of which has been linked with secrecy, conducted hearings in private. 5 Holdsworth 156, and nn. 5 and 7, and 163; Radin, The Right to a Public Trial, 6 Temp. L. Q. 381, 386–387 (1932). Rather, the unbroken tradition of the English common law was that criminal trials were conducted "openlie in the presence of the Judges, the Justices, the enquest, the prisoner, and so manie as will or can come so neare as to heare it, and all depositions and witnesses given aloude, that all men may heare from the mouth of the depositors and witnesses what is saide." T. Smith, De Republica Anglorum 101 (Alston ed. 1972).

In the light of this history, it is most doubtful that the tradition of publicity ever was associated with the rights of the accused. The practice of conducting the trial in public was established as a feature of English justice long before the defendant was afforded even the most rudimentary rights. For example, during the century preceding the English Civil War, the defendant was kept in secret confinement and could not prepare a defense. He was not provided with counsel either before or at the trial. He was given no prior notice of the charge or evidence against him. He probably could not call witnesses on his behalf. Even if he could, he had no means to procure their attendance. Witnesses were not necessarily confronted with the prisoner. Document originals

---

[12] See, e. g., T. Smith, de Republica Anglorum 79, 101 (Alston ed. 1972), published in 1583, where the author, in contrasting the English common law with the civil law system of the Continent, stressed that in England all adjudications were open to the public as a matter of course. See also *Trial of John Lilburne* (1649), reported in 4 How. State Trials 1270, 1274 (1816).

GANNETT CO. v. DePASQUALE

were not required to be produced. There were no rules of evidence. The confessions of accomplices were admitted against each other and regarded as specially cogent evidence. And the defendant was compelled to submit to examination. 1 J. Stephen, A History of the Criminal Law of England 350 (1883). Yet the trial itself, without exception, was public.

It is not surprising, therefore, that both Hale and Blackstone, in identifying the function of publicity at common law, discussed the open-trial requirement not in terms of individual liberties but in terms of the effectiveness of the trial process. Each recognized publicity as an essential of trial at common law. And each emphasized that the requirement that evidence be given in open court deterred perjury, since "a witness may frequently depose that in private which he will be ashamed to testify in a public and solemn tribunal." 3 W. Blackstone, Commentaries *373. See M. Hale, The History of the Common Law of England 343, 345 (6th ed. 1820). Similarly, both recognized that publicity was an effective check on judicial abuse, since publicity made it certain that "if the judge be PARTIAL, his partiality and injustice will be evident to all by-standers." *Id.*, at 344. See 3 W. Blackstone, Commentaries *372.[14]

In the same vein, Bentham stressed that publicity was "the most effectual safeguard of testimony, and of the decisions depending on it; it is the soul of justice; it ought to be extended to every part of the procedure, and to all causes." J. Bentham, Treatise On Judicial Evidence 67 (1825). Bent-

---

[14] Similarly, the Solicitor General, Sir John Hawles, in 1685 in his *Remarks upon Mr. Cornish's Trial*, 11 How. State Trials 455, 460 (1816), stated:

"The reason that all matters of law are, or ought to be transacted publicly, is, That any person, unconcerned as well as concerned, may, as *amicus curiae*, inform the court better, if he thinks they are in an error, that justice may be done; and the reason that all trials are public, is, that any person may inform in point of fact, though not *subpoena'd*, that truth may be discovered in civil as well as criminal matters."

GANNETT CO. *v.* DePASQUALE

ham believed that, above all, publicity was the most effectual safeguard against judicial abuse, without which all other checks on misuse of judicial power became ineffectual. 1 J. Bentham, The Rationale of Judicial Evidence 525 (1824). And he contended that publicity was of such importance to the administration of justice, especially in criminal cases, that it should not be dispensed with even at the request of the defendant. "The reason is . . . there is a party interested (viz. the public at large) whose interest might, by means of the privacy in question, and a sort of conspiracy, more or less explicit, between the other persons concerned (the judge included) be made a sacrifice." *Id.,* at 576–577

This English common-law tradition concerning public trials out of which the Sixth Amendment provision grew is not made up of "shreds of English legal history and early state constitutional and statutory provisions," see *Faretta* v. *California,* 422 U. S., at 843 (dissenting opinion describing the right of self-representation), pieced together to produce the desired result. Whatever may be said of the historical analysis of other Sixth Amendment provisions, history in this case reveals an unbroken tradition at English common law of open judicial proceedings in criminal cases. In publicity, we "have one tradition, at any rate, which has persisted through all changes" from Anglo-Saxon times through the development of the modern common law. Pollock, at 31–32. See E. Jencks, The Book of English Law 73–74. (6th ed. 1967). There is no evidence that criminal trials of any sort ever were conducted in private at common law, whether at the request of the defendant or over his objection. And there is strong evidence that the public trial, which developed before other procedural rights now routinely afforded the accused, widely was perceived as serving important social interests, relating to the integrity of the trial process, that exist apart from, and conceivably in opposition to, the interests of the individual defendant. Accordingly, we find no support in the common-law antecedents of the Sixth Amendment public trial provi-

GANNETT CO. *v.* DePASQUALE

sion for the view that the guarantee of a public trial carries with it a correlative right to compel a private proceeding.[11]

2. This English common-law view of the public trial early was transplanted to the American colonies, largely through the influence of the common-law writers whose views shaped the early American legal systems. "Coke's Institutes were read in the American Colonies by virtually every student of the law," *Klopfer v. North Carolina*, 386 U. S. 213, 225 (1967), and no citation is needed to establish the impact of Hale and Blackstone on colonial legal thought. Early colonial charters reflected the view that open proceedings were an essential

---

[11] The continuing development in England of the common-law notion of publicity during the years since the founding of our own Nation casts light upon the function of publicity in our system of justice. For example, in a series of cases establishing a privilege for the reporting of judicial proceedings, the courts recognized: "Though the publication of such proceedings may be to the disadvantage of the particular individual concerned, yet it is of vast importance to the public that the proceedings of Courts of Justice should be universally known. The general advantage to the country in having these proceedings made public, more than counterbalances the inconveniences to the private persons whose conduct may be the subject of such proceedings." *The King v. Wright*, 8 D. & E. 293, 298, 101 Eng. Rep. 1396, 1399 (K. B. 1799). See *Davison v. Duncan*, 7 El. & Bl. 229, 230–231, 119 Eng. Rep. 1233, 1234 (Q. B. 1857), *Wason v. Walter*, 4 L. R. 73, 88 (Q. B. 1868).

Important for our purposes is the decision in *Daubney v. Cooper*, 10 B. & C. 237, 109 Eng. Rep. 438 (K. B. 1829). There the court upheld a verdict for damages in an action by a spectator, who had been ejected from a criminal proceeding, against the magistrate who had ejected him. The court stated:

[I]t is one of the essential qualities of a court of justice that its proceedings should be public, and that all parties who may be desirous of hearing what is going on, if there be room in the place for that purpose,—provided they do not interrupt the proceedings, and provided there is no specific reason why they should be removed,—have a right to be present for the purpose of hearing what is going on." *Id.*, at 240, 109 Eng. Rep., at 440.

See also *Scott v. Scott*, [1913] A. C. 417, 438–439 (Haldane, L. C.), 440–441 (Earl of Halsbury).

GANNETT CO. *v.* DePASQUALE

quality of a court of justice, and they cast the concept of a
public trial in terms of a characteristic of the system of justice, rather than of a right of the accused. Indeed, the first
public trial provision to appear in America spoke in terms
of the right of the public, not the accused, to attend trials:

> "That in all publick courts of justice for tryals of
> causes, civil or criminal, any person or persons, inhabit-
> ants of the said Province may freely come into, and
> attend the said courts, and hear and be present, at all or
> any such tryals as shall be there had or passed, that jus-
> tice may not be done in a corner nor in any covert man-
> ner." Concessions and Agreements of West New Jersey
> (1677), ch. XXIII, quoted in 1 B. Schwartz, The Bill of
> Rights: A Documentary History 129 (1971) (hereinafter
> Schwartz).

Similarly, the Pennsylvania Frame of Government of 1682,
which Professor Schwartz described as, "[i]n many ways,
[one of] the most influential of the Colonial documents protecting individual rights," 1 Schwartz, at 130, provided that in
William Penn's colony "all courts shall be open." *Id.*, at 140.

This practice of conducting judicial proceedings in criminal
cases in public took firm hold in all the American colonies.
There is no evidence that any colonial court conducted criminal trials behind closed doors or that any recognized the right
of an accused to compel a private trial.

Neither is there any evidence that casting the public trial
concept in terms of a right of the accused signaled a departure
from the common-law practice by granting the accused the
power to compel a private proceeding. The first provision
to speak of the public trial as an entitlement of the accused
apparently was that in ¶ IX of the Pennsylvania Declaration
of Rights of 1776. It said that "in all prosecutions for criminal offenses, a man hath a right . . . a speedy public trial."
See 1 Schwartz, at 265. The provision was borrowed almost
verbatim from the Virginia Declaration of Rights, adopted

GANNETT CO. *v.* DePASQUALE

earlier the same year, with one change: the word "public" was added. Virginia's Declaration had provided only that the accused "hath a right to . . . a speedy trial." See 1 Schwartz, at 235. It is doubtful that, by adding this single word, Pennsylvania intended to depart from its historic practice by creating a right waivable by the defendant, for at the time its Declaration of Rights was adopted, Pennsylvania also adopted its Constitution of 1776, providing, in § 26, that "[a]ll courts shall be open." See 1 Schwartz, at 271. And there is no evidence that after 1776 Pennsylvania departed from earlier practice, either by conducting trials in private or by recognizing a power in the accused to compel a nonpublic proceeding.[15]

Similarly, there is no indication that the First Congress, in proposing what became the Sixth Amendment, meant to depart from the common-law practice by creating a power in an accused to compel a private proceeding. The Constitution as originally adopted, of course, did not contain a public trial guarantee. And though several States proposed amendments to Congress along the lines of the Virginia Declaration, only New York mentioned a "public" trial. See E. Dumbauld, The Bill of Rights, 173–205 and, specifically, 190 (1957); 1 Elliot's Debates 328 (2d ed. 1836). But New York did not follow Virginia's language by casting the right as one belonging only to the accused; *but* urged rather that Congress should propose an amendment providing that the "trial should be speedy,

---

[15] Although a number of States followed the language of Virginia's Declaration, only Vermont copied the Pennsylvania emendation by adding the word "public" to the speedy trial provision. Vt. Const., Declaration of Rights § X (1777), quoted in 1 Schwartz, at 323. Once again, however, there is no evidence that by so doing Vermont intended to depart from the common-law practice of holding court in public. Indeed, the Vermont Declaration, adopted by the revolutionary legislature in haste, was "virtually [a] verbatim repetition [ ] of the revelant Pennsylvania" article. 1 Schwartz, at 319. It is thus doubtful that by adding the word "public" Vermont, any more than Pennsylvania, intended to alter existing practice.

GANNETT CO *v* DePASQUALE

public, and by an impartial jury. . . ." Amendments Proposed by New York (1788), quoted in 1 Elliott's Debates, at 328

We are thus persuaded that Congress, modeling the proposed amendment on the cognate provision in the Virginia Declaration, as many States had urged, did merely what Pennsylvania had done in 1776, namely, added the word "public" to the Virginia language without at all intending thereby to create a correlative right to compel a private proceeding. Indeed, in light of the settled practice at common law, one may also say here that "if there had been recognition of such a right, it would be difficult to understand why [the Sixth Amendment was] not drafted in terms which recognized an option." *Singer v. United States*, 380 U. S., at 31. And, to use the language of the Court in *Faretta v. California*, 422 U. S., at 832: "If anyone had thought that the Sixth Amendment, as drafted," departed from the common-law principle of publicity in criminal proceedings, "there would undoubtedly have been some debate or comment on the issue. But there was none." Mr. Justice Story, writing when the adoption of the Sixth Amendment was within the memory of living man, noted that "in declaring, that the accused shall enjoy the right to a speedy and public trial [the Sixth Amendment] does but follow out the established course of the common law in all trials for crimes. The trial is always public." 3 J. Story, Commentaries on the Constitution of the United States 662 (1833).

We consequently find no evidence in the development of the public trial concept in the American colonies and in the adoption of the Sixth Amendment to indicate that there was any recognition in this country, any more than in England, of a right to a private proceeding or a power to compel a private trial arising out of the ability to waive the grant of a public one. We shall not indulge in a mere mechanical inference that, by phrasing the public trial as one belonging to the

GANNETT CO. *v.* DePASQUALE

accused, the framers of the Amendment must have meant the accused to have the power to dispense with publicity.

3. We thus conclude that there is no basis in the Sixth Amendment for the suggested inference. We also find that, because there is a societal interest in the public trial that exists separately from, and at times in opposition to, the interests of the accused, cf. *Barker* v. *Wingo*, 407 U. S., at 519, a court may give effect to an accused's attempt to waive his public trial right only in certain circumstances.

The courts and the scholars of the common law perceived the public trial tradition as one serving to protect the integrity of the trial and to guard against partiality on the part of the court. The same concerns are generally served by the public trial today. The protection against perjury which publicity provides, and the opportunity publicity offers to unknown witnesses to make themselves known, do not necessarily serve the defendant. See 6 J. Wigmore, Evidence in Trials in Common Law § 1834 (Chadbourn rev. 1976) (hereinafter Wigmore). The public has an interest in having criminal prosecutions decided on truthful and complete records, and this interest, too, does not necessarily coincide with that of the accused.

Nor does the protection against judicial partiality serve only the defendant. It is true that the public trial provisions serves to protect every accused from the abuses to which secret tribunals would be prone. But the defendant himself may benefit from the partiality of a corrupt, biased, or incompetent judge, "for a secret trial can result in favor to as well as unjust prosecution of a defendant." *Lewis* v. *Peyton*, 352 F. 2d 791, 792 (CA4 1965).

Open trials also enable the public to scrutinize the performance of police and prosecutors in the conduct of public judicial business. Trials and particularly suppression hearings typically involve questions concerning the propriety of police and government conduct that took place hidden from

GANNETT CO. *v.* DePASQUALE

the public view. Any interest on the part of the prosecution in hiding police or prosecutorial misconduct or ineptitude may coincide with the defendant's desire to keep the proceedings private, with the result that the public interest is sacrificed from both sides.

Public judicial proceedings have an important educative role as well. The victim of the crime, the family of the victim, others who have suffered similarly, or others accused of like crimes, have an interest in observing the course of a prosecution. Beyond this, however, is the interest of the general public in observing the operation of the criminal justice system. Judges, prosecutors, and police officials often are elected or are subject to some control by elected officials, and a main source of information about how these officials perform is the open trial. And the manner in which criminal justice is administered in this country is in and of itself of interest to all citizens. In *Cox Broadcasting Corp.* v. *Cohn,* 420 U. S., at 495, it was noted that information about the criminal justice system "appears to us to be of critical importance to our type of government in which the citizenry is the final judge of the proper conduct of public business."

Important in this regard, of course, is the appearance of justice. "Secret hearings—though they be scrupulously fair in reality—are suspect by nature. Public confidence cannot long be maintained where important judicial decisions are made behind closed doors and then announced in conclusive terms to the public, with the record supporting the court's decisions sealed from public view." *United States* v. *Cianfrani,* 573 F. 2d 835, 851 (CA3 1978). The ability of the courts to administer the criminal laws depends in no small part on the confidence of the public in judicial remedies, and on respect for and acquaintance with the processes and deliberations of those courts. 6 Wigmore § 1834, at 438. Anything that impairs the open nature of judicial proceedings

GANNETT CO. *v.* DePASQUALE

threatens to undermine this confidence and to impede the ability of the courts to function.

These societal values secured by the public trial are fundamental to the system of justice on both the state and federal levels. As such, they have been recognized by the large majority of both state [16] and federal [17] courts that have con-

---

[16] Nearly every State that has considered the issue has recognized that the public has a strong interest in maintaining open trials. Most of these cases have involved state constitutional provisions modeled on the Sixth Amendment in that the public trial right is phrased in terms of a guarantee to the accused. See, e. g., *Jackson* v. *Mobley*, 157 Ala. 408, 411–412, 47 So. 590, 592 (1908); *Commercial Printing Co.* v. *Lee*, —— Ark. ——, ——, 553 S. W. 2d 270, 273–274 (1977); *Lincoln* v. *Denver Post*, 31 Colo. App. 283, 285–286, 501 P. 2d 152, 154 (1972); *State ex rel. Gore Newspapers Co.* v. *Tyson*, 313 So. 2d 777, 785–788 (Fla. App. 1975); *Gannett Pacific Corp.* v. *Richardson*, —— Haw. ——, ——, 580 P. 2d 49, 55 (1978); *State* v. *Beaudoin*, 386 A. 2d 731, 733 (Me. 1978); *Cox* v. *State*, 3 Md. App. 136, 139–140, 238 A. 2d 157, 158–159 (1968); *State* v. *Schmit*, 273 Minn. 78, 86–88, 139 N. W. 2d 800, 805–807 (1966); *State* v. *Keeler*, 52 Mont. 205, 218–219, 156 P. 1080, 1083–1084 (1916); *Keene Publishing Corp.* v. *Keene District Court*, —— N. H. ——, ——, 380 A. 2d 261, 263–264 (1977); *State* v. *Allen*, 73 N. J. 132, 157–160, 373 A. 2d 377, 382–383 (1977); *Neal* v. *State*, 86 Okla. Cr. App. 283, 289, 192 P. 2d 294, 297 (1948); *State* v. *Holm*, 67 Wyo. 360, 382–385, 224 P. 2d 500, 508–509 (1950).

Several States have recognized such an interest under constitutional provisions establishing open courts. E. g., *State* v. *White*, 97 Ariz. 196, 198, 398 P. 2d 903, 904 (1965); *Smith* v. *State*, 317 A. 2d 20, 23–24 (Del. 1974); *Johnson* v. *Simpson*, 433 S. W. 2d 644, 646 (Ky. 1968); *Brown* v. *State*, 222 Miss. 863, 869, 77 So. 2d 694, 696 (1955); *In re Edens*, 290 N. C. 299, 306, 226 S. E. 2d 5, 9–10 (1976); *E. W. Scripps Co.* v. *Fulton*, 100 Ohio App. 157, 160–169, 125 N. E. 2d 896, 899–904 (1955); *State ex rel. Varney* v. *Ellis*, 149 W. Va. 522, 523–524, 142 S. E. 2d 63, 65 (1965).

Massachusetts appears to have no case precisely on point. But in *Cowley* v. *Pulsifer*, 137 Mass. 392 (1884), the Supreme Judicial Court, in an opinion by Mr. Justice Holmes, stated that the chief advantage of permitting a privilege for publication of reports of judicial proceedings

[*Footnote 17 is on p. 451*]

GANNETT CO. *v.* DePASQUALE

sidered the issue over the years since the adoption of the
Constitution. Indeed, in those States with constitutional provisions modeled on the Sixth Amendment, guaranteeing the
right to a public trial literally only to the accused, there has
been widespread recognition that such provisions serve the
interests of the public as well as those of the defendant.[18]

We therefore conclude that the Due Process Clause of the
Fourteenth Amendment, insofar as it incorporates the public
trial provision of the Sixth Amendment, prohibits the States
from excluding the public from a proceeding within the ambit

---

is the security which publicity gives for the proper administration of
justice." *Id.,* at 394. The court continued.

[This] privilege and the access to the public to the courts stand in
reason upon common ground. . . . It is desirable that the trial of
causes should take place under the public eye, not because the controversies of one citizen with another are of public concern, but because it
is of the highest moment that those who administer justice should always
act under the sense of public responsibility, and that every citizen should
be able to satisfy himself with his own eyes as to the mode in which a
public duty is performed." *Ibid.*

[17] See, *e. g.,* *United States* v. *Clark,* 475 F. 2d 240, 246–247 (CA2 1973),
Stamicarbon, N. V. v. *American Cyanamid Co.,* 506 F. 2d 532, 540–542
(CA2 1974); *United States* v. *Cianfrani,* 573 F. 2d 835, 852–854 (CA3
1978), *Lewis* v. *Peyton,* 352 F. 2d 791, 792 (CA4 1965).

[18] See cases cited, at n. 16, *supra.* For example, in *Commercial Printing Co.* v. *Lee,* —— Ark. ——, 553 S. W. 2d 270 (1977), the Supreme Court
of Arkansas held that the exclusion of the public from the *voir dire* phase
of a criminal trial violated the State's public trial constitutional provision, even though it, like the Sixth Amendment, literally read in favor
of only the accused. The court found that members of the public have
a strong interest in observing criminal proceedings, inasmuch as they involve crimes against society. And it added that since courthouses, prosecutors, judges, and often defense attorneys are paid for with public funds,
the public "has every right to ascertain by personal observation whether
its officials are properly carrying out their duties and responsibilities and
capably administering justice, and it would require unusual circumstances
for this right to be held subordinate to the contention of a defendant that
he is prejudiced by a public trial (or any part thereof)." *Id.,* at ——,
553 S. W. 2d, at 274.

GANNETT CO. *v.* DePASQUALE

of the Sixth Amendment's guarantee without affording full and fair consideration to the public's interests in maintaining an open proceeding. And we believe that the Sixth and Fourteenth Amendments require this conclusion notwithstanding the fact it is the accused who seeks to close the trial.[19]

D

Before considering whether and under what circumstances a court may conduct a criminal proceeding in private, we must first decide whether the Sixth Amendment, as applied through the Fourteenth, encompasses the type of pretrial hearing contemplated by *Jackson* v. *Denno*, 378 U. S. 368 (1964), and at issue in this case. The Amendment, of course, speaks only of a public "trial." Both the County Court and the New York Court of Appeals emphasized that exclusion from the formal trial on the merits was not at issue, apparently in the belief that the Sixth Amendment's public trial provision applies with less force, or not at all, to a pretrial proceeding.

We find good reason to hold that even if a State, as it may, chooses to hold a *Jackson* v. *Denno* or other suppression

---

[19] The ABA standards adopt the view that the public has a strong interest in maintaining the openness of criminal trials, and that the Sixth Amendment protects that interest:

"The sixth amendment speaks in terms of the right of the accused to a public trial, but this right does not belong solely to the accused to assert or forgo as he or she desires. . . . The defendant's interest, primarily, is to ensure fair treatment in his or her particular case. While the public's more generalized interest in open trials includes a concern for justice to individual defendants, it goes beyond that. The transcendent reason for public trials is to ensure efficiency, competence, and integrity in the overall operation of the judicial system. Thus, the defendant's willingness to waive the right to a public trial in a criminal case cannot be the deciding factor. . . . It is just as important to the public to guard against undue favoritism or leniency as to guard against undue harshness or discrimination." American Bar Association, Standards Relating to the Administration of Criminal Justice, Fair Trial and Free Press, Standard 8-3.2, at 15 (Approved Draft 1978). (Footnotes omitted.)

GANNETT CO. *v.* DePASQUALE

hearing separate from and prior to the full trial, the Sixth Amendment's public trial provision applies to that hearing. First, the suppression hearing resembles and relates to the full trial in almost every particular. Evidence is presented by means of live testimony, witnesses are sworn, and those witnesses are subject to cross-examination. Determination of the ultimate issue depends in most cases upon the trier of fact's evaluation of the evidence, and credibility is often crucial. Each side has incentive to prevail, with the result that the role of publicity as a testimonial safeguard, as a mechanism to encourage the parties, the witnesses, and the court to a strict conscientiousness in the performance of their duties, and in providing a means whereby unknown witnesses may become known, are just as important for the suppression hearing as they are for the full trial.

Moreover, the pretrial suppression hearing often is critical, and it may be decisive, in the prosecution of a criminal case. If the defendant prevails, he will have dealt the prosecution's case a serious, perhaps fatal, blow; the proceeding often then will be dismissed or negotiated on terms favorable to the defense. If the prosecution successfully resists the motion to suppress, the defendant may have little hope of success at trial (especially where a confession is in issue), with the result that the likelihood of a guilty plea is substantially increased. *United States* v. *Clark,* 475 F. 2d 240, 246–247 (CA2 1973); *United States* v. *Cianfrani,* 573 F. 2d. at 848–851.

The suppression hearing often is the only judicial proceeding of substantial importance that takes place during a criminal prosecution. In this very case, the hearing from which the public was excluded was the only one in which the important factual and legal issues in the prosecution of respondents Greathouse and Jones were considered. It was the only proceeding at which the conduct of the police, prosecution, and the court itself were exposed to scrutiny. Indeed, in 1976, when this case was processed, every-felony prosecution in

GANNETT CO. *v.* DePASQUALE

Seneca County—and we say this without criticism—was terminated without a trial on the merits. Judicial Conference of the State of New York, 22d Annual Report 55 (1977). This statistic is characteristic of our state and federal criminal justice systems as a whole,[20] and it underscores the importance of the suppression hearing in the functioning of those systems.

Further, the issues considered at such hearings are of great moment beyond their importance to the outcome of a particular prosecution. A motion to suppress typically involves, as in this case, allegations of misconduct by police and prosecution that raise constitutional issues. Allegations of this kind, although they may prove to be unfounded, are of importance to the public as well as to the defendant. The searches and interrogations that such hearings evaluate do not take place in public. The hearing therefore usually presents the only opportunity the public has to learn about police and prosecutorial conduct, and about allegations that those responsible to the public for the enforcement of laws themselves are breaking it.

A decision to suppress often involves the exclusion of highly relevant evidence. Because this is so, the decision may generate controversy. See *Bivens* v. *Six Unknown Fed. Narcotics Agents*, 403 U. S. 388, 412–420 (1971) (dissenting opinion). It is important that any such decision be made on the basis of evidence and argument offered in open court, so that all

[20] In 1976, the Supreme Court for the City of New York, 89.7% of all criminal cases were terminated by dismissal (25.6%) or by plea of guilty (64.1%). Judicial Conference of the State of New York, 22d Annual Report 52 (1977). In the Supreme Courts and County Courts outside New York City, 93.4% of the criminal cases were disposed of by dismissal (18.9%) or by plea of guilty (74.5%). *Id.*, at 56.

As noted, these statistics are characteristic of the criminal justice system across the country. See generally, National Institute of Law Enforcement and Criminal Justice, Law Enforcement Assistance Administration, Plea Bargaining in the United States Appendix A (1978).

GANNETT CO. *v* DePASQUALE

who care to see or read about the case may evaluate for themselves the propriety of the exclusion.

These factors lead us to conclude that a pretrial suppression hearing is the close equivalent of the trial on the merits
for purposes of applying the public trial provision of the Sixth
Amendment. Unlike almost any other proceeding apart from
the trial itself, the suppression hearing implicates all the policies that require that the trial be public. For this reason, we
would be loath to hold that a State could conduct a pretrial
Jackson v. *Denno* hearing in private over the *objection* of the
defendant. And for this same reason, the public's interest
in the openness of judicial proceedings is implicated fully
when it is the accused who seeks to exclude the public from
such a hearing. Accordingly, we hold that the Sixth and
Fourteenth Amendments prohibit a State from conducting a
~~preliminary~~ hearing in private, even at the request of the
accused, unless full and fair consideration is first given to the
public's interest, protected by the Amendments, in open
trials.[21]

IV

At the same time, we cannot deny that the publication of
information learned in an open proceeding may harm irreparably, under certain circumstances, the ability of a defendant
to obtain a fair trial. This is especially true in the context
of a pretrial hearing, where disclosure of information, determined to be inadmissible at trial, may severely affect a
defendant's rights. Although the Sixth Amendment's public
trial provision establishes a strong presumption in favor of
open proceedings, it does not require that all proceedings be

---

[21] The ABA standards take the position that pretrial suppression hearings are within the scope of the Sixth Amendment's public trial provision. American Bar Association, Standards Relating to the Administration of Criminal Justice, Fair Trial and Free Press, Standard 8–3.2, at
15 and n. 1 (Approved Draft 1978).

GANNETT CO. *v.* DePASQUALE

held in open court when to do so would deprive a defendant of a fair trial.

No court has held that the Sixth Amendment imposes an absolute requirement that court be open at all times. On the contrary, courts on both the state and federal levels have recognized exceptions to the public trial requirement even when it is the accused who objects to the exclusion of the public or a portion thereof. Thus it is clear that the court may exclude unruly spectators or limit the number of spectators. And in both *Estes v. Texas*, 381 U. S. 532 (1965), and *Sheppard v. Maxwell*, 384 U. S. 333 (1966), this Court held that a court may place restrictions on the access of the electronic media in particular, and certain types of news gathering in general, within the courthouse doors. There are a number of instances where the courts have gone further and upheld the exclusion of the public for limited periods of time. Examples are when it was necessary to preserve the confidentiality of the Government's "skyjacker profile," *United States v. Bell*, 464 F. 2d 667 (CA2), cert. denied, 409 U. S. 991 (1972), and when it was necessary to effectuate Congress' determination that the confidentiality of communications intercepted under Tit. III of the Omnibus Crime and Safe Streets Act of 1968, 18 U. S. C. § 2510 *et seq.*, be preserved prior to the determination that such communications were lawfully intercepted. *United States v. Cianfrani*, 573 F. 2d 835 (CA3 1978).

---

[22] This holding is confined to cases where the defendant seeks to close the hearing on the ground that his fair trial rights will be infringed by an open proceeding. We express no opinion as to whether or when a proceeding subject to the command of the Sixth Amendment may be closed over the objection of the defendant. Nor do we decide what interests other than those of the defendant in a fair trial may support an order of closure. Our holding today is also confined to rulings within the ambit of the Sixth Amendment's public trial provision. We thus express no opinion about the application of our holding to proceedings, such as those in juvenile court, not otherwise subject to the requirement of the Sixth Amendment. See *McKeiver v. Pennsylvania*, 403 U S 528, 540–541 (1971) (plurality opinion)

GANNETT CO. *v.* DePASQUALE

We need express no opinion on the correctness of such decisions. But they illustrate that courts have been willing to
permit limited exceptions to the principle of publicity where
necessary to protect some other interest. Because of the importance we attach to a fair trial, it is clear that whatever
restrictions on access the Sixth Amendment may prohibit in
another context, it does not prevent a trial court from restrict-
ing access to a pretrial suppression hearing where such restriction is necessary in order to ensure that a defendant not be
denied a fair trial as a result of prejudicial publicity flowing
from that hearing. See *Branzburg* v. *Hayes*, 408 U. S. 665,
685 (1972).

At the same time, however, the public's interest in maintaining open courts requires that any exception to the rule
be narrowly drawn. It comports with the Sixth Amendment
to require an accused who seeks closure to establish that it is
strictly and inescapably necessary in order to protect the fair
trial guarantee. That finding must be made in the first
instance, of course, by the trial court. We cannot detail here
all the factors to be taken into account in evaluating the
defendant's closure request, nor can we predict how the balance should be struck in every hypothetical case. The accused who seeks closure must establish, however, at a minimum the following.

First, he must provide an adequate basis to support a finding that there is a substantial probability that irreparable
damage to his fair trial right will result from conducting the
proceeding in public. This showing will depend on the facts.
But we think it requires evidence of the nature and extent of
the publicity prior to the motion to close in order to establish
a basis for the trial court to conclude that further coverage will
result in the harm sought to be prevented. In most cases,
this will involve a showing of the impact on the jury pool.
This seldom can be measured with exactness, but information
relating to the size of the pool, the extent of media coverage

GANNETT CO. *v.* DEPASQUALE

in the pertinent locality, and the ease with which change of venire can be accomplished or searching *voir dire* instituted to protect against prejudice, would be relevant. The court also should consider the extent to which the information sought to be suppressed is already known to the public, and the extent to which publication of such information, if unknown, would have an impact in the context of the publicity that has preceded the motion to close.

Second, the accused must show a substantial probability that alternatives to closure will not protect adequately his right to a fair trial. One may suggest numerous alternatives, but we think the following should be considered: continuance, severance, change of venue, change of venire, *voir dire*, peremptory challenges, sequestration, and admonition of the jury. ABA Project on Standards Relating to the Administration of Criminal Justice, Fair Trial and Free Press Standard 8-3. 2, at 16 (App. Draft 1978). See *Nebraska Press Assn.* v. *Stuart*, 427 U. S., at 562–565; *Sheppard* v. *Maxwell*, 384 U. S., at 354 n. 9, 358–362. One or more of these alternatives may adequately protect the accused's interests and relieve the court of any need to close the proceeding in advance.[23]

---

[23] It has been suggested that the public's interest will be served adequately by permitting delayed access to the transcript of the closed proceeding once the danger to the accused's fair trial right has dissipated. A transcript, however, does not always adequately substitute for presence at the proceeding itself. Also, the inherent delay may defeat the purpose of the public trial requirement. Later events may crowd news of yesterday's proceeding out of the public view. "As a practical matter . . . the element of time is not unimportant if press coverage is to fulfill its traditional function of bringing news to the public promptly." *Nebraska Press Assn.* v. *Stuart*, 427 U. S., at 561. Public access is restricted precisely at the time when public interest is at its height. *Bridges* v. *California*, 314 U. S. 252, 268 (1941). Moreover, an important event, such as a judicial election or the selection of a prosecuting attorney, may occur when the public is ignorant of the details of judicial and prosecutorial conduct. Finally, although a record is kept for later relesae, when the proceeding itself is kept secret, it is impossible to know what it would

GANNETT CO. *v.* DePASQUALE.

We note, too, that for suppression hearings alternatives to closures exist that would enable the public to attend but that would limit dissemination of the information sought to be suppressed. At most such hearings, the issues concern not so much the contents of a confession or of a wiretap, or the nature of the evidence seized, but the circumstances under which the prosecution obtained this material. Many hearings, with care, could be conducted in public with little risk that prejudicial information would be disclosed.

Third, the accused must demonstrate that there is a substantial probability that closure will be effective in protecting against the perceived harm. Where significantly prejudicial information already has been made public, there might well be little justification for closing a pretrial hearing in order to prevent only the disclosure of details.

We emphasize that the trial court should begin with the assumption that the Sixth Amendment requires that a pretrial suppression hearing be conducted in open court unless a defendant carries his burden to demonstrate a strict and inescapable necessity for closure. There is no need for a representative of the public to demonstrate that the public interest is legitimate or genuine, or that the public seeks access out of something more than mere curiosity. Trials and suppression hearings by their nature are events of legitimate public interest, and the public need demonstrate no threshold of respectability in order to attend. This is not to say, of course, that a court should not take into account heightened public interest in cases of unusual importance to the community or to the public at large. The prosecution of an important office holder could intensify public interest in observing the proceedings, and the court should take that interest into account where it is warranted. It is also true, however, that as the public interest intensifies, so does the potential for prejudice

have been like had the pressure of publicity been brought to bear on the parties during the proceeding itself.

GANNETT CO. *v.* DePASQUALE

As a rule, the right of the accused to a fair trial is compatible with the interest of the public in maintaining the publicity of pretrial proceedings. "In the overwhelming majority of criminal trials, pretrial publicity presents few unmanageable threats to this important right." *Nebraska Press Assn. v. Stuart*, 427 U. S., at 551. Our cases "cannot be made to stand for the proposition that juror exposure to information about a state defendant's prior convictions or to news accounts of the crime with which he is charged alone presumptively deprives the defendant of due process." *Murphy v. Florida*, 421 U. S. 794, 799 (1975). A high level of publicity is not necessarily inconsistent with the ability of the defendant to obtain a fair trial where the publicity has been largely factual in nature. *id.*, at 802; *Beck v. Washington*, 369 U. S. 541, 542–545, 557–558 (1962), or where it abated some time prior to trial. See *Stroble v. California*, 343 U. S. 181, 191–194 (1952).

In those cases where the court has found publicity sufficiently prejudicial as to warrant reversal on due process grounds, the publicity went far beyond the normal bounds of coverage. In *Irvin v. Dowd*, 366 U. S. 717 (1961), for example, there was a barrage of adverse publicity about the defendant's offer to plead guilty and his confession to several murders and burglaries. In *Rideau v. Louisiana*, 373 U. S. 723 (1963), there was live pretrial television coverage of the defendant's confession. And in *Estes v. Texas*, 381 U. S. 532 (1965), and *Sheppard v. Maxwell*, 384 U. S. 333 (1966), the press, and especially the electronic media, intruded to such an extent on the courtroom proceedings that all semblance of decorum and sobriety was lost. See *Nebraska Press Assn. v. Stuart*, 427 U. S., at 551–556; *Murphy v. Florida*, 421 U. S., at 798–799.

But "[c]ases such as these are relatively rare." *Nebraska Press*, 427 U. S., at 554. All our decisions in this area, "[t]aken together, . . . demonstrate that pretrial publicity—even pervasive, adverse publicity—does not inevitably lead to

GANNETT CO. *v.* DePASQUALE

an unfair trial." *Ibid.* The cases provide the background
against which a trial judge must evaluate a motion to close a
hearing on the ground that an open hearing will result in publicity so prejudicial that a defendant will be deprived of his
due process right to a fair trial. In *Stroble, Murphy,* and
Beck, of course, the sharpened vision of hindsight helped the
Court to see that the trial had been fair notwithstanding the
publicity. The trial judge faced with a closure motion has
the more difficult task of looking into the future. We do not
mean to suggest that only in the egregious circumstances of
cases such as *Estes* and *Sheppard* would closure be permissible. But to some extent the harm that the defendant fears
from publicity is also speculative.[24]

If, after considering the essential factors, the trial court
determines that the accused has carried his burden of establishing that closure is necessary, the Sixth Amendment is no
barrier to reasonable restrictions on public access designed to
meet that need. Any restrictions imposed, however, must extend no further than the circumstances reasonably require.
Thus, it may be possible to exclude the public from only those
portions of the proceeding at which the prejudicial information will be disclosed, while admitting it to other portions
where the information the accused seeks to suppress is not
revealed. *United States v. Cianfrani,* 573 F. 2d, at 854.
Further, closure should be temporary in that the court should

---

[24] Although we hold today that a pretrial suppression hearing is the
equivalent of the trial on the merits for purposes of evaluating when
closure is permitted under the Sixth Amendment, it should be clear that
the fact closure is sought at the pretrial hearing will be of importance to
the trial court. The potential for prejudice is greater in the case of the
pretrial hearing. Release of potentially prejudicial information prior to
the swearing of the jury presents the primary threat to the accused's fair
trial right. Once the jury is sworn, there is less risk that disclosure
during the trial itself will result in injury. The court's powers to
sequester and to admonish should be sufficient to meet any threat in
this respect.

GANNETT CO. *v.* DePASQUALE

ensure that an accurate record is made of those proceedings held *in camera* and that the public is permitted proper access to the record as soon as the threat to the defendant's fair trial right has passed.

We thus reject the suggestion that the defendant alone may determine when closure should occur. We also reject any notion that the decision whether to permit closure should be in the hands of the prosecutor on the theory that he is the representative of the public's interest. It is in part the public's interest in observing the conduct of the prosecutor, and the police with whom he is closely associated, that the public trial provision serves. To cloak his own actions or those of his associates from public scrutiny, a prosecutor thus may choose to close a hearing where the facts do not warrant it. Moreover, prosecutors often are elected, and the public has a strong interest, as noted, in observing the conduct of elected officials. In addition, the prosecutor may fear reversal on appeal if he too strenuously resists the motion of a defendant to close a hearing. Conversely, a prosecutor may wrap in the mantle of the public interest his desire to disseminate prejudicial information about an accused prior to trial, and so resist a motion to close where the circumstances warrant some restrictions on access. We thus are unwilling to commit to the discretion of the prosecutor, against whose own misconduct or incompetence the public trial requirement is designed in part to protect, the decision as to whether an accused's motion to close will be granted.

As a final safeguard, we conclude that any person removed from a court should be given a reasonable opportunity to state his objections prior to the effectiveness of the order. This opportunity need not take the form of an evidentiary hearing; it need not encompass extended legal argument that results in delay; and the public need not be given prior notice that a closure order will be considered at a given time and place. But where a member of the public contemporaneously

GANNETT CO. *v.* DePASQUALE

objects, the court should provide a reasonable opportunity to that person to state his objection. Finally, the court should state on the record its findings concerning the need for closure so that a reviewing court may be adequately informed

V

The Sixth Amendment, in establishing the public's right of access to a criminal trial and a pretrial proceeding also fixes the rights of the press in this regard. Petitioner, as a newspaper publisher, enjoys (the same) right of access to the *Jackson v. Denno* hearing at issue in this case as does the general public. And what petitioner sees and hears in the courtroom it may, like any other citizen, publish or report consistent with the First Amendment. "Of course, there is nothing that proscribes the press from reporting events that transpire in the courtroom." *Sheppard* v. *Maxwell,* 384 U. S., at 362–363. Newspaper, television, and radio reporters "are entitled to the same rights as the general public" to have access to the courtroom, *Estes* v. *Texas,* 381 U. S., at 540, where they "are always present if they wish to be and are plainly free to report whatever occurs in open court through their respective media. *Id.,* at 541–542. "[O]nce a public hearing ha[s] been held what transpired there could not be subject to prior restraint. *Nebraska Press Assn.* v. *Stuart,* 427 U. S., at 568

Petitioner acknowledges that it seeks no greater rights than those due the general public. But it argues that, the Sixth Amendment aside, the First Amendment protects the free flow of information about judicial proceedings, and that this flow may not be cut off without meeting the standards required to justify the imposition of a prior restraint under the First Amendment. Specifically, petitioner argues that the First Amendment prohibits closure of a pretrial proceeding except in accord with the standards established in *Nebraska Press* and only after notice and hearing and a stay pending appeal.

We do not agree. As we have noted, this case involves no

GANNETT CO. *v.* DePASQUALE

restraint upon publication or upon comment about information already in the possession of the public or the press. It involves an issue of access to a judicial proceeding. To the extent the Constitution protects a right of public access to the proceeding, the standards enunciated under the Sixth Amendment suffice to protect that right. We therefore need not reach the issue of First Amendment access.

VI

We turn, at long last, to the exclusion order entered by Judge DePasquale. It is clear that the judge entered the order because of his concern for the fair trial rights of the defendants and his belief that those rights would be threatened if the hearing were public. We acknowledge that concern, but we conclude that the order was not justified on the facts of this case.

There was no factual basis upon which the court could conclude that a substantial probability existed that an open proceeding would result in harm to the defendants' rights to a fair trial. The coverage in petitioner's newspapers of Clapp's disappearance and the subsequent arrest and prosecution of Greathouse and Jones was circumspect. Stories appeared on only 7 of the 18 days between Clapp's disappearance and the arraignments. All coverage ceased on August 6 and did not resume until after the suppression hearing three months later. The stories that appeared were largely factual in nature. The reporting was restrained, and free from editorializing or sensationalism. There was no screaming headline, no lurid photograph, no front page overemphasis. The stories were of moderate length and were linked to factual developments in the case. And petitioner's newspapers had only a small circulation in Seneca County. See n. 2, *supra.*

In addition, counsel for respondents stated that the only fact not known to petitioner prior to the suppression hearing was the content of the confessions. Tr. of Oral Arg. 40.

GANNETT CO. *v.* DePASQUALE

Prior to the hearing, petitioner had learned of the confessions and of the existence and nature of the physical evidence sought to be suppressed. It is thus not at all likely that the openness of the suppression hearing would have resulted in the divulgence of additional information that would have made it more probable that Greathouse and Jones would be denied a fair trial.

On this record, we cannot conclude, as a matter of law, that there was a sufficient showing to establish the strict and inescapable necessity that would support an exclusion order. The circumstances also would not have justified a holding by the trial court that there was substantial probability that alternatives to closure would not have sufficed to protect the rights of the accused.

It has been said that publicity "is the soul of justice." J. Bentham, A Treatise on Judicial Evidence 67 (1825). And in many ways it is: open judicial processes, especially in the criminal field, protect against judicial, prosecutorial, and police abuse, provide a means for citizens to obtain information about the criminal justice system and the performance of public officials; and safeguard the integrity of the courts. Publicity is essential to the preservation of public confidence in the rule of law and in the operation of courts. Only in rare circumstances does this principle clash with the rights of the criminal defendant to a fair trial so as to justify exclusion. The Sixth and Fourteenth Amendments require that the States take care to determine that those circumstances exist before excluding the public from a hearing to which it otherwise is entitled to come freely. Those circumstances did not exist in this case.

The judgment of the Court of Appeals of New York, accordingly, is reversed.

It is so ordered

1st DRAFT

SUPREME COURT OF THE UNITED STATES

No. 77–1301

Gannett Co., Inc., Petitioner, *v.* Daniel A. DePasquale, Etc., et al.	On Writ of Certiorari to the Court of Appeals of New York.

[April —, 1979]

Mr. Justice Stewart, dissenting.

The Sixth Amendment to the Constitution provides that "In all criminal prosecutions, *the accused* shall enjoy the right to a speedy and public trial, by an impartial jury. . . ." (Emphasis added.) The question presented in this case is whether, under the Sixth and Fourteenth Amendments, members of *the public* have an independent constitutional right to insist upon access to a pretrial judicial proceeding, even though the accused, the prosecutor and the trial judge all have agreed to the closure of that proceeding in order to assure a fair trial.[1]

The trial court in this murder case excluded the public from a pretrial suppression hearing. This ruling was made after defense attorneys had argued that the unabated buildup of publicity about the murder had jeopardized the prospect of a fair trial for their clients. The prosecutor did not oppose the

---

[1] The question in this case is not, as the Court repeatedly suggests, *ante*, at 2, 13, 17–18, 20–21, 25–26, 28, 29, 30, 34, whether the Sixth and Fourteenth Amendments give a defendant the right to compel a secret trial. In this case the defendants, the prosecutor, and the judge all agreed that closure of the pretrial suppression hearing was necessary to protect the defendants' right to a fair trial. Moreover, a transcript of the proceedings was later made available to the public. Thus there is no need to decide the question framed by the Court. If that question were presented, I would agree that the defendant has no such right. See *Singer* v. *United States*, 380 U. S. 24, 35 ("[A]lthough a defendant can, under some circumstances, waive his constitutional right to a public trial, he has no absolute right to compel a private trial").

GANNETT CO. *v.* DePASQUALE

motion to exclude the public. The motion was granted by the trial judge after finding that "there was a reasonable probability of prejudice to these defendants" that would endanger their constitutional right to a fair trial. The New York Court of Appeals upheld the trial court's exclusion order, premised upon the conclusion that continued publicity in the community "would threaten the impaneling of a constitutionally impartial jury in the county of venue."[2]

The Court today reverses the judgment of the New York Court of Appeals, holding that a constitutional right of public access requires a general rule that pretrial suppression hearings must be kept open. The inevitable result of this decision will be to increase the probability that defendants will be unfairly convicted as a result of prejudicial pretrial publicity.

In effect, the Court has somewhere discovered a new constitutional right of public access and then exalted this right over the explicit constitutional right of the accused to receive a fair trial by an impartial jury. Because of my profound disagreement with this result, I respectfully dissent.

I

This Court has long recognized that adverse publicity can endanger the ability of a defendant to receive a fair trial.

---

[2] I am far less confident than the Court that an open suppression hearing would have posed no real threat to the prospects of a fair trial. This case involved a highly publicized murder in a small community. The suppression hearing was closed to prevent further dissemination of information concerning allegedly unlawfully obtained confessions and unlawfully seized items of evidence. Newspaper, radio, and television coverage of the hearing might well have been intense, had the hearing been opened to the public. The extent of television and radio coverage before the suppression hearing is not disclosed by the record. Under these circumstances, we should be extremely hesitant to second-guess the finding of the local trial judge who was undoubtedly in the best position to know whether a public suppression hearing would pose a "reasonable probability of prejudice to these defendants."

GANNETT CO. *v.* DePASQUALE

E. g., Sheppard v. *Maxwell,* 384 U. S. 333; *Irvin* v. *Dowd,* 366 U. S. 717; *Maxwell* v. *United States,* 360 U. S. 310. Cf. *Estes* v. *Texas,* 381 U. S. 532. To safeguard the due process rights of the accused, a trial judge has an affirmative constitutional duty to minimize the effects of prejudicial pretrial publicity. *Sheppard* v. *Maxwell, supra.* And because of the Constitution's pervasive concern for these due process rights, a trial judge may surely take protective measures even when they are not "strictly and inescapably necessary."

Publicity concerning pretrial suppression hearings such as the one involved in the present case poses special risks of unfairness. The whole purpose of such hearings is to screen out unreliable or illegally obtained evidence and insure that this evidence does not become known to the jury. Cf. *Jackson* v. *Denno,* 378 U. S. 368. Publicity concerning the proceedings at a pretrial hearing, however, could easily influence public opinion against a defendant and inform potential jurors of inculpatory information wholly inadmissable at the actual trial.

The danger of publicity concerning pretrial suppression hearings is particularly acute, because it is impossible to measure with any degree of certainty the effects of such publicity on the fairness of the trial. After the commencement of the trial itself, inadmissible prejudicial information about a defendant can be kept from a jury by a variety of means.[3] When such information is publicized during a pretrial proceeding, however, it may never be altogether kept from potential jurors. Closure of pretrial proceedings is really the only method that a trial judge can employ to attempt to insure that the fairness of a trial will not be jeopardized by the dissemination of such information throughout the com-

---

[3] In addition to excluding inadmissible evidence, a trial judge may order sequestration of the jury or take any of a variety of protective measures. See *Nebraska Press Assn.* v. *Stuart,* 427 U. S. 562–565; *Sheppard* v. *Maxwell,* 384 U. S. 333, 358–362.

GANNETT CO. *v.* DePASQUALE

munity before the trial itself has even begun. Cf. *Rideau* v.
Louisiana, 373 U. S. 723.[4]

II

A

The Sixth Amendment surrounds a criminal trial with
guarantees such as the rights to notice, confrontation, and
compulsory process that have as their overriding purpose the
protection of the accused from prosecutorial and judicial
abuses.[5] Among the guarantees that the Amendment provides

---

[4] The future power of a trial judge to order closure of a pretrial proceeding to protect the right of an accused to a fair trial is far from clear
from the opinion of the Court. The Court states that because of the
importance of a fair trial, a judge can restrict access to a pretrial suppression hearing "where such restriction is necessary in order to ensure that a
defendant not be denied a fair trial as a result of prejudicial publicity
flowing from that hearing." *Ante,* at 39. But closure can be ordered only
if it is "strictly and inescapably necessary" to protect the right of the
accused to a fair trial. *Ante,* at 39.

In making this determination, the trial judge must first decide whether
the accused has established that there is a "substantial probability that
irreparable damage to his fair trial right will result." Factors such as the
size of the jury pool, the extent of media coverage, and the extent to which
information sought to be suppressed is already known to the public must
be considered. *Ante,* at 39–40. Second, the accused must show a "substantial probability that alternatives to closure will not protect adequately
his right to a fair trial." *Ante,* at 39–40. Finally, "the accused must
demonstrate that there is a substantial probability that closure will be
effective in protecting against the perceived harm." *Ante,* at 41. As a
final safeguard "any person removed from a court should be given a
reasonable opportunity to state his objections . . . ." *Ante,* at 44.

In all likelihood, the burden and delay imposed by this complicated
and multifaceted inquiry, coupled with the virtually unattainable "strictly
and inescapably necessary" standard, will make it all but impossible for a
judge constitutionally to order closure of a pretrial suppression hearing.

[5] The Sixth Amendment provides:

"In all criminal prosecutions, the accused shall enjoy the right to a
speedy and public trial, by an impartial jury of the State and district
wherein the crime shall have been committed, which district shall have
been previously ascertained by law, and to be informed of the nature and

GANNETT CO. *v.* DePASQUALE

to a person charged with the commission of a criminal offense, and to him alone, is the right to a public trial. The Constitution nowhere mentions any right of access to a criminal trial on the part of the public; its guarantee, like the others enumerated, is personal to the accused.

Our cases have uniformly recognized the public trial guarantee as one created for the benefit of the defendant. In *In re Oliver*, 333 U. S. 257, this Court held that the secrecy of a criminal contempt trial violated the accused's right to a public trial under the Fourteenth Amendment. The right to a public trial, the Court stated, "has always been recognized as a safeguard against any attempt to employ the courts as instruments of persecution. The knowledge that every criminal trial is subject to contemporaneous review in the forum of public opinion is an effective restraint on possible abuse of judicial power." *Id.*, at 270. In an explanatory footnote, the Court stated that the public trial guarantee:

> ". . . 'is for the protection of all persons accused of crime—the innocently accused, that they may not become the victim of an unjust prosecution, as well as the guilty, that they may be awarded a fair trial—that one rule [as to public trials] must be observed and applied to all.' Frequently quoted is the statement in 1 Cooley, Constitutional Limitations (8th ed. 1927) at 647: 'The requirement of a public trial is for the benefit of the accused; that the public may see he is fairly dealt with and not unjustly condemned, and that the presence of interested spectators may keep his triers keenly alive to a sense of their responsibility and to the importance of their functions . . . .' " *Id.*, at 270 25.[6]

_____

cause of the accusation; to be confronted with the witnesses against him; to have compulsory process for obtaining witnesses in his favor, and to have the Assistance of Counsel for his defence."

[6] The Court also recognized that while the right to a public trial is guaranteed to an accused, publicity also provides various benefits to the public. *In re Oliver*, 333 U. S. 257, 270 n. 24.

GANNETT CO. *v.* DePASQUALE

Similarly, in *Estes* v. *Texas*, 381 U. S. 532, the Court held that a defendant was deprived of his right to due process of law under the Fourteenth Amendment by the televising and broadcasting of his trial. In rejecting the claim that the media representatives had a constitutional right to televise the trial, the Court stated that "[t]he purpose of the requirement of a public trial was to guarantee that the accused be fairly dealt with and not unjustly condemned." *Id.*, at 539. See also *id.*, at 588 ("Thus the right of 'public trial is not one belonging to the public, but one belonging to the accused, and inhering in the institutional process by which justice is administered.") (concurring opinion of Harlan, J.); *id.*, at 583 ("The public trial provision of the Sixth Amendment is a 'guarantee of an accused'. . . [and] a necessary component of an accused's right to a fair trial . . .") (concurring opinion of Warren, C. J.).

Thus both the *Oliver* and *Estes* cases recognized that the constitutional guarantee of a public trial is for the benefit of the defendant. There is not the slightest suggestion in either case that there is any correlative right in members of the public to insist upon a public trial.[7]

---

[7] Numerous commentators have also recognized that only a defendant has a right to a public trial under the Sixth Amendment. *E. g.*, Radin, The Right to a Public Trial, 6 Temple L. Q. 381, 392 (a public right to a public trial "cannot be derived from the Constitution because the Constitution certainly does not mention a public trial as a privilege of the public, but expressly that of the accused."); Boldt, Should Canon 35 Be Amended?, 35 A. B. A. J. 55 (1955) ("[T]he guarantee of public trial is for the benefit of persons charged with crime . . . . It is significant that the Constitution does not say that the public has the right to 'enjoy' or even attend trials. There is nothing in the constitutional language indicating that any individual other than the accused in a criminal trial . . . [has] either a right to attend the trial or to publicity emanating from the trial."); Note, The Right to Attend Criminal Hearings, 78 Colum. L. Rev. 1308, 1321 (1978) (since the Sixth Amendment confers a right to a public trial to the accused, "to elaborate a parallel and possibly adverse public right of access from the public trial guarantee clause strains even flexible

GANNETT CO. *v.* DePASQUALE

B

While the Sixth Amendment guarantees to a defendant in a criminal case the right to a public trial, it does not guarantee the right to compel a private trial. "The ability to waive a constitutional right does not ordinarily carry with it the right to insist upon the opposite of that right." *Singer* v. *United States*, 380 U. S. 24, 34.ˣ But the issue here is not whether the defendant can compel a private trial. See n. 1, *supra*. Rather the issue is whether members of the public have an enforceable right to a public trial that can be asserted independently of the parties in the litigation.[9]

constitutional language beyond its proper bounds."): Note, The Right to a Public Trial in Criminal Cases, 41 N. Y. U. L. Rev. 1138, 1156 (1966) ("Despite the importance of the public interest, however, it does not appear that a public right is so 'rooted in the traditions and conscience of our people as to be ranked as fundamental,'. . . particularly in view of the uncertain status of this right in the majority of state courts.").

See also Powell, The Right to a Fair Trial, 51 A. B. A. J. (1965) ("We must bear in mind that the primary purpose of a public trial and of the media's right as a part of the public to attend and report what occurs there is to protect the accused."); 1 Cooley, Constitutional Limitations 647 (8th ed. 1927) ("The requirement of a public trial is for the benefit of the accused. . . .").

It appears that before today, only one court, state or federal, has ever held that the Sixth and Fourteenth Amendments confer upon members of the public a right of access to a criminal trial. *United States* v. *Cianfrani*, 573 F. 2d 835 (CA3 1978). The *Cianfrani* case has been criticized for its departure from the plain meaning of the Sixth Amendment. See Columbia Note *supra*, at 1321–1322.

[8] In *Faretta* v. *California*, 422 U. S. 806, by contrast, the Court held that the Sixth and Fourteenth Amendments guarantee that an accused has a right to proceed without counsel in a criminal case when he voluntarily and intelligently elects to do so. In reaching this result, the Court relied on the language and structure of the Sixth Amendment which grants to the accused the right to make a defense. As part of this right to make a defense, the Amendment speaks of the "assistance of counsel," thus contemplating a norm in which the accused, and not a lawyer, is master of his own defense. *Id.*, at 819–820.

[9] One of the ironies embodied in the Court's opinion is that the public

GANNETT CO. *v.* DePASQUALE

There can be no blinking the fact that there is a strong societal interest in public trials. Openness in court proceedings may improve the quality of testimony, induce unknown witnesses to come forward with relevant testimony, cause all trial participants to perform their duties more conscientiously, and generally give the public an opportunity to observe the judicial system. *Estes* v. *Texas, supra,* at 583 (Warren, C. J., concurring). But there is a strong societal interest in other constitutional guarantees extended to the accused as well. The public, for example, has a definite and concrete interest in seeing that justice is swiftly and fairly administered. As the Court noted in *Barker* v. *Wingo*, 407 U. S. 514, 519, "there is a societal interest in providing a speedy trial which exists separate from, and at times in opposition to, the interests of the accused." Similarly, the public has an interest in having a criminal case heard by a jury, an interest distinct from the defendant's interest in being tried by a jury of his peers. *Patton* v. *United States*, 281 U. S. 276, 312.

Recognition of an independent public interest in the enforcement of Sixth Amendment guarantees is a far cry, however, from the creation of a constitutional right on the part of the public. In an adversary system of criminal justice, the public interest in the administration of justice is protected by the participants in the litigation. Thus, because of the great public interest in jury trials as the preferred mode of fact-finding in criminal cases, a defendant cannot waive a jury

---

now has an enforceable right to a public trial even if nobody ever asserts the right. Thus even if nobody objects to closure, the judge can still not close the suppression hearing unless he finds that it is "strictly and inescapably necessary" to protect the right of the accused to a fair trial. This is true even if all participants in the litigation, including the judge, agree that closure is appropriate. In effect, therefore, the newly created public right to a public trial cannot be waived under any circumstances. Since even explicit constitutional guarantees (such as the right of an accused to a public trial) can be waived, this is truly an extraordinary result.

GANNETT CO. *v.* DePASQUALE

trial without the consent of the prosecutor and judge. *Singer*
v. *United States, supra,* at 38; *Patton* v. *United States, supra,*
at 312. But if the defendant waives his right to a jury trial,
and the prosecutor and the judge consent, it could hardly be
seriously argued that a member of the public could demand a
jury trial because of the societal interest in that mode of fact-
finding. Cf. Fed. Rule Crim. Proc. 23 (a) (trials to be by
jury unless waived by a defendant, but the court must approve
and the prosecution must consent to the waiver). Similarly,
while a defendant cannot convert his right to a speedy trial
into a right to compel an indefinite postponement, a member
of the general public surely has no right to prevent a continuance in order to vindicate the public interest in the efficient
administration of justice. In short, our adversary system of
criminal justice is premised upon the proposition that the
public interest is fully protected by the participants in the
litigation.[10]

---

[10] The Court has recognized that a prosecutor "is the representative not
of an ordinary party to a controversy, but of a sovereignty whose obligation to govern impartially is as compelling as its obligation to govern at
all; and whose interest, therefore, in a criminal prosecution is not that it
shall win a case, but that justice shall be done. As such, he is in a
particular and very definite sense the servant of the law. . . ." *Berger* v.
United States. 295 U. S. 78, 88. The responsibility of the prosecutor as a
representative of the public surely encompasses a duty to protect the
societal interest in an open trial. But this responsibility also requires him
to be sensitive to the due process rights of a defendant to a fair trial.
A fortiori, the trial judge has the same dual obligation.

There is some force to the suggestion of the Court, *ante,* at 44, that the
prosecutor cannot always be trusted with protecting the public interest in
open proceedings. But in the situation presented here the public interest
was protected by more than the prosecutor alone—both adversaries and
the trial judge agreed in this case that closure was required to protect the
right of the defendants to a fair trial. The public interest was further
protected by subsequent access to a transcript of the proceedings, thus
assuring the public an opportunity to scrutinize the conduct of the
participants in the litigation.

GANNETT CO. *v.* DePASQUALE

III

In conferring upon members of the general public a constitutional right to attend a criminal trial, despite the obvious lack of support for such a right in the structure or text of the Sixth Amendment, the Court relies heavily on the history of the public trial guarantee. In my view, the Court has ultimately demonstrated no more than the existence of a common-law rule of open civil and criminal proceedings.

A

Not many common-law rules have been elevated to the status of constitutional rights. The provisions of our Constitution do reflect an incorporation of certain few common-law rules and a rejection of others. The common-law right to a jury trial, for example, is explicitly embodied in the Sixth and Seventh Amendments. The common-law rule that looked upon jurors as interested parties who could give evidence against a defendant [11] was explicitly rejected by the Sixth Amendment provision that a defendant is entitled to be tried by an "impartial jury." But the vast majority of common-law rules were neither made part of the Constitution nor explicitly rejected by it.

Our judicial duty in this case is to determine whether the common-law rule of open proceedings was incorporated, rejected, or left undisturbed by the Sixth Amendment. Instead of pursuing that course, the Court simply states that there is no "evidence that casting the public trial concept in terms of the right of the accused signaled a departure from the common law practice. . . ," *ante,* at 27, and that "there is no indication that the First Congress, in proposing what became the Sixth Amendment, meant to depart from the common law practice . . . ." *Ante,* at 28. Similarly, when discussing the

---

[11] Blackstone, for example, stated that it "universally obtains" that if a juror knows of a matter in issue, he may "give his evidence publicly in court." 3 W. Blackstone, Commentaries 374.

GANNETT CO. *v.* DePASQUALE

evolution of the various state constitutions, the Court says that there is no evidence that they "intended to depart from the common law practice of holding court in public." *Ante,* at 28 n. 15.

The fundamental defect in the Court's analysis lies in its confusion of what the Constitution permits with what it requires. It has never been suggested that by phrasing the public trial guarantee as a right of the accused, the Framers intended to reject the common-law rule of open proceedings. There is no question that the Sixth Amendment permits and even presumes open trials as a norm. But the issue here is whether the Constitution *requires* that a pretrial proceeding such as this one be opened to the public, even though the participants in the litigation agree that it should be closed to protect the defendants' right to a fair trial. The Court's opinion totally fails to demonstrate that the Framers of the Sixth Amendment intended to create a constitutional right in strangers to attend a pretrial proceeding, when all that they actually did was to confer upon the accused an explicit right to demand a public trial.[12] In conspicuous contrast with some

---

[12] An additional problem with the Court's historical analysis is that it is equally applicable to civil and criminal cases and therefore proves too much. For many centuries, both civil and criminal trials have traditionally been open to the public. As early as 1685, Sir John Hawles, quoted *ante,* at 24 n. 13, commented that open proceedings were necessary so "that truth may be discovered in civil *and* criminal matters" (emphasis added). English commentators also assumed that the common-law rule was that the public could attend civil and criminal trials without distinguishing between the two. *E. g.,* 2 E. Coke, Institutes of the Laws of England 103 (6th ed. 1681) ("all Causes ought to be heard . . . openly in the Kings Courts"); 3 W. Blackstone, Commentaries 372 (1768); M. Hale, The History of the Common Law of England 343, 345 (6th ed. 1820); E. Jenks, The Book of English Law 73–74 (6th ed. 1967).

The experience in the American colonies was analogous. From the beginning, the norm was open trials. Indeed, the 1677 New Jersey Constitution, quoted *ante,* at 27, provided that any person could attend a trial whether it was "civil *or* criminal" (emphasis added). Similarly, the 1682

GANNETT CO. *v.* DePASQUALE

of the early state constitutions that provided for a public right
to open civil and criminal trials,[13] the Sixth Amendment
confers the right to a public trial only upon a defendant and
only in a criminal case.

B

But even if the Sixth and Fourteenth Amendments could
properly be viewed as embodying the common-law right of the
public to attend criminal trials, I think the decision of the
Court today would still be wrong. For there exists no persuasive evidence that at common-law members of the public
had any right to attend pretrial proceedings; indeed, there is
substantial evidence to the contrary.[14] By the time of the
adoption of the Constitution, public trials were clearly asso-

---

and 1776 Pennsylvania Constitutions, quoted *ante,* at 17, 28, both provided
that *"all* courts shall be open" (emphasis added).

If the existence of a common-law rule were the test for whether there
is a Sixth Amendment public right to a public trial, therefore, there would
be such a right in civil as well as criminal cases. But the Sixth Amendment does not speak in terms of civil cases at all; by its terms it is
limited to providing rights to an accused in criminal cases. In short, I
see no principled basis upon which a public right of access to judicial
proceedings can be limited to criminal cases if the scope of the right is
defined by the common law rather than the text and structure of the
Constitution.

Indeed, many of the advantages of public criminal trials are equally
applicable in the civil trial context. While the operation of the judicial
process in civil cases is often of interest only to the parties in the litigation,
this is not always the case. *E. g., Dred Scott v. Sandford,* 60 U. S. (19
How.) 393; *Plessy v. Ferguson,* 163 U. S. 537; *Brown v. Board of Education,* 347 U. S. 483; *Regents of the University of California v. Bakke,* ——
U. S. ——. Thus in some civil cases, the public interest in access, and the
salutary effect of publicity, may be as strong or stronger than in most
criminal cases.

[13] See n. 12, *supra.*

[14] Although pretrial suppression hearings were unknown at common law,
other preliminary hearings were formalized by statute as early as 1554
and 1555. 1 & 2 Phil. & M., ch. 13 (1554); 2 & 3 Phil. & M., ch. 10
(1555).

GANNETT CO. *v.* DePASQUALE

ciated with the protection of the defendant.[15] And pretrial proceedings, precisely because of the same concern for a fair trial, were never characterized by the same degree of openness as were actual trials.[16]

[15] I do not agree with the Court's assertion, *ante*, at 23–24, that the tradition of publicity was not associated with the interests of the defendant. What the Court says was probably true until the abolition of the Star Chamber, but not thereafter.

After the abolition of the Star Chamber in 1641, defendants in criminal cases began to acquire many of the rights that are presently embodied in the Sixth Amendment. Thus the accused now had the right to confront witnesses, call witnesses in his own behalf, and generally to a fair trial as we now know it. It was during this period that the public trial first became identified as a right of the accused. As one commentator has stated:

"The public trial, although it had always been the custom, acquired new significance. It gave the individual protection against being denied any of his other fundamental rights. A public trial would make it difficult for a judge to abuse a jury or the accused. Any such abuses would cause much public indignation. Thus, it must have seemed implicit that the public trial was as much an essential element of a fair trial as any of the newer conventions." Note, Legal History: Origins of the Public Trial, 35 Ind. L. J. 251, 255 (1960).

It was during this period that we first find defendants demanding a public trial. See, *The Trial of John Lilbourne*, 4 How. St. 1270, 1274 (1649), in which Lilbourne, on trial for treason, referred to a public trial as "the first Fundamental liberty of an Englishman." Indeed, the fact that the Framers guaranteed to an accused the right to a public trial in the same Amendment that contains the other fair trial rights of an accused also suggests that open trials were by then clearly associated with the rights of a defendant.

[16] Even with respect to trials themselves, the tradition of publicity has not been as universal as the Court suggests. Exclusion of the general public has been upheld, for example, in cases involving violent crimes against minors. *Geise v. United States*, 262 F. 2d 151 (CA9 1958). The public has also been temporarily excluded from trials during testimony of certain witnesses. *E. g., Beauchamp v. Cahill*, 297 Ky. 505, 180 S. W. 2d 423 (1944) (exclusion justified when children forced to testify to revolting facts); *State v. Callahan*, 100 Minn. 63, 110 N. W. 342 (1907) (exclusion justified when embarrassment could prevent effective testimony). Exclu-

GANNETT CO. *v.* DePASQUALE

Under English common law, the public had no right to attend pretrial proceedings. *E. g.,* E. Jencks, The Book of English Law 75 (6th ed. 1967) ("It must, of course, be remembered that the principle of publicity only applies to the actual trial of a case, not necessarily to the preliminary or prefactory stages of the proceedings . . ."); F. W. Maitland, Justice and Police 129 (1885) (The "preliminary trial of accused persons has gradually assumed a very judicial form . . . The place in which it is held is indeed no 'open court'; the public can be excluded if the magistrate thinks the ends of justice will thus be best answered . . ."). See also Indictable Offenses Act. 11 § 12 Vict., ch. 42, § 19 (1848) (providing that pretrial proceedings should not be deemed an open court and that the public could therefore be excluded); Magistrate's Court Act. 15 & 16 Geo. 621 Eliz 2, ch. 55, § 4 (2) (1952) (same).[17]

----

sion has also been permitted when the evidence in a case was expected to be obscene. *State v. Croak,* 167 La. 92, 118 So. 703 (1928). Finally, trial judges have been given broad discretion to exclude spectators to protect order in their courtrooms. *United States ex rel. Orlando v. Fay,* 350 F. 2d 967 (CA2 1965) (exclusion of general public justified after an outburst in court by defendant and his mother).

Approximately half the States also have statutory or constitutional provisions containing limitations upon public trials. *E. g.,* Alabama Constit. 1901, Art. VI § 169 (public can be excluded in rape cases); Ga. Code § 81-1006 (1972) (public can be excluded where evidence is vulgar); Mass. Gen. Laws Ann. ch. 278, § 16A (1958) (general public can be excluded from all trials of designated crimes); Minn. Stat. § 631.04 (1971) (no person under 17 who is not a party shall be present in a criminal trial); Va. Code § 19.1-246 (1960) (court may in its discretion exclude all persons "not deemed necessary" in all felony and misdemeanor prosecutions).

[17] The Court relies on the development in England of a common law "privilege for the reporting of judicial proceedings," *ante,* at 26 n. 14, to support its argument that trials were always open to the public. The Court, however, overlooks the fact that this privilege did not extend to the reporting of pretrial proceedings. Thus in the well-known case of *Rex v. Fisher,* 2 Camp. 563, 170 Eng. Rep. 1253 (1811), the court forbad the dissemination of information about a pretrial hearing to protect the right

GANNETT CO. *v.* DePASQUALE

Closed pretrial proceedings have been a familiar part of the judicial landscape in this country as well. The original Field Code published in 1850, for example, provided that pretrial hearings should be closed to the public "upon the request of a defendant." [18] The explanatory report made clear that this provision was designed to protect defendants from prejudicial pretrial publicity:

> "[I]f the examination must necessarily be public, the consequence may be that the testimony upon the merely preliminary examination will be spread before the community, and a state of opinion created, which, in cases of great public interest, will render it difficult to obtain an unprejudiced jury. The interests of justice require that the case of the defendant should not be prejudiced, if it can be avoided; and no one can justly complain, that until he is put upon his trial, the dangers of this prejudgment are obviated." [19]

of the accused to receive a fair trial. In distinguishing between the privilege accorded the reporting of trials, and the absence of such a privilege of reporting pretrial proceedings, Lord Ellenborough declared:

"If anything is more important than another in the administration of justice, it is that jurymen should come to the trial of persons on whose guilt or innocence they are to decide, with minds pure and unprejudiced . . . . Trials at law, fairly reported, although they may occasionally prove injurious to individuals, have been held to be privileged. Let them continue to be so privileged . . . . But these preliminary examinations have no such privilege. Their only tendency is to prejudge those whom the law still presumes to be innocent, and to poison the sources of justice." 170 Eng. Rep., at 1255.

See also *The King* v. *Parke*, [1903] 2 K. B. 432, 438.

[18] Commissioners of Practice and Pleadings, Code of Criminal Procedure, Final Rep., § 202 (1850).

[19] *Id.*, at 94. To protect a defendant's right to a public trial, however, closure could be ordered only at the request of the defendant:

"To guard the rights of the defendant against a secret examination, the section provides that it shall not be conducted in private, unless at his request." *Id.*, at 95.

GANNETT CO. *v.* DePASQUALE

Indeed, eight of the States that have retained all or part of the Field Code have kept the explicit provision relating to closed pretrial hearings.[20]

IV

The petitioners also argue that they, as members of the press, had a right of access to this judicial proceeding under the First and Fourteenth Amendments. This Court has held, however, that "[t]he First Amendment . . . grants the press no right to information about a trial superior to that of the general public." *Nixon v. Warner Communications, Inc.*, 435 U. S. 589, 609. See also *Saxbe v. Washington Post Co.*, 417 U. S. 843; *Pell v. Procunier*, 417 U. S. 817; *Zemel v. Rusk*, 381 U. S. 1, 16–17; *Estes v. Texas, supra*, at 540. If the public had no enforceable right to attend the pretrial proceeding in this case, it necessarily follows that the petitioners had no such right under the First and Fourteenth Amendments.

---

[20] Ariz. Rev. Stat. Ann., Rule 27 (1956); Cal. Penal Code § 868 (1970); Idaho Code Ann. § 19–811 (1948); Iowa Code § 761.13 (1973); Mont. Rev. Codes Ann. § 95–1202 (1) (1969); Nev. Rev. Stat. § 171.445 (1959); N. D. Code Ann. § 29–07–14 (1974); Utah Code Ann. § 77j–15–13 (1953). Other States have similar provisions. *E. g.*, Pa. Rule Crim. Proc. 323 (f) (providing that suppression hearings shall be open "unless defendant, by his counsel, moves that it be held in the presence of only the defendant, counsel for the parties, court officers, and necessary witnesses."). Still other States allow closure of pretrial hearings without statutory authorization. *Nebraska Press Assn. v. Stuart, supra*, at 568.

Until a year ago, the American Bar Association also endorsed the view that presiding officers should close pretrial hearings at the request of a defendant unless there was no "substantial likelihood" that the defendant would be prejudiced by an open proceeding. ABA Advisory Committee on Fair Trial and Free Press, Project on Standards Relating to Fair Trial and Free Press § 3.1 (1968 draft). The ABA, following the "approach taken by the Supreme Court in *Nebraska Press Association v. Stuart*," has now changed this standard. American Bar Association, Standards Relating to the Administration of Criminal Justice, Fair Trial and Free Press, § 8–3.2, at p. 16 (Approved Draft 1978). The *Nebraska Press* case, however, is irrelevant to the question presented here.

GANNETT CO. *v.* DePASQUALE

V

I certainly do not disparage the general desirability of open judicial proceedings, so effectively demonstrated by the Court. But we are not asked here to declare whether open proceedings represent beneficial social policy, or whether there would be a constitutional barrier to a state law that imposed a stricter standard of closure than the one here employed by the New York courts. Rather, we are asked to hold that the Constitution itself gave the petitioners an affirmative right of access to this pretrial proceeding, even though all the participants in the litigation agreed that it should be closed to protect the fair trial rights of the defendants. That I cannot do.

I would affirm the judgment of the New York Court of Appeals.

77–1301—GANNETT *v.* DEPASQUALE

MR. JUSTICE STEVENS, dissenting.†

Unless one assumes that the prosecutor, the defendant's lawyer and the trial judge are parties to a conspiracy to conceal, the risks that the Court's new rule is intended to avoid are relatively unimportant. Ironically, in that class of cases the new rule may well be ineffective. For the right to object to a closure order is extended only to those persons who happen to be in the courtroom when a closure motion is made.* And in all but the most highly publicized cases—those in which closure is most apt to be justified by the danger of prejudice—conspirators could surely plan the timing of their motion in a way that would frustrate any meaningful objection. Moreover, if we put the notorious cases to one side, it is unlikely that appellate review could often be had in time to remedy an erroneous order.

These observations are not intended to demean the important interests at stake, but rather to highlight the difficulty of fashioning third party rights and remedies to regulate judicial proceedings that historically have involved only the adversaries, the judge, and the jury. Like MR. JUSTICE STEWART—and like most trial judges, prosecutors, and defense counsel—I recognize the great value of public access to judicial proceedings, but I remain convinced that these values will continue to receive their most effective protection from self-interested adversaries. For the reasons stated by MR. JUSTICE STEWART, I do not believe the Court has the authority to create this novel remedy for a random selection of bystanders.

---

† Original in typescript.

* Although I recognize that theoretically the rule applies even when no potential objector is present, in practice the absence of an objection would vitiate the value of the rule.

Had the Blackmun draft opinion of the Court come down as the final *Gannett* opinion, it would have completely resolved the issue of access to criminal proceedings in favor of a wide right on the part of the public and the press. Such a broad holding would have made the *Richmond Newspapers* decision[5] (to be discussed at the end of this chapter) unnecessary. It would also have answered the question left unanswered by *Richmond Newspapers*—does the press have a right of access to pretrial proceedings as well as to criminal trials?—with a strong affirmative.

But the Blackmun draft was not able to secure the fives votes needed to make it into a Court opinion. The day after it was circulated, April 5, 1979, Justice Stewart sent its author a "Dear Harry" note: "I shall in due course circulate a dissenting opinion."

The same day, Justice Blackmun received a letter from Justice Stevens indicating that, "Although I agree with a good deal of what you say in your opinion," he would not change his conference vote. "I probably will adhere to my view that the public interest in open proceedings can be adequately vindicated by the combined efforts of the two adversaries and the trial judge, coupled with a right of access to a transcript promptly after the risk of prejudice has passed." Stevens saw dangers to defendants in the Blackmun holding. "I am fearful that your holding will tolerate prejudice that may not be serious enough to violate the defendant's constitutional rights but will nevertheless enhance his risk of conviction."

On April 18, the promised Stewart draft dissent was circulated. It is reprinted on p. 465. The draft is an abbreviated version of the opinion of the Court that ultimately came down in *Gannett*, with changes made in the latter to convert the draft dissent into the Court opinion (this time changing the "I" in the draft to the "we" of the opinion of the Court). The main omission is the statement of facts, needed only in the final Stewart opinion. The draft dissent starts with the question to which the Blackmun dissent was to object. "The question presented in this case is whether, under the Sixth and Fourteenth Amendments, members of *the public* have an independent constitutional right to insist upon access to a pretrial judicial proceeding, even though the accused, the prosecutor and the trial judge all have agreed to the closure of that proceeding in order to assure a fair trial." (Interestingly, the italics were removed in the final *Gannett* opinion).

The Stewart draft stresses that the Sixth Amendment public trial guaranty is one created for the benefit of the defendant alone. "The Constitution nowhere mentions any right of access to a criminal trial on the part of the public; its guarantee, like the others enumerated, is personal to the accused."

Stewart recognizes that the Sixth Amendment does not guarantee a right in defendant to compel a private trial. But that is not the issue here. "Rather, the issue is whether members of the public have an enforceable right to a public trial that can be asserted independently of the parties in the litigation." The draft, like the final opinion, denies that any such right exists. In our system, "the public interest in the administration of justice is protected by the participants in the litigation." Nor, despite the lengthy historical excursus in the Blackmun draft, does the history of the public trial guaranty justify a different result. "In my view, the Court has ultimately demonstrated no more than the existence of a common-law rule of open civil and criminal proceedings"—not a right elevated to the constitutional plane by the Sixth Amendment.

The Stewart draft concludes by asserting, "even if the Sixth and Fourteenth Amendments could properly be viewed as embodying the common-law right of the public to attend criminal trials, I think the decision of the Court today would still be wrong." The public trial guaranty applies only to trials, not to pretrial proceedings. Nor, under this approach, does the First Amendment compel a different result, since it gives the press no right superior to that of the public. "If the public had no enforceable right to attend the pretrial proceeding in this case, it necessarily follows that the petitioners had no such right under the First and Fourteenth Amendments."

The Stewart draft concludes by noting the general desirability of open judicial proceedings. But the Court is not asked to declare whether open proceedings are a beneficial policy. "Rather, we are asked to hold that the Constitution itself gave the petitioners an affirmative right of access to this pretrial proceeding, even though all the participants in the litigation agreed that it should be closed to protect the fair trial rights of the defendants. That I cannot do."

On April 19, Justice Stevens circulated a two-page typed draft dissent. It is reprinted on p. 482 as an unpublished opinion in the case since Stevens withdrew it before the decision was announced. The Stevens draft argues that "the risks that the Court's new rule is intended to avoid are relatively unimportant. Ironically, in that class of cases the new rule may well be ineffective." Stevens opposes "fashioning third party rights and remedies to regulate judicial proceedings that historically have involved only the adversaries, the judge, and the jury." Instead, the values involved in open courts will be protected most effectively by "self-interested adversaries. . . . I do not believe the Court has the authority to create this novel remedy for a random selection of bystanders."

There the matter stood for over a month, with the general expectation that the Blackmun draft would ultimately come down as the *Gannet* opinion. Then, on May 31, Justice Powell informed Justice Blackmun that he had finally concluded to change his vote. Powell noted that he had earlier indicated in his already-quoted May 9 letter that "I was inclined to view this case as presenting primarily a First Amendment rather than a Sixth Amendment issue." As far as the basis of the Blackmun opinion was concerned, "I had become persuaded that my views as to the Sixth Amendment coincide substantially with those expressed by Potter. . . . I therefore will join his opinion." Powell also noted that he had written a draft, originally as a dissent, which would be issued as a concurring opinion, "in which I address the First Amendment issue."

The Powell letter concluded with an apology, "I am sorry to end up being the 'swing vote.' At Conference I voted to reverse. But upon a more careful examination of the facts, I have concluded that the trial court substantially did what in my view the First Amendment requires."

The Powell switch completely altered the *Gannett* situation in the Court. It led to the following *MEMORANDUM TO THE CONFERENCE* circulated the next day, June 1, by the Chief Justice, "In light of the most recent developments in this case, I am assigning it to Potter for a Court opinion."

On June 7, Justice Stewart circulated a revised version of his draft dissent (supra p. 465), now redrafted as the *Gannett* opinion of the Court. The one substantial addition was pointed out in the Justice's covering memorandum: "You will note that I have unabashedly plagiarized Harry Blackmun's statement of facts in Part I and discussion of mootness in Part II. I offer two excuses: (1) the pressure of time, and (2) more importantly, I could not have said it better."

The Stewart opinion of the Court was quickly joined by the Chief Justice and Justices Powell, Rehnquist, and Stevens. The latter's letter of joinder noted, "I have withdrawn the short separate opinion that I circulated some time ago."

By then Justice Blackmun recognized that he had definitely lost his Court. On June 20, he wrote a "Dear Bill, Byron, and Thurgood" letter, "You were kind enough to join me when I attempted an opinion for the Court. Please feel free to unhook, if you wish, in my conversion of that opinion to a concurrence in part and a dissent in part." As it turned out, none of the Blackmun supporters wanted "to unhook," and all four joined the *Gannett* dissent that he issued.

The *Gannett* decision did not, however, finally resolve the issue of public and press access to criminal proceedings in the Burger Court. The next year, in 1980, the Justices were again presented with the issue in *Richmond Newspapers* v. *Virginia*.[6] Once again, the trial court had closed a criminal proceeding to the public and the press and refused to grant a newspaper's motion to vacate the closure offer. This time, however, it was the trial itself that was closed. The closure order was upheld by the highest state court.

According to Chief Justice Burger at the postargument conference in mid-February 1980, the fact that the case involved the trial and not a pretrial proceeding differentiated this case from *Gannett*. Hence, he began his presentation, "*Gannett* didn't decide this case." The Chief Justice noted that open trials were always the practice in our system. "The assumption has been that trials must be public. They were taken for granted from 1787 to 1791"—that is, from the drafting of the Constitution to the ratification of the Bill of Rights. Thus, Burger concluded, "[t]here's a common thread for public trials." But that still left the question: "What's the constitutional handle?"[7]

The Chief Justice's answer was different from that given by the other Justices. "I'm not persuaded," Burger said, "it's in the First Amendment either as an access right or an associational right." Then the Chief Justice indicated the constitutional approach he would favor, "I would rely on the fact it was part of judicial procedure before adoption of the Bill of Rights. The Ninth Amendment is as good a handle as any."

Had the Burger suggestion of reliance on the Ninth Amendment ("The enumeration in the Constitution, of certain rights, shall not be construed to deny or disparage others retained by the people") been followed, *Richmond Newspapers* might have become a leading case in the revival of what used to be termed "the forgotten amendment."[8] But the Chief Justice's suggestion was not supported by the others and the Burger *Richmond Newspapers* opinion does not discuss the Ninth Amendment beyond a brief reference to it in a footnote[9]—and even that, we shall see, evoked opposition from at least one Justice.

Justice Rehnquist, who alone spoke for affirmance, asserted, "There are tensions between *Gannett* and this case." But the others (with the exception of Justice Powell, who did not participate) all agreed with the Chief Justice that *Gannett* did not apply and that the lower court decision in *Richmond Newspapers* should be reversed. At the argument, Professor Lawrence Tribe, speaking for the appellants, had relied on the Sixth as well as the First Amendment, despite the categorical *Gannett* restriction of the public trial guaranty's scope. Justice White alone said that the Court "might get some mileage out of the Sixth." The others who spoke on the matter, however, agreed with Justice Stewart when he said, "Tribe's Sixth Amendment argument is not appealing."

Instead, the others relied on the First Amendment to support the public and press right of access. Once again, their view was best expressed by Justice Stewart, who pointed out, "The Sixth was resolved against public trials in *Gannett*. The press has no right superior to the public of access to institutions like prisons which are traditionally closed." On the other hand, Stewart recognized, "trials have been open traditionally subject to time, place, and manner regulations." The Justice then concluded that the First Amendment furnished the basis for a reversal. "I agree there is a First Amendment right, subject to the overriding interest in a fair trial."

The ultimate conference conclusion was, as stated by Justice Stevens, that "the First Amendment protected some right of access. . . . I'd be prepared to hold that, in the absence of any rational basis for denying access, the benefits of openness argue for it."

The *Richmond Newspapers* draft opinion of the Court was circulated by Chief Justice Burger on May 27, 1980. He realized by then that none of the others supported his conference reliance on the Ninth Amendment. Therefore, he wrote in his covering memorandum, "I have refrained from relying on the Ninth Amendment but the discussion of its genesis gives at least 'lateral support' to the central theme." The discussion referred to was relegated to a footnote in the Burger opinion. Even so, Justice White wrote to the Chief Justice "that as I see it, your invocation of the Ninth Amendment is unnecessary, and in any event, it may be that I shall disassociate myself from that portion of the opinion." There were also animadversions against the Burger reference to the Ninth Amendment in the opinions issued by Justices Blackmun[10] and Rehnquist.[11]

The White letter also repeated the Justice's preference for the Sixth Amendment approach, "Although I thought, and still do, that the Sixth Amendment is the preferable approach to the issue of public access to both pre-trial and trial proceedings, particularly the latter, it does not appear that the Conference is prepared to proceed on this basis." Because of this, White went on, "I join your opinion based on the First Amendment and would expect to stay hitched if three or more Justices in addition to myself join your opinion. If there is a Court only for the judgment, I may leave you and say my own piece."

As it turned out, the Burger opinion could attract only two others (Justices White and Stevens). Except for Justice Rehnquist, who dissented, the others issued separate opinions concurring in the judgment. This included Justice White, who wrote the short concurrence quoted at the beginning of this chapter, pointing out that the *Richmond Newspapers* case would have been unnecessary, had *Gannett* ruled that the Sixth Amendment gave the public and the press a right of access to criminal proceedings—that is, the approach taken in Justice Blackmun's draft *Gannett* opinion of the Court (supra p. 418). That approach would also have answered the question still left open by *Richmond Newspapers*—whether the First Amendment right of access recognized by the decision there is limited to trials or extends to pretrial proceedings, such as that closed in *Gannett*.

We can end our discussion of *Gannett* and *Richmond Newspapers* with a human-interest touch. In his *Richmond Newspapers* concurrence, Justice Brennan stated that the First Amendment plays a structural role in securing and fostering our system of self-government. "Implicit in this structural role is . . . the antecedent assumption that valuable public debate—as well as other civil behavior—must be informed."[12] In a recirculation of his opinion, Brennan added a new footnote 3, "This idea has been foreshadowed in Mr. Justice Powell's dissent in [another case]"[13] and quoted a paragraph from the Powell opinion.[14]

Justice Powell was so pleased by this that he sent a written note to Brennan:

June 6th

Dear Bill,
Thank you so much for your new Note 3 in *Richmond Newspapers*. You are a scholar and a gentleman—and a generous one!

Lewis

I had intended to conclude this chapter with this Powell note. A word must, however, be added about *Press-Enterprise Co.* v. *Superior Court*,[15] which was decided in 1986. The Supreme Court there held that the First Amendment right of access to criminal proceedings applied to a preliminary hearing in a California criminal case. The question left open by *Richmond Newspapers* has thus been answered in favor of a First Amendment right of access to pretrial proceedings. But the Burger *Press-Enterprise* opinion was not nearly as forthright in upholding that right as Justice Blackmun's draft *Gannett* opinion. The Chief Justice stressed that the right of access applied to preliminary hearings as conducted in California, where there had been a tradition of public accessibility. There is an implication here that the same result might not be reached in a case from a state with a different tradition. Despite *Press-Enterprise*, then, the law on the matter may still not be where it would have been if the Blackmun draft had come down as the *Gannett* opinion of the Court.

Notes

1. 448 U.S. 555 (1980).
2. Id. at 581–82.
3. *Gannett Co.* v. *DePasquale*, 443 U.S. 368 (1979).
4. Id. at 406.
5. Supra note 1.
6. Supra note 1.
7. I have changed the order of the Burger statements as they are contained in the conference notes made available to me.
8. *Griswold v. Connecticut*, 381 U.S. 479, 490, n.6 (1965).
9. 448 U.S. at 579, n.15.
10. Id. at 603.
11. Id. at 605.
12. Id. at 587.
13. *Saxbe* v. *Washington Post Co.*, 417 U.S. 843 (1974).
14. 448 U.S. at 587.
15. 106 S. Ct. 2735 (1986).